Repertory
Movie Theaters
of New York City

Repertory Movie Theaters of New York City

Havens for Revivals, Indies and the Avant-Garde, 1960–1994

BEN DAVIS

McFarland & Company, Inc., Publishers
Jefferson, North Carolina

ISBN (print) 978-1-4766-6720-1
ISBN (ebook) 978-1-4766-2720-5

LIBRARY OF CONGRESS CATALOGUING-IN-PUBLICATION DATA

British Library cataloguing data are available

© 2017 Ben Davis. All rights reserved

No part of this book may be reproduced or transmitted in any form or by any means, electronic or mechanical, including photocopying or recording, or by any information storage and retrieval system, without permission in writing from the publisher.

Front cover: The Regency Theater, 1982

Printed in the United States of America

*McFarland & Company, Inc., Publishers
Box 611, Jefferson, North Carolina 28640
www.mcfarlandpub.com*

In memory of Thomas Cole, my first editor,
and Richard Kersche, a gentle friend.

Table of Contents

Acknowledgments   ix
Preface   1

Part One: The First Wave

1. The Roots of Repertory Programming in New York   5
2. The First Wave of the Repertory Theater Movement   18
3. The New Yorker Theater: Art over Commerce   23
4. The Bleecker Street Cinema: From Repertory Theater to Independent Film Showcase   38
5. The Charles Theater: The Underground Film in the Heyday of the East Village   49
6. The Thalia: Grand Dame of Repertory Houses   63

Part Two: The Second Wave

7. New York Film Scene, 1970s On   77
8. The Second Wave of the Repertory Theater Movement   86
9. The Elgin Theater: Midnight Movies and the Countercultural Craze   93
10. Theatre 80 St. Marks: Joan Crawford, Grauman's Chinese Theater and Other Memorabilia of Hollywood's Golden Age   113
11. The Regency: MGM Reigns Supreme   130
12. The Thalia: A Temple to B Films, Trashy Films and Other Critical Rejects   145

13. Carnegie Hall Cinema and Bleecker Street Cinema: Classic Revivals, American Independents, Godard and Company—A Smorgasbord of Riches   166

14. Repertory Programming: A Return to Its Roots   200

Chronology of the Repertory Movie Theaters, New York City, 1960–1994   207
Chapter Notes   209
Bibliography   229
Index   231

Acknowledgments

This book could not have been written without the generous, wholehearted contributions of the former owners, managers, and programmers of these repertory movie theaters. Their memories have enriched and deepened the history of their theaters and the alternative exhibition scene of the era. Some of them have supplemented their memories with calendars, posters, and other primary material from their personal collections. Jackie Raynal, Dan Talbot, Howard Mandelbaum, Frank Rowley, Greg Ford, and Lorcan Otway provided a face to the people and theaters with their photographs. Jackie went to special efforts to obtain photos from the Cinémathèque de Toulouse, where she had deposited her memorabilia from the Carnegie Hall and Bleecker Street Cinemas. My thanks to her and the Cinémathèque de Toulouse.

The calendars, posters, and other printed material in the collections of Ed and Mary Maguire, Walter Langsford, John Pierson, and Jim Harvey filled in the gaps in their memories. Larry Chadbourne's collection of the *Thousand Eyes* magazines gave me invaluable information about Sid Geffen's three theaters. Last, but not least, Deborah Sutherland and her brothers, John and Tom Lewis, have provided this book with rare glimpses of their parents, Martin and Ursula Lewis, and the venerable Thalia, through their family photographs and their mother's unpublished memoir.

Finding the former participants, many of whom were scattered throughout the country, has been a fascinating adventure. Two stand out for my unexpected success in locating them. Walter Langsford seemed to have disappeared after the close of the Charles Theater in 1962. One day, I had a truly creative idea—look in my outdated telephone directory; there, miraculously, was his name. I contacted him and found a generous friend, who opened his home and collection of calendars and posters to me. The telephone directory proved just as valuable in locating still another name that I thought was lost to me, Van Sommer. Van had another surprise in store when we finally began our interview; he brought greetings from my former employer, who is his best friend.

Locating Ted Ostrow and John Pierson did require genuine detective work through the internet since both no longer lived in New York. The exact details of my detecting in both cases are misty now, but I remember, in Ted's case, somehow finding a link to a former place of employment. His ex-employer, after receiving permission from Ted, gave me his contact information; and I had the pleasure of interviewing an interesting, very

Acknowledgments

nice man. I recently learned the sad news that Ted had since died. In John's case I discovered his wife's website and through her, met John by phone. John's knowledge of the alternative exhibition scene and his enthusiastic sharing of information and collection of calendars from the Bleecker Street Cinema was a welcome experience.

Serendipity is the only word to describe my initial contacts with Steve Gould and Deborah Sutherland. My first encounter with Steve has already been described in the preface. The one with Deborah seems to me like a fortunate whim of fate. A couple of months before my June deadline with my publisher, as I was putting the final touches on the manuscript, I was browsing the *Cinema Treasures* website for some reason I cannot now remember, probably unimportant, and went on the Thalia section. The first comment was from someone named Deborah Sutherland; and happening to read her first sentence, I discovered the daughter of Martin and Ursula Lewis. My contact with her led as well to her two brothers and a wealth of memories of the three and, most surprising, of their mother, through her unpublished memoir. This has been a major addition to the existing information on the first revival movie theater in New York and perhaps the nation.

Most of my interviews were conducted by telephone or in the offices of my sources. Howard Mandelbaum's office at Photofest was always open to me and I spent several informative sessions with him and his staff, surrounded by fascinating movie posters often of B pictures, talking about the repertory theaters and, later, picking photos for the book. Bruce Goldstein kindly took time twice from his busy schedule preparing the repertory programs for Film Forum 2, to talk to me about the Thalia and Richard Schwarz.

On several occasions the interviews took place in my sources' homes. I spent two enjoyable days with Walter Langsford and Janet Cooper in their home in the Berkshires, and had invitations to dinners with Bill Thompson and his wife Joyce, who were delightful hosts. Jackie Raynal introduced me to interesting friends in the film industry at dinners in her elegant apartment on Central Park South and graciously invited me to her farewell party before leaving permanently for Paris. Tom Lewis invited me to his home in upstate New York to see his photos of his parents and the Thalia. I spent an afternoon with him and his wife Susan, reviewing the photos and engaging in a stimulating conversation with them over coffee and cake.

Four of my sources have sadly passed away: Florence Otway, Ted Ostrow, Mary Kelly, and film critic Elliot Stein.

I want to make special mention of Jim Harvey, whose incisive comments on an early draft of my manuscript led me to rethink my approach, the result of which is the current book. Similarly, Ron Magliozzi's comments on an earlier version of the final chapter helped me to strengthen it. Dan Talbot was my first contact on this project and continued his support to the end.

The owners, managers, and programmers who contributed to this book have been generous with their remembrances and I thank them all: Gail Aronow, Ben Barenholtz, Henry Fera, Greg Ford, Rudy Franchi, Steve Gould, Bruce Goldstein, Peter Haratonik, Jim Harvey, Mary Kelly, Walter Langsford, John Lewis, Tom Lewis, Miller Lide, Phillip Lopate, Ed and Mary Maguire, Howard Mandelbaum, Barbara Nitke, Ted Ostrow, Florence and Lorcan Otway, John Pierson, Paul Power, Jackie Raynal, Michael Rogosin, Jonathan Rosenbaum, Frank Rowley, Marty Rubin, Andrew Sarris, Michael Silberman, Van Sommer, Elliot Stein, Deborah Sutherland, Dan Talbot, Morton Tankus, Bill Thompson, Marc Weiss, William Wolf, Chuck Zlatkin.

Ron Magliozzi and Ashley Swinnerton of the Department of Film at the Museum of Modern Art and the staff of the Research Collection of the Billy Rose Theater Division of the New York Public Library for the Performing Arts (LPA) have been unfailingly gracious and supportive with my constant requests. They have been an invaluable resource.

My friend Bill Cipolla volunteered to edit the final version. I couldn't have asked for a more qualified editor and appreciated this support. Of course, I took advantage of his offer and have benefited from his feedback.

Finally, I want to thank my companion of twenty years, Russ O'Donnell for his love and support through the years of research and writing.

Preface

Discovering the repertory cinemas shortly after my arrival in New York in 1987 is a special memory of my first years in the city.

These theaters were a revelation to me. The Film Forum on Watts Street was showing its varied programs of independent films and retrospectives, and the two repertory houses in Greenwich Village, the area where I settled—the Bleecker Street Cinema between Thompson Street and LaGuardia Place and Theatre 80 St. Marks in the East Village—were screening either daily changes of double features of older Hollywood films or longer runs of neglected foreign imports. I loved their dowdy, but authentic, ambiance that breathed film history and a love of film. I felt part of a special community of film lovers watching unusual films like Isaac Julien's *Looking for Langston* at the Bleecker, a film noir classic like Fritz Lang's *Ministry of Fear* at Theatre 80, or Marcel Carne's *Children of Paradise* at the Thalia on the Upper West Side. Often in the oddest places, like the shiva (mourning) house for a friend's mother, I met middle-age people who would reminisce about their Saturday night outings to the Elgin in the Chelsea area or some other repertory house of their youth.

Something similar to these alternative cinemas had also existed in Baltimore where I come from. The regional theater, Center Stage, filled its house during the summer off-season with classics like *Gilda,* and the Walters Art Gallery ran its own summer film programs, usually thematic series. Two young movie mavens operated a local *cinematheque*, the Bijou, on weekends on the Johns Hopkins University campus, showing everything from B movies like *Murder at the Vanities* to classics like *The Third Man*; and the Baltimore Film Forum ran thematic series in its home in the Baltimore Museum of Art. I devotedly attended the Bijou programs every Saturday evening and stood in line with a friend, Neal, each Wednesday evening one summer for the Hitchcock-Truffaut series at the Walters Art Gallery. My most intense experience was with the Baltimore Film Forum, where for one season, I had created a series on film noir and wrote the program notes for that and several other series. One of these program notes, my "interpretation" of the closing line in Billy Wilder's *Some Like It Hot*, was my crowning achievement. On the night of the screening, sitting behind two strangers, I overheard one of them tell the other, after reading my program notes, that he finally understood the film. This marked the tentative beginning of my own more earnest approach to film.

When my partner Bill and I came to New York in 1987, I discovered that what was relatively limited fare in Baltimore had been a staple of the New York film scene since the 1960s. At its height in the seventies and early eighties, the repertory theater movement served up a banquet of alternative movie theaters for New Yorkers, such as the Thalia, the New Yorker, the Elgin, the Regency, the Bleecker Street Cinema, Theatre 80 St. Marks, to mention just a few. By the time of my arrival, however, only a few of these theaters remained, victims of changing economic conditions and audience interests. By the early nineties, they would all vanish.

I was curious about these unique neighborhood theaters; but my thoughts were inchoate and I put them aside to take advantage of the educational benefits of the City University of New York, where I had begun working as a writer for its admissions office, and matriculated in the master's program in film studies at the College of Staten Island/CUNY. An independent project for Professor Jerry Carlson led to a published paper after graduation in the film journal *Film & History* on the first two film societies in the United States, both of which had had brief existences in New York (the article is listed in the bibliography in the *Wikipedia* entry on *film societies*).

Now ready to tackle another project, I turned once again to the idea of researching the now-extinct commercial repertory movie theaters. My idea was to rescue their histories from oblivion. But where to start my research? That question was soon answered for me serendipitously. One Saturday as I was walking on Sheridan Square in the Village with a friend, Ed, he briefly stopped to talk to a lanky, animated man; and as we walked on, Ed casually mentioned that his friend was Steve Gould, who used to operate the Elgin, one of the better known repertory movie houses of the 1970s. I immediately contacted Steve and his former partner in the Elgin, Chuck Zlatkin. A generous, open pair, they allowed me to interview them a total of four times, in one joint interview and three individual ones. (Later, when I was in the midst of writing this book, Steve submitted himself willingly to two more interviews.) I synthesized the four interviews into one, which *Film Quarterly* published in its Summer 2000 issue.

With this encouraging beginning, I spent the next years, in between my full-time job, researching the collections at the Department of Film at the Museum of Modern Art and the Research Collection of the Billy Rose Theater Division of the New York Public Library for the Performing Arts (LPA). Ron Magliozzi, assistant curator at MoMA's Department of Film, had been my first resource in researching the early film societies and continued this valuable service. We soon worked together to build the archive of memorabilia of the repertory houses. The staff at the LPA came to recognize me from my frequent visits and also provided valuable assistance. Early on, I made contact with Dan Talbot, the former owner of the New Yorker Theater, who kindly allowed me to interview him twice in his apartment on the Upper West Side, and has continued to be interested in my project over the years. Another early contact was Florence Otway and her son Lawrence, the wife and son of the deceased owner of Theatre 80 St. Marks, Howard Otway. Mrs. Otway and Lawrence (who has since adopted the Irish version of his name, Lorcan) invited me to their apartment above the theater, which was then home to a theatrical company, the Pearl Theatre (the Otways had closed Theatre 80 after the death of Howard and rented the space to the Pearl); they spent a couple of hours talking about Howard and Theatre 80, often overlapping each other, and then gave me a tour of the rest of the building, all of which Howard had constructed himself. It was an impressive multifloor apartment. Several years of stops and starts followed; then on my retirement around 2007, I began serious efforts to track down other former owners, managers, and freelance programmers of these movie houses.

Finding the former participants, many of whom were scattered throughout the country, sometimes required detective work, other times, networking. Some, modest about their accomplishments, were surprised that I was even bothering with the topic. Others enjoyed going back in time and talking about their past in repertory cinema. All have been munificent in sharing their memories of their past, their time, and their memorabilia from the theaters. They are all identified throughout the book. I am deeply grateful to them.

These repertory movie theaters occupied a unique, but largely unrecognized, place in film history and alternative exhibition. Besides contemporary newspaper and magazine articles, the bulk of the literature on these theaters consists of anecdotes buried in memoirs by a small number of film critics, scholars, and others who grew up or were young adults during the years of the repertory houses. Among these memoirs is the only full-length one—limited, however, to only one of these theaters: Toby Talbot's *The New Yorker Theater and Other Scenes from a Life at the Movies*. Research work on the repertory movement is even scarcer. Douglas Gomery, in his seminal work on commercial film exhibition in the United States, *Shared Pleasures: A History of Movie Presentation in the United States*, briefly discusses what he terms the repertory film movement without defining it, other than naming the nonprofit film societies and the for-profit repertory movie theaters as its constituents and inflating the influence of the midnight movies of the 1970s on the commercial repertory theaters. Raymond Haberski's *Freedom to Offend: How New York Remade Movie Culture* describes the roles of the New Yorker Theater, the film society Cinema 16, and the avant-garde exhibition efforts of Jonas Mekas in the mid–twentieth century censorship wars in New York City. The piece missing from the literature is a comprehensive examination of the repertory theater movement in New York.[1]

I learned much in the process of writing this history. Input from Dan Talbot, Jim Harvey, and others helped me to refine my original concept and relate the movement to the larger cultural context in which they operated. Connecting these theaters to my previous work on nonprofit film societies, I came to realize that these movie theaters operated as commercial versions of the nonprofit film societies. How did they carry out this role in the commercial arena? What were the cultural, economic, and intellectual contexts that enabled them to arise and flourish in the commercial market, and what were the changes that eventually led to their demise? What were their contributions to movie culture of the period? Finally, now that they are gone, what is the contemporary state of repertory programming?

These are the questions that I have attempted to answer.

PART ONE: THE FIRST WAVE

Chapter 1

The Roots of Repertory Programming in New York

New York City, January to March 1960.[1] The art scene in the city was lively. On Broadway, the long-running *My Fair Lady* was delighting audiences at the Mark Hellinger Theater. Tucked away in upper-floor lofts, small cafes, and minuscule theaters, jazz bands, Off Off Broadway groups, and dance troupes performed. Off Broadway theater was blooming, with thirty theaters scattered throughout the city. The Actors Repertory Theatre Workshop was performing Samuel Beckett's *Waiting for Godot* in a loft on Third Avenue; Theatre 1960 was previewing Beckett's *Krapp's Last Tape* and Edward Albee's *The Zoo Story* for $2 admission at the Provincetown Playhouse; *Three Penny Opera* was in its fifth smash year at Theatre De Lys on Christopher Street; and Julian Beck and Judith Malina's Living Theatre Repertory was performing a double bill of Pirandello's *Tonight We Improvise* and Jack Gelber's *The Connection*.

Jazz fans had their choice of the Village Gate, where they could hear the Max Roach Quintet, or the Village Vanguard, for an evening with Prof. Irwin Corey and Miriam Makeba. Count Basie and his jazz band were playing a gig at Birdland in midtown. Night life in the Village was enlivened by the Kenny Dorham Quintet at the Half Note on Hudson Street and the Slide Hampton Orchestra and Roland Hanna Trio at the Jazz Gallery on St. Mark's Place. For those who preferred folk music, there was Gerdes, billed as New York's first folk music cabaret on West 4th Street, where the Tarriers and Charlotte Daniels were singing. And for lovers of words, the International on Greenwich Street, "New York's Most Unusual Café," offered poetry readings every Sunday evening.

Movies were just as vibrant. In January the art cinema screens were playing François Truffaut's *400 Blows* (1959) at the Fine Arts, J. Lee Thompson's *Tiger Bay* (1959) at the Baronet, Jack Arnold's *The Mouse That Roared* (1959) with Peter Sellers and Jean Seberg at the Guild 50th, Claude Chabrol's *Les Cousins* (1959) at the Beekman, Louis Malle's *The Lovers* (1958) with Jeanne Moreau at the Paris, Ingmar Bergman's *The Magician* (1958) at the Fifth Avenue Cinema and *Wild Strawberries* (1957) at the Art, Joseph L. Mankewicz's *Suddenly Last Summer* (1959) at the Sutton, Basil Dearden's *Sapphire* (1959) at the Murray Hill Theatre, and Akira Kurosawa's *Drunken Angel* (1948) at the Little Carnegie.

Then there were the special film events for cinema connoisseurs. In March at the

Art on East 8th Street in the Village, the complete, three-hour version of Marcel Carne's *Children of Paradise* (1945) was receiving its U.S. premiere, while Bert Stern's *Jazz on a Summer's Day* (1959) was premiering at the 55th Street Playhouse and Fifth Avenue Cinema. Major postwar avant-garde advocate Jonas Mekas, whose column for *The Village Voice* favored the cutting-edge film, proclaimed *Jazz on a Summer's Day* a harbinger of the new generation of filmmakers, along with Lionel Rogosin's *Come Back, Africa* (1959) at the new Bleecker Street Cinema and Robert Frank and Alfred Leslie's independent film *Pull My Daisy* (1959), a Beat Generation riff written by Jack Kerouac, at the Film Center of the 92nd Street YMHA (in a double bill with John Cassavetes's *Shadows,* 1960).[2]

Meanwhile, a brief mention appeared in Mekas's March 9 column of a new "art" theater on the Upper West Side, simply informing his readers of its opening. Arthur Knight, then film critic for *Saturday Review*, though, devoted his entire June 18 column to this new addition to the New York cinema scene. What impressed him was the owner's singular goal to screen only films he deemed worthwhile; Knight considered it a unique type of movie theater. But neither the dismissive Mekas nor the enthusiastic Knight could foresee that the New Yorker Theater signaled the beginning of an alternative, commercial cinema movement in New York that would last thirty-four years—the repertory movie theater movement.[3]

The repertory movie theaters operated in New York from 1960 to 1994. They were part of the postwar rise of film culture, which began with the extraordinary popularity of Italian neo-realism and the French New Wave and ushered in "the golden age of the foreign film" from 1945 to 1965, which embraced an international movement of film as the leading art form on both sides of the Atlantic. Following the Second World War, the American film audience had shifted from a mostly middle-aged, modestly educated, middle- to lower-middle-class group to a smaller, younger, better educated, more affluent, and predominantly middle-class segment of the population. This new audience demanded more serious fare, Robert Sklar noted in his cultural history of American movies, than the "overglamorized, manipulative Hollywood products, full of the crashing Max Steiner scores, gauzy photography, and implausible happy endings." It was turning to the foreign film and its distinct alternative to the synthetic look and engineered narratives of the Hollywood film. Seeing a market for foreign films, a number of small, independent distributors began to import them, leading in turn to the art cinemas, mostly in the larger cities, to exhibit them.[4]

The art cinema movement arose first in New York, then spread nationwide. Specializing in contemporary foreign art films, the art cinemas introduced the work of rising European directors such as François Truffaut, Satyajit Ray, and Jean-Luc Godard, as well as the latest masterpieces of older directors, like Jean Renoir, Akira Kurosawa, and Vittorio de Sica. The number of art cinemas nationwide grew to approximately 470 by January 1952. "To be young and in love with films in the early 1960s," Phillip Lopate, essayist and film critic, wrote in his memoir as a young cineaste, "was to participate in what felt like an international youth movement."[5]

While the art theaters were the most visible part of this cinemaphilia, a parallel complex of alternative exhibition venues slowly appeared in the early sixties and blossomed in the early seventies, specializing in the wide range of noncommercial cinema that the art houses and first-run theaters ignored. Most were nonprofits, but one cluster, the repertory movie theaters, were for-profit enterprises. These are traditionally known as revival houses or sometimes as countercultural ones in the literature. *Revival* or *countercultural*,

1. The Roots of Repertory Programming in New York 7

The Fine Arts Theatre, located on West 58th Street in Manhattan, was one of the principal art cinemas in New York in the 1950s. Photofest.

however, are insufficient descriptions. As a body they brought to their screens a wide range of films that rarely, if ever, appeared on the screens of the mainstream and art theaters, a type of programming known as repertory programming since the 1920s. In addition to the vintage foreign and Hollywood reruns and countercultural films for which they were mostly known, their reach spread to independent American films, experimental films, documentaries, first-run failures to which they gave a second chance, and cutting-edge foreign films that distributors considered noncommercial.[6]

Repertory programming was normally associated with the nonprofit film societies, membership clubs that offered "screenings of films which would otherwise not be shown in mainstream cinemas ... through an organized and prepared program...." The nonprofit field was a natural fit for repertory programming, since it could tap into the grants, donations, and membership subscriptions to supplement the limited income from the specialized audience for non–Hollywood films. The repertory theaters, on the other hand, ventured into the commercial arena as for-profit versions of the nonprofit film societies. They were a rare undertaking that mixed art with commerce.[7]

Like the film societies, the repertory theaters curated rather than simply booked their programs. "[Y]ou went to the theater," recalled Peter Haratonik, associate professor of Media Studies at the New School, "because there was a film noir festival somewhere, or a Marx Brothers festival, or a Bogart festival, [or ones] around artists or themes." Programs were curated, Haratonik explained, "in the way that museum people would curate what paintings got hung or librarians what books got purchased."[8]

The programs of the repertory theaters typically consisted of double features, two films that were purposely linked, most often by a common theme such as director or star, but sometimes by other concepts. The double features played in one of two formats: series (also called festivals or retrospectives) or randomly scheduled double features (a film noir double bill one day might be followed by a screwball comedy double bill the next day). The series, or festival, approach organized retrospectives around a star (Bette Davis festival), a director (Alfred Hitchcock series), a genre (B western series), a studio (RKO festival), a theme (the bicentennial), a country (French series), or any other category conjured up in the imagination of the programmer. They were generally as comprehensive as possible, depending usually on what films were available and in what condition: a Bette Davis retrospective might show her earlier, obscure films as well as her later, better known ones. Festivals were scheduled either vertically—they took place on specific days of the week (a Tuesday or a Wednesday, for example) for a scheduled number of weeks—or, less often, horizontally: they were screened for part of a week or an entire week or more.

By placing films in context, the double features and, especially, the festivals at the repertory houses replicated the invaluable educational function of the film societies. Hitchcock's *Rear Window* as part of a Grace Kelly retrospective "read differently than *Rear Window* as part of a Cornell Woolrich series," David Schwartz, Chief Curator at the Museum of the Moving Image, pointed out in *Cineaste* magazine's symposium on repertory programming. Jason Rapfogel, programmer at Anthology Film Archives, further elucidated in the same symposium that festivals educated audiences in seeing "individual works as part of an oeuvre, a tradition, an historical era, or a nexus of relationships and interconnections." Furthermore, the festivals were often enriched with essays, film notes, and personal appearances by film critics and scholars, directors and stars. Program notes might be distributed with each film. These short essays, written by film scholars, film buffs, or film critics, treated some aspect—historical, thematic, or formal—of the films. "The humble program note," wrote the film journal *Bright Lights* in a tribute to the species, had "a long and noble history ... cheered as often as they were reviled, these brief, ephemeral, often illuminating handouts, likely destined for the dustbin the same night they appeared, offer[ed] wisdom in a nutshell."[9]

The repertory houses, like the film societies, were in effect creating courses of study before film study lost its backwater status in academia. "In those days [the late fifties and early sixties]," remembered Lopate, who was a regular habitué of the various repertory venues in his youth, "you could acquire the same education [as in a university]—or better—by going to the revival houses around town: the New Yorker, the Charles and, most venerable of all, the Thalia."[10]

Yet there was a significant difference between the repertory movie theaters and the nonprofit venues—the film societies and MoMA's film department. A number of obstacles made attendance difficult at the programs of the latter organizations: the odd, erratic, part-time scheduling of show times; the nuisance in getting tickets; and the unfamiliar, often remote locations. The commercial repertory houses, on the other hand, democratized repertory programming. Located mostly on the Upper West Side and in Greenwich Village with their large populations of students and young professionals, they operated in easily accessible, affordable neighborhood movie houses, with a full-time, daily schedule of films, and calendars printed in advance so patrons could plan what they wanted to see.[11]

The repertory houses published seasonal (winter or summer, for example) calendars, which were part of the total adventure of patronizing these theaters. Out-of-town devotees used the calendars as an imaginative substitute for the actual experience. "I, too, collected and devoured the repertory schedules from several Manhattan sites," a Pittsburgh native wrote on the *Cinema Treasures* website, reminiscing about his semiannual visits to New York. "Thalia, Elgin, Bleecker Street ... the Regency.... I loved reading the descriptions, scrutinizing the feature times, spotting the occasional error in show times and keeping them all handy so that at any hour of the afternoon or evening back here in Pittsburgh, I could envision what was going on on every screen." And if you did not have the current calendar from any of the repertory theaters, you would probably bump into Ed Maguire on the street handing them out. Maguire was a well-known figure among the circle of film aficionados of the period as "the man with the schedules ... a one-man *Cue* magazine," Howard Mandelbaum related in the *Bright Lights Film Journal*, "with a gentle smile and an easygoing manner.... He always listens sympathetically to the complaints of others [about faded color prints or rotten projection] ... and then reaches into his battered *Sunday Times* doubling for a portfolio and removes another brochure. Theatre managers are only too pleased to give him stacks because he will make sure they get into the right hands."[12]

A broad swath of the public received an education in film through these theaters. In an era with few college film programs, young film buffs, many of whom grew up to become film professors like Haratonik, film critics like Andrew Sarris and Phillip Lopate, repertory programmers like Dan Talbot, and important film directors like Martin Scorsese and Paul Mazursky, haunted the repertory houses throughout the city, often obsessively consulting lists of must-see films culled from Andrew Sarris's *The American Cinema* or Arthur Knight's *The Liveliest Art*; the lay public broadened and deepened their knowledge of film sitting in their neighborhood repertory houses watching the festivals, reading the film notes, and listening to the visiting film directors and stars; the no-longer-young revisited, in a convenient neighborhood theater, the films of their youth. And enriching this experience was the communal nature of these movie theaters—sharing film experiences with like-minded spectators.

The commercial repertory houses were much more than a passing reference in a major period of film culture. In effect, they were part of a complex that kept alive the past of film and its noncommercial present and helped to prepare many young neophytes for their future in film.

* * *

New York City had long had a love affair with film and its heritage, even after the flight of the motion picture industry to California. It was here that the idea of film as the newest art form was nurtured. In 1922, the National Board of Review (NBR), located in New York, first proposed a national chain of small movie theaters for screening pictures of artistic merit for special audiences. Between 1932 and 1940, NBR promoted cinema art throughout the nation through its Exceptional Photoplays Committee, which published recommendations in the NBR Magazine of "films of originality, art, social relevance from European and American directors [that] were never released for public showings, or ... died quickly for want of popular support." It favored "social cause" films.[13]

NBR also joined entrepreneurs in New York to create exhibition alternatives to the first-run, downtown movie palaces and the subsequent-run neighborhood theaters. The Little Cinema movement began in New York with the opening of Symon Gould's International Film Arts Guild in 1925, showing older and newer foreign films to sophisticated audiences at the George M. Cohan and Central Theatres, and then spread to other cities. Another New York pioneer was Michael Mindlin, president of the Fifth Avenue Playhouse Group, known as "The Aristocrats of the Cinema," who added to his chain of theaters the 55th Street Playhouse in New York in 1927 as well as other playhouses in New York, Brooklyn, and outside the city. His theaters showed British, French, and German films. Unfortunately, the Little Cinema movement collapsed with the coming of sound.[14]

In the 1930s repertory programming returned. The first two film societies in the United States—the Film Society and the Film Forum—sprang up simultaneously in 1933 in New York. Both were modeled after the cine-club (or film society as it was later called in England) movement, which originated in Paris in 1920 with the Club des amis du septième art [Club of Friends of the Seventh Art]. The cine-club sprang from the desire of a small group of Parisian artists, critics, and students to see the worthwhile, usually foreign, films especially German and Japanese, that the theaters in Paris neglected. The Parisian cine-club was soon replicated in London with the London Film Society.[15]

The two American film societies also offered screenings of important foreign and American films ignored by New York theaters, often adding lectures and film notes to their programs. In addition, the Film Forum, in cooperation with the Picture Collection department of the New York Public Library, prepared the first public exhibition in the United States on the art and history of the cinema. The organization, reported the *New York Times*, was "concerned with the artistic and social possibilities of the motion picture, which, it believes, have only begun to be realized."[16]

While they shared a common interest in rarely seen, important films, they differed in the types of films they favored. The "pinkish" Film Forum, reflecting the leanings of its founder, Thomas Brandon, a member of the leftwing Workers' Film and Photo League, emphasized foreign films with political themes, such as the Russian satire *Bed and Sofa* (1928) and the British anti-war film, *High Treason* (1929). The elitist Film Society, on the other hand, mirrored the aesthetic interests of its founder, Julien Levy, the owner of an art gallery that was soon to become an important center of surrealist art in the United States. Levy's desire to import Luis Buñuel's surrealist comedy *L'Âge d'or*, which he had first seen and fallen in love with in Europe, led to his founding the Film Society. Such foreign films as G.W. Pabst's *L'Opéra de quat' sous* (1931) and Jean Cocteau's *Le Sang d'un poète* (1930) dominated the Film Society's calendar. Unfortunately, both societies quickly folded primarily because of internal personnel problems.[17]

There was a link among the London Film Society, New York's Film Society, and the next major development in alternative film exhibition, the Film Library of the Museum of Modern Art (MoMA). British-born Iris Barry, one of the founders of the London Film Society, and later, an active board member of the New York Film Society, became the museum's first film librarian in 1933. MoMA's Film Department was an innovation among museums. The brainchild of Alfred H. Barr, Jr., the longtime director of MoMA, and Barry, the film department opened in 1935 "to assemble and preserve for all time the outstanding films and important literature associated with the development of motion pictures."[18]

Including film among the visual arts was a radical idea for museums. Barr and Barry had to wage a strenuous, two-year campaign to persuade the museum's board and public to incorporate film collection and exhibition in the museum's mission. Arguing that film was the newest art form, they proposed treating film as the museum did its other arts: "trace, catalog, assemble, exhibit and circulate to museums and colleges single films or programs of films in exactly the same manner in which the museum traces, catalogs, exhibits and circulates paintings, sculpture, architectural photographs and modes or reproductions of works of art, so that the film may be studied and enjoyed as any other one of the arts is studied and enjoyed." Basing their argument on the bias among both intellectuals and the public towards the foreign film as the only film art, Barry and Barr singled out the European art film as the equal of the other arts; they contended that it had a single author of a coherent film text, namely, the director (anticipating the French auteurist theory by at least a decade), thus giving the art film both the necessary author and a European origin, which "elevated [it] from the perceived vulgarity and provincialism of American popular culture to the more cosmopolitan realm of high art." A curator would supervise the selection of films for inclusion in the museum's collection and arrange exhibition programs to promote education as well as entertainment.[19]

The Film Department began by offering silent and early sound film programs to New York cultural, academic, and nonprofit institutions and in 1939 started screening programs in its own theaters in MoMA's new building on West 53rd Street. Over the years its programming grew to cover the spectrum of noncommercial cinema, from series and retrospectives of individual film artists and national cinemas to experimental, avant-garde, and independent films and works in new genres, such as the self-reflexive cinema or the diary film.[20]

MoMA's Film Department was one of the few institutions devoted to repertory programming until the late 1940s when film societies reappeared, concurrently with the art theaters. During the war, the film society movement in Europe had folded, and in New York, institution-based cinemas like MoMA's and one at the 92nd Street Y were the only alternative film exhibition venues. Following the war, with the burgeoning interest in the foreign art film, the film society movement reemerged. By 1949 there were approximately 200 film societies in the nation, "organized," reported the *New York Times*, "by persons whose interests in the film medium goes [sic] beyond the purely entertainment functions of the commercial theatre"; and by 1954, according to *New York Times* film critic Bosley Crowther, they had become a large-sized educational and art-world trend. In the United States, most were linked to colleges or museums. MoMA was the pioneer among museums, but soon popular film societies were organized at the San Francisco Museum of Art, the George Eastman House in Rochester, the Museum of Art in Cleveland, and the Art Museum in Worcester, Massachusetts.[21]

In addition to the institution-based film societies, there were a number of free-standing ones founded and operated usually by one person or a small group of cineastes, who put their individual stamp on their enterprise, as the founders of the defunct Film Forum and Film Society had once done. New York was the home to two of the more important free-standing film societies in the country—Cinema 16, the largest one in the nation in the fifties and early sixties (at its peak it had a membership subscription of over 7,000) and the Theodore Huff Memorial Film Society, a much smaller but well-known one. They were part of a small, active film society scene in New York, which also included Film Directions; radio film-reporter Gideon Bachmann's Group for Film Study, which also published the pioneering *Cinemages* journal; and college groups like the one at Fordham University.[22]

Cinema 16 was founded by Amos Vogel in 1947. Originally a for-profit entity, it was soon converted by Vogel into a nonprofit film society because of censorship problems and the undependability of the box office revenues. As a nonprofit, membership society, it was supported solely by annual subscriptions: private foundations then were not interested in supporting this type of activity, and Vogel was not willing to solicit donations. Nevertheless, the subscriptions gave him a steady, predictable income for most of the sixteen years of its existence.[23]

Vogel, who had emigrated from Austria in 1938 as a teenager with his parents, began Cinema 16 to show the vast range of 16mm films that were, at that time, limited to schools and professional and civic groups. The economical 16mm camera, originally aimed at home enthusiasts, had been used since the mid–1930s to produce a vast range of important films for government, business, medical, education, and industrial clients, and by the 1940s had spurred the rise of the avant-garde movement. During the war the availability of inexpensive 16mm films allowed community groups—labor unions, churches, women's clubs, civic organizations, social clubs, and home consumers—to show them for educational and informational purposes: studies of animal life, scientific subjects, and discussions of labor-management relations were among their subjects.[24]

Vogel's interest in this little-known body of nonfiction and avant-garde films had been sparked as a teenager in his native Austria on seeing the subversive, experimental films *Votiv Kino* and *Urania*, and the English documentary *Night Mail* (1936), a surprisingly moving film about the unlikely subject of a mail train from London to Scotland. He believed there were thousands of superior nonfiction films languishing in libraries that would appeal to a large audience. Proceeding on that belief and inspired by pioneer avant-garde filmmaker Maya Deren, who had rented the Provincetown Playhouse for a program of her films, he and his wife established their film society and named it after the 16mm film. Its audience ranged from artists and intellectuals to school teachers and secretaries. Vogel divided his audience into two groups: one that preferred documentaries and nonfiction and another that leaned toward the avant-garde and experimental films.[25]

His programs were designed to explore the full range of the film medium and to screen every interesting, challenging form of film he could find. They extended from scientific films (documents of medical procedures, psychological treatments, and anthropological studies), government-sponsored and independent documentaries, and films about visual artists to experimental, avant-garde films (including a wide range of animation), commercially made, controversial films, and out-of-circulation, long-unseen classics, such as Val Lewton's *Cat People* (1942) and Carl Dreyer's *Day of Wrath* (1943).

He was the first to introduce the work of independent filmmakers such as Kenneth Anger and Stan Brakhage to American audiences, and of foreign directors such as Robert Bresson, Michelangelo Antonioni, and Mikio Naruse. Jonas Mekas, in a 1961 *Village Voice* column, praised Cinema 16 for showing some films of Ozu, "whom our art theaters have yet to 'discover.'" Independent filmmakers submitted their 16mm projects for screening. Hearing of interesting work being done at the Lodz film school in Poland, Vogel had some student films sent to him, including ones by a young, unknown filmmaker, Roman Polanski. "The very first things he did in 35mm," he related in an interview for *Film Quarterly*, "*Two Men and a Wardrobe* [1958], *The Fat and the Thin* [1959], five or six titles." This was the first time Polanski's films were screened in America. Vogel was also in contact, he told the interviewer, with young filmmakers from other countries, like Dusan Makavejev in Yugoslavia and Nagisa Oshima in Japan.[26]

The Theodore Huff Memorial Film Society, originally called the Film Circle, on the other hand, was dedicated to the rare silent film and early film history. It was, in fact, what Vogel thought a film society should *not* be. Vogel's concept was based, according to his biographer, Scott MacDonald, on the European film society tradition, which strives to build an audience for the appreciation of the full range of film rather than limit itself to a small coterie group that already liked the kinds of films being shown. The latter, however, was the model on which the Huff Society was founded. The intent was always to restrict its audience to those who were "*genuinely* interested in film history, as opposed to the transient nostalgia, trivia, and 'camp' hounds" (emphasis in original). While Cinema 16 attracted a broad audience of artists, intellectuals, and the lay public, the Huff Film Society's hardcore audience was characterized by William K. Everson, its longtime director and programmer, as the serious film students (like the teenaged Leonard Maltin), who would see almost anything from a masterpiece to an obscure piece of film history, and what he loosely termed *losers*, "escapists who were reliving an imagined happy past through the films of that time."[27]

A cadre of historians and film fans attended Huff Society screenings. Harvey Deneroff, a film historian who started visiting the Society as a high school student around 1956, remembered that "intellectual-in-waiting Susan Sontag (often accompanied by film critic and historian Carlos Clarens), and sometimes Andrew Sarris" attended. Filmmakers Stanley Kubrick and Radley Metzger came, as well as every film historian in the area and a miscellany of old-time film stars and directors who dropped in to see their films. For that small coterie, the society served an important educational function: "they [Huff Society program notes] were an important part of my cinematic education," Deneroff recalled. "And I think there are perhaps a few others who might also agree."[28]

The Huff Society was started by Charles Turner, a film stills collector and filmmaker, around late 1951, and run by a small group of his friends in the film business, including Theodore (Ted) Huff, whose name the society adopted after his death in March 1953. By October 1953, however, Everson, eventually an important film collector, film historian, and professor at New York University, took over its operation, assuming all programming and administrative responsibilities. Turner later told an interviewer that this had been a necessary move. "A film society," he said, "must be run by one person who sets the tone and makes selections. It can't be run by a committee."[29]

Everson distinguished between film art and film education/appreciation on the one hand and film history on the other. Film history was the focus of the society. It meant for him the total gamut of silent and early sound films, bad as well as good, from those that represented the "lesser aspects of film history—the programmers, the B pictures, the interesting failures that never seem to get much attention elsewhere" to the masterpieces. Because the recognized masterpieces like D.W. Griffith's *Intolerance* (1916) or Sergei Eisenstein's *Potemkin* (1925) were easily available in other venues, Everson concentrated primarily on the obscure and forgotten silent and early sound films; it was preferable, he believed, to fill gaps in one's knowledge with an unknown film by Robert Florey or Walter Forde than "adding further cement to existing pedestals." The introductory note of the October 18, 1955, program represents his curatorial approach: "tonight the society was taking a risk playing films that are not great or even terribly important but are typical, enjoyable, examples of the 'bread and butter' pictures of 1922–29, and have a definite place in the history of the *film*, even if not in the history of the film *art*" (emphasis in original).[30]

The two societies designed their programs to reflect their educational objectives. Vogel wanted to overturn conventional thinking. Intelligent programming, he once explained to a *Village Voice* reporter, could be a means of consciousness-raising, of making "people question an existing value system" and of opening their minds to other possibilities. To accomplish this, he chose a dialectical editing process that was unique in combining educational and informational functions with the study of cinematic art. In another interview, he discussed how specific films were chosen for each program to collide with one another so as to "create maximum intellectual engagement on the part of the audience." An abstract film, a scientific film, an avant-garde film, and a political documentary would appear on the same program, because, he told the interviewer, "my intention at all times was to subvert audience expectations by showing such diverse and different films on one and the same programme."[31]

According to Haberski, in his book on postwar movie culture and censorship in New York, Vogel's audience actively responded to the films, including shouting at the screen, booing, and even stomping out in the middle. Nat Hentoff, *Village Voice* columnist, wrote at the time of Cinema 16's closing that "Vogel exacerbates every member at least six or seven times a season, but at the same time other members are surprised into intensity by the same feature or short."[32]

One example of this varied audience reaction was his presentation in 1958 of an anti–Semitic Nazi-era film, Fritz Hippler's *The Eternal Jew* (1940), accompanied by extensive notes written by Siegfried Kracauer, the author of a major work on German film, *From Caligari to Hitler*. "I saw this in Europe," Vogel remembered, "and I decided that I had to show this film here, because I think that even when the message of a film is evil, if it represents the ideology of a particular political group—in fact one that was strong enough to not only take over a country but start a world war—then it was important to show it." Some audience members objected to its presentation while for others it shook up some unquestioned principles. Ed Emschwiller, avant-garde filmmaker and censorship foe, for example, found himself considering the possible value of censorship when such a presentation as this one could have the potential for doing harm as well as educating.[33]

Everson, on the other hand, organized his programs around topics of film history, such as the February 1958 program devoted to "the great stars of the silent era—those who made a successful switch to the new medium, and those who didn't, like Laura LaPlante, who *should* have made it, but never managed to pull it off." In a 1958 program with an interesting historical slant, he screened a two-reeler, *Sleeping Wives* (1927), made by Laurel and Hardy just before they were established as a team, with its 1935 remake when the comedy team was now well-known.[34]

Supporting the educational objectives of both film societies were schedules of their programs, information sheets, and program notes. Everson wrote extensive program notes for each screening, which are now part of the William K. Everson Collection of New York University's Cinema Studies Department of the Tisch School of the Arts. Vogel also supplied program notes, at first written by him, then by such critics and film scholars as Arthur Knight, Parker Tyler, Siegfried Kracauer, Everson, and Richard Griffith. Many of their programs also featured guest speakers and open discussions following the programs.

Cinema 16 closed in 1963 because of financial difficulties. Its subscription income had been large enough for most of its sixteen years to cover the cost of operations plus reasonable salaries for Vogel and his wife and a small staff, including two high-priced union projectionists per show as the union demanded. (He was proud it was always a union operation.) From 1960 to 1963, however, Cinema 16 was running a deficit because of rising costs barely covered by the stagnant subscription list.[35]

The Huff Society shut down twenty years later in May 1983 on the retirement of Everson. Even though Everson's operation had a very limited income based solely on the sale of individual tickets rather than subscriptions (the ticket price stayed at the low rate of one dollar throughout most of its existence), it managed to exist longer than Cinema 16 partly because of its modest operating costs. There were no salary expenses: Everson did not rely on the Huff Society for an income, volunteers carried out the administrative functions under Everson's supervision, and nonunion, volunteer projectionists could be used since Everson tried to find spaces that did not have contracts with the union. The principal cost of hall rentals was eliminated when the society finally settled in the New School for Social Research at the invitation of Everson's friend and fellow Huff Society member Joseph Goldberg, a professor at the New School. Finally, Everson mostly avoided film rentals by borrowing from private collections as well as relying on his own extensive collection.[36]

At the time of their respective closings, both Vogel and Everson also cited competition as another factor in their decisions. Vogel, for instance, noted that by the early 1960s, films that previously could only be seen at Cinema 16 were now screening in other venues. Among these venues was the New York Film Festival, which Vogel moved to shortly after shutting down Cinema 16. Begun as one of Lincoln Center's annual activities in the same year, 1963, that witnessed the closing of Cinema 16, the New York Film Festival screened both cutting edge foreign films and the classics. Richard Roud, the director of the London Film Festival, performed similar duties with the New York one and Vogel served as the New York–based program coordinator. Together with the San Francisco Film Festival, which began six years earlier, and the Montreal International Film Festival, already four years old, the New York Film Festival became part of a strengthened distribution infrastructure for art cinema; films from the festivals were sometimes picked up by distributors.[37]

Perhaps, though, the most vigorous competition came from nascent trends in alternative film exhibition, trends that would come of age in the next decade: the avant-garde and the repertory theater movement. In 1962, Jonas Mekas and his brother Adolfas, in conjunction with about twenty other avant-garde/independent filmmakers, formed the Film-makers' Cooperative, a distribution center for independent films, a distribution center for independent films, in reaction to Cinema 16's rejection of avant-garde filmmaker Stan Brakhage's *Anticipation of the Night* (1958), which Mekas saw as heralding a totally new, subjective cinema. Beginning with a catalogue of twenty names and sixty titles, the Film-Makers' Cooperative accepted *all* 16mm experimental films regardless of quality; distributed them to nontheatrical venues, such as film societies, colleges and universities, museums, media centers, corporations, individuals, and local organizations; and returned seventy-five percent of the rental fees to the filmmakers, with the other twenty-five percent covering costs. The New York Film-Makers' Cooperative marked the eventual start of other film cooperatives around the country, such as the Northwest Film-Makers' Cooperative, the Los Angeles Film-Makers' Cooperative, the Gulf Coast Film-Makers' Cooperative, and the Canyon Cinema Film-Makers' Cooperative on the West Coast.[38]

Since the fifties, Mekas had been promoting the avant-garde through his *Village Voice* column, "Movie Journal," and in his influential magazine *Film Culture,* which he started

A scene being shot of the satirical comedy *President's Analyst* (1967) with James Coburn, on location on Bleecker Street. The Garrick Cinema is in foreground and Bleecker Street Cinema in background. Photofest.

in 1955 with his brother. In the late fifties, before the Film-Makers' Cooperative, he had founded, together with twenty-three independent filmmakers (both experimental filmmakers, later known as avant-garde filmmakers, and low-budget, semi-commercial ones), the New American Cinema group. Promoting new forms of cinema, the group's manifesto emphasized the personal cinema (expression of personal visions), rejection of censorship, and the "abolition of the budget myth," principles that Mekas continued to push throughout the sixties and the seventies, after the group itself, a loosely organized collection that met frequently at the Bleecker Street Cinema in its early days, dissolved.[39]

Mekas began moving into film exhibition in the early sixties, and kept the New American Cinema name as a marketing tool for the films and filmmakers he was supporting. He used the term again in the title of an article he wrote for *Film Culture* in 1962, surveying the new directions taken by filmmakers such as John Cassavetes, Richard Leacock, Stan Vanderbeek, and Stan Brakhage, in the fifties. In 1961, Mekas helped the young owners of the Charles Theater to set up pioneering theatrical programs of avant-garde films, which became a model for future exhibitors of the genre. Following the closing of the Charles in late 1962, he and his brother held Monday midnight screenings at the Bleecker Street Cinema in the first six months of 1963 under the rubric of Film-Makers'

Showcase, until the theater's manager evicted them; they then moved their operation to the Gramercy Arts Theatre on 138 East 27th Street. In 1964 Mekas formed the Film-Makers' Cinematheque as a venue exclusively for screening contemporary, avant-garde works. The Cinematheque held its first program at the New Yorker Theater and then relocated to other temporary host sites, finally settling in on the first floor of 80 Wooster Street in 1967.[40]

The other important competition with Cinema 16 was the emerging repertory movie theater movement. A month after Dan Talbot's New Yorker Theater on the Upper West Side opened in March 1960 with a dynamic schedule of American and foreign classics, the independent filmmaker Lionel Rogosin launched the Bleecker Street Cinema in Greenwich Village, and was soon followed in 1961 by the Charles Theater in the East Village; by Cinema Village in 1965; and by the Garrick in the same year, another revival house practically next door to the Bleecker Street Cinema. Finally, there was the original repertory theater, the venerable Thalia, which had been running continuously since the early 1940s. These comprised the first wave of repertory movie houses.

Chapter 2

The First Wave of the Repertory Theater Movement

The repertory movie theater movement came in two waves: the first lasted from 1960 to 1974, and the second, from 1968 to 1994. Although the Thalia on the Upper West Side was the oldest of the repertory houses, it was the opening of the New Yorker Theater that signaled the beginning of the repertory movement in New York. In his *Saturday Review* column, Knight anointed it "a new concept in presenting motion pictures," a theater that was "operated by a man who knows enough and cares enough about the movies to put together genuinely exciting programs."[1]

A few full-time revival/repertory theaters had earlier cropped up in the forties and fifties in other American cities—notably the Clark Theater in Chicago; the Cinema-Guild in Berkeley, California; and the Brattle Theater in Cambridge, Massachusetts. The Clark Theater in downtown Chicago was owned and operated by Bruce S. Trinz, who joined the family business in 1946 after service in the air force and took over management of the Clark from his father and uncles. The Clark screened a different double feature of 35mm prints every day. "Under Mr. Trinz's guidance," *Chicago Sun-Times* film critic Roger Ebert wrote in an obituary on Trinz, "the Clark became one of the first repertory movie theaters in the United States." Trinz published a monthly movie schedule entitled, "Hark! Hark! the Clark" with two-line rhymes about each showing ("Sled is the bane/Of Citizen Kane."). The theater closed in 1969, a victim of the suburban drift typical of many cities at the time.[2]

The Cinema-Guild in Berkeley California was created in the 1950s by Ed Landberg, who opened it as the first two-screen art/repertory theater in the nation. Cinema-Guild was run for five years from 1955 to 1960 by Landberg's then wife, Pauline Kael, in her pre–*New Yorker* days. Her program notes were remembered by many Berkleyites as "providing the basics of a film education."[3]

Also in the 1950s Bryant Halliday and Cy Harvey converted the Brattle Theatre in Cambridge, Massachusetts, to a repertory/art cinema. Halliday and Harvey created a programming strategy of combining foreign films and older American films. The theater's U.S. premieres of such films as Eisenstein's *Ivan the Terrible, Part II* (1958) and many of Ingmar Bergman's films from the fifties and sixties made it a vital force in the expanding foreign film market of the fifties and sixties; its revivals of older American films contributed to a developing relationship with the Harvard student community and the postwar student film societies. A particular favorite of the student community was the Brattle's famous Bogart ("Bogey") festivals in the mid-fifties, which ran during the week of final exams at Harvard.[4]

What was unique about New York, however, was the large number of these theaters that arose in a seventeen-year period and lasted as a movement for almost thirty years. It was an exciting time in New York for budding entrepreneurs, when anyone with a vision of their ideal theater and a little capital could open their own repertory theater (usually in a seedy venue), book films that the mainstream movie palaces and second-run theaters ignored, and draw large enough numbers to make their artistically adventurous enterprises commercially viable, albeit often marginally.

How did the nonprofit film society prototype survive as a commercial enterprise for over thirty years in New York, especially with owners who were novice entrepreneurs with no background in theater management and with little capital? "We were lucky," Toby Talbot, the wife of Dan Talbot, wrote in her memoir of the New Yorker. "The time was ripe, cinema was ripe, and audiences were ready." The excitement in the New York film scene of the fifties and early sixties created an important audience for repertory programming. The film societies had nurtured a readymade audience for the repertory houses, and the art house movement was spreading the gospel of film, at least of the foreign film, as the newest art.[5]

Contributing to this intellectual excitement was the auteurist theory of the French film magazine, *Cahiers du cinema,* which Andrew Sarris introduced to America in 1963 in an article in *Film Culture* and then expanded into a full-length book, *The American Cinema.* The issue in which the article appeared, film critic Roger Greenspun wrote, "sold out very quickly and began changing the way in which a great many people think about movies." Proposing that film, like the other arts, had an author, the director, as Barr and Barry had done fifteen years earlier, the auteurist theory went beyond Barr and Barry's stance; according to Steve Neale in his work on film genres in Hollywood, it argued that directorial authorship was found not only in foreign films and the occasional maverick Hollywood film but also in Hollywood's routine output. This was a radical proposal and a revelation to many. The studio films of certain directors like John Ford, Alfred Hitchcock, Orson Welles, and Howard Hawks, and even B movie directors like Samuel Fuller and Bud Boetticher, were hailed as authentic works of art and studied by young film buffs, even if they were still being disparaged by their professors. "The intellectual mainstream," Andrew Sarris remembered, "treated movies as a joke; they liked them but they didn't want to take them too seriously."[6]

But the young cineastes, like the future director Martin Scorsese, did take film seriously. Scorsese remembered congregating with fellow students at the Thalia or the Bleecker Street Cinema or the New Yorker, as well as at the first- and second- and third-run theaters all over town, where "[w]e would look at everything new from all around the world, and we would also look at older pictures with new eyes, pictures we always loved, by people like Hawks and Hitchcock and Lang and Ford." The world, he wrote, "was separated between people who liked to go to the movies to pass the time and people who went for the same reasons that lovers of dance would go to see a Balanchine performance, that lovers of literature would spend their weekends scouring the bookstores." Sarris's book *The American Cinema* would become the bible of these young cineastes, and the auteurist theory would underpin much of the programming of the repertory houses.[7]

Early television was another formative influence in creating an audience for the repertory theaters. New York City had seven channels, including the three network channels and four independent channels, which filled their schedules with old movies that were easily and cheaply available because they had little value then. "In the Fifties and Sixties, and now in the Seventies," observed Sarris in an interview in 1973, "television stations in the big cities were showing 125 movies each week.... This situation has never existed before.... Even the great critics of the Thirties and Forties, critics like Ferguson and Agee, didn't have that opportunity. They would sneak off to the Museum of Modern Art and see one or two films, but they couldn't fill in so massively as people can today."[8]

By the mid–1950s with *Million Dollar Movies* and the early 1960s with *Saturday Night at the Movies*, older feature films from the Hollywood studios were one of television's main programming forms. These movies fascinated the baby boomers. Watching them on television, paradoxically, whetted their appetite for seeing the same films on the big screen. "[F]or me," recalled Haratonik, "it was watching movies on television that got me wanting to watch them in the movie theater, knowing that they would be bigger." Howard Mandelbaum, who later ran the Thousand Eyes Film Society with Roger McNiven, remembered that watching movies on television as a teen was a frustrating experience that pushed him to search for classic films on the big screen. "We grew up watching movies on TV," he said, "but it was clear that they were cut into impossible time slots. My brother and I would watch a film repeatedly because we would see scenes we hadn't seen before. The first time I went to a revival—it was at the New Yorker—I saw *Tale of Two Cities* and was amazed by the beautiful print. I got hooked and I came from the suburbs to see revivals. I loved the movies and I wanted to see them properly." The reigning movie critic of the era, the *New York Times*'s Bosley Crowther, speculated that repeated exposure of these films on television contributed to the success of a classic in the theater; he cited as examples the successful screenings at the New Yorker Theater and the Bleecker Street Cinema of the Marx Brothers' *A Night at the Opera* (1935) and four Humphrey Bogart films, all of which had had "uncounted showings" on television.[9]

The economy was favorable to the unconventional repertory business. Most important, the inexpensive real estate of the period offered an abundant supply of cut-rate neighborhood theaters in deteriorating areas. These theaters were disappearing because of the postwar decline in movie attendance. "Theaters all over the city were closing," Walter Langsford, who ran the Charles with Edwin Stein, recalled. "The buildings were becoming supermarkets; their marquees now advertised leg of lamb for 79 cents."[10]

Also at the time the salaries (except for those of the union projectionists) were minimal; the staff generally consisted of college students or young graduates. Ted Ostrow, for example, who worked as house manager for the Bleecker Street Cinema in the mid-sixties, earned $1.35 an hour. Finally, rentals for the obscure films that the repertory houses favored were affordable. While Talbot at the New Yorker, for example, paid percentages for certain films like Laurence Olivier's *Henry V* (1944; total cost $1,432) and Vittorio De Sica's *Shoeshine* (1946; total cost $828.54), he only had to pay inexpensive flat rates for other films like Alfred Hitchcock's *Strangers on a Train* (1951; $75 a week) and Orson Welles's *Touch of Evil* (1958; $50 a week).[11]

There was a downside, however, to these bargain films—the often poor quality of the prints. They would have scratches, missing dialogue, and even missing scenes. But the repertory theaters were stuck with them. The six major studios, which had depots, or exchanges, in key cities throughout the country for distributing prints, were typically reluctant to strike new prints to replace deteriorating ones, since the revival theaters were unable to recoup the cost of striking a new 35mm print quickly enough. In the past, Bruce Goldstein explained in the *Cineaste* magazine's symposium on repertory programming, most repertory houses only played films for a day or two and most often on a split bill, so there was not enough box office take to recoup their costs.[12] (Later, though, when the reputation of older Hollywood films soared, the studios were more eager to mine this goldmine with new prints and higher rentals. Mandelbaum, who later worked for one of the depots, remembered how *Touch of Evil* went from a budget film at $15 a week to an international film classic at $75 weekly.)

The prints of regional distributors could be equally problematic. Under the states' rights system, these distributors bought prints outright and kept them in circulation until they wore out completely. To get around this problem, the revival house managers would often warn each other of the worst prints of a certain film.[13]

Locating films could also be difficult, sometimes forcing the theaters to use 16mm prints because of the unavailability of 35mm ones. Some films had disappeared—no prints, no negatives, no rights existed. Prints of vintage films from the thirties and early forties were dropping out of circulation or difficult to find. Talbot also found that television companies such as MCA, which had bought the rights to many old movies, refused to rent them because they were not million-dollar deals. In addition, private owners were sometimes unwilling to lend their prints.

Another victim of their threadbare operations was the physical condition of the theaters. Having limited capital, the young entrepreneurs kept renovations to a minimum. The New Yorker's plush, burgundy-velvet seats had been purchased for a dollar apiece from the old Roxy Theater. The physical settings were usually described by patrons as funky, ratty, or seedy. They were "privately owned movie houses with worn-out seats and dubious popcorn," described a *Variety* reporter. Mandelbaum recalled that the New Yorker "was okay until they turned on the lights after the last show and you could see how decayed and peeling the walls were. They kept it kind of damp." The Charles in the East Village was described by J. Hoberman and Jonathan Rosenbaum in their book *Midnight Movies* as "a decrepit movie house on New York's Lower East Side," while Elliott Stein, retired film critic, remembered it as "a flea pit with rats and mice often scurrying around the place." The Thalia, according to one former patron, "was the seediest. Decorated in 1930s ocean-liner motif, it had the faded optimism of an aging chorus girl with over-rouged cheeks." It also had soundproofing problems: with the lack of doors between its lobby and auditorium, loud discussions from the lobby, refreshment stand, and even the street could be heard inside. The Thalia's outstanding physical feature was the auditorium's parabolic floor, a swayback floor that sloped down for two-thirds of the way to the front and then uphill the rest of the way to the screen. "It was a disorienting experience for the moviegoer," Pete Delaney, a historian of the theater, reported, "who thought they were seeing an optical illusion on first entering the surrealistic world of the Thalia theater."[14]

Yet the funky settings were paradoxically part of the charm and attraction of these repertory houses. They fit into a youthful subculture that set itself apart from the more respectable, conservative one of their elders. Reminiscing about his days as a youngster attending films at the Thalia, the novelist E.L. Doctorow told a *New York Times* reporter that "the fact that it was rundown was what made it attractive to young people. We flocked to it, young people with—oh, I don't know what you'd call them—aspirations or pretensions. There was a sense of past in film at the Thalia." The ambiance and audience of the repertory theaters were an unforgettable experience for Laurence Kardish, senior curator in MoMA's Department of Film. "When I first came to New York in the late Sixties," he remembered in the *Cineaste* symposium, "there was a wealth of 'repertory' theaters in Manhattan—there were great films in lousy cinemas (meaning they all needed repairs, and had seen better days), but somehow the seedy ambiance ... and the absolute passion of the filmgoers made moviegoing memorable." Gary Palmucci, general manager of Kino International, a leading distributor at the time of repertory house favorites, mourned the demise of the atmosphere of the revival houses. "Venues like the museums, the Film Forum, and the Walter Reade," he reminisced in a *Variety* interview, "don't have the funky life of the old theaters." The funky life of these theaters was also well-known for their balconies and bathrooms, which were often choice places for anonymous, generally gay, sex, although heterosexual groping was also an occurrence.[15]

While the "mom and pop" operation of the repertory houses often meant an amateurism that, Lopate complained in a *Times* interview, led to "late starts, poor queuing up procedures, drunken projectionists, lunatic customers," it also lent an intimate, home-like atmosphere to these unpretentious settings. Regular patrons came to know the front-line staff. Toby Talbot described the New Yorker as a family store where her elderly father Joe, "eyes alert, hands slightly quivering," stood as a sort of sentry in the center of the lobby while her mother, Bella, nonjudgmental and stoic, listened patiently to the personal stories and woes of patrons as she presided over the candy stand. At the Thalia there were Teddy Feiffer, an elderly, Jewish ex-boxer, and Gladys DiPillo, longtime managers of the theater.[16]

Overriding the rundown settings, the poor prints, and the sometimes irritating incompetence was the one essential quality of these theaters—their unique programming. "They showed things," said Lopate, "that you absolutely had to see." Furthermore, one was seeing them in a communal setting. "In those days," reminisced Woody Allen with a *Times* reporter, "part of the pleasure of going to the movies was the whole ritual: standing in line to buy tickets with a whole lot of like-minded people, listening to them talk. You'd go in and the lights would be on and you'd hear Vivaldi or Stravinsky on the speakers while you waited for the reels to be put up and you'd see *Earth* by Dovzhenko or *Rashomon* by Kurosawa."[17]

Chapter 3

The New Yorker Theater: Art over Commerce

When the New Yorker opened on March 17, 1960, on Broadway between 88th and 89th Streets, Arthur Knight described it in his *Saturday Review* article as neither an art house nor a revival house but one that was open to every worthwhile film. "I have a policy of no policy," Dan Talbot, the thirty-five-year-old manager and programmer of the theater, told him. "I'll play new films, old films, foreign films, American films—whatever I think merits being shown." He envisioned his theater, as he later expressed in an interview with this author, as "my 900-seat living room. I wanted to see on the screen the movies that I wanted to see. And if the audience agreed with me, great. If they didn't, too bad." His vision worked. For thirteen years, audiences came to the New Yorker to discover the films that Talbot believed in.[1]

In his book on the censorship battles in New York in the twentieth century, Haberski contrasted Talbot's laissez-faire approach to Vogel's confrontational approach. "It was as if New Yorkers," he wrote, "having received their primary education through MoMA's programs and taken advanced courses in movie viewing at Cinema 16, had now graduated into the world of the New Yorker, where they were expected to use their filmic wisdom to appreciate the diversity of the movie culture all around them."[2]

Movies had been an important part of Talbot's youth, along with baseball and piano. But the latter two eventually fell by the wayside. "When I was younger," Talbot recalled in our interview in his apartment on the Upper West Side, where he has lived since 1965 with his wife and three daughters (until they grew up and moved out), "I had been training to be a concert pianist. But I was also involved in baseball, and there was a conflict between the two." The conflict was resolved, however, by a key influence in his life then—his mother. When a scout from the New York Giants wanted to recruit him and send him to training camp in the South, she grew hysterical. "Her 16-year-old Jewish son going to a baseball training camp in the South where there are shiksas [non-Jewish young women] and God knows what else and—the remark that ended it all for me—'You know that they eat fried food in the South,' she screamed." His career as a concert pianist, on the other hand, ended after stage fright ruined his concert at Stuyvesant Hall.

The Victory on West 42nd Street, ca. 1952. As the area began declining in the early 1950s, the first-run theaters began screening "art" films and second-run movies and gradually sank to grindhouse, exploitative films. Photofest.

Films, however, remained a lifelong passion, from his childhood when he spent Saturdays with his friends at the local movie theater in the Bronx seeing all kinds of movies—Buck Rogers, adventure films, the Phantom—into his marriage, when going to the movies was the principal recreation of the young couple. "[W]e went a lot to the movies," Talbot recalled, "and one of our favorite hangouts—that was a great age of movie-going—was the Beverly Theater. It was a charming, tacky, old theater that specialized in British films, like *Brief Encounter* and *Colonel Blimp*. It was heaven." Other favorite movie haunts were the 42nd Street grindhouses for old comedies, westerns, newsreels, and art movies; the East Side theaters like the Paris, the Sutton, and the Normandie for first runs of the Ingmar Bergman and other art films; and the Thalia for its foreign revivals.

By the time he opened the New Yorker Theater, he had seen the works of all the great American directors—Lubitsch, Sturges, and von Sternberg were among his favorites—as well as a great number of foreign films. He especially loved the American films of the 1930s, which he considered one of the great periods of filmmaking. "I know those films to this day," he said. "They're in my bloodstream." Film, for him, was a collective enterprise among the directors, the stars (Carole Lombard, Katherine Hepburn, the Marx Brothers, W.C. Fields, and Buster Keaton were ones he particularly named), and the screenwriters.

While he was knowledgeable about film, he had no experience operating a movie theater. Instead, he had had a varied, restless professional career mostly in publishing—as an editor for Gold Medal Books and then Avon Books and as a freelance editor of seven anthologies, including *Treasury of Mountaineering Stories* and the first serious anthology of film criticism, *Film: An Anthology,* which was published by Simon and Schuster in 1959. It included an early piece by Pauline Kael, "Movies: The Desperate Art," which he had read in *Partisan Review* and thought revealed a new voice. "So I contacted her," he recalled, "and made arrangements to get the rights to publish it as part of the anthology. She was very pleased to be in that book." He spent three years on the anthology. "It was a labor of love," he said.

His interesting, eclectic background also included a stint with Warner Bros. as an Eastern story editor; a business operating a small, offbeat booth selling textiles; and, after a yearlong sojourn in Spain with his wife and two daughters (his third came later), a job as film critic for *The Progressive* magazine, where he reviewed such foreign films as Akira Kurosawa's *Ikiru* (1952), on which he wrote a long, passionate piece, and Hollywood films such as Stanley Kramer's *On the Beach* (1959) and Robert Wise's *Odds Against Tomorrow* (1959).

With a family to support, Talbot needed a regular income, but he also wanted independence. "I didn't want to work in an office," he said, "and I needed steady work. And this came up." What came up was the idea of turning the Yorktown Theater on the Upper West Side into a revival house. The Yorktown had been a fourth-run, sub-run house, which his accountant, Henry Rosenberg, was thinking of adding to his chain of Spanish-language movie theaters. Talbot explained to Knight that he had concluded from observing his neighborhood that the young married couples in the arts and professions who were moving into the old apartment houses, brownstones, and large, inexpensive flats were turning the Upper West Side into an extension of Greenwich Village and a potential location for a revival movie theater. "By then," he said, "I had a dictionary of movies in my head." He convinced Rosenberg to experiment with the theater as a repertory house for a year with him as manager, "running the best films of all time on a carefully, intelligently balanced program." If it failed to turn a profit after the year, it would be added to Rosenberg's Hispanic chain. Talbot's salary was to be $125 a week, plus one-third of the profits.[3]

Knowing nothing about film exhibition, he was working twenty hours a day at the theater, learning the business. He and Rosenberg made some minor improvements, especially their purchase of the burgundy-velvet, plush seats of the recently defunct Roxy Theater. Wanting to rename the theater, Rosenberg suggested preserving the neon tubing for "York" in the theater's original name as an economy measure; so the Yorktown became the New Yorker. The 900-seat theater was "a really stunning theater," Talbot recalled. "It had gorgeous medallions on the wall of dancing girls right out of Busby Berkley." Three red-and-gold banquettes from the old Roxy Theater flanked the area. The inner lobby door had a black-and-white Jules Feiffer mural of the faces of a movie audience intently watching an invisible screen. The auditorium had 800 seats, and the balcony, an additional 100 seats, plus a men's room and a ladies' room. There was a small staircase from the balcony, which led to a projection booth containing a huge century projector with a Peerless carbon-arc lamphouse, framer, exhaust, and sound system. Three projectionists covered the ninety-hour week. (One of them, Melvin, liked to masturbate during Marilyn Monroe movies.) An early innovation of Talbot's, which Mekas lauded in his *Village Voice* column, were the huge posters in front of the theater, with texts explaining the backgrounds of the films and directors instead of the usual publicity blurbs and quotes.[4]

The opening double bill, Laurence Olivier's *Henry V* (1944) and French director Albert Lamorisse's *The Red Balloon* (1956), ran for two weeks, drew over 2,000 paying customers, and grossed $11,165.00. As a high school senior, Lopate remembered learning about the New Yorker Theater through a promotional letter that Talbot sent to the English high school departments in the city, promoting the debut film, *Henry V*, as a Shakespearian film that the students should see. He came for the opening and returned. "The next presentation," he recalled, "was a double bill of *Harvest* [1937] by Pagnol and *Day of Wrath* [1943] by Dreyer. *Day of Wrath* really hit me. I began going to the New Yorker after that." The third double feature, Orson Welles's *Magnificent Ambersons* (1942) and the independent film about the Beats, *Pull My Daisy* (1959), which Talbot booked on the suggestion of its promoter, Emile de Antonio, sold over 7,300 tickets in its two-week run and grossed $8,045.42 (despite a negative review of *Pull My Daisy* by Archer Winsten of the *New York Post*, as noted by Mekas in his *Village Voice* column).[5]

In its first year, 1960, the theater drew 700 patrons on Friday nights and close to 1,000 on Saturdays and Sundays, and grossed around $211,000 that year, making the theater financially viable. Seeing the success of his idea, Talbot persuaded Rosenberg to sell him the lease. He borrowed money from friends, his in-laws, and "from wherever I could put my hands on money," he told Ron Magliozzi of MoMA's Film Study Center. In May 1962, two years after the opening, he noted in the New York Theater box-office log book that he now owned the theater.[6]

Unfortunately, his first year as owner ended badly with a newspaper strike on December 9, which involved all the New York newspapers and lasted 114 days until April 1, 1963. Deprived of newspaper advertising, the box office declined significantly, grossing $16,337 less than that of the previous four-month period and nearly $10,000 less than that of the comparable time period a year later. Still, the New Yorker survived. Its eclectic series of festivals continued through 1963—an "Easter Festival," a "Science Fiction Festival," a "Comedy Series," a "Horror Cycle" and a "Thriller Cycle"—and ended the year with a "Winter Repertory." The year 1964 saw a "Humphrey Bogart Festival" earlier in the year and concluded with "American Dada," featuring *Henry Geldzahlen* (1964), an early Andy Warhol film.

The range of Talbot's "discoveries" was indeed wide. In the first half of the theater's existence, what specially interested him were the rarely seen, neglected films from cinema's history, both American and foreign. In its first six months patrons saw Buster Keaton's 1921 shorts *The Playhouse* and *The Boat*; Chaplin's 1917 silent films *Easy Street*, *The Cure*, and *The Immigrant* and his 1935 masterpiece *Modern Times*; Max Reinhardt's *Midsummer Night's Dream* (1935); two 1950 Oscar contenders, Billy Wilder's *Sunset Boulevard* and Joseph Mankiewicz's *All About Eve*; John Huston's *Treasure of the Sierra Madre* (1948); and Rene Clement's *Forbidden Games* (1952). A series in 1962 of unknown Warner Bros. films from the 1930s gave him an opportunity to screen "some interesting movies [that] sneaked across [the studio factory system]." The opening of *Sunset Boulevard* recreated the old-time excitement of a Hollywood premiere—Gloria Swanson arrived in a white limousine and white ermine. "She was still smashing," Talbot remembered. The film had lines around the block and ran for three weeks, netting slightly over $12,000 for its run.[7]

The six-edition "Forgotten Films" series were high points in the New Yorker's resurrection of long-unseen gems of the Hollywood studio era. The concept was the brainchild of the twenty-year-old Peter Bogdanovich, who was at one time a neighbor of the Talbots and later one of Dan's assistants. "Peter, who was just the craziest of the craziest film fans in the world," Talbot recalled, "used to throw his window open in the morning when he was younger and holler across the street for me, and say, 'Can I come over?'" As a teenager, he wanted to work for Talbot, but not in a modest position like usher since he considered himself a scholar. "I put him on the payroll," Talbot said, "and gave him $35 a week, just to hang around, just to talk to me. And I let him write some program notes, which he did on a mimeograph paper and sold for five cents apiece." Already a disciple of the auteurist approach, Bogdanovich eventually persuaded Talbot to screen some of the lesser known American films by studio directors like Howard Hawks and Raoul Walsh. Talbot liked Bogdanovich's idea. "These were films, like *The Crowd Roars*," Talbot said, "that nobody knew about. Some of them were B movies, but they were wonderful and should be shown." One advantage of their obscurity was their low flat fees, which ranged from $15 to $50.

Dan Talbot (left) had arranged to meet Alfred Hitchcock when he was in town around 1964. Courtesy Dan Talbot.

Playing in January and February 1961, the first "Forgotten Films" series stressed mostly Hollywood directors whose critical reputations were emerging: Orson Welles (*Journey into Fear*, 1943), John Ford (*Wagon Master*, 1950), Jules Dassin (*Thieves' Highway*, 1949), John Huston (*Across the Pacific*, 1942), and Howard Hawks (eight films, from the 1930 *The Dawn Patrol* to the 1951 *The Thing*). Among Hawks's films that were relatively little known at the time but are now considered classics of their respective genres were his screwball comedy *Bringing Up Baby* (1938) and his films noirs *To Have and Have Not* (1944) and *The Big Sleep* (1946). The opening double feature was Richard Thorpe's *The Crowd Roars* (1938), paired with Robert Aldrich's *Kiss Me Deadly* (1955); the closing one was *The Big Sleep* with *Wagon Master*.[8]

Bogdanovich, in his book *Who the Devil Made It*, claims that the New Yorker was the first revival house to program the classic American films that were being proselytized by Andrew Sarris and *New York Times* film critic Eugene Archer. "This was the time, remember," he wrote, "when everyone chic was talking about Antonioni and Fellini and hardly anyone talked about Hitchcock (except the public) or knew about Hawks (except in Hollywood). Revival houses in those days mainly programmed foreign films, and if there was an occasional homegrown film it had to be serious and weighty in some seemingly social-minded way, like *The Informer* [1935] or *Grapes of Wrath* [1940], say from John Ford, as opposed to [Ford's] *The Quiet Man* [1952] or *The Searchers* [1956]. Talbot's New Yorker policy, aided and abetted by the French-influenced Archer, Sarris, and me, started to change all that." Despite the extravagance of the claim (Sarris wrote an angry article in the *Village Voice* denying any association with Bogdanovich), the New Yorker did play an important role in bringing these films to the attention of the public and critics.[9]

While the critics praised the first series, the audiences generally panned it. The films seemed outdated to them. Negative responses like "What kind of silly pictures are these," and "I can do better" appeared in the guest books that Talbot kept in the lobby for audience comments. The series' box-office take was below average. Its gross of $8,576 in its two-week run, for instance, was approximately $2,260 less than that of the two-week "First Anniversary Program," which took place a month later. But Talbot felt they gave the theater certain panache. "People who knew what the score was," he said, "recognized the beauty of them. They were beautiful programs, and the texts were nice, too. But they weren't popular enough to draw a general audience, not like *Henry V* or *Sunset Boulevard*." They were popular, though, with the young film cineastes, like Lopate. "There was no promotion," he remembered, "just the names of these films, really obscure, the more obscure the better. This was the allure of the obscure, which, I think, was important to us in the sixties. It was a kind of occult knowledge."[10]

Despite the negative responses, Talbot scheduled "Forgotten Films II" three months later in June 1961, keeping his promise to prioritize a film's worth over its commercial appeal. "Forgotten Films II" had a different angle, featuring 28 films from the late 1940s and 1950s that were critical failures in America but whose directors were popular in Europe, particularly among the young, French New Wave directors. The series included three John Ford westerns, Otto Preminger's *Saint Joan* (1957), Alfred Hitchcock's *The Wrong Man* (1956), Howard Hawks's *Rio Bravo* (1959), Max Ophuls' *Letter from an Unknown Woman* (1948), Josef von Sternberg's *Jet Pilot* (1957), Douglas Sirk's *A Time to Love and a Time to Die* (1958), and Nicholas Ray's *Johnny Guitar* (1954). Bogdanovich's rationale for the second series underscored his auteurist approach. "We think the films at least deserve another look. Perhaps by paying less attention to the dialogue and more to their visual and symbolic qualities, we can discover what the Europeans see in American films that we miss."[11]

Talbot considered the series worth the investment (Bogdanovich may have added some push) since four more "Forgotten Films" series took place. Although the second and third ones did even worse financially than the first (the second grossed almost $2,000 less and the third did even slightly worse than the second), the final three fortunately did comparatively better. "Forgotten Films IV" grossed the highest of the six, $9,383; and surprisingly, "Forgotten Films V," which occurred in the middle of the New York newspaper strike, did a respectable $8,337. The final one grossed $8,799 in January 1964.

Even in the early years of the New Yorker, Talbot was interested in films other than the Hollywood classics. One of the theater's most successful shows in the early period was Leni Riefenstahl's *Triumph of the Will* (1935), the movie of the 1934 Nuremberg rally, which had never been commercially exhibited in New York. This screening of a controversial, Nazi film was reminiscent of Vogel's run of *The Eternal Jew*, but the motivations were different. Whereas Vogel used the film to force the audience to actively engage with its content, Talbot felt it deserved to be shown for its artistry, despite its reprehensible content.[12] (Since then, however, Talbot has changed his mind about the film. "As I grow older," he wrote to this author in an e-mail, "and know more about the Shoah I'm not comfortable with her film, no matter how well it was made. She was a diehard Nazi and my bottom line is that substance [the murder of Jews] is more significant than 'Art.'")

Shown on a Monday evening in June 1960, *Triumph of the Will* was a surprising success. "Suddenly 3,000 people showed up at 6 o'clock," Talbot recalled, "and they were all young Jewish kids in their twenties who had heard about this *racha movis*—that means *the angel of death* in Yiddish—and they wanted to see it on the screen." To accommodate the overflow crowd, he staged extra shows until three o'clock in the morning. The enthusiastic crowd had heard about Hitler, read about Hitler, but had never seen any films about Hitler. Their response to the film was unanticipated. "We thought that there was going to be some rioting or people accusing us of being neo–Nazis, but there was nothing like that," he once told an interviewer. "On the contrary, they came in very curious, and they were absorbed in it." Following this successful one-night presentation, which grossed $2,500, Talbot scheduled it for a first-run engagement in the fall on a double bill with Alain Resnais's *Nuit et Brouillard* (1955; *Night and Fog*), a thirty-minute French documentary survey of the Nazi extermination camps at Auschwitz and Dachau. The film was chosen, Talbot explained to a reporter, to counterbalance any suggestion of sensationalism in the programming.[13]

An ironic incident on the opening night was once recalled by Talbot. "I was at that time friends with Isaac Bashevis Singer. He used to come by to the New Yorker bookstore, to buy his newspapers. He liked to walk at night along Broadway. I was out in front of the theater when he came by. Of course he knew nothing about the cinema, let alone this picture, but he was so happy to see all these people lining up in the streets that he came over to me and said, 'Oh, Dan, what a pleasure it is to see people lining up for culture and not bread. Isn't that wonderful?' Little did he know."[14]

Triumph of the Will was the first in a ten-week experiment on Monday evenings in the summer of 1960, traditionally the slowest night for motion picture business. Talbot created the New Yorker Film Society to show very old, seldom-seen classics in this time period. The Nazi film was not the only controversial program in the Monday night series. *Operation Abolition* (1960), the notorious forty-five-minute film of the San Francisco student demonstrations in May 1960, which was prepared by the House Committee on Un-American Activities (HUAC), played on January 29, 1962. Screened with this film were the rejoinder from the ACLU of San Francisco, *Operation Correction* (1960), and Michael and Philip Burton's *Wasn't That a Time* (1961), showing some of the effects of HUAC's investigations.[15]

Avant-garde films also screened in the Monday evening series. Five successive Monday evenings of "Underground Movies" were advertised on the New Yorker calendar for May to June 1967. Included in the series were Michael Putnam's *The Hard Swing* (1962), Ron Rice's *Senseless* (1962), Robert Breer's *Pat's Birthday* (1962), and Ed Emshwiller's *George Dumpson's Place* (1965), among others. This was not the first time underground films showed at the New Yorker. Three years earlier in November 1964 the New Yorker had hosted Mekas's Film-Makers' Cinematheque, which had just resurfaced after a hiatus of seven months forced on it by the police for screening films like Jack Smith's notorious

Flaming Creatures (1963). In the following month, what Mekas described as another precedent in his *Village Voice* column, Talbot scheduled screenings of works by avant-garde filmmakers Stan Vanderbeek, Robert Breer, Bruce Conner, and Andy Warhol in his regular program rather than squirreling them away in the Monday evening series. Yet ten years later, at the closing of the New Yorker, Mekas disparaged the part that the theater, along with other rep houses (other than the Charles), played in supporting underground films. "We never really felt at home there [the New Yorker, the Bleecker, the 55th Street Playhouse, the Elgin, etc.], we always felt like we were in an enemy camp."[16]

Talbot hired two young film buffs, Marshall Lewis and Rudy Franchi, to help him curate the Monday evening programs. Both would later go on to program the Bleecker Street Cinema for Lionel Rogosin. "Marshall and I were always very close," Talbot said. "He died last year; he had become a homeless man." But at that time he was in good health and running the successful series, for which well-known film critics, scholars, and filmmakers, who were friends of Talbot's, wrote film notes. Bill Everson wrote on Paul Wegener's *The Golem* (1920); the *Village Voice* cartoonist Jules Feiffer, on Mervyn LeRoy's *Gold Diggers of 1933*; the novelist Terry Southern, on William A. Wellman's *A Star Is Born* (1937); Robert Brustein, founder of Yale Repertory Theatre, on *Never Give a Sucker an Even Break* with W.C. Fields (1941); the playwright Jack Gelber, on Erich von Stroheim's *Foolish Wives* (1922); Harold Humes, co-originator of *The Paris Review* literary magazine, on F.W. Murnau's *The Last Laugh* (1924); and Beat novelist Jack Kerouac, on Murnau's *Nosferatu* (1922).[17]

The Monday evening and the "Forgotten Films" programs were unusual in that they were programmed by others than Talbot, who normally kept curatorial responsibilities in his hands. Talbot's unconventional curatorial approach eschewed thematic programming, such as pairing two Joan Crawford vehicles or two films noirs, for fragmented programming, bringing together disconnected pairings where, Toby Talbot described in her memoir, "[o]pposites attracted, ... our audiences ... found that exhilarating." It was evocative of Vogel's technique at Cinema 16. Typical of this approach, the Winter 1967 calendar paired a Shakespearian film, Laurence Olivier's *Hamlet* (1948), with an Ealing Studios comedy, *The Lavender Hill Mob* (1951) starring Alec Guinness; and the "Winter Repertory 1971" calendar coupled the early Warners musical *42nd Street* (1933) with Sam Peckinpah's unconventional western *Ballad of Cable Hogue* (1970). "Dan Talbot used to do offbeat double bills," Bruce Goldstein, programmer for Film Forum 2, recalled. "He would show *Pull My Daisy* and *The Magnificent Ambersons*. That's another approach, which is difficult to pull off. You don't thematically link; you have two different things for people to discover." Mary Maguire, a regular patron, remembered that "the New Yorker used to put these incredible series together and made them so glamorous and romantic that you'd want to see every film." Mandelbaum, a regular patron of the theater as a teenager and young adult, liked the variety of the New Yorker's programming and its inventive double bills. "Their most famous double bill," he said, "was Buñuel's *El* [1953] with Lang's *M* [1931]. They had a sense of humor."[18]

While Talbot kept control of his programs, nevertheless, he did have help and advice. Everson, for example, assisted with the "D.W. Griffith Cycle" in the Monday evening series in 1962 "because he was an expert on these kinds of films [silent films]." Pauline Kael, with whom he had become friends, discussed business with him weekly by phone from California where she was still programming her husband's repertory theater, the Cinema-Guild. They talked "about where to get that print, how did you do with that show, I thought that was a good combination you put together," Talbot remembered. "You know,

An example of Talbot's fragmented programming. Courtesy Dan Talbot.

trade talk. We spoke for several years and helped each other; she helped me more than I helped her because she was in the business before me."

Later when Kael was fired by her husband, Talbot encouraged her to come to New York. "I told her," he said, "maybe you might have some nice orange trees in California, but if you want to be a movie critic you've got to come to the Big Apple." When she first came to New York, he helped her to find an apartment and advised her financially. "Not that I knew that much about money, but I knew more than she did." They continued their friendship often in late night, liquor-fueled sessions in his apartment arguing over films. "My wife, me, and her would just sit around—we both drank a lot, she drank more than I did—till three o'clock in the morning, arguing about movies, fighting: this movie's a piece of junk, this is a masterpiece, who was a good director. You know, the same kind of coffee shop arguments that you have with your pals. Nothing original."[19]

Kael with her long experience was probably a help to the more inexperienced Talbot in choosing films for his audience, which was a rich mix of film lovers. Talbot recalled that "[f]ilm cinephiles, film buffs, filmmakers came. Woody Allen used to come, and I didn't know who he was at that time. Writers came, critics came." In her memoir, Toby Talbot wrote that film buffs from all walks of life hung out at the theater: Columbia students Phillip Lopate and Morris Dickstein; critics such as Vincent Canby, Stanley Kauffmann, Dwight Macdonald, and Susan Sontag. Manny Farber, one of the few, contemporary film critics writing about American studio directors, had attached himself to the New Yorker Theater, where he became interested in foreign films. (Farber later dedicated his collection of essays, *Negative Space*, to the New Yorker Theater.) Film critic and author James Monaco, who frequented the theater as a student at Columbia University, remembered the audiences as mostly students, who "had a hunger for film that couldn't be satisfied with Times Square junk." They came from all over the city, he recalled, "down from Columbia or City [City College of New York] or up from NYU or over from Hunter College to escape from absurdity for a while."[20]

Most of the audience, however, were ordinary moviegoers: neighborhood people; people from the boroughs who loved older films; people of all ages, young, middle-aged, elderly. "At the New Yorker Theater," *New York Times* film critic Vincent Canby wrote in 1970, "little old ladies rattle their candy wrappers as loudly as they please and weep through Frank Borzage's 1927 version of 'Seventh Heaven.'" The daytime, regular patrons seemed an assorted collection, from Toby Talbot's description in her memoir: "Unemployed actors, a cop/part-time opera singer from Brooklyn, a farmer from upstate NY, a NJ architect between jobs, a blind man from our block, elderly retirees, blue-haired women living on fixed incomes, the Belgian from Great Neck who left home each morning with dispatch case and gray flannel suit, giving his wife the impression that he had a full-time job, even inventing office tales and handing her a 'paycheck' each Friday, drawn from a bank account set up by his rich parents—wife never suspicious. Every once in a while, he and Dan would link up at the Lyric or some other 42nd Street fleabag movie house, for a Melville, Walsh, Franju, or Preminger."[21]

The theater was integrated into the fabric of the neighborhood. The nearby New Yorker Bookstore where Singer came regularly for his newspaper gave a cultural cachet to the neighborhood. Talbot, Peter Martin, and Austen Laber, a friend and neighbor of the Talbots, opened it in 1965. Martin, who was the illegitimate son of Carlo Tresca, the anarchist leader from the 1930s, and who had co-founded the City Lights Bookstore in San Francisco with Lawrence Ferlinghetti, ran the bookstore for five years until it went into decline under his increasingly unstable management (he was an alcoholic) and finally closed. Martin and his wife then left New York and eventually moved to San Francisco where they both died within two years of each other of cirrhosis of the liver.[22]

The New Yorker also became peripherally involved in the political unrest in the late 1960s because of its proximity to Columbia University. In 1968 during the height of the protests against the Vietnam War, Mark Rudd, the leader of the Columbia University chapter of Students for a Democratic Society (SDS), and his followers one night commandeered the New Yorker—in a friendly way, Talbot noted. Rudd, who knew Talbot, announced to the audience that the theater was a liberated area. "They liked us," Talbot said. "It meant 'We don't want any funny stuff here, we want the theater to continue to run, and we don't want anyone to interfere with the operation of the theater.' He was like a little red guard in the theater."[23]

The day before the Columbia University demonstrations began in April 1968, Talbot had coincidentally scheduled a double feature, Jean-Luc Godard's political film about war and its inhumanity, *Les Carabiniers* (1963), with an eighteen-minute newsreel of a draft resistance movement in the summer of 1968, *Boston Resist*. During its two-week run, Talbot noted the local and international developments in his box office record: "the students take over buildings"; "Cops invade bldgs. Students strike." "Peace talks begin in Paris. Rain all day. French crisis begins."[24]

For its admirers, the theater was the cultural center of the Upper West Side. "It had a larger meaning than just film," Lopate said, "partly because Talbot aggressively drew in cultural figures, like Susan Sontag." It wasn't just that star-struck patrons could sight these celebrities; they could also listen in on their discussions with Talbot, who would station himself in the lobby. Film director Jonathan Demme remembered, in a *New York Times* article, that "there was a definite advantage to going to the New Yorker: after the screening you could loiter in the lobby and hear Dan Talbot exchanging views with learned cineastes. I never knew who they were. I just listened." His theater was his private salon. "The New Yorker myth," Sarris once said, as quoted in Talbot's memoir, "was born … because Dan initiated a dialogue with the audience. Dan believed an audience is always as intelligent as you want it to be. It was a lot of fun holding discussions in the lobby."[25]

Not only could audience members listen in on conversations, they could also participate through the guest books in the lobby, writing their opinions about movies, making suggestions for programs, even revealing personal issues. "Someone said that in these books," Talbot recalled, "you've got some of the psychic life of New York City. They would write things about their lives that the films suggested. Or there were angry comments, people who were just disturbed." Assertive comments on individual films ("Don't ever show anything like *The Magnificent Ambersons*!!!") or on the theater itself ("Your camera is noisy!!") were some entries. The film critic John Simon was always complaining about the bathrooms or the seats or the sound, Talbot remembered. Audience members made curatorial suggestions ("Bill together remakes & originals, e.g., Dietrich's & Britt's *Blue Angel*; Chaney & Laughton's *Hunchback*; the MGM & Italian versions of *Postman Always Rings Twice*."). Even political opinions, such as "Who needs red rat Chaplin?," would appear in the pages. Requests came from celebrities like W.H. Auden, who seemed predisposed to any of the films of Carole Lombard, Jean Harlow, or early Marilyn Monroe. Talbot remembered cases, he told Dan Yakir for a *Thousand Eyes* magazine interview, where overzealous cinephiles would use different penmanship to create the impression that their obscure object of desire was shared by others as well.[26]

Audience members also carried on mini-dialogues, often passionately, with each other. For example, in one exchange three patrons disagreed over Sergei Eisenstein's *Alexander Nevsky*: Patron #1: "Let's concentrate on Eisenstein and Pudovkin for the next two or three weeks, but we could do well without *Alexander Nevsky*"; Patron #2: (on the same page) "I agree with above, with the exception of *Nevsky*. Show it!"; Patron #3: (same page) "The damned fool who wrote the above wouldn't know a classic if he saw one." Even Talbot, who was not shy about expressing his opinions, engaged in the dialogues, especially when their jottings provoked him. To a sarcastic remark about Lionel Rogosin's film *Come Back Africa*, Talbot wrote "Idiot!" To a request for *Sink the Bismarck*, his reply was "This film stinks." And to a request for Val Lewton films, he wrote "Yes, they're very good."

Many of Talbot's ideas for programming came from the guest books, which he carefully read. He paid special attention to the frequently requested films. One of his most important finds through the guest books was *Sunset Boulevard*, which had been a commercial disappointment on its release and had not been seen in ten years in New York. "It was a film that had an underground cachet to it," Talbot remembered. "Don't ask me why. I don't know how these films develop it, but that film did. I sensed from my guest books that there were a lot of people interested in it. Every second or third page had *Sunset Boulevard*. I thought, 'What's going on here? There's something to this.'"

Locating the film, though, was difficult. When none of his distributors claimed to have a print or knew where to locate one, he turned to Kael for help. In one of their weekly phone conversations, she told him there was a print sitting in the Texas depot. "That was part of running a repertory theater," Talbot explained. "You had to know where the prints were because the studios didn't give a damn about booking your theater." In an interview with James Monaco, he talked about discovering prints through bills of lading that might pinpoint their location, for example, at some forgotten railroad siding in deepest Texas. Then when he confronted the studio with the location of the print, the studio would get the film for him.[27]

The year 1964 marked the beginning of changes for Talbot. First, there was the theatrical premiere of his one and only venture into filmmaking, *Point of Order*, which he had made with the independent filmmaker Emile de Antonio. Based on an idea by Talbot and one of the early examples of the emerging trend in the early sixties of the cinéma vérité documentary, the ninety-seven-minute film had been culled by de Antonio and Talbot from the 188 hours of television kinescopes of the Army-McCarthy Senate hearings of 1954 and then edited by de Antonio (it took him almost a year) into the final film. The film premiered at the Beekman.[28]

In that same year Talbot came across a film that would take him in a new direction and eventually out of the New Yorker. He had been experimenting with foreign films since 1961 after seeing Jean-Luc Godard's *Breathless* (1960) with Bogdanovich, who did not like the film. But it astounded Talbot, who thought Godard was a genius. From that point he started showing the occasional European film. In 1961 he premiered Andrzej Wajda's *Kanal* (1957). A year later, some more "unsold" foreign films that had been deemed too "noncommercial" by distributors were unveiled at the New Yorker: Orson Welles's *Mr. Arkadin* (1955), Michelangelo Antonioni's *Cronaca di un Amore* (1950; *Story of a Love*) and *Le Amiche* (1955; *The Girlfriend*), Akira Kurosawa's *The Idiot* (1951), Robert Bresson's *Pickpocket* (1959), and Luis Buñuel's *Criminal Life of Archibaldo de La Cruz* (1955). Except for *Mr. Arkadin*, which grossed $18,792 in its almost four-week run in October 1962, they did not make money (as the distributors had predicted). But Talbot was not discouraged. He began increasing his bookings of these unsold, "noncommercial" films, a trend that Vincent Canby, movie critic for the *New York Times*, said was "a natural follow-up to the pioneering work of film societies, which have been the only U.S. showcase for 'unsold' foreign pictures to this time."[29]

Then he and his wife saw *Before the Revolution* (1964), directed by a young Italian director, Bernardo Bertolucci, at the 1964 New York Film Festival. The film moved them. Talbot was determined to open it at the New Yorker, but the producer was not interested in a single exhibition of the film at a small art theater; however, he was open to selling Talbot the distribution rights. Talbot agreed and New Yorker Films, his new distribution company, was born, with *Before the Revolution* as its first acquisition. The film opened in July 1965 to good reviews but poor box office, doing respectable business in its first week ($5,526.70) and falling off in the second week ($2,127.43). (Two months later Talbot raised admission prices to $1.50.) Nevertheless, he continued to acquire distribution rights to other works of both unknown and known directors, and over the years New Yorker Films became one of the largest distributors of foreign art films. The crowning achievement of his career as a distributor, he felt, was Claude Lanzmann's *Shoah* in 1985.[30]

Talbot started off slowly with distribution, but by 1967 he had become more invested in it. He was also growing angrier with the tepid reception of critics and the public to "a lot of the new European cinema, a lot of the directors whom I construed to be very important." In 1969 he threw down the gauntlet, so to speak, to both groups. The challenge was a fifteen-week series, *One Dollar at All Times,* of fifteen mostly foreign films and short subjects, some new to the United States and others with previous limited exposure. Admission to all screenings—for critics as well as public—was one dollar. Talbot's idea, reported the *New York Times,* was "to offer some interesting, worthwhile, experimental movies at reasonable prices to an audience in between cultists and mass-audience moviegoers." Not afraid to express his displeasure in public against critics, distributors, and even the public, he vented a passionate critique, in a full-page, self-financed ad for the series in the *New York Times,* against the "senseless and archaic, traditional system of launching films," which was prohibitively expensive for important, noncommercial filmmakers. In another interview with a *Times* reporter, he estimated that the cost of opening a new or unknown film amounted to about $35,000 for advertising and publicity just for the pre-opening campaign and opening week. "The problem," he wrote, "is to find a thrifty and commonsensical way of joining interesting work with audiences who are tired of being seduced day in and day out."[31]

As the distributor for most of the films in the series, Talbot tested a new way of premiering foreign art films: he launched them collectively rather than in the more expensive, traditional manner of picture by picture and without the aggressive, prohibitively expensive publicity that usually preceded premieres. Instead, he wrote the *New York Times* ad himself without the typical hype. "[T]he films in this series represent some of the novel directions taking place in movies today," but, he acknowledged, "we cannot offer unqualified raves ourselves." Among the premieres were African director Ousmane Sembene's *Black Girl* (1966), Robert Bresson's *Pickpocket* (1959), Robert Frank's *Me and My Brother* (1969), and Jean-Marie Straub's *Chronicle of Anna Magdalena Bach* (1968), as well as short films by Jean-Luc Godard, Eric Rohmer, and Claude Chabrol. Each film ran for a week.[32]

Devoting almost four months to fifteen unknown features was a risky venture. The series' average weekly gross of $4,326 did not cover the weekly expenses of $4,500, without including advertising. It was "a total disaster," Talbot admitted to the *Thousand Eyes* magazine interviewer, "and I almost went down with it." Inclement weather contributed to its poor box office. Heavy snowstorms blanketed the city during two weeks of the run, and cold and sleet another week, sometimes cutting grosses in half.[33]

Nevertheless, Talbot stubbornly continued to bring in foreign premieres, often through New Yorker Films. A second series of independent foreign premieres in May 1972, what one journalist called a kind of last hurrah in America for independently made foreign films, again tested the public's interest. The result, Talbot apprised a *New York Times* reporter, would tell him "whether or not there is a future and a market for first-run foreign films." Again he complained of the "ferocious economics" of opening a new or unknown film. Talbot promoted the series with ads in the *New York Times, Village Voice,* and *After Dark,* and with a print of ten thousand flyers. Each film in the series played an open-end run as long as business warranted; Alain Resnais's *Je t'aime, je t'aime* (1968), for example, ran two weeks. The series lasted through August 30, but unfortunately, also did poorly at the box office. Its total gross was $73,664 for the slightly more than 15-week run.[34]

That year, 1972, however, was not a total failure for foreign films. Yasujiro Ozu's *Tokyo Story* (1953), an elegiac film about the last years in the life of an elderly couple on a final, disappointing visit to their children in different cities, had a seven-week run at the New Yorker in its American premiere. "Donald Richie [author and scholar of Japanese cinema] put me on to Ozu," Talbot recalled. "He had come back at that time from Japan to do a curating gig at MoMA. I remember screening *Tokyo Story* with Donald in the theater one morning. I tell you, I was just wiped out. I was in tears at the end of that movie. It was a huge success when I opened it."

In between these foreign premieres, which were sometimes paired with popular films to pull in the audience, Talbot continued his eclectic programming. Silent films and early sound films from Europe and Hollywood were still a draw. "The Vaults Are Open," a festival in April 1970 of early 20th Century–Fox films from the studio's vaults, was an interesting example of Talbot's digging for long-forgotten films. "Most of these films," noted the series calendar, "have not been seen theatrically for between 20 and 40 years, and most of them have never appeared on Television." The importance of the series, the calendar explained in its informative introduction, related to the campaign to convince studios to transfer their older nitrate films to acetate stock, in order to preserve them from disintegration. 20th Century–Fox, notoriously neglectful of its older films, was finally transferring some from its vault to acetate stock for the series. Included were rarely seen works by John Ford (*Judge Priest*; 1934), Preston Sturges (*Unfaithfully Yours*; 1948), F. W. Murnau (*Sunrise*; 1927), Raoul Walsh (*Me and My Gal*; 1932), Rowland Brown (*Quick Millions*; 1931), Howard Hawks (*The Road to Glory*; 1936), Erich von Stroheim (*Hello Sister*; 1933), Frank Borzage (*Seventh Heaven*; 1937), and Ernst Lubitsch (*Cluny Brown*; 1946).[35]

The end of the New Yorker came in 1973 when Talbot decided to give up exhibition despite the "sensational" business of that year and concentrate on distribution. Beginning with a four-week run of Bertolucci's *The Spider's Stratagem* (1970), which grossed a respectable $33,365, the larger part of the year screened mostly week runs of other single foreign art films and double features, which required less of Talbot's time and effort than did the series format, probably as he was spending more time on New Yorker Films. The theater ended its thirteen-year run in December 1973 with David Lean's *Lawrence of Arabia* (1962), and was then turned over to its new owner, the Walter Reade Organization.

In explaining his move, Talbot said he had lost rapport with the audience about three years previously. He couldn't show the outré, cutting-edge films that interested him because of a shift, he felt, in audience taste and in the cultural climate towards a more conservative, less adventurous bent. "New York," he told *Variety* in rather apocalyptic terms, "does not have a film culture."[36]

Perhaps, though, the critical factor was his need to make a decision whether to stay in exhibition or commit full time to distribution. By 1970 he had acquired sixty to seventy films and had also developed a small distribution network of repertory houses across the country—Max and Bob Laemmle's Los Feliz in Los Angeles, Mel Novikoff's Surf theatre in San Francisco, Art Carduner's Bandbox in Philadelphia, and Cy Harvey's Brattle Theatre in Boston. He had come to know most of the interesting young European filmmakers over the past ten years and felt he owed them something. Feeling ready to move on, he took the plunge and sold the theater, a move that his wife strongly objected to and that, he admitted in later years, he also deeply regretted.[37]

In fact, he eventually returned to film exhibition while running New Yorker Films. In 1982 he reopened the Midtown Theater on the Upper West Side as the Metro, a repertory movie house similar to the old New Yorker, showing many films from his New Yorker Films catalogue. At the same time he was also running Cinema Studio, a small two-screen movie house near Lincoln Center that showed a mix of foreign and offbeat first-run films. Over the years, these enterprises folded for various reasons. In 1986, disgusted with the poor quality of the prints he was getting from distributors, he decided to discontinue with repertory screening and converted the Metro to a twin cinema, which he closed in 2003. Cinema Studio closed in 1990 when the landlord took over the property for demolition and resale. In 2009 New Yorker Films went out of business. Talbot now owns a multiplex art theater, Lincoln Plaza Cinemas, in the Lincoln Center area of the Upper West Side.

Talbot's legacy for film culture in New York was enormous—premiering little-known foreign and American films, reviving older favorites like the Marx Brothers and W.C. Fields, uncovering unknown works by Welles, Buñuel, and Bresson, and placing priority on the merits of the films rather than their commercial value. "Talbot's policy of showing old, new, good, bad, and indifferent films," wrote Judith Crist in the last year of the New Yorker, "that are of interest to someone in the film community, [has earned him] the well-deserved epithet of patron saint of the neglected film.... What separated him from other exhibitors is a sense of obligation to both the artist and audience that is not predicated on box office results or advertising draw, as in his booking Alain Resnais's *Je T'aime, Je t'aime*, lambasted after its festival showing, because he owed it both to a great filmmaker and to his followers."[38]

Jonas Mekas's tribute in the *Village Voice* captures the essence of Talbot's talent: "What Talbot did ... he did from his own passion and he did it singlehandedly.... He did it as an Artist. That was his work of art that he had to do and he did it."[39]

Chapter 4

The Bleecker Street Cinema: From Repertory Theater to Independent Film Showcase

When the Bleecker Street Cinema opened on April 4, 1960, a month after the New Yorker Theater, in Greenwich Village, it had a different mission from the New Yorker's. Independent filmmaker Lionel Rogosin, frustrated by the indifference of U.S. distributors to his two award-winning films, intended it to showcase his films as well as those of other independent filmmakers that distributors ignored—"the sort," he told a *New York Times* reporter, "that may not be commercial precisely [sic] but ones which do deserve to be seen." Jonas Mekas proclaimed the theater in his *Village Voice* column a filmmaker's theater, which would bypass distributors and their power to select the films for theatrical release and to decide the shape of their release, uncut or mangled. The theater premiered Rogosin's second film *Come Back, Africa* (1959). Less than a month later, on April 28, in a show of support for Rogosin, whose film had received negative reviews from the New York film critics, Talbot also screened *Come Back, Africa* at the New Yorker.[1]

Rogosin was the son of a wealthy Jewish producer of rayon yarns; the company, Beaunit Mills, was based in New York and New Jersey. The young Rogosin had been president of the textile division of his father's firm, but eventually left to pursue his interests in social and political issues and in film as a means of fighting for social justice. His interest in film had been aroused at the age of ten or eleven by Robert Flaherty's *Man of Aran* (1934), which, Rogosin wrote in his unpublished autobiography, "reached the core of my emotions … [it] made the romantic Hollywood feature films of the time seem insipid and insignificant." While working for his father's company, he taught himself to use the 16mm Bolex camera. Like Amos Vogel, he wanted to use film to raise social consciousness about social and political issues, especially those of racism and fascism, which he saw as interconnected.[2]

In 1954, the thirty-year-old Rogosin left the firm, a move that caused a rift with his father that was never fully healed. Living in New York's Greenwich Village where he saw firsthand the underbelly of society, he decided to make a documentary-like fictional film set on the Bowery, using real life denizens of the area. He learned his craft as a filmmaker in directing and producing *On the Bowery* (1956), a 65-minute portrayal of skid-row life, with $60,000 of his own money and the help of three friends. The film, heavily influenced by Flaherty's documentaries, became the first American film to win a Grand Prize, for documentary feature, at the Venice Film Festival, as well as earning the British Film Academy Award for the best documentary of the year and an Academy Award nomination in Hollywood. With this experience, he then felt ready to embark on his dream project, a film on apartheid. His second film, *Come Back, Africa*, was a dramatized documentary on South African apartheid, which he made undercover by convincing the South African authorities it was a documentary on the nation's music. The film introduced Miriam Makeba to the world and received the Italian Critics Award at the 1960 Venice Film Festival. Even with this international attention, neither film was picked up by a U.S. distributor. Deciding to open his own theater, he took a ten-year lease in 1960 on the Renata Theater at 144 Bleecker Street, spent $40,000 to renovate it, and renamed it the Bleecker Street Cinema.[3]

Situated in the heart of the Village, the Bleecker Street Cinema was an icon of the bohemian scene of the 1960s, along with the Bitter End nightclub, where young people listened to folk singers Pete Seeger and Peter, Paul and Mary and laughed at the self-deprecating monologues of Woody Allen; Art D'Lugoff's Village Gate, which headlined jazz greats Thelonious Monk and Charlie "Bird" Parker; and Café Figaro at the corner of Bleecker and MacDougal Streets and Café Reggio a block north on MacDougal Street, two legendary cafes that served as watering holes for the struggling young writers and painters who crowded into the Village as well as the students from neighboring New York University.

The Bleecker Street Cinema's audience was mostly the downtown young people, disdainful of their uptown, square counterparts. They were loud and boisterous and indifferent to rules. "Having to run things," remembered Mary Kelly, Rogosin's assistant in the mid-sixties, "was a little tough." Drinking and drugs were part of the scene. There was one afternoon Kelly heard noise in the lobby and looked in to see a young man, "who was maybe on uppers and downers," raging and ranting, while some people were holding him by his arms and others were standing around, watching the scene as if it were a movie. Extracurricular spectacles could also play out inside the theater, such as the antics of the theater's jet-black, small house cat, Breathless (named in homage to Godard's film). Breathless would regularly escape from the office area and start to climb the movie screen, which, like most screens at the time, had small holes in it. Rudy Franchi, the house manager (who had by then followed Marshall Lewis from the New Yorker to the Bleecker), would get a signal on the house phone from the projectionist with the short message "cat's on the screen." Climbing onto the small stage in front of the screen, he would grab the cat, who was usually about two-thirds of the way up. Regulars in the audience would root for the cat to get to the top, but, as far as Franchi remembered, it never reached it.[4]

The Bleecker was not large; it had a very small marquee outside and a small and shabby, but clean, interior, according to Kelly. Inside, past a little colonnade, were the lower lobby and one tiny, wooden desk for the ticket seller. Its operation was primitive. The wait between screenings in a little, upper lobby to the left of the ticket desk was often interminable because the films would start later than scheduled, leaving people grumbling and pushing when it was time to go into the theater. About ten steps beyond the desk were the doors to the long and narrow, 250-seat theater. "Like many of the old

NYC revival houses," one former patron wrote on the *Cinema Treasures* website, "it offered a less than ideal viewing experience (long and narrow like a shoebox and barely a floor slant to speak of.... I'm getting claustrophobic even as I sit here recalling it, but hey, that was all part of the experience: we were roughing it for art's sake)." Also to the left of the desk on the same level were large curtains hanging from the upper level, which separated the lobby from the office.[5]

After the inaugural presentation of his *Come Back, Africa,* Rogosin seemed to be minimally involved in operating the theater; filmmaking was his principal interest. A series of general managers ran the theater (the first one was Adolfas Mekas, Jonas's brother) while he went on a three-month tour of Europe and Asia in the summer of 1960 to prepare his third independent film and to confer with European directors and distributors about obtaining their films for his theater. The calendar for the first year consisted mostly of foreign revivals with some of these first-run, neglected European films.[6]

Despite Rogosin's initial stated intentions, independent films were not a regular feature until later in the theater's existence. There were some programs of that nature in the early years. In March 1961 the Bleecker inaugurated a new, special Monday night series of "very rarely seen first-rate cinema," consisting of short subjects and experimental films (similar to the Monday night series Lewis and Franchi had worked on at the New Yorker) that Rogosin had probably obtained on his European tour of the previous year. One program comprised three short films from the British Free Cinema movement, directed by Tony Richardson and Karel Reisz, Lindsay Anderson, and Alain Tanner. The following week a group of Polish short subjects was shown, and the third week, a revival of Hans Richter's avant-garde feature, *8 × 8: A Chess Sonata in 8 Movements* (1957).[7]

As the prime mover behind the short-lived New American Cinema Group and avant-garde film exhibition, Mekas most likely had expected the Bleecker Cinema to be an important theatrical venue for independent and avant-garde films. Rogosin had been one of the founding filmmakers of the Group, and the theater had been designated the venue for their films. But Mekas did not program any independent films at the Bleecker until around February 1963, after the Charles Theater, where he had been helping the owners program avant-garde work, closed. He and his brother then moved their programs to the Bleecker. Under the auspices of their earliest film exhibition organization, Film-Makers' Showcase, they introduced "Monday Midnights," a weekly series that included retrospectives of the work of New York filmmaker Ed Emschwiller and San Francisco filmmaker Larry Jordan; new documentaries from New York, San Francisco, and Cuba; and the world premiere of Stan Brakhage's *Dog Star Man, Part I* (1962).[8]

On midnight, April 29, 1963, however, they crossed the line with their premiere of Jack Smith's controversial *Flaming Creatures*. Scenes such as elaborate, hilarious dance and orgy sequences and a discussion of makeup and penises with the drag-queen heroine, Francis Francine, one of the stars of Andy Warhol's *Lonesome Cowboys* (1968), contributed to its scandalous reputation. Smith was part of a group of avant-garde filmmakers which, according to Hoberman and Rosenbaum in their book *Midnight Movies*, "was distinguished ... by a combination of willful primitivism, taboo-breaking sexuality, and obsessive ambivalence toward American popular culture (mainly Hollywood)." Emerging in the early 1960s, they constituted the mythopoeic strand of the avant-garde (a term invented by P. Adams Sitney for his history of the visionary avant-garde), which based their creations on different mythological or mystical systems. Smith's source for *Flaming Creatures* was the mythology of the movies, Sklar wrote in *Movie-Made America*, particularly "a commentary on, an elaboration of, and a homage to the visual images and structures of Josef von Sternberg's 1930s films with Marlene Dietrich and to the 'B'-movie actress Maria Montez."[9]

Screening *Flaming Creatures* was a brazen move that almost seemed to dare the Bleecker management to react; and react it did. Marshall Lewis, who was by then the general manager, sent them an eviction letter. In his June 13, 1963, *Village Voice* column, Mekas gave an evasive explanation for the eviction. "The Bleecker Cinema people," he wrote, "did not like our movies. They thought the independent cinema was ruining the 'reputation of the theater.'" Eleven years later, however, he was more forthright in acknowledging that it was his particular films, not independent cinema, which had led to the eviction: "[W]e premiered 'Flaming Creatures' there and 'The Blonde Cobra,'" he wrote, "and then they threw us out ... they told us we were ruining the reputation of the theatre with our movies, and we were scaring the 'regular' public away." In his eviction letter, Lewis expressed his conflicted feelings about the eviction. "I regret ... that the experiment [screening avant-garde films] has not been successful," he wrote; "however, my concern for the reputation of the theatre comes before any personal feelings I might hold about *every* film-maker (good or bad) having access to a showing place." (Jack Smith's *Flaming Creatures* served as a weapon in Mekas's continuing battle against the licensing and censorship forces in New York in the 1960s and 1970s. Challenging a whole set of artistic and sexual norms, it was soon declared obscene by a New York Criminal Court and became the focus of police raids. Mekas, who championed the film as "one of the most beautiful and original films made recently anywhere," defiantly continued screening it at different venues despite the danger of police raids. In March 1964, he and three others were arrested for showing the film at the Bowery Theater. The film was even censored at the 3rd International Experimental Film Competition in Knokke-Le Zoute, Belgium.)[10]

In 1961 Rogosin departed for Europe to film his third feature, leaving the operation of the theater with Lewis. He remained abroad for approximately two years making the antiwar film, *Good Times, Wonderful Times* (1966). With Lewis in charge, the Bleecker became known as the repertory movie theater with an auteurist emphasis on the great foreign directors. Lewis was especially interested in French films. His auteurist approach spoke to the passions of the young downtown audience, among them New York University film students like Martin Scorsese, all of whom embraced the writings of Sarris and the films of the foreign and American auteur directors.[11]

Lewis had run a film society in Philadelphia before joining Talbot at the New Yorker. He moved to the Bleecker around the winter or spring of 1961; Franchi followed him a little later. Kelly described him as "very intelligent, affable. He knew a lot about films. At that time [working at the theater] he must have been in his mid-thirties. He was a good businessman. He knew how to run the business." Others painted him as strange or shy, but all agreed that he loved film. Ben Barenholtz, who employed him after he left the Bleecker, remembered him as one of those who "may have been crazy and had different tastes but they had a real love for film." Barenholtz credits Lewis with helping to launch *Bonnie and Clyde* (1967), which Warner Bros. was reluctant to release because of its violence, by managing to get a print from the studio and showing it at the Montreal Film Festival. (*Bonnie and Clyde* premiered at the Montreal Film Festival on April 8, 1967.)[12]

Lewis's partiality to the auteurist approach was reflected, for instance, in an early program, "Hollywood: On and Off-Beat," which put together musicals and low-budget psychological suspense films by six American directors admired by the French New Wave critics; Stanley Donen's *Funny Face* (1957) and Orson Welles's *Touch of Evil* was the first double bill in the series. Generally, he concentrated on revivals of works of older foreign directors such as Jean Renoir and Kenji Mizoguchi and contemporary European star directors and art house favorites, like Federico Fellini, Ingmar Bergman, and François Truffaut, with some revivals of works of favorite American auteur directors. Ted Ostrow, house manager in Lewis's last years at the Bleecker, remembered that "[t]he films were almost exclusively European and Asian: French, Russian, Italian, Japanese productions; directors like Godard, Truffaut, Renoir, Eisenstein, Fellini, Bergman, Kurosawa, Buñuel, Antonioni, Jacques Tati." The films were shown in double bills, two changes a week on Tuesdays and Fridays.[13]

Lewis adopted a unique curatorial method: each year he selected a group of works by the great directors that he would show throughout the year in different combinations. "We recycled films on a yearly basis," said Ostrow. "We had a list that had been established by Marshall. We knew what we had played, we knew what was available, and we said, for instance, that we hadn't played *Breathless* for eight months, let's book it together with a Truffaut." The double bills were carefully fashioned. Lewis had a knack, recalled Franchi, for creating interesting combinations. Films were paired in the manner preferred by most repertory curators (other than Talbot and Vogel), according to themes or other commonalities. "We wouldn't put a comedy together with a real tearjerker," Ostrow remembered, "but a comedy together with another comedy or a romance would work very well. Doing a double bill is a kind of art. You try to make sense out of what you're doing in the hope that the audience sees the appeal." One could go at different times to see Ingmar Bergman's *Naked Night* (1953) with Kenji Mizoguchi's *Ugetsu* (1953), *Ugetsu* with Jean Renoir's *La Grande Illusion* (1937), *La Grande Illusion* with Akira Kursosawa's *Sanjuro* (1962). Kelly remembers that Lewis was admired for the way he chose films. "It worked," she said. "We had packed houses."

This curatorial approach was, in Talbot's opinion, a successful and rewarding concept. "Bleecker was running very successfully under his [Lewis's] tutelage quite a few years," Talbot remembered. "To take a hundred of the great movies and show them all year round, recycling the double bills into other double bills, other combinations, was a great idea. It was like going to a film academy." Lewis may have had a practical reason as well for this curatorial approach. Franchi told this author that Lewis was forced to adopt this method because "[w]e had a limited pool of available films from the distributors," he said. "This was the reason why we showed the same films repeatedly."

The films were often packaged as festivals. In January 1964, for example, as a counterpoint to the Thalia's summer festivals, Lewis scheduled a 46-film "Winter Revival Showcase," which presented familiar classics like Sergei Eisenstein's *Alexander Nevsky* (1938) and infrequently revived French New Wave features—Jacques Demy's *Lola* (1961), Jean-Luc Godard's *My Life to Live* (1962), Georges Franju's *Thérèse* (1962), and Jacques Rivette's *Paris Belongs to Us* (1961). Films from Brandon Films, Inc., an independent distributor, were sometimes booked into the theater as a "Brandon Film Festival." For its sixth anniversary the theater featured exclusive revivals from Brandon Films, including films by Akira Kurosawa (*Throne of Blood*, 1957), Luis Buñuel (*Young and the Damned*, 1950), Sergei Eisenstein (*Ten Days that Shook the World*, 1928), Marcel Carné (*Bizarre, Bizarre*, 1937), F. W. Murnau (*Nosferatu*, 1922), Fritz Lang (*Metropolis*, 1927, *M*), René Clair (*Under the*

Roofs of Paris, 1930), Robert Bresson (*Les Dames du Bois de Boulogne*, 1945), and Jean Cocteau (*The Testament of Orpheus*, 1960). Following this series, a weeklong tribute to the foremost American auteurist Orson Welles and the 25th anniversary of the release of his masterpiece, *Citizen Kane* (1941), took place in anticipation of its withdrawal from U.S. distribution by RKO.[14]

Lewis constantly replenished his repertoire so as not to become stagnant. New films were introduced and added to the lineup if they proved successful. "We always worked to expand our repertoire," Franchi remembered. "We would incorporate new films when they became available, like *Jules and Jim* (1962)." Their mission, he said, was to see and screen as many important, but often obscure, films as they could. "Andy Sarris would select films [from local distributors' lists], often obscure ones, like a Losey film, that he knew about but had never seen, and we would book them for the theater. If they were a success, they would go into the repertoire." They also began premiering films. In February 1962, Lewis launched the New York premiere of Akira Kurosawa's five-year-old *The Lower Depths* (1957). Following this successful run, he booked a double bill of Jean Vigo's *L'Atalante* (1934) and *Zéro de conduite* (1933), both of which had not been distributed locally since their original U.S. release in 1947.[15]

In October 1962 Lewis announced plans to increase the number of new, unconventional foreign films. His first two bookings were *The Lady with a Dog* (1960), a Soviet adaptation of a Chekhov short story, and *Tire au flanc* (1960; *The Army Game*), a New Wave French comedy by Claude de Givray. Montreal was their principal source for new French films, according to Franchi. Lewis and Franchi would travel there to obtain the U.S. rights from Quebec distributors, with whom they would arrange a first-run showing with the idea of hopefully finding a U.S. distributor. Ideas for new features sometimes came from the Montreal Film Festival; one such borrowing was a festival of "TV commercials and documentaries to illustrate the art—and pop art—influences of television."[16]

The cavernous office of the Bleecker soon became the salon for the fans of auteurism and the French New Wave, and its basement, the home of the auteurist magazine, *The New York Film Bulletin*, which was published by Franchi. Sarris came down on Sundays to meet with eight to ten people to talk about film. He fondly remembered the "many convivial hours of Francophilia and cinemaphilia" he spent at the Bleecker Street Cinema with "Village visionaries like Rafe Blasi, Rudy Franchi, and Marshall Lewis." Reminiscing on the *Cinema Treasures* website, Franchi recalled the heated discussions on the auteur theory, which "was quite controversial at the time and not at all accepted by most of the movie establishment. Pauline Kael was strongly against it as was ... Bosley Crowther and Dwight MacDonald." His magazine, following the auteurist approach of the British magazine *Movie* and the French *Cahiers du Cinéma*, was the first in the U.S. to translate and publish articles from the French magazine. Interestingly, the *Bulletin*'s aesthetic diverged from the theater's programming preferences, favoring the cutting-edge, minor American auteurs over the European directors. "The magazine was not auteurist in the sense of Ingmar Bergman," Lopate elucidated in his memoir, "but in the sense of Joseph H. Lewis [a B movie director admired by the auteurists]." Franchi's antagonism towards the rapid-cutting editing technique of montage, which had been pioneered by the early Soviet director Serge Eisenstein, Lopate wrote, led him to proclaim that he preferred any one sequence in a Stanley Donen musical to all of Eisenstein.[17]

Many of the New Wave French directors counted the Bleecker as their favorite theater in New York. François Truffaut, who once declared that the Bleecker was to New York what the Cinémathèque Française was to Paris, met Lewis through Helen Scott, the then public relations person for the French film office in the United States, Unifrance Film. Lewis had become friends with Scott after she helped him to get a print of Jean Renoir's *Rules of the Game* (1939), which he regarded as the greatest film of all time and which had not been shown in years after its rights had lapsed. Scott, who lived in the Village, introduced Truffaut to Lewis and the Bleecker during one of her walks with the French director on his visit to New York. Later, she also introduced Jean-Luc Godard to Lewis and the theater. Truffaut would often act as mediator to persuade friends and acquaintances in France who owned the rights to films that were unavailable in the States to release them to the Bleecker. Godard, years later when he was given an award by New York critics, refused it and instead said "Give it to the Bleecker."[18]

An intimacy had grown between the theater and these New Wave directors. One of Franchi's fond anecdotes involved Truffaut. "We were fanatical about proper projection and proper screen ratio for the three screen formats," he reminisced once on *Cinema Treasures*. "We had evolved a system of mattes that would work by pulleys so as to change from CinemaScope to standard ratio to what was known then as VistaVision (and is now known as wide-screen.). Since we always showed double bills, we would have to go backstage and re-arrange the mattes, if they were in different formats. On one of Truffaut's visits we were showing a CinemaScope film (actually it was *Jules and Jim*) and a second feature in standard format. I excused myself, telling him I had to change the screen ratio. He asked if he could come and watch. He stepped behind the screen as I worked the pulleys, and as soon as I finished, the film started. Truffaut was fascinated by seeing the film projected through the screen and also by watching the audience watch a film. He stayed back there for quite a while. The result of that experience can be seen in his next film, *The Soft Skin* (1964; *La Peau douce*), when the lead actor goes behind a movie screen."[19]

Around 1963 or early 1964 Rogosin returned to New York to find distribution for his latest film, the antiwar *Good Times, Wonderful Times*. The Vietnam War was raging and antiwar fever was high. The times were ripe, he felt, for his film, and he wanted to reach a wider audience at an uptown theater than his small, out-of-the-way movie house could provide. "We had to get prints and start the campaign," Kelly, whom Rogosin hired to help him with the opening of the film, remembered. "He wanted a regular, commercial New York opening. He wanted a big splash." Lewis continued to run the theater while Rogosin concentrated on his film and antiwar efforts. He returned to England in 1965 to help organize, along with Bertrand Russell (a fan of *Good Times, Wonderful Times*) and others, the British Artists' Protest and the European Artists' Protest against the Vietnam War.[20]

Rogosin's return in early 1966 marked the beginning of the theater's switch from a principally repertory theater to one that mixed premieres of neglected foreign and independent films with repertory. The plan, according to Lewis in a March 1966 *New York Post* article, was to sell these films to 16mm distributors if other theaters did not follow the Bleecker Street's lead. Certain developments precipitated this change. Rogosin's expectation that his latest film would have a premiere in an uptown theater was frustrated. The scheduled premiere at the Carnegie Hall Cinema was delayed due to scheduling glitches. (The film was finally screened at the Carnegie in July 1966.) In addition, the theater was experiencing greater difficulty in renting the standard films in its repertory because of Janus Films, a prominent distributor of foreign films in the United States; the distributor was acquiring the rights to many of these films and taking them out of circulation for a time, then re-releasing them in what it called "festival packages." Whereas previously Lewis could easily book a single film, he now found that more of his films were no longer available as single rentals but only as part of a festival package. Since the smaller Bleecker could not generate the grosses that the larger repertory houses like the Elgin could, it was less attractive to Janus Films. Looking back on the theater in later years, Rogosin wrote that what was particularly devastating was that "they [Janus Films] obtained exclusive rights to show some of our favorite and successful standbys, which we had shown for years, such as *Black Orpheus* (1959) and *The Queen of Hearts* [he probably meant Philippe de Broca's *King of Hearts*, 1966]. After that the distributors refused to rent us the films."[21]

As a result of these trends, Rogosin returned to the idea of using his theater as a showcase for independent films. "The Janus [took away] the repertoire that was the Bleecker's bread and butter," Ostrow said, "so Lionel started moving in the direction of releasing new, independent films and made deals for a variety of films." Another reason for the shift may have been the growing staleness of the programming. The repertory did not change, according to Ostrow, during Lewis's final years at the Bleecker. "We'd show *Breathless* a few times, *Potemkin* a few times; they just seemed to repeat. I don't remember any innovation until we started with *Scorpio Rising*."

Kenneth Anger's *Scorpio Rising* (1963), another mythopoeic film based on Hollywood mythology, inaugurated the new, first-run change in April 1966. Commenting on Hollywood's mythical creations of James Dean and Marlon Brando as motorcyclists, the film was a great success, with lines snaking around the block. Adding to its appeal was its pre-show attraction. "*Scorpio Rising* starred a guy named Bruce Byron," recalled Ostrow, "who showed up at the premiere on his Harley Davidson; he had on a leather vest with silver studs on the back that said *Scorpio Rising*.... He was a character, kind of short, stocky, nice guy.... Then he showed up just every night during the run of the film, parked his Harley Davidson out front, came in and struck a pose in the lobby in his leather vest, much to the delight of the moviegoers."

Rogosin obtained *Scorpio Rising* through the Film-Makers' Distribution Center, one of the two small distribution companies for independent films that he had been involved with Mekas in establishing (the other was the Film-Makers' Cooperative). He was turning to these small distributors—Dan Talbot's New Yorker Films, Brandon Films, the Film-Makers' Cooperative—for his new thrust. Late in 1966 he created his own distribution company, Rogosin (later Impact) Films, which soon began booking 16mm prints of independent works by Kenneth Anger, Emile de Antonio, Robert Downey, and Joris Ivens as well as films from Czechoslovakia, Hungary, and China, for universities, cultural groups, and his own theater. Impact Films became an organ for antiwar and civil rights films as well.[22]

A second premiere, also in April, followed *Scorpio Rising*—Jonas Mekas's 1964 Venice Film Festival Grand Prize-winning *The Brig* (1964), which, unlike the former film, was panned by the critics. "Leonard Nimoy had some interest in it [*The Brig*]," said Ostrow. "It was a grim, tragic, black-and-white film about men in prison, and nobody wanted to open it. Leonard Nimoy and I had a cup of coffee across the street at the coffee shop and he convinced me to take a chance and I did and it bombed. It was awful, didn't get good reviews."

More underground films came next. Robert Downey, Sr.'s two films—*Chafed Elbows* (1966), a quasi-underground comedy about a man who goes on welfare and marries his mother, and *Putney Swope* (1969), a satire of the advertising world—did well critically and financially. "Downey was a Madison Avenue ad exec," Ostrow recalled, "who was making these commercials that nobody would put on TV 'cause they were too outrageous. So he spliced them together and put a film around them and came out with a feature." Another important underground film that played at the theater was Shirley Clarke's *Portrait of Jason* (1967), a monologue by a bespectacled, aging African-American hustler. Other independent films, like Sheldon Rochlin's *Vali, the Witch of Positano* (1965), were not as well received by the public or critics.[23]

Along with these independent films, Rogosin had an interest in the contemporary films and directors of Eastern Europe. He acquired seven Czech films through his distribution company, including the Czech New Wave *Diamonds of the Night* (1964) and *Transport from Paradise* (1962), a prizewinning film about the Nazi persecution of Jews of Middle Europe. Other American premieres included Jerzy Skolimowski's *Le Départ* (1967); Jean-Luc Godard's *Les Carabiniers* (1963), which opened simultaneously at the Bleecker and the New Yorker; and Kenji Mizoguchi's *Sansho, the Bailiff* (1954). Rogosin also booked antiwar films, like *17th Parallel: Vietnam in War* (1968), through Impact Films.

Where the Bleecker had once been the meeting place for auteurist fans, it was now the hangout for independent filmmakers, who congregated in the theater's office to talk with Rogosin about distribution of their films as well as screening opportunities at the theater. "Bob Downey and Jonas Mekas used to come over a lot," Kelly recalled. "I was watching this parade of filmmakers talking about their unusual films with Lionel in his office." Downey was always planning new projects; he hired Ostrow once to be in a little film he was making for an off–Broadway play. Sheldon Rochlin was in the office preparing for the opening of his film *Vali*. A particularly important outlet for young filmmakers was the open screenings at midnight of their films, similar to the pioneering paradigm of the defunct Charles Theater. "I met one of the people," recalled Michael Rogosin, Lionel's son, "who said his whole life changed because he came up to Dad with a roll of film that he said he had made, and Lionel told him he could show it at the Bleecker." The early films of the acclaimed underground filmmaker Warren Sonbert, made while he was a student at New York University, were first shown at the Bleecker and the Film-makers' Cinematheque on Wooster Street. "I spent the better part of my ill-spent youth at the Bleecker," David Ehrenstein wrote on *Cinema Treasures*. "And most of all I remember Sunday mornings when Warren Sonbert showed his films to all his friends."[24]

For Lewis, though, the changes marked the beginning of his end at the Bleecker. He was not interested in the avant-garde or the socially conscious films that Rogosin favored. Ostrow sensed that he was feeling resentful, although he avoided any confrontation with Rogosin. "He was a bit of a whiner behind the scenes and under his breath," Ostrow remembered. "He acted like he was in a constant state of frustration. My impression was that he and Lionel were somehow at loggerheads. I think Marshall was solidly behind keeping the theater in repertory and Lionel was pushing for something new."

Some of his behavior was puzzling to Ostrow. One time Lewis sent him and his girlfriend in his place to the Montreal Film Festival (it was probably the summer 1966 festival for which he had served as the U.S. representative on the festival committee) without giving him any idea of his role there. He may have been disengaging from the theater; Bob Downey, who later employed Lewis as his publicist, thought he was tired of booking films. Lewis probably left in early 1969 and worked as a publicist for Barenholtz and Downey. About twelve years later, he suffered from HIV/AIDS along with a drug problem and eventually became destitute. Friends once found him sleeping on a park bench. According to Barenholtz, at the end of his life, Jonathan Demme, the director, took care of him until his death from AIDS.

While a series of general managers, including Ostrow, ran the Bleecker, Rogosin was spending time on his filmmaking and increasingly less time with the theater. Finally, in October 1969, he rented the Bleecker to Grove Press, which advertised it as the Evergreen Bleecker Street Cinema. By September 1970 Grove Press had left and Rogosin used the Bleecker for the official opening of his new film *Black Roots* (1970). In January 1972 he temporarily closed it, then opened only on weekends, showing films like a Busby Berkeley series. Finally, in 1974 he sold it to Sidney Geffen, who also owned the Carnegie Hall Cinema.

Rogosin wrote in his unpublished autobiography that "I finally gave it up because I started to lose money." He blamed his money problems on Janus Films and the competition from several other repertory cinemas, especially the Elgin; but Barenholtz dismissed Rogosin's complaint. "There was certainly enough film around that you didn't have to depend on the Janus," he said. "Janus didn't own the Marx Brothers or W.C. Fields." This rebuttal, however, misses the point that the foreign, not American, revivals were the crux of the Bleecker's repertoire. Other factors, Barenholtz believed, contributed to the theater's demise. Rogosin, he pointed out, was more interested in filmmaking than in programming. Furthermore, Barenholtz felt that the theater had lost its inventive edge.[25]

Rogosin's troubled personal life may have also played a part in giving up the theater. He had separated from his wife in the mid–1960s and was living for a while in the basement of the theater, where he drank, according to Ostrow, and occasionally came upstairs to the office after hours, pulled plants from their pots, and spilled liquid on the bills.

Finally, the environment for independent film distribution was dispiriting. The Film-Makers' Distribution Center had closed in 1970 due to lack of funds; and Impact Films, Rogosin wrote in his autobiography, was struggling against the overt and covert "grey list" of independent films by the three commercial television networks and public television. What Rogosin seemed to mean was that these television outlets, uninterested in screening independent films, were ignoring, rather than deliberately banning, them. A receptive policy on the part of the stations would have made Impact Films financially viable, Rogosin claimed. All these frustrations with exhibition and distribution made filmmaking more attractive to Rogosin: "[B]y that time [1973–4] I began to sense," he wrote, "that my filmmaking was being neglected because of all this enterprise ... my creative work was suffering." He sold Impact Films in 1978.[26]

* * *

In comparing the Bleecker Street Cinema to Henri Langlois's Cinémathèque Française in Paris, Truffaut seemed to imply that the Bleecker, like the Cinémathèque Française, served as a film school for future directors. Certainly, this is what Scorsese once told Michael Rogosin; the Bleecker, he had said, was the film academy, the classroom for New York University film students. Ostrow remembers it as "a place where you could find a dependable program of great merit. It was not so much interested in money as in, really, public service. It's where I got my film education. I had not seen any of the repertoire before I went to the Bleecker." For young filmmakers it also gave them their first opportunity to screen their films. Tom Luddy of the Pacifica Foundation told Rogosin years later, "You not only made films but you made filmmakers." And it was part of the exciting bohemian spirit of the Village. "If I were a filmmaker I'd create a homage to the bygone days of the truly bohemian Bleecker Street," Marco Acevedo conjured up on *Cinema Treasures*. "My characters would meet at the Bleecker Cinema, argue about the movies over espressos at Le Figaro and end the evening getting blasted over martinis at the Village Gate while Dizzy Gillespie and Tito Puente jam onstage."[27]

In his unpublished autobiography, Rogosin told of receiving his highest accolade in 1995 in Los Angeles where he had settled: "I was sitting in a restaurant on Sunset Blvd when my waitress asked me if I was Lionel Rogosin. Slightly mystified I naturally said yes, and I was told that the young woman at a nearby table used to work at the Bleecker St. She waved to me; I recognized her and waved back. When she and her party left they came over to my table and gave me a marvelous compliment. One of her companions volubly said to me, the Bleecker St. Cinema was the greatest cinema in the world."[28]

Chapter 5

The Charles Theater: The Underground Film in the Heyday of the East Village

When Walter Langsford and Edwin Stein, Jr., opened the Charles Theater at 193 Avenue B in the East Village, they were the youngest of the first-wave entrepreneurs of New York repertory houses (Langsford was 26 and Stein, 30). Operating in the early sixties when the East Village was becoming a countercultural center for artists and writers, they made their theater part of the movement and gave American avant-garde filmmakers their first stable, commercial venue. Langsford, who came from Boston, Kentucky, "which has 300 people," he told a *New York Herald Tribune* reporter, "when I'm home for a visit," had left college in January 1959, a semester before graduating, and came to New York in pursuit of a young dancer with whom he had fallen in love. The romance didn't work out, but his love affair with New York did. "I got off the plane in Newark," he said, "that wonderful old airport that looked like Grand Central, took a bus to Eighth Avenue, where more things were happening than all the time I was growing up in Kentucky: prostitutes with skirts up to here, drunks laying in the door, cops screaming by, sirens going by. 'Wow,' I thought, 'this has got to be the greatest place in the world.'"[1]

Through the friend of a colleague in Kentucky, with whom he had interned in Paul Green's outdoor symphonic drama, *The Stephen Foster Story,* he obtained a summer job at the Sharon Playhouse in Connecticut, and there became friends with John Griggs, the silent film buff who ran the Sutton Cinema Society in the city (Griggs was operating a weekend silent film program during the summer in the area). Griggs, in turn, introduced him to Dan Talbot, who hired him as a manager at his New Yorker Theater. A few months later, in March 1961, Talbot assigned him to manage the Charles Theater, which he had opened as an East Village version of the New Yorker. The Charles, formerly the Bijou, had been "an action house with whatever Hollywood was sending out," Langsford said. The opening double feature was *Sunset Boulevard* and Jacques Becker's *Casque d'or* (1952). Unfortunately, the revival policy of the New Yorker did not do well in the area, and the theater closed after nineteen weeks on July 17, 1961, with Irvin Kershner's *Hoodlum Priest* (1961) and Robert Mulligan's *The Great Imposter* (1961).

Langsford, who was living on 12th Street in the East Village, stayed in the neighborhood. It was an exciting place that was transitioning into a bohemian area for young, creative people. Writers, artists, actors, and young filmmakers, as well as a number of middle-class, young people without a lot of money who wanted to live in New York, were beginning to move there for its low rents; there they mingled with the long-established ethnic, working-class residents. "I loved that polyglot population," recalled Langsford, "because in Kentucky everybody's the same; my family's been there since 1790. To see the Jewish neighborhood further down on the Lower East Side and the contiguous Ukrainian, Russian, and Spanish neighborhoods was very exciting to me." The Mafia was part of this ethnic neighborhood; Langsford had encountered a Mafia member shortly after relocating to the Charles as its manager. "The Charles theater building," remembered Langsford, "had a little taxpayer in the corner of it [*taxpayer* refers to extra street-front space that a building rents out as a store to pay the taxes on the building] that was rented out as a restaurant and bar, George's Greek Restaurant. In the bar, hoods from the Mafia were running numbers. One of my first encounters with them was Louie, this strong-arm man, who came over and said, 'Hey Walter, if you have any trouble, don't call the cops, call me. I'll take care of it.' He didn't want the police down there."

On the corner of 12th Street and Avenue B was a local saloon called Stanley's, which many of the newer residents in the neighborhood used as a gathering place. "It was like an early version of the TV show *Cheers*," said Langsford. "A lot of young intellectuals, at least we liked to think of ourselves as that—artists, musicians, actors, filmmakers, sculptors—hung out there, so we had many friendships." At Stanley's he struck up a friendship with Ed Stein (known to his friends as Ted), who also lived on East 12th Street. New York–born Stein had grown up on Park Avenue, gone to Fieldston School, then to Yale for a master's degree in English literature, where he had been an editor at Yale University Press; he had also served two years in the Army. He was taking a year's sabbatical between his master's and doctoral studies at Yale.

Sitting in the bar with the darkened Charles Theater in full view (it was located diagonally across from Stanley's), the two young men decided to reopen the theater, this time as a "new movement" for the Lower East Side. They were not interested in making money but in being, in their words, "at the forefront of film." Hollywood films, they felt, were moribund, other than those of the auteurist directors; they wanted their theater to be a showcase for a different kind of film than the "dying" Hollywood product of the mainstream theaters. A creative ferment was bubbling in the area with the influx of the new residents, who saw themselves as rebels against the oppressive institutions of postwar American society; and they felt a part of it. Stein put up the money to open the theater, which was a Mickey Rooney–Judy Garland "Come on, kids, let's put on a show" type of venture. "At that point in our lives," Langsford remembered, "we didn't make long-range plans, we made short-range ones. We thought the theater might catch on and pay for itself and continue." The year of operation during Stein's leave from school would be a test to see if the theater could become self-supporting.

Langsford and Stein leased the theater from Harry Brock, whose advice to the novice entrepreneurs was to "put lots of salt on the popcorn so they'll buy more soda." Being the anti-establishment entrepreneurs that they were, they reversed his advice and provided free coffee to their patrons. Stein's family lawyer, Victor Gettner, who was also the attorney for the New York Civil Liberties Union, established them as a corporation, The Tenth Muse, Inc., and also set up the Midnight Film Society. On their letterhead Edwin

Stein, Jr., was listed as president, Walter Langsford as vice president, and Fred von Bernewitz as manager.

Getting the theater ready for opening was a do-it-yourself job, described by *Cue* writer Jesse Zunser: "They cleaned out the dusty old building and washed it down. They bought paint and brushes, and gave the landmark a new surface inside and out. They bought hammers, nails, and a Do It Yourself booklet, and set about doing their own carpentering, plumbing, electrical mending and sign making, roof-leak plugging, floor-hole repairing, cement patching, marquee fixing, etcetera. They fixed up the cashier's coop, whitewashed the cellar, scrubbed out the steam boiler—and, one cold wintry night, says Ed, Walt napped in the furnace because it was the only warm spot in the house. He had been cleaning it out—and besides it was four o'clock in the morning." Finally came the logo for their theater, which was designed by George Maciunas, a Lithuanian-born, experimental American artist and a founding member of Fluxus, an international community of artists, architects, composers, and designers. Maciunas, who lived in the neighborhood, designed a logo that fit their drive to be different.[2]

The Charles opened on October 1, 1961, with a double feature, the French adventure-comedy *Fanfan La Tulipe* (1953) and the 1954 British animated film *Animal Farm*. The standard, weekday schedule of double features was their concession to commercial considerations, even though it turned out to be the least profitable part of their programming. Langsford borrowed some ideas from the New Yorker, one of them being books displayed in the lobby for audience input. Suggestions from these books gave them ideas for bookings, as they had for Talbot. Their weekly programs, extending from great classics through a wide-ranging selection of recent films, were similar, according to Hoberman and Rosenbaum in their book, *Midnight Movies*, to "a handful of other Manhattan revival theaters (the Thalia, the New Yorker, the Bleecker Street Cinema) that catered to the rising interest in offbeat movies." Classic works by Orson Welles (*Touch of Evil* and *Citizen Kane*), John Ford (*Grapes of Wrath* and *Tobacco Road*, 1941), John Huston (*The Maltese Falcon*, 1941 and *The Treasure of the Sierra Madre*, 1948), as well as long-unseen ones by foreign directors like Roberto Rossellini (*Flowers of St. Francis*, 1950), Yves Allegret (*Les Orgueilleux*, 1953) and Luis Buñuel (*Los Olvidados*, 1950) appeared on the Charles's screen. More recent films included ones from Britain (Carol Reed's *Outcast of the Islands*, 1951; Alexander Mackendrick's *The Lady Killers*, 1955; and Joseph Losey's *Chance Meeting*, 1959) and Hollywood productions (Elia Kazan's *Face in the Crowd*, 1957; George Steven's *Shane*, 1953; and Joshua Logan's *Bus Stop*, 1956).[3]

American films took up a large part of the weekday programs. Langsford and Stein once encountered the same problem in obtaining a film for a seventeen-day Humphrey Bogart festival that Talbot had experienced in locating *Sunset Boulevard*. "Most [of Bogart's films] were available, except for *Beat the Devil* [1953]," Langsford said. "All the distribution companies said that the film was unavailable; they didn't have a copy of it." The two men and their friends were not discouraged. "We thought it must be somewhere. So we were brainstorming one night, and somebody said, 'Let's call John Huston and see where it is.'" That Huston was in Africa did not deter them. "I don't know how we got the connection," Langsford marveled, "but we found the hotel where he was staying and we called him. He answered the phone and we said, 'We'd like to show *Beat the Devil* with some other Bogart film,' and he told us where we could find it." The festival took place in October 1962 with *Beat the Devil* in the schedule.[4]

Phillip Lopate remembered that the Charles was particularly good for showing the

Ed Stein, left, and Walter Langsford lugging reels into the theater for a future program, circa 1962. Charles Theater Collection, MoMA Department of Film Archives, New York.

work of obscure American auteurs, including young American directors who had been singled out by the *Cahiers du Cinéma* critics as promising filmmakers. "That would be the place," he said, "where you would see movies like Paul Wendkos's *The Burglar* (1957) and *The Case Against Brooklyn* (1958). Wherever there was a rumor of a young director like Irv Kershner that might be worth checking out, they would show those movies. So they showed things that nobody else was showing, and largely American." For Lopate, the screenings helped him to "fill in the gaps" in his film education. The young entrepreneurs used the French New Wave angle in curating a major series on French-praised American directors, such as established B directors Allan Dwan and Samuel Fuller and a young American director, Gerd Oswald. The highlight of the series was the "Edgar G. Ulmer Festival," which, according to the theater's press release, was a response to a recent claim made by François Truffaut that Ulmer was "the best American film director today." The series was intended to test Truffaut's assertion.[5]

Separately from the regular weekday schedule, Langsford and Stein carried out their dream of operating an unconventional movie theater. From the beginning, they wanted their theater to be receptive to all the forms of creative activity that were beginning to flourish in the neighborhood and city. "We opened the theater to everything," Langsford said. Robert Downey, Sr., produced a couple of his plays at the theater; one, which played weekends at midnight in November 1962, *What Else Is There?*, was a short play "written with wit and charm," wrote a *Village Voice* theater critic, which "you either swing with, as I did, or you find it repellent." Other activities included an art gallery, which was started by the neighborhood 10th Street Gallery, and jazz concerts and children's movies on Sundays. "There was a spark in the neighborhood of creative activity," Langsford said. (A Wednesday program in January 1962 that was devoted to peace films brought them a visit from the FBI.)[6]

Their principal goal, however, was to experiment with films that did not fit into the format of the daily programs. One outlet for such films was their Midnight Film Society. There were precedents for the Midnight Film Society. Talbot had already set up his own New Yorker Film Society to screen special films on Monday evenings; and Rogosin had allowed independent filmmakers, including Jonas and Adolfas Mekas, to screen their

Poster for a "Jazz at the Charles Theatre" program, March 4, 1962. Donated by Walter Langsford. In the Charles Theater Collection, MoMA Department of Film Archives, New York.

films at midnight at the Bleecker Street Cinema. Langsford remembered that the idea for the society came up in discussions that most likely included Jonas Mekas. "We didn't want to do a conventional film policy," said Langsford. "We decided that the only time that could be done would be after the regular features and on Saturday, so we started the Saturday midnight shows. That was a good choice and it became a popular event." The midnight events, which became all the rage even outside the anti-establishment East Village, soon expanded to Fridays.

As part of these midnight shows of rarely and never-before seen films, Langsford and Stein screened uncommon classics, such as Mikhail Romm's *Boule de suif*, a 1934 Russian silent version of the de Maupassant story that had never been shown in the United States; it drew 400 customers to its midnight screening. Over the course of the next year other unusual older films included the first films of Alfred Hitchcock (*The Pleasure Garden* 1925) and Stanley Kubrick (*Fear and Desire*, 1953), James Cruze's *The Covered Wagon* (1923; "Perhaps *the* classic Western"), Rene Clair's *I Married a Witch* (1942; "one of the finest of Rene Clair's films"), King Vidor's *Our Daily Bread* (1934; "Considered one of the first artistic achievements after the introduction of sound"), and *The Black Sleep* (1956; "a horror film with Rathbone, Chaney, Tamiroff, Lugosi").[7]

The midnight series' reputation, however, (and, by extension, that of the Charles) rested on its dedication to the underground (also referred to as avant-garde or experimental) movies. "Reaching out to more experimental movies," said Langsford, "was what we were trying to do." These low-budget, underground films could take risks that explored new artistic territory outside of the classical Hollywood narrative and stylistic conventions. The 1940s saw their rise, and by the late 1950s they were becoming recognized as the New American Cinema. The early independent filmmakers first operated in San Francisco and New York City. "There was a whole side-show of what we called experimental filmmakers," Ben Barenholtz remembered, "who were not like filmmakers now who are thinking of doing their first film and then going to Hollywood. They never dreamed of Hollywood; the last thing on their minds was to do that. They were basically interested in furthering the concept of film and how to view films. Jack Smith was a total genius; Warhol got most of his ideas from Smith."[8]

Langsford and Stein came to know a number of these experimental filmmakers. "Stan Vanderbeek was a good friend, great guy," recalled Langsford. "He lived on Cherry Street with his wife, Joanna, and a couple of blond-headed kids. We loved his films because they were about politics: Nixon was shown with stuff coming out of his head. Stan Brakhage and Bob Breer came occasionally to the theater and we got to know them. These guys were making films ready to go to the theater; they weren't Hollywood professionals, but their films were professional, finished products. Richard Preston, Carmen D'Avino. We knew these guys."

The opportunities for theatrical presentations of these films were sporadic. Commercial theaters would not book them, since they were outside the mainstream, characterized by the absence of linear narrative, by the use of various abstracting techniques and asynchronous sound or even the absence of any sound track, and often by an oppositional stance toward mainstream culture. The filmmakers would often self-exhibit. Maya Deren had booked the Provincetown Playhouse in Greenwich Village in 1946 for a public exhibition of three of her films, including her most famous one, *Meshes of the Afternoon* (1943). This particular exhibition, in fact, inspired Amos Vogel to begin Cinema 16. Vanderbeek's American Underground Cinema "was a peripatetic exhibition center that floated from storefront to storefront," much like Mekas's Film-Makers' Cinematheque. Nonmainstream venues like Cinema 16 and the Living Theater occasionally screened experimental films. While repertory theaters, such as the Bleecker Street Cinema and the New Yorker Theater, premiered independent films sporadically, they were mostly unreceptive, according to Mekas, to the experimental films that he was promoting. The Charles was the first commercial theater to provide these filmmakers with a semi-permanent base of operation in New York. The crown jewels of the midnight series were the avant-garde works. "The policy," Langsford said, "if you can call it policy—only after we did it awhile did it become a policy—was experimental films by established filmmakers Fridays and Saturdays midnight."[9]

Mekas was a major asset in helping them to program the experimental works. He introduced Langsford and Stein to many of the filmmakers, provided ideas for programs, and recruited filmmakers. The works of a rich variety of independent directors appeared in the midnight programs: documentary filmmakers of the thirties (Willard Van Dyke, Lewis Jacobs, Herman G. Weinberg); and contemporary independents, such as the social satirists Stan Vanderbeek and Richard Preston, the Colorado filmmaker Stan Brakhage (considered at the time too radical for Cinema 16), the animators Robert Breer (a recent expatriate from Paris) and San Franciscan Larry Jordan, Gregory Markopoulos (another recently returned expatriate), and New Yorker Marie Menken.[10]

Usually curated as one-person shows ("I'm not sure," said Langsford, "who suggested we start performances of the work of a single artist"), the midnight series were groundbreaking in screening the first complete retrospectives of a number of these seasoned professionals. Among the first-time retrospectives (with personal appearances by the filmmakers) publicized in the Charles's press releases, was one for Shirley Clarke, "fast-rising light among independent and documentary filmmakers," who had been making one film a year since 1953 (her controversial film, *The Connection*, 1961, was not included in the retrospective since it was scheduled for release in a mainstream theater). Other first-time retrospectives promoted in the press releases featured the works of Humphrey Jennings, "the only real poet the British cinema has yet produced"; Nicholas Webster, "one of the most promising TV documentarists"; Rudy Burkhardt, a documentarist who "has caught the poetry of the Lower East Side as no one else has"; and Joseph Marzano, "a member of the Film Workshop, a group of experimental New York film-makers … considered one of the more promising figures of the New American Cinema." Older independent filmmakers were not neglected. Willard Van Dyke, then president of the Screen Director's Guild and "one of the giants of the American documentary film—a founder of the classic tradition in this country," had a festival of his works.[11]

Poster for the Shirley Clarke retrospective, April 1962. Donated by Walter Langsford. In the Charles Theater Collection, MoMA Department of Film Archives, New York.

Langsford and Stein also made room for premieres of individual films. Stan Brakhage's first full-length feature, *Anticipation of the Night* (1958), an attempt by the filmmaker to capture a child's view of the visual sensations of the world around it, premiered on October 21, 1961, and was repeated the following year as part of a series of first runs (it was mistakenly advertised as a premiere). San Franciscan Ron Rice's *The Flower Thief* (1960) ran an unprecedented three weeks, achieving a milestone in experimental film: it was one of the first avant-garde films to have a successful commercial run. The 70-minute feature, *New York Times* film critic Eugene Archer enthused, bore "all the trademarks of the American avant-garde"—plotless, ultra-symbolic, and determinedly obscure. "But for filmgoers with an appreciation of the potentialities of the medium," he countered, "and a smattering acquaintance with recent experiments in the American theatre, music, painting, and literature, it is an original and exciting piece of work. In the highly specialized area of experimental films, he has produced a major work."[12]

People came from all over the city and metropolitan area for the popular midnight programs and then stayed, if they wanted, for the symposia that usually followed. The filmmakers, plus an invited group of people in the film industry, would discuss the films and the state of filmmaking. The *New York Post*'s Archer Winsten and Eugene Archer from the *New York Times* were frequent visitors; the *Village Voice* would also send a reviewer, sometimes Andrew Sarris. One reviewer, however, who did not come was Pauline Kael, who, said Langsford, "asked us not to send her any invitations and warned us that she would write negative reviews." He continued, nevertheless, to send her invitations. Otherwise, "[e]verybody came to the midnight shows," remembered Langsford. "Judith Malina and Julian Beck [of the Living Theatre] came after their performances were over. Merce Cunningham and John Cage came; John played electronic music, moog, and somebody else played a synthesizer. They hung out, we didn't care how long the show went on, just until people got tired. And usually they stayed all night on Saturday watching movies. Then we'd go from there to some party at a loft. That was the spirit of the times. We just had tons of energy, we could sleep through the morning."

The two co-proprietors were open to new ideas for their theater, even unplanned ones. One such accidental event that turned into a permanent fixture was the trailblazing monthly Film-Makers' Festival. It came about through a fortuitous oversight on the part of Langsford and Stein. On ten Wednesday evenings until the end of December 1961, a Ukrainian in the neighborhood, Gregory Markovich, had rented the theater for screenings of Ukrainian films for his compatriots in the area. "It was a culture shock for us," remembered Langsford. "The Ukrainians were neat and well-behaved in contrast to our friends, who were pretty raucous and would leave the theater in a mess with half-eaten sandwiches, beer bottles, cans all over the floor. But the Ukrainians were orderly: they first filed in, filled the back rows forward; and when they left they turned the seats up and there wasn't a candy wrapper on the floor." Having forgotten to book a film on the eleventh Wednesday, Langsford and Stein invited some friends to bring their films that afternoon and screen them. "A lot of these kids," said Langsford, "were making films on nothing. They'd gotten movie cameras for Christmas, portable Bolexes and 8mm and 16mm cameras, and suddenly were doing something with them; some were fairly credible films." They thought nothing more about the invitation. Then, on that Wednesday afternoon, 12-year-old Amador Martinez, Jr., who lived in the neighborhood and had adopted the Charles Theater, rushed into the cluttered office back of the screen and shouted, "Hey! Look at all the people!" Stein and Langsford went out to face a line of people—many clutching cans of film—that reached all the way down to the corner. Word had spread rapidly. The filmmakers had come with ten or fifteen of their friends to screen their films. "We were showing their movies for the first time," said Langsford. "Some of their friends had helped them on their film and wanted to see it as well. There was no place that they could show them, in a room maybe, but not to an audience. That was such a spontaneous hit that we continued it for the life of the theater." The price of admission was either a can of film that the filmmaker had shot or 95 cents. "If you brought a film," said Langsford, "you got in; but your friends had to pay. It was a loose arrangement. That was interesting and fun."[13]

In contrast to the weekend midnight series, the monthly Film-Makers' Festival, which took place the first Wednesday of every month, was the preserve of mostly amateur filmmakers. They were a diverse group. At one showing the entrants included a young still-photographer, a parking lot attendant, a salesman, a clerk, and an unemployed artist. Their films were made on a shoestring. While a commercial documentary cost at that time around $1,000 a minute of showing time, these amateur filmmakers figured their costs closer to $15 a minute. One filmmaker, Stein told the *Herald Tribune* reporter, boasted he had made his film for $77.86. Ranging in style from the experimental to the conventional, the films consisted of documentaries of the city, mood pieces, comic chases, and parodies of well-known film directors. "We'll take anything from anyone with a can of film," Stein explained in a *New York Post* interview. The proprietors eventually created an application form for filmmakers, but at the end of each evening, time was set aside for unscheduled films by latecomers. "We'd never seen the films we put on in front of an audience," said Langsford. "Mostly they were films that came in uncensored. Some of them were pretty good; some were not so great." Films in all stages of production were accepted—complete, incomplete, titled, untitled, finished prints, uncorrected work prints. It was, a *Villager* reporter wrote, a "[m]arvelous grab-bag of talent and fun, resembling the old-time amateur night at the movies where you never knew whether the next act was going to be a stumbling tap dancer or a someday Fred Astaire."[14]

The Film-Makers' Festival became the Charles's best attended weekday event. Approximately five hundred fans would cram into the Charles each month for a three-hour look at its programs of twenty experimental shorts on average, from 60 seconds to 30 minutes in length. Each program started when Stein pushed his way through the mob to a microphone at the side of the screen and read a list of the films to be shown that evening, and then the titles of late entries. Some of the films, the *Villager* reporter noted in the program she attended, "appeared as finished and expert as works ready and able for art house booking." She singled out for special mention Bill Powers's *Fight Game*, a short film about training as a fighter, which had "the sharp impact of a swift uppercut"; Madeline Tourtelot's *Reflections*, an abstract study of the patterns made by leaves and branches reflected in the water, which "was a truly lovely thing"; and *Perils of Pauly*, a "funny, homey take-off on the villain, innocent beauty, and inspired hero serials." The festival on June 6, 1962, included a thirty-five-minute silent film, *Icarus* (1960), by the young neophyte Brian de Palma.[15]

For the tyro filmmakers, the important part of the evening was the responses of the audience. "What the filmmakers liked," said Langsford, "was that they got a reaction. It wasn't always what they wanted, but it was honest. We had a pretty fair audience." Audience reactions could be demonstrative. "[F]ireworks began," wrote a *New York Times* movie critic, "with hissing of two experimental numbers. Feet pounded the floor with Rockette precision at the sight of revolving, lighted matches, a kewpie doll's head inside a cantaloupe, and an occasional stream of ball bearings." The young filmmakers may have wanted the feedback, but it could, nevertheless, hurt. "Standing outside in the lobby and looking in [at the hissing audience]," observed the same reviewer, "was a student whose picture had been applauded. His schoolmate's movie, almost as imaginative, had provoked laughter and some catcalls. The boy quivered with rage. 'Listen to them,' he said. 'It's the hissing that really hurts. The girl in his picture just came out crying. After I showed some of my rushes here, I felt like committing suicide.'"[16]

The audiences at these monthly screenings were a young and lively, motley crowd of filmmakers, directors, writers, assistants, girlfriends, relatives, and angels. "A fairly well-known television and movie actor," said Langsford, "came frequently." The atmosphere was informal and somewhat anarchic, but warm and friendly. In one meeting, half the audience juggled paper cups of coffee furnished free in the lobby, while others pulled sandwiches or chicken legs from pockets or bags. The theater was full of seat-changing, visiting, and talking before the show started and during the two coffee breaks.[17]

After six months of open screenings came the climax—a single, grand Film-Makers' Festival, cosponsored with *Show Business* magazine. By June 1962 Langsford, and probably Stein as well, decided there should be a weeklong competition with prizes, as a major publicity splash for the work of these young filmmakers. Langsford contacted Ira Bilowit, the managing editor of *Show Business*, who liked the idea and, through his contacts in the film community, obtained free prizes, such as film processing and a used 16mm film projector; in turn, he promised to feature the contributors in future stories.

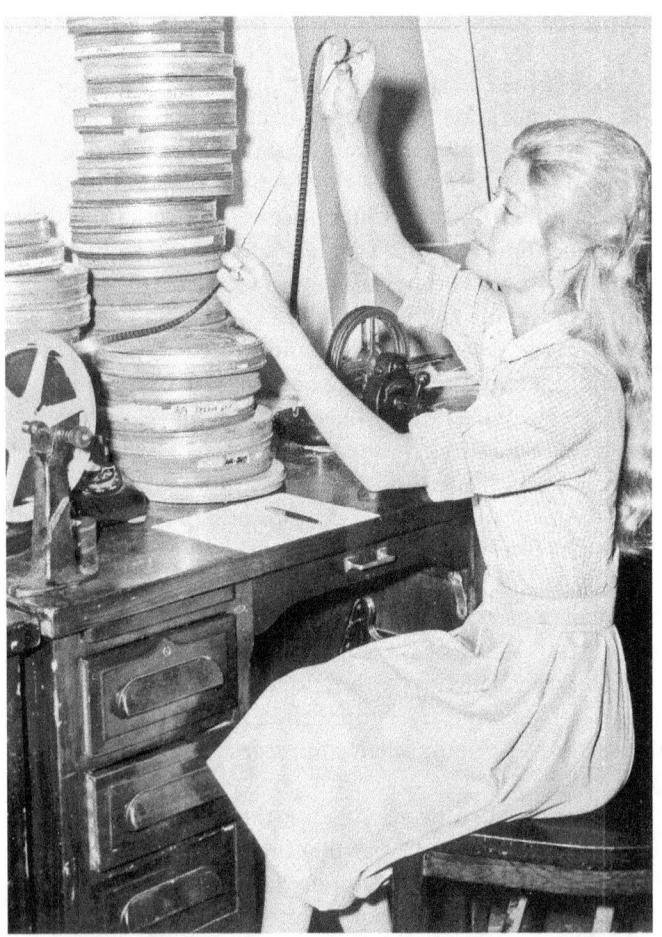

Wilhelmina Pfeiffer, Charles Theater program director, sorts some of the more than one hundred films already received for the eighth Film-Makers' Festival. Photograph by Braun Photo Service. Charles Theater Collection, MoMA Department of Film Archives, New York.

The grand festival ran from June 28 to July 4, 1962. Among the filmmakers featured were such future luminaries as Brian de Palma (*6602-24B44* and, again, *Icarus*), Paul Morrissey (*Mary Martin Does It*), and Nestor Almendros (*People on the Beach*). Because of its popularity the festival was extended four days to July 8. On the final day two awards were given out: one for The Best Film and the other for The Most Promising Filmmaker. The Most Promising Filmmaker Award was presented by Herman G. Weinberg to Ron Rice, the director of *The Flower Thief,* which subsequently had its successful run at the Charles. Sadly, Rice died two years later of pneumonia in Mexico. The prize for Best Film, presented by Bilowit, went to Michael Putnam's *The Hard Swing* (1962), a twenty-four-minute cinéma vérité account of a San Francisco stripper.

A second Film-Makers' Festival, held from September 1 to September 19, 1962, generated a lively debate in the *Village Voice* on the merits of the current avant-garde (at least as manifested in the festival). Andrew Sarris, one of the judges in the festival, dismissed the films as inept with unfocussed images and inaudible soundtracks. "Since I have always been dubious about the inflated claims of the New American Cinema [usually claims made by Mekas]," he wrote in the *Village Voice*, "I bent over backwards to be fair to new filmmakers.... Its [New American Cinema's] art is so marginal that any critical evaluation degenerates into trivialities." Mekas, the committed defender of the avant-garde, rebutted Sarris's critique in the following issue by questioning whether Sarris, a critic specializing in dramatic (snidely defining it as "commercial") cinema, was qualified to appraise poetic-experimental film, "just as in literary criticism," he wrote, "most fiction critics are insufficiently knowledgeable about poetry, and vice versa."[18]

A third festival was planned and advertised for January 1963. Unfortunately, before it could take place, the Charles closed.

By September 1962, the Charles was in financial difficulties with its future bleak, and Langsford was trying to find some way to salvage the dream of running a radical cinema, if not the Charles. In September 1962 with moral, and perhaps some financial, support from Stein, who was returning to Yale, Langsford rented the Windsor, a movie house that was further east on the Lower East Side at Grand and Clinton, while still operating the Charles. The Windsor had been one of the oldest, continuously operating theaters in the nation until it closed down a few months previously. Langsford intended it to be a backup in case the Charles should fail. "We thought that if the Charles went under," Langsford said, "maybe we could keep that one going." The move seemed financially feasible at the time. "The Windsor was an effort to reduce the cost. I'm not even sure it was smart, but the rent at the Charles was $750 a month, which was a lot then, while the Windsor's rent was $250 a month, which included the loft where my family and I lived. [Sometime after moving to New York, Langsford married and had a child.] We also thought that moving downtown would be a better location, and a smaller theater would have a better chance of surviving."

An article by film critic Eugene Archer in the *New York Times*, announcing the opening of the Windsor, described the new plan for the Windsor and the Charles: the Windsor would become the "old American cinema," featuring mostly early talkies and silent films from Hollywood, "the rare kind that are seldom available for theatres," while the Charles would continue its successful policy of alternating the amateur filmmakers' festivals with first runs of avant-garde films by little-known American directors. The plan seemed to be an effort by Langsford and Stein to capitalize on the successful parts of their programming.[19]

It was no coincidence that the plans for the Windsor bore a decided resemblance to the silent film programming of Bill Everson's Huff Film Society. To curate the Windsor programs, Langsford had enlisted the help of his friend and silent film buff John Griggs, who had a film collection that rivaled Everson's. Through his friendship with Griggs, Langsford had developed an interest in silent films, often spending evenings in Griggs's home with other Sutton Cinema Society participants watching films from his collection. "John had a theater in his basement," recalled Langsford, "and a couple of projectors so he could watch an entire film without stopping to rewind. I spent hours and days there watching silent films." The collector had helped to program silent films at the Charles at no charge, just out of a love of doing it. Under Griggs's guidance, the Charles had featured a number of rare silent films, like *Boule de Suif*, in the midnight shows and ran a series of long-unseen silent films in the weekday programs. These had been fairly successful. In addition, the proprietors had once arranged with Madame Malthete-Méliès, the granddaughter of the French silent film pioneer, Georges Méliès, to screen a program of her grandfather's films that she was taking on tour in the U.S. "Ted found out about it," said Langsford, "and contacted her. He was fluent in French so they had a long, warm conversation, a little bit of correspondence."

The Windsor with its interesting history was a perfect site, Langsford thought, for silent and early sound films. According to its original, and still current, owner, Harold Forma, it had started out as two separate, but adjacent, nickelodeons that were eventually combined into one movie theater. One nickelodeon was owned by Forma and the other, by Marcus Loew. "Forma told me," Langsford said, "that there was a window high up on the common wall [between the two nickelodeons] and he could climb up on a chair and look into Loew's nickelodeon to see what reels he had, how many people were coming, so he could get the same entertainment." Loew eventually moved from this location, according to Forma, and opened his first movie theater on 3rd Street and Avenue B.

Langsford had ambitious plans for the Windsor. The theater would include a film reference library, a film bookstore and print shop, and a film museum illustrating the history of film. "The Windsor was this treasure trove of old stuff," said Langsford. "It had synchronized wheels for showing silent movies. It wasn't a tape player exactly, but you could put records on them and play sound with the movie that was to some extent synchronized. The discs were put out with the films. I had learned to operate the projectors and went through the business of getting a license and passed the city test because the union operators were expensive. Don't ask me how I thought I could do that and be downstairs, too."

He worked hard to prepare for the opening. A skilled carpenter, he fixed up the loft as living quarters for his wife and child. He also made repairs to the theater. In a letter to Stein, who was now back at Yale, Langsford wrote that the front of the building was now a startling white and he was beginning to paint the inside. He had some help from a friend of Stein's, Roger Greenspun, who was on leave for a semester from his graduate studies.[20]

The theater finally opened on October 19, 1962, with Charlie Chaplin's *The Cure* (1917) and Erich von Stroheim's *Foolish Wives* (1922). The Windsor, however, lasted only a short time. "There was some business," Langsford said, "but this whole thing was collapsing. We owed money, we weren't getting the revenue, debts were increasing. We couldn't go on with it.... It's a shame because we had a great source of films. We had access to every silent film, many of the ones that were still in currency then, identical to the Museum of Modern Art's collection, incidentally." His principal sources were the three major private collectors—Griggs, Everson, and Joe Franklin. The Windsor closed in October or early November 1962.

The fate of the Charles, meanwhile, was also in jeopardy. It had been losing money every month of its existence, according to Langsford. The regular audience for the poorly attended weekday programs were usually eccentric characters, like "this mad lady, we called the 'God love you lady,'" Langsford recalled, "who would put cold cream over her face and wash it off when the movie was over, and a man who sat in the back yawning, putting everyone to sleep." The best attended programs were the evening shows, the midnight series, and the Film-Makers' Festivals. But ticket sales alone did not generate enough income to cover all the costs.

By November 1962 the operation had consumed $36,000 and was nearly $5,000 in debt; closure was looming, the *Village Voice* reported, if Langsford and Stein did not raise a significant part of that amount by the end of November. They had already loaned the corporation considerable amounts of money: Stein, $21,000; and Langsford, $7,500. A last-minute fundraising effort supported by such celebrities as actor Darren McGavin and *Esquire* critic Dwight MacDonald was unsuccessful. Jerome Hill, a wealthy supporter of the arts and humanities, also tried to find donors for the Charles as an interim measure. Langsford was most disappointed in Mekas, who, he thought, could have helped to save the Charles, but chose not to. There was interest among foundations and individual donors at the time in supporting struggling arts organizations. Langsford had learned of a meeting in Hill's apartment that was being organized by Mekas to give arts organizations an opportunity to present their case to potential donors, like the Ford Foundation. Mekas, however, had not invited him. "A grant to us at that point," he said, "might have saved us." But, Langsford believes, Mekas "decided that he wanted to be in line for the grant awards rather than the Charles." A brief mention in his November 22nd column in the *Village Voice* was the only plug Mekas gave to the Charles's fundraising efforts. The Charles closed shortly after in December 1962.[21]

What contributed to the Charles's failure? Location was probably an important factor. The area could not support an art or repertory theater, as the fate of the Charles under New Yorker auspices had demonstrated. The indigenous, immigrant neighborhoods were not likely patrons for this type of theater. The incoming population of young, middle-class people and artists frequented the Film-Makers' Festivals and midnight shows, but the theater needed patronage at other times as well to be sustainable. The film buffs who were an important audience of the other repertory houses found the theater in a remote and dangerous area; Ed Maguire had been mugged in Tompkins Square Park one night on his way home from the Charles.

Equally important, the two co-proprietors went into their business venture with an idealism that did not include a practical business sense. One *Village Voice* reviewer described the two as "doting grandfathers who cannot bear to let you go home without another gum drop or piece of halvah." They did not offer patrons gum drops or halvah, but they did provide them with free coffee and, as an extra bonus, allowed the customers of a regular Friday or Saturday evening performance to attend that night's midnight show for free. These casual bonuses fit into the counterestablishment ethos but were not good business practices. Collecting admission at the Film-Makers' Festivals could be chaotic, according to Jack Smith, one of the independent filmmakers nurtured by the Charles. The golden age of the Charles ended, he told J. Hoberman for his history of the Charles, "when the ecstasy got out of hand and it became difficult to collect admissions because of the confusion of filmmakers and audience." But in this instance, the Charles and its owners may have been wrongly criticized. "It was not true [what Smith had reported]," Langsford told the author. "The festivals were well-organized and the most profitable part of our operation. The friends and relatives of the filmmakers all paid."[22]

Langsford continued to live in the East Village with his family for a time, using his carpentering skills to build a set for the Living Theatre and to rehab an abandoned building in the East Village for squatters, unfortunately a failed experiment. He also worked as a carpenter for Oscar Zurer after Zurer sold the Bleecker to Rogosin, helping him build a loft and 162-seat Off–Broadway theater at 53 East 11th Street. Langsford and his family eventually left New York, and sometime later, he and his wife divorced. He has since retired from the construction business he built and has been living for the last thirty-two years in the Berkshires, "happily unmarried," with Janet Cooper.

Langsford and Stein lost track of each other. Several years ago Langsford attempted to reestablish contact with his former partner. He learned that Stein received his Ph.D. in literature from Yale and an M.D. from Case Western and finally settled down at Whitman College in Walla Walla, Washington. On his retirement from the college, he may have moved to Boulder, Colorado; but after that, Langsford could discover nothing more about him.

The theater had a short life; but it, nevertheless, left an impressive legacy. By being the first commercial showcase for avant-garde films, it effectively put them on the cultural map. Newspapers began reviewing them, and the greater public had the opportunity to view them. Underground filmmakers were no longer "underground," and their innovative styles would soon influence mainstream filmmaking. The Charles's dual-pronged, innovative programming of independent films was picked up soon after by nonprofit groups like the Millennium Film Workshop. The Charles pioneered the midnight movie cult that would flourish during the seventies; and as the theater that invented the avant-garde tradition of the open screening, it "was the spiritual home of a particular utopian ideology," Hoberman wrote in his brief history of the Charles, "a place where the audience was not just the passive recipient of mass-produced fantasies, but an active community, producing movies for itself." Even the Windsor earned a footnote in the history of the underground movies: it was on the roof of the theater that Jack Smith filmed *Flaming Creatures*, the most notorious underground movie of them all.[23]

"In its one year of existence," Hoberman summed up, "the Charles had become a landmark of sorts in the creation of an American counterculture."[24]

Chapter 6

The Thalia: Grand Dame of Repertory Houses

The Thalia was the grand old lady of the New York repertory movie theaters. In its more than thirty-one years screening double-feature foreign classics (with some American revivals) and staging summer festivals, it occupied an intimate place in the lives of many New Yorkers. "Wherever I go," Ursula Lewis, the wife of its deceased owner, Martin J. Lewis, and owner/manager after her husband's death in 1955, would later tell the *New York Post*, "I would meet some kids and they tell me that the Thalia was part of their upbringing. It's great to hear that." Kids like M. Farricker, who frequented both the Symphony Theater and the Thalia as a teenager. "The Symphony," he wrote on the *Cinema Treasures* website, "showed mostly English films and many old classics. The Thalia showed mostly foreign films and some silent movies, too. I was enthralled with all of them and I learned so much about life and the world from them." Delaney, the theater's historian, described its audience as "[c]ollege students from Columbia University, senior citizens, long time residents and movie buffs [who] flocked to the Thalia almost monthly." For film students and future filmmakers, the Thalia was their classroom. "That's where I learned about films," Martin Scorcese told a *Times* reporter. "It was better than film school."[1]

Located in the Symphony theater building on Broadway at 95th Street, with its entrance on 95th Street, the Thalia was "a reassuring neighborhood landmark along with its folksy 95th Street neighbors…—a hand laundry, a print shop, a lunch counter and a used bookstore." The Lewises' son John described it as a distinctive, small theater with an interesting marquee, in contrast to the much larger Symphony Theater around the corner on Broadway.[2]

Martin Lewis, a cultured, German-Jewish, naturalized citizen, presented programs that reflected his intellectual and esthetic interests. In addition to his preference for foreign films, he included films on music and dance, the lives of great composers and artists, and operas. Similar to the later programs of Cinema 16, he also presented festivals on art, psychology, and the world of nature: "Secrets of Nature," "Art in Films," and "Psychology in Films." The character of the Upper West Side also determined the kinds of films the Thalia showed. "Its emphasis on French, Russian, Italian, and German films,"

Lopate speculated in our interview, "reflected the demographics of the postwar Upper West Side, with its abundance of European refugees and elderly residents." John Lewis described the area as composed of liberal Europeans who generally belonged to the Democratic Party. A number were blacklisted artists, such as Zero Mostel, who lived around the corner from the Lewises.[3]

Lewis was born in 1904 in Germany to a Jewish, middle-class family named Lewy. He changed his name to Lewis upon settling in the United States. Much of the information on his background comes from the stories Lewis told his wife, who wrote down what she knew in a short, unpublished memoir, and his three children. (Mrs. Lewis acknowledged in her memoir that she could not vouch for his history prior to 1943, when they met and married.) As a youngster he studied Latin and Greek. He loved music, a lifelong passion, and played the violin; as an adult he was particularly fond of playing chamber music in his leisure time. His older brother, Hans, was raised to be an academic while Lewis was expected to take over his father's wholesale business. (His brother, a famous classicist specializing in the works of Philo of Alexandria, a Hellenized, Jewish philosopher and historian, emigrated in 1933 to what was then Palestine, where he became Yohanan Lewy.) Uninterested in the business, Lewis convinced his father to let him attend university and study economics and business administration. After graduation, he interned in the wholesale business of a competitor of his father's, from which he was soon fired. Lewis wanted to become a film producer; but his father disapproved of this disreputable, young industry, sending him instead on a Grand Tour, with the idea that when he returned, he would settle down.[4]

When his ship docked in New York in 1926, however, he remained in the city, a twenty-two-year-old young man with no knowledge of English and no particular skills, but managing to survive and learn the language. His first important foothold in the film industry came in 1930 or 1931 as publicity director for the 55th Street Playhouse. From that start he went on to pioneer the importation and screening of foreign films in the U.S. as owner and/or operator of a number of art theaters in New York. The Fifth Avenue Cinema, the 55th Street Playhouse, the Little Carnegie, the 72nd Street Playhouse, the Heights, and the Beverly Theater were among the theaters that he owned at various times. In the fall of 1938 Lewis and his partner, H.S. Rosenwald, bought the Thalia and transformed it into an art house, specializing in foreign films that had completed first runs at centrally located Broadway theaters.[5]

Lewis was an innovative programmer. In July 1938, ten years after the start of sound pictures, he introduced the first international film festival of sound films in the United States. The idea for the festival, he told a *New York Times* reporter, had been sparked by "the recent renewed public interest in the revival of old silent and early talking pictures." A June 1938 item in *Cue*, the first consumer guide to the cultural life of New York City, also noted this rise in revivals. It was due, the *Cue* columnist wrote, to audiences' weariness with the "B" and "C" pictures that were filling the double-feature theaters, aggravated by the drastic reduction of "A" features that year. The reissue of past hits had begun in the thirties by the Big Five Hollywood studios, to cover slow periods when there were not enough new releases for all first-run theaters. Mostly sound films from the earlier thirties were reissued. In May 1936, for example, *Twentieth Century* (1934) played at the Alden; *Imitation of Life* (1934), at the Madison; and *Dr. Jekyll and Mr. Hyde* (1931), at the Rose. Revivals became so popular that in February 1938, *Cue* polled its readers on their preferred ones. *Birth of a Nation* (1915), *The Thin Man* (1934), and *Cavalcade* (1933) headed the final list, published in May 1938, of the top "fifteen pictures which ten thousand voters in *Cue*'s giant double-feature poll would like to see again."[6]

Taking place at his Fifth Avenue Cinema, Lewis's first international festival featured forty-four films from sixteen film-producing countries. The United States, France, U.S.S.R., and England sent the largest number, while one to two films came from countries such as Ireland, Poland, Sweden and Denmark, Palestine, and Mexico. In the advertisement for the festival, the two German films—Leontine Sagan's *Mädchen in Uniform* (1931) and Fritz Lang's *M* (1931)—and the one Austrian film, *Tales from the Vienna Woods*, were followed by the letters "B.H.," standing for "Before Hitler," a touch insisted on by Lewis, probably to meet a restrictive clause in his lease, which prohibited screening any film not endorsed by the many anti–Nazi boycott committees in existence at the time. Because of this clause, he had been unable to show the prize-winning *La Kermesse héroïque* (*Carnival in Flanders*, 1935), which was on several non–Aryan blacklists.[7]

Foreshadowing the educational component of the later repertory movie theaters, Lewis enriched the screenings with post-film discussions by guest speakers from different countries. The *Cue* columnist listed such speakers as Paul Charles Bivers, director of France-Amerique Films; Dr. Curt Pinthus, ex–film editor of 8-Uhr Abendblatt, Berlin, and "now professor at the University of Exile in the New School of Social Research"; and Dudley Digges, "of New York, Hollywood, and Dublin...." The extensive publicity that Lewis and his partners generated paid off; more than ten thousand programs were distributed throughout the metropolitan area to hotels and public libraries, as well as through some 750 educational, social, and political organizations. The public response to the festival was great enough to warrant a 15-day extension, with a focus on films from the French section, which had generated the largest audience.[8]

Despite the stressful six weeks of selecting films, making booking arrangements, and encountering last-minute delays when prints became unavailable because of their poor quality or for other reasons (he was assisted by Oliver M. Sayler, Rosenwald, and Marjorie Barkentin), Lewis produced two more international festivals. He had the hope, he had told the *Times* interviewer at the first festival, that an "annual international film festival comparable to the ones held each year in Venice and Brussels" would be a future possibility for the United States. It was an idea that he held on to over the years. In July 1939 he brought out an even more ambitious international festival, the Second International Film Festival, which increased its screenings to fifty-four films from about twenty-one countries, including countries represented for the first time—Egypt, Italy, China, Greece, and Finland. The Third International Film Festival was again a major event from May to August 1940.[9]

Unfortunately, the rise of Hitler and the growing conflict in Europe unsettled the future of the art theaters. They found that the flow of foreign films had dried up. Hitler forbade the export of most German films, and the fall of France brought an end to the golden age of French cinema. The Nazi-Soviet Pact cut off Russian films, which became available again after Russia went to war against Germany, but which were, nonetheless, unable to fill the gap. The art theaters shrank from a high of 150 theaters nationwide in the 1930s, a *Times* reporter noted in 1942, to mostly twenty in New York City and the larger Northeastern cities by the early 1940s. The remaining ones tried various solutions to fill their screens. The Little Carnegie Playhouse, for example, converted into an "intimate-type newsreel and television house." The Thalia, on the other hand, gave birth to the first full-time, for-profit revival movie theatre in New York.[10]

The change came about gradually. Lewis and Rosenwald began relying on revivals of foreign and American films in a double-feature format to supplement the ever-scarcer first-run screenings at the Thalia and Fifth Avenue Cinema. June 1939 saw Frank Capra's *Lady for a Day* (1933) and Alfred Hitchcock's *The Man Who Knew Too Much* (1934) at the former and G.W. Pabst's *Kameradschaft* (1931) and Jean Cocteau's *Blood of a Poet* (1930) at the latter. Eventually, the partners began screening festivals. The first was a "Music Film Festival" at the 55th Street Playhouse, in February 1939. In July 1939 the Thalia put on "The London and Paris Film Parade," a retrospective program of the best French and British movies of the previous two decades. Immediately afterwards in August 1939, also at the Thalia, "The Charles Boyer Revival Month," the first retrospective of a single star, appeared on the marquee. At the same time a "Foreign Film Festival" played most of July 1939 at the Fifth Avenue Cinema and was immediately followed by a "Revival Festival" at the same theater. Lewis attempted to establish an annual revival festival at the Fifth Avenue Cinema; in May 1940, an announcement appeared in the *New York Times* of the theater's "annual revival program," based on recommendations from a survey of 5,000 patrons. Other art theaters soon imitated the festival concept. Joseph Green, owner of the Irving Place Theatre, screened a French and Russian film festival honoring the United States' wartime allies; the Bridge Theater in upper Manhattan presented a film festival of selected Soviet, French, English, and American films.[11]

The success of "The London and Paris Film Parade" and "The Charles Boyer Revival Month," reported the *New York Times* in 1942, convinced Lewis and Rosenwald that "there was a large and steady audience for revivals of outstanding films of the past, provided that the films were grouped in a sort of 'festival' and were properly exploited." Thus, according to this article, the first full-time, revival movie house was born. On the other hand, Lillian Gerard, Lewis's publicist at the time, had a somewhat different version of the beginning. In an interview with Archer Winsten of the *New York Post* in 1977, she claimed that the "Charlie Chaplin Festival" in April 1941 marked the start of the Thalia as a revival theater. According to her, Lewis, who was scrounging around for replacements for new foreign films, found some famous Chaplin shorts in the public domain. Their success in bringing in a large audience led to the idea of a revival house. Whichever version is accurate, both credited the triumph of the festival concept for generating the Thalia's conversion. The festival concept, in turn, became the principal curatorial approach of the repertory movie theaters twenty years later.[12]

By January 1942 the two directors scheduled festival programs primarily at the Thalia and Fifth Avenue Cinema, in between the regular programs of daily, stand-alone double features. "Russian Victory Month" at the Thalia coupled Russian revivals with American, British, and French classics. In that same month the Fifth Avenue Cinema screened the most famous of the series, "The Surrealist Film Festival," which, Delaney reported, was described by a *New York Times* critic as "a night at the movies that surely will drive you crazy." Lewis and Rosenwald, however, reassured patrons in one of their frequent messages to them that this festival was "not intended to conjure nightmares" but "is designed to purposely disturb and shock one's balance." Other festivals during the war years included "March of Time Month," "A Night at the Nickelodeon," "Documentary Film Festival," "Avant-garde Film Festival," and "Dance Film Program."[13]

It was also in 1942 that the Summer Film Festival, the Thalia's signature event, first made its appearance, inaugurating an annual festival that New Yorkers would eagerly look forward to every year between the months of June and October for the next thirty-one years. The format was unvarying: a mind-boggling number of double features of foreign and some American classics that changed daily. Mrs. Lewis noted in her memoir that her husband picked the summer for the film festival to attract the tourists as well as the natives, who had few television programs in the summer to keep them at home.[14]

The Summer Film Festival probably represented the fulfillment of Lewis's dream of an annual international film festival, similar to the European ones. He billed it as "The Thalia International Film Festival" and even went so far in the 1947 summer calendar to group "Thalia's Own International Film Festival" with those in Cannes, Venice, Locarno, Lucerne, Vichy, Edinburgh, and "even Berlin."[15]

Following the war, when films began to flow again between Europe and the United States, Lewis traveled once a year to Europe to seek out films at festivals and other venues to bring back to the States. He was part of a group of distributors who initiated the foreign-film movement in the fifties. Arthur Mayer, another of these distributors and a friend of Lewis's, who spoke at his funeral, had introduced Roberto Rossellini's *Rome, Open City* (1945) and Vittorio De Sica's *Bicycle Thief* (1948) to the American public. The Fifth Avenue Cinema started alternating new films from Europe, especially Germany, with its festival repertory, while the Thalia remained a revival house, presenting, Delaney rhapsodized, "an unprecedented schedule of 14 different movies a week ... and displaying a range of world cinema unparalleled at any theater in the country." One could see British films like David Lean's *Great Expectations* (1946) and *Brief Encounter* (1945); French films like Jacques Feyder's *Carnival in Flanders* (1935) and Jean Renoir's *Grand Illusion* (1937); Russian films like Mark Donskoy's anti–Nazi *Rainbow* 1944; and even American double features, like Henry Hathaway's *House on 92nd Street* (1945) and Fritz Lang's *Ministry of Fear* (1944). The most requested films at that time, Mrs. Lewis later told a *Times* reporter, were *Grand Illusion* and Rene Clair's *Under the Roofs of Paris* (1930). Lewis's two sons remember especially the George K. Arthur shorts that their father programmed for the 55th Street Playhouse and the Thalia. "Arthur was a great shorts filmmaker," John Lewis recalled. "My father would spend a night just watching his shorts. They were really powerful." Another unforgettable memory was the UPA cartoons starring Gerald McBoing-Boing and Mr. Magoo, often in a double feature with Charlie Chaplin shorts. When John Lewis was in the third grade, his father invited his class to a special showing of the cartoons with the Chaplin shorts. It was an outstanding experience for the class.[16]

One of the Thalia's draws was its repeated screenings of selected classic films, a strategy similar to Marshall Lewis's approach at the Bleecker Street Cinema, but without his slant on auteurist directors and New Wave films. "When I came to New York in the fifties," recalled William Wolf, former film critic for *Cue* and currently reviewer on the website *Wolf Entertainment Guide*, "I used to spend so much time at the Thalia, because they had everything there and showed them over and over. That's where you could see *Potemkin* every year ... great Italian neorealist films, French films of the thirties—all these things that were part of a wonderful education. And I'm not the only one. I've talked to many who did that." Two others who appreciated the repeated screenings were Lillian Ross, writer for the *New Yorker*, and William Shawn, its editor. "We went there repeatedly," Ross recalled in a *Times* interview, "to see Jean Renoir's *Rules of the Game* (1939)—we must have seen it there about 15 times. Bill Shawn's favorite of all time forever was Jacques Demy's *The Umbrellas of Cherbourg* (1964), so we saw it there a couple dozen times, too." For many young enthusiasts, this opportunity to study a film through the repeated screenings was critical to their film education.[17]

The UPA cartoons and George K. Arthur's films were popular not only with Martin Lewis's sons but also with the public, as demonstrated by the long line for the 55th Street Theater's program, ca. 1950s. Photofest.

Lewis was ambitious. Believing that art theaters would work outside New York City, he invested in movie theaters in cities like Baltimore, Maryland, and Hartford, Connecticut. But these theaters went through a cycle of boom and bust, where he made money, then lost it. Two or three years before he died, he bought the 72nd Street Playhouse on the Upper East Side, thinking that the then slum neighborhood in which it was located would soon gentrify and become an ideal location for art films. Unfortunately, Mrs. Lewis wrote in her memoir, he was ten years too early. He tried festivals and first runs at the theater, but nothing worked; he was losing money that he could not afford. By 1954, Lewis began divesting himself of some of his theaters, including the Fifth Avenue Cinema, which he sold to Pathé Cinema, and the Beverly. Two weeks preceding his death, Mrs. Lewis noted in her memoir, he was nervous and apprehensive. "Martin was beginning to get frightened," she wrote. "Things were not working out the way he saw it, and he was no longer that young that he could take it in his stride." Looking back, she blamed it mostly on the financial disaster with the 72nd Street Playhouse and "a general fear in the air."[18]

He may have also been disheartened by his lack of success in getting financing for his latest production effort. In her memoir, Mrs. Lewis described her husband as wanting to expand beyond distribution and exhibition to film production, his early ambition. Lewis had worked as a film editor in his early years in the country. He had edited Jean Benoit-Levy and Marie Epstein's *La Maternelle* (1933) for its 1935 American release and also wrote its subtitles, as well as worked on Julien Duvivier's *Der Golem* (1936). Later in life, he produced a burlesque film called *Striporama* (1953), starring Lili St. Cyr, which was directed by Jerry Intrator, who worked with Lewis on various production projects. The film had a successful opening at the Rialto in New York; but because Lewis put a large amount of money into color prints, he could not recoup his investment.[19]

Around two years before his death, he intended to produce a movie based on the life of Mozart. Since the 1940s he had been involved in the Tanglewood Music Center in the Berkshires and friendly with the director of its opera department, Boris Goldovsky.

Martin Lewis holding his newborn daughter Deborah, shortly before his death, 1955. Courtesy the Lewis/Sutherland family.

He and Goldovsky dreamt up the idea for the movie. Goldovsky put together the music, and a blacklisted screenwriter (whose name neither of Lewis's two sons could remember nor did Mrs. Lewis mention in her memoir) wrote the script; a friend of the family, Sandy Jason, acted as the front for the writer. At the time of his death, Lewis was still looking for financing for the film. It was never produced, although the family still retains the script.[20]

Lewis died suddenly on November 13, 1955. He was fifty-one years old and, as far as the family knew, in good health. The day of his death he was screening one of his imports, *Don Giovanni* (1954), at the 55th Street Playhouse for the managers of his theaters and some family members, including his son John. Complaining of a sudden, intense headache, he left the room and was standing in the lobby when his wife came by with their newborn baby, Deborah, and their dog. She later believed she had had a premonition about Lewis and decided to drop by the theater. Leaving the baby and dog with a cousin who was at the screening, she took him home and called the doctor, who came but could not diagnose the problem. Lewis yelled that another attack was coming on, went into his bedroom, collapsed on his bed, and died from a cerebral hemorrhage.[21]

The family was in shock; Mrs. Lewis had no idea what to do. Her husband had kept her separated from his businesses, which in one instant had suddenly become her responsibility. During their twelve years of marriage, she played the role of wife and mother that Lewis had wanted and that she had accepted, carrying it, she admitted in her memoir, to an extreme. She never interested herself in the theater or her husband's work. The Lewises had met at a New Year's Eve party in 1942 and married on July 22, 1943. Both had been married before. Mrs. Lewis had emigrated in 1937 or 1938 with her former husband, Walter Brenner, from Nazi Germany. Lewis had returned to Germany sometime in the 1930s, after he had become established, to "collect his bride" (as Mrs. Lewis phrased it in her memoir), Natasha Lytess, who later became the acting coach for Marilyn Monroe.

The new couple settled on 71st Street between Columbus Avenue and Central Park West. They had three children: Thomas, born in 1944; John, in 1946; and Deborah, in 1955.[22]

Left with three young children to raise; loads of debt; no life insurance, which Lewis had canceled because of cash-flow problems; and little money, she relied in the immediate aftermath of her husband's death on two longtime friends from Germany. One, Herman Jacobson, urged her to maintain the business while the other, Walter Zarek, advised her to sell everything. After some time going over her options, she decided to continue at least parts of her husband's businesses. Lewis had left four theaters, the distribution company, and several films that were owned by seven or eight corporations that he either had headed or was involved with. She kept the profitable Thalia and the Heights in Washington Heights, which ran a mix of first runs and revivals in a good neighborhood, and sold the leases to the poorly performing 72nd Street Playhouse and the 55th Street Playhouse, which, she felt, needed a showman to sell the outré first runs it tended to screen. Where her husband was always looking to expand, Mrs. Lewis took the opposite tack and consolidated.[23]

The crisis awoke her dormant capabilities. In her memoir, she described her metamorphosis from homemaker to entrepreneur as coming out of cold storage. An anecdote in the manuscript captures the essence of her transformation. When she had been operating the theater for a number of years, one of her longtime distributors invited her to lunch. During the lunch he asked her a question that he said had been bothering him for fifteen years. "About 15 [sic] years ago," she wrote that he began his inquiry, "I came to your house and I had to discuss some business with Martin, and there was a young woman sort of flitting in and out, like a frightened little mouse bringing in refreshments ... but never stopping to talk and sort of trying to make herself as invisible as possible. Was that YOU?" Mrs. Lewis replied, "Ja, it was." Later, when she tried to explain to herself how she was able to mobilize herself following the night of his death, she wrote that it was "because there was no alternative and I knew I must keep the theatres and my family alive." But she recognized the price for her blossoming. "The horror, however, was that the knowledge of what I had to do and would do and ultimately was able to do had to be tied

Ursula Lewis, ca. 1945 or 1946. Courtesy the Lewis/Sutherland family.

in with the fact that a death was responsible for the fact that I became alive. I always felt this was a terrible price to pay." She solved her immediate financial problems, including settling the debts, by selling her husband's distribution rights to the film *Don Giovanni* to Times Films with the help of Intrator and by holding out for the amounts she felt she needed from the sales of the two theaters, despite warnings from a potential buyer that she would never do better than the lower offer he was making. But she knew she needed those amounts to clear her debts and have enough remaining to live on. Her resolve worked; she finally received what she was asking for: $17,000 for the 72nd Street Playhouse lease and $55,000 for the 55th Street Playhouse one. Her perseverance also won her the respect of the film exhibition business as someone to take seriously; this was especially important since she was the only female in a male-dominated industry.[24]

Bryan Haliday and Cyrus Harvey, Jr., owners of the Brattle Theater in Cambridge, Massachusetts, bought the lease to the 55th Street Playhouse and turned it into the first-run venue for the films of their new distribution company, Janus Films, which became a major distributor of foreign films during the fifties and sixties. Haliday and Harvey were supportive of her and the Thalia over the years. While the repertory houses could only book the entire Janus package of films (a tactic similar to the Hollywood studios' pre–1948 blind booking policy and one that Rogosin blamed for the Bleecker Cinema's later problems), John Lewis explained that Janus Films allowed his mother to book individual films, but only for the Thalia.[25]

Mrs. Lewis had indispensable help in running the Thalia. Its daily operation was in the capable hands of the longtime manager, seventy-six-year-old Teddy Feiffer, his older brother, Ed, and Gladys DiPillo, the cashier of the theater for the past twenty-five years. The three worked well together. Teddy managed the crises that were always cropping up at Thalia, and Gladys DiPillo controlled the influx of patrons into the theater.

Teddy and Abe, who had been boxers in their younger

Gladys DiPillo, left, and Ursula Lewis in front of the box office and glass-enclosed poster of the current program schedule, ca. early 1970s. Courtesy the Lewis/Sutherland family.

days, also served informally as the theater's security guards. In her memoir, Mrs. Lewis related several incidents in which they thwarted robberies. One time Teddy fought two hoodlums who tried to rob him when he was making a night deposit at the bank. The police car came while he was struggling with them. Another time he foiled a robber who was holding up the cashier. When Mrs. Lewis asked him not to fight these thieves because he might get hurt, his reply was "Nobody gets away with my money!" she wrote. "That was the answer he gave me." It was gratifying to her that he and Ed felt possessive about the theater, which they treated as if it were theirs. She relates another incident when Ed was vacationing in Florida and happened to hear people at a nearby table talking about a little theater in New York "where you could see all the pictures you had missed. And he turned around and he said, 'You're talking about the Thalia theater, and they said, 'Yes.' He said, 'Well me and my brother run this.'" When Ed died, she sadly noted, "Teddy sort of lost heart, and did not want the full responsibility any more." Gladys DiPillo took over as manager for the last years of the Thalia.[26]

Her right hand, though, was Max Zipperman. What his business relationship with Lewis was is uncertain. In her memoir Mrs. Lewis identified him as her husband's longtime friend and partner in a number of theaters over twenty-five years, including the one in Hartford, another in Detroit, and the Schuyler on Eighth Avenue in New York. Many of their theaters, she noted, did not succeed, but their relationship survived because of Zipperman's mild, tolerant temperament, which weathered Lewis's frequent outbursts of temper. John Lewis called him a junior partner, while he was listed on the Summer Film Festival calendars as director along with Mrs. Lewis. Zipperman eased the transition for her into her new role. He knew Lewis's methods and the mechanics of running a theater, and helped her deal with distributors, merchants, and other exhibitors, a group that Tom Lewis described as a fraternity, where all knew each other. "Max was solid," he said. "He was liked by the people in the business." Most important, he taught her programming techniques: how to secure films, what considerations went into selecting films, and how to put together a festival. Because of his high blood pressure and generally poor health, Zipperman worked mostly in their office, which was located in the Paramount Building on Times Square until they moved to a smaller space uptown.[27]

The Thalia was doing well under Mrs. Lewis and Zipperman. Between 1955 and 1958 they enlarged the summer festivals from about eighty films to three hundred and added Hollywood classics in 1955, which apparently increased the Thalia's success. "Bogart always sold out," she explained in a newspaper interview. "Garbo and Dietrich films [also] have done well for the last 20 years. And Bette Davis is still a favorite. So are the Marx Brothers and W.C. Fields." They also adopted a new advertising technique in the calendars—treating specific double features as special events. The calendar for 1959, for example, publicized two John Ford films about Depression-era farmers, *Tobacco Road* (1941) and *Grapes of Wrath* (1940), as "Two Mighty American Classics," and Alfred Hitchcock's *The Trouble with Harry* (1955) with Guy Hamilton's *An Inspector Calls* (1954) as "Two Masterpieces of Suspense!"[28]

Several months of concentrated work beginning in April preceded the summer festivals. In curating a festival, Mrs. Lewis seemed to have two guiding principles. First, to create and sustain a mood in the audience, the double features had to blend—two Greek tragedies, for example, not a Greek tragedy with a French farce. Second, the festival must have a sense of continuity. She and Zipperman first compiled a list of previous festival films that were still available, then a list of films shown in movie theaters since the last festival. "So we tried to give the festival some kind of history," she explained in her memoir. Her idea was to provide the public with a sense of the history and development of motion pictures. The Summer 1964 festival, for instance, featured pre–World War II classics like Marcel Carné's *Quai des brumes* (1938) and Sergei Eisenstein's *Alexander Nevsky* (1938) and well-regarded, popular postwar films like Helmut Kautner's *The Last Bridge* (for which Maria Schell won the 1954 Cannes Festival Award as Best Actress) and the international hit of that year, Phillipe de Broca's *That Man from Rio* (1964), with Jean-Paul Belmondo.[29]

Next came scheduling the festival. Certain types of films were scheduled for certain days of the week. For instance, Russian films were scheduled on Thursdays. For some reason, they found that these films performed well on that day. After this, they dealt with the distributors, who had to be convinced to reserve films in April for screening sometime between June and October.

Ursula Lewis on 95th Street under the Thalia marquee listing the current day's program in the Summer Film Festival, ca. late 1960s. Courtesy the Lewis/Sutherland family.

In an interview with a *New York Times* reporter in 1963, Zipperman discussed the difficulties in arranging the 341 features and short subjects for that summer's festival. He specifically talked about two obstacles that were similar to those encountered by Talbot at the New Yorker and, incidentally, every other repertory house programmer. "Very often, in the case of particularly vintage films," he said, "we find that distribution rights have lapsed, and the pictures are simply unobtainable." The other problem involved the quality of available prints. "In some cases," he continued, "the prints are too bad to use. Last summer, for instance, there were 30 or 40 interesting pictures we were unable to get. For the new program, however, we've managed to obtain quite a few of the ones we missed." Poor quality prints were always a problem. "Thalia prints were notoriously bad," recalled a patron who was interviewed by the *New York Times* at the theater's closing. "They broke. Voices would evaporate; the screen darken." For that reason, Mrs. Lewis added 16mm projection so she could substitute a 16mm print for a defective 35mm one.

Sixteen millimeter prints had become abundant because of television, which was showing older films in that format.[30]

The granddaughter of Gladys DiPillo had stories to tell about working at the theater during the summer festivals. "In the late 60s and early 70s," she wrote on the *Cinema Treasures* website, "I ushered there in the Summer and changed the marquee every night for the Summer Film Festival. She [her grandmother] was delighted because I wouldn't misspell anything as others had done in the past to her great embarrassment as it would stay up there all day! When she played Fellini's '8½' the marquee would read '812' since she didn't have a '½.' I couldn't stand for that so I fashioned a '½' by sawing other pieces and gluing them together. It looked great! She loved it.... I have such stories of the place and really miss it."[31]

The Thalia was at its peak during the summer, the *New Yorker* magazine reflected in its obituary on the theater's closing in 1973. "It is during the summer months…" it commented, "that one's memories of the Thalia are likely to be formed." For those film buffs who stayed in the city during the summer, the Thalia's summer festival was as eagerly anticipated as a summer vacation; and preparing for it took as much thought as arranging travel plans to Paris or some other foreign city. "Snagging a copy of the Thalia's schedule in the 1960s was a rite of summer," one man reminisced on the *Cinema Treasures* website. "One could spend hours poring over the incredible scheduling of classic double features." Joseph Michalak, another habitué of the theater in his youth, wrote an article for the *New York Times* explaining the ritual of planning one's summer around the Thalia's schedule: "You got three copies of the schedule. You taped two on your refrigerator door (showing front and back—both ends of the schedule). You circled the must-sees. Remaining dates, if any, were available for lower-priority summer activities. (The third copy was sent to a friend back home, where the existence of films not made in Hollywood was still pretty much a rumor, and revivals of anything flickered only occasionally across a film-club or film-class screen.)" Getting in line early for a weekend night at the summer festival was a necessity. "Before an evening dedicated to the Thalia," explained Michalak, "you and any companions ate early and often (two movies *are* longer than one and you might want to see them twice). You got on line early (there were only 296 seats, and the people who got in first were sure to know as well as you did which seats were missing vital parts). And there was always the chance that the rule about not sitting on the floor might actually be enforced."[32]

Despite the theater's success, when the lease came up for renewal in November 1958, Mrs. Lewis and Zipperman encountered problems with the landlord, William Bodine. The whole area—Symphony Space, Thalia, Pomander Walk—was owned by an estate and managed by Bodine. For years, Bodine had made problems for her husband with the lease, which he insisted be renewed every five years, at which time he would demand a large increase in the rent. She and her husband would always take him out for an expensive dinner as part of the routine. This time Bodine did not want to lease to her as a single woman. "He could not permit me," she wrote in her memoir, "to fall under the influence of another man, whether by marriage or by professional association." Bodine finally agreed to renew the lease on the condition that she sell half of her stocks to Zipperman, whom he trusted as a guide and mentor for her. The sexism underlying his demand would not be tolerated today but was inescapable then. Infuriated by his intrusion into her private life, she, nevertheless, had no choice.[33]

Fortunately, her relationship with Zipperman remained collegial; they continued to work together to improve the Thalia. They rebuilt the front of the theater, but they could not improve the projection system because of the small auditorium or replace the uncomfortable, small seats with modern, larger ones because the fewer number of seats would further reduce the profits. Yet, she proudly explained in her memoir, the audience loved the theater despite its drawbacks: "...this was the beauty of running the Thalia Theatre," she wrote, "the old prints would break down, the seats would creak and you would be uncomfortable and you had to crane your neck to see the picture, but you loved it because there was a certain atmosphere, you got the shows you wanted, and they didn't care. They just accepted it."[34]

In 1960 Dan Talbot's New Yorker Theater caused her some concern because of the competition it represented. Until that time her revival house had had the Upper West Side to itself, except for Symphony Theater in the same building, which was more of a sister theater than a competitor. Talbot met with her to reassure her. "She was very apprehensive about my starting the theater," he said. "And I asked to meet with her, because I admired her, what she was doing. I said to her when we met, 'Ursula, don't worry, I'm not going to hurt you, I just want to try and do my thing here. I'm going to show things that you're not showing; and sometimes I'll wind up showing them later or earlier. And I'm sure it's not going to hurt you.'" He turned out to be right. "After I started the New Yorker," he said, "her business went up. It brought people into the neighborhood, and there was a certain electric thing going on between these two theaters. People knew that this was the one part of town that they could see really great stuff."

On the fourth of July weekend, 1965, another abrupt shock happened. Zipperman had a stroke and could not continue working. For the first time in her life, Mrs. Lewis wrote, "I now was really completely alone."[35]

Once over the shock of being without Max's protection and calming influence, however, she realized she knew how to run a theater. On her own, she found the freedom to implement other ideas. Changes in programming, she thought, needed to be made in order to attract a new generation. Max and she had already introduced American films to the festival, which, under her husband, had been primarily a foreign festival. Now she felt strongly that experimental films and ones made by young filmmakers also had to be included. She did not stop there, though. She introduced weekly and monthly festivals from March through May, something, she wrote, that had not been done either by her husband or in her work with Zipperman. Festivals like "A Review of Experimental and/or Controversial Films" screened in 1966 with films of the independent filmmakers Shirley Clarke (*The Cool World*, 1963, and *The Connection*, 1961) and Lionel Rogosin, (*On the Bowery* and *Come Back, Africa*). "Way Out and Wild—Films in a New Idiom" was shown in 1968, featuring "far-out" and "off-beat" double features, like Richard Lester's *The Knack—and How to Get It* (1965) with Jean Genet's *The Balcony* (1963).[36]

In her memoir, Mrs. Lewis contrasted the new weekly programs with the "all-comprising" summer festivals: the weekly programs were thematic series as opposed to the random daily changes of the summer film festival. In March and April each year, she ran programs on topics like a week of Shakespeare on film. One that she cites in her memoir was a series on the great films of Germany, Japan, and Russia. It opened with Vsevolod Pudovkin's *Mother* (1926), based on Maxim Gorky's novel, and Akira Kurosawa's *Yojimbo* (1961) and included Joseph von Sternberg's *Blue Angel* (1930) with Werner Hochbaum's *The Eternal Mask* (1935). Finally, in the "Merry Month of May," immediately preceding the summer film festival, patrons were entertained with lighter festivals of musicals or comedies.[37]

These weekly programs, she explained, had educational objectives. The series "18 Days Around the World," for example, showed pictures from eighteen countries, "compar[ing] them and their ideology and what was outstanding in these different countries and why these particular pictures were chosen to represent that particular country." Each month, the audience, she wrote, came to expect a program on a subject that would be explored from different angles. Eventually, schools approached her with requests for films to complement their curriculum and would bring their classes to the theater. Her year-round programs, she believed, added to the stature and success of the theater.[38]

Throughout the sixties, the Thalia's familiar printed schedules were a fixture on bulletin boards and refrigerator doors all over the metropolitan area. Then, in September 1973, the final schedule was printed and the theater closed at the conclusion of its 31st Summer Film Festival on September 28, 1973. The newspaper reports about her poor health, Tom Lewis said, were mistaken. Although she had suffered a mild heart attack a few years previously, she had recovered. But she had just remarried, and her husband wanted to retire to Florida. Her son also speculated that she was ready to leave because she found the work more stressful. Managing the theater had always been taxing. Her daughter, Mrs. Sutherland, remembered her constant complaints about being cheated by distributors and about getting bad prints.

Part of the stress may have also related to the retirement of most of her long-time staff. Zipperman had left in 1965. By 1972, Teddy Feiffer was no longer managing, but only periodically helping DiPillo, who was now, according to the 1972 summer calendar, the manager. She and Mrs. Lewis were the only ones left. Still, Mrs. Lewis found it hard to leave. "I love the theater," she told the *New York Post*. "Believe me, it's a difficult decision to make." But she finally made it. On September 28, 1973, the theater was taken over by the landlord of the Symphony Space, who began showing first-run films, bringing the revival policy to an end. Lewis and her husband moved to Florida, but two years later she developed pancreatic cancer and died in November 1975 in Palm Beach.[39]

In the month of its closing, the *New Yorker* magazine defined what the loss of the Thalia meant. Unless someone carried on Mrs. Lewis's work, it wrote, "the Thalia may relinquish its role as a preserver of the most stirring and most artful of American and foreign films ... many young people first encountered them there."

What did the Thalia mean to these young people? The magic of the Thalia may have been best encapsulated in this personal tribute at the end of its career. "That Thalia was mythic.... The theater was tiny—the archetypal revival house. It exuded shabbiness like a backstage, or a third-rate hotel. It had more grace than the Elgin.... It was not so decadent as Theater 80 St. Marks.... You were anonymous there. Somehow, that seemed right.... You have not been down and out and an artist in New York until you have been down and out and unshaven and broke with two bucks in your hand at the box office of the Thalia.... I saw more great movies at the Thalia. *Sundays and Cybele, Loving, The Wild Child, The Virgin Spring, La Guerre Est Finie, Strangers on a Train....* Liv Ullmann, Liv Ullmann in *The Passion of Anna* or *Hour of the Wolf*.... She is the Thalia to me. I sat in the second row, my knees up, taken away by her eyes, the doubt on the corner of her lips, the tremor at the end of a word to Max von Sydow. Because of her, I can feel more deeply, even though I am now more aware of my loss."[40]

Part Two: The Second Wave

Chapter 7

New York Film Scene, 1970s On

The mid- to late-1960s represented a break from the first half of the decade. The youthful rebellion and anti-establishment trends normally associated with the sixties actually began around 1965 and climaxed in the 1970s. The New Left, a mostly white student movement centered on the Students for a Democratic Society (SDS), advocated for civil rights, democracy, and university reforms, while also protesting against the Vietnam War. On the campus of the University of California, Berkeley, the student Free Speech Movement erupted in the academic 1964-65 year, challenging the administrative authority of the university. These student protest movements captured the public's attention. An advertisement for the *New Republic* magazine in *The Village Voice* in 1966 highlighted the magazine's regular coverage of the "new left" and the student protest movements from Texas, California, and Alabama. The Civil Rights Movement moved into a new, separatist phase with the rise of the Black Power Movement. In an article for the *Village Voice*, essayist Vivian Gornick wrote about her experience with the confrontational nature of the Black Power Movement at a presentation by Leroi Jones, the African-American poet and black cultural nationalist who soon changed his name to Amiri Baraka, before an overflowing "white, liberal, middle-class" audience in the small basement room of the Village Vanguard in New York.[1]

By the second half of the decade, local social and political issues were upending New York. On April 23, 1968, an SDS demonstration against Columbia University's plan to build a gymnasium in Morningside Park, led by Mark Rudd, occupied several university buildings (the same demonstration that also occupied the New Yorker Theater) until they were evicted seven days later by one thousand police in riot gear. In the same period two hundred thousand high school and college students struck to protest the Vietnam War, and a month later ten thousand sanitation workers began a nine-day strike. The Knapp Commission to investigate police corruption was set up in 1970 by Mayor Lindsay, following a *New York Times* story based on information from policemen David Durk and Frank Serpico. Serpico's story of his years as a New York police officer was dramatized three years later in Sidney Lumet's film *Serpico*.[2]

Perhaps the most traumatic crisis was the fiscal one, which brought the city to the brink of bankruptcy and social collapse in the mid–1970s. By 1974, the city had a growing municipal debt, which was exacerbated by a worldwide recession. New York's revenue was flat because of a diminishing job market and a declining population, while its growing budget was supporting a large workforce and expanded services for an aging population and an increasing number of poor. In addition, the recession was creating a demand for more social services. After years of urging the city to increase its borrowing when its bonds were low risk and high yield, its largest creditors, the commercial banks, refused to lend it the money needed to cover the budget gap; and when the city turned to the federal government, the latter's refusal to help was memorably captured in a 1975 *Daily News* headline, "Ford to City: Drop Dead." The city was more demoralized than it had ever been.[3]

Yet not everything was bleak. "I think this idea that New York was hell on earth in the late seventies has been mythologized," Marty Rubin, who lived in New York then and programmed for several repertory theaters, opined. "Okay, there were problems, but I remember it as being an extremely lively time, a time of intellectual, cultural excitement. People could still live in Manhattan and not be rich. Eighth Street in the Village had tons of bookstores. And there were great coffee shops that were funky and individualistic. The New York City that I knew, that I programmed for, was the greatest time and the greatest place to be a film programmer."[4]

Rubin's memories were not outlandish. The negative image of New York as a haven for undesirable minorities and arrogant intellectuals and artists, an image that partly accounted for Washington's refusal to help the city, paradoxically made the city an affordable haven for a creative class of artists and quirky entrepreneurs. In a *New York Times Magazine* article in 2012, Adam Davidson recalled a New York of cultural and creative excitement, specifically the Greenwich Village of his youth before gentrification, which was distinctive for its "artists, weirdos and blue-collar families." During the 1970s and 1980s, he wrote, "the Village was the Jane Jacobs ideal, a neighborhood crammed with small mom-and-pop stores … the Village was dense and walkable and, more important, cheap … there was a low barrier to any new idea. Countless dreamers could open shops, clubs, restaurants and oddball stores, even if they didn't have a lot of money or financial moxie."[5]

Among these "countless" impecunious, inexperienced dreamers were the young cineastes who took up the cause of the noncommercial film. They ran small, mostly non-profit film venues dedicated to the non–Hollywood, alternative cinema. Peter Feinstein and Sandy Miller, two young film buffs, opened the Film Forum in November 1970 in a second-floor loft with fifty folding chairs, a rented 16mm projector, and a movable screen. Located on the Upper West Side at West 88th Street, around the corner from the New Yorker Theater and operating only on weekends, the mini-theater of 16mm films showed independent works that were too esoteric or controversial to open commercially. "One of the few places in New York (other than the Millennium, the Jewish Museum Wednesday series, and MoMA's Cineprobes)," Mekas wrote in his *Village Voice* column, "to see Off-Hollywood films." Two years later, moving out of town, the two owners turned the operation over to a twenty-three-year-old Smith College graduate, Karen Cooper, who assumed the responsibility with trepidation, having no previous experience. Despite her initial qualms, she matured into a savvy business person, and by 1990, accomplished the miraculous transformation of the Film Forum from a makeshift, part-time venue into a three-screen, full-time theater, the only autonomous, nonprofit movie theatre in New

Film Forum in its former location, 57 Watts Street, ca. 1987. Photofest.

York: one screen was dedicated to American independent and contemporary foreign art films; the second, a repertory screen reserved for American and foreign classics, genres, festivals and retrospectives; and the third, a holdover for the more popular films from the two theaters as well as new films for longer engagements. As a nonprofit partly supported by government and private grants, the Film Forum was able to screen commercially risky independent films, some of which went on to mainstream theaters. In the early 1970s Cooper introduced the then little-known films of the "big three" of the German New Wave—Rainer Werner Fassbinder, Werner Herzog, and Wim Wenders. "I think we broke a lot of ground in the mid-'70s," she told an interviewer for the magazine *American Film* in 1981, "when we presented work from all over the world—when perhaps an important Truffaut would open in midtown, but not something from Argentina or Japan."[6]

Also in 1970, a fecund year for nonprofit ventures, the more seasoned Jonas Mekas opened his definitive organization, Anthology Film Archives, on December 1, at Joseph Papp's Public Theater, on the invitation of Joseph Martinson, chairman of Papp's New York Shakespeare Festival, and with the financial support of his longtime friend and benefactor, the wealthy filmmaker Jerome Hill. Anthology was different from Mekas's other efforts. Whereas the Film-Makers' Cooperative and the Film-Makers' Cinematheque were democratic in orientation, open to all independent (mostly avant-garde) filmmakers irrespective of competence, Anthology was an elitist, standard-setting "academy," founded on the premise of film as a high art. It restricted its programs to a permanent collection of films carefully selected by a committee composed of P. Adams Sitney, Mekas, Kenneth Kelman, Peter Kubelka, and James Broughton, which was intended to define the art of film. From this collection of classics of film history and landmark experimental films, named the Essential Cinema, programs were drawn and screened in a five- to six-week repertory cycle, allowing a serious study by the public of these outstanding films through their multiple viewings. With Hill's death in 1972, Anthology found it could no longer afford the rent at the Public and relocated in 1974 to 80 Wooster Street in the Village, where the Film-Makers' Cinematheque already resided. A few years later Mekas purchased the Second Avenue Courthouse building in Manhattan with money from the sale of land left to Anthology by Hill and spent a number of years raising money for its renovation. In October 1988, Mekas finally opened Anthology Film Archives in its permanent home in the newly renovated Courthouse building, with two motion picture theaters, a reference library, a film preservation department, offices, and its Essential Cinema Repertory collection. He finally realized his dream of a stable home for his brand of cinema art.[7]

By the middle sixties, other nonprofit ventures dedicated to the independent film and filmmaker were established. In 1966, during the countercultural period in the East Village, St. Marks Church and the New School set up the Millennium Film Workshop as part of the federal government's antipoverty program, with filmmaker Ken Jacobs as its first director. Jacobs instituted one-person programs for any filmmaker with a body of work and "open screenings" for novice filmmakers, much like the pioneering programs of the long-gone Charles Theater. Filmmaker Howard Guttenplan, who succeeded Jacobs and led Millennium for forty years beginning in 1971, added the "Personal Cinema" series, which brought emerging filmmakers from around the nation and world to New York, filmmakers such as Jon Jost, Kenneth Anger, Valie Export, Michael Snow, Yvonne Rainer, and Rudy Burckhardt. Stan Brakhage, a passionate supporter of Millennium, made it his preferred New York City exhibition venue. Its multifaceted programs eventually included low-cost classes in lighting, sound, and camera for beginners, and the periodical *Millennium Film Journal*, which is now the oldest continuously published journal in the world on the theory and practice of avant-garde and independent cinema.[8]

Another offbeat endeavor whose operations and film choices were similar to those at the Millennium was founded in 1973 by a group of former film students from the State University of New York at Binghamton, probably acolytes of the Hollywood director Nicholas Ray, who was teaching at the college. The Collective for Living Cinema started in rental space in two Manhattan churches, then with a growing audience, moved in 1975 to a permanent location in a storefront at Two White Street in Tribeca. Characterized by *Village Voice* film critic Amy Taubin as "[t]he most eclectic of New York's independent film venues," the Collective screened a wide range of films, from Hollywood rarities to new avant-garde productions. Its showpiece, the "New Film-Makers' Showcase," became a regular forum for young, independent filmmakers, who often made personal appearances with their works. By 1983, film scholar David Sterritt reported in the *Christian Science Monitor*, more than 800 independent filmmakers had exhibited work there. In its Tribeca location, the Collective, like Millennium, offered filmmaking classes and published a magazine in addition to its regular weekend program schedule. Unfortunately, by February 1991, the organization was forced to close due to falling attendance, cuts in government funding, and real estate problems, among other factors.[9]

Finally, scattered throughout the city in churches, colleges, and even apartments, young film buffs established their own small cinematheques. The Undercroft Coffeehouse at Christ and St. Stephen's Church, an independent project of a group of young people, was listed in the *New York Times*'s "Going out Guide" for its weekly programs of classic musicals and dramas, such as *The Good Earth* (1937) and *The Lost Weekend* (1945). The Cooperative Film Society at Joe's Place on West 40th Street, Ed Maguire remembered, was operated by Puerto Rican Joe Guidice, who screened prints from his tremendous collection of 16mm B westerns in an all-day format devoted either to serials or to westerns.[10]

"The real underground film," Mary Maguire opined, "was in people's apartments." Most of these apartment-based cinematheques were simple setups, but others were described by Charles Turner in a *Film History* interview, as "elaborate little theaters with velvet rope, upholstered seats, and wall hangings." Between the modest and extravagant operations were ones like that of Don Malkames, "whose screening room had theater seats and a railing before a curved screen." Mary Maguire remembered the simple operation of Don Cole, an actor who showed 1930s films, especially those that were too minor for television packages; he would drag rented reels of film up five flights to his coldwater flat on East 3rd Street for evenings with other fans of these obscure films. Another modestly run cinematheque was John Griggs's Sutton Cinema Society, which began in Griggs's apartment on Sutton Place but kept the name as he moved to different residences. In what was probably his last one, a house rather than apartment, he reserved an area in his basement with a built-in booth for the screenings, where Walter Langsford had spent many evenings watching silent films, along with the writers and actors who mostly made up his audience. Over the years, celebrities like Lillian and Dorothy Gish, Vivien Leigh, and Anthony Perkins also attended.[11]

One of the best known of these small cineclubs was the Thousand Eyes Film Society, run by Howard Mandelbaum and Roger McNiven out of four different apartments over a period of years. "[Roger] and Howie moved to better and better apartments," one fan reminisced on a blog, "presumably as their economic situation improved; the first screening I went to was on the Lower East Side, with the screen in the kitchen and the projector in the hallway. Then there was a studio-loft on 13th Street, and finally a larger loft, I think in the 20s." The two were famous among the cognoscenti for their schedules of Hollywood films from the 1930s to the 1950s. They even advertised their schedules in *Cue*. "The Howard and Roger screenings," wrote another fan, "are the stuff of New York legend."[12]

In 1969 film historian Richard Schickel proclaimed the era a time when film was reigning as the premiere art for the mostly younger, educated public under the age of 40 who comprised the new, moviegoing audience. Literary critic Irving Howe noted in a 1973 *New York Times* article that "movies have recently carried a sharper air of excitement than have books." Susan Sontag remembered the late 1960s and 1970s as "this specific moment in the 100-year history of cinema that going to the movies, thinking about movies, talking about movies became a passion among university students and other young people. You fell in love not just with actors but with cinema itself."[13]

What was attracting the young to film over the other arts? Just as the year 1965 represented a generational break from the conformist ethos of the fifties, it also represented an abrupt transition in film culture. The golden age of the foreign film had ended by 1965. "[O]ne should not confuse the early sixties with the late," Lopate wrote in his memoir of the period. By 1970 the art cinema movement was in decline as audience attendance had diminished. One of the first art house pioneers, the Walter Reade chain, declared bankruptcy in the early 1970s. In addition, the foreign art film had changed. Major U.S. studios, which had taken over the financing and distribution of foreign films, Deac Russell wrote in an essay in *Boston After Dark* in 1970, were now obligating foreign directors who wanted financing and distribution to make their type of commercial film rather than the kind they, the filmmakers, once believed in. Independent foreign directors found themselves locked out of the market.[14]

Furthermore, interest among the young had shifted from stylistic innovation to social content. "By 1968," Lopate wrote in his memoir, "the students at Columbia would have more important things to argue about than the merits of Gerd Oswald's *Screaming Mimi*." Between 1968 and 1974, the assassinations of Martin Luther King, Jr., and Robert Kennedy and the Watergate scandal traumatized the nation, protests over the Vietnam War intensified, and drug use and changing, more lenient sexual behaviors characterized the new generation. Political and social content in film now took precedence over style. Gary Crowdus, reviewing the 1969 New York Film Festival for *Film Society Review*, criticized the festival for including films that showed a preoccupation with artistic personality over subject matter and noted with satisfaction the presence of films that showed the influence of the "Cinepolitical Age." "[M]ore than half of the films screened this year," he wrote, "had themes of an underlying socio-political character. Filmmakers everywhere, reflecting current political preoccupations, are quite naturally turning to subjects with prominent social and political themes."[15]

Documentaries condemning the Vietnam War, illuminating urban problems, and documenting Third World movements were produced and distributed to colleges, churches, and community organizations. They also became the natural home for feminist filmmakers, who were shut out of the Hollywood system. *Antonia: A Portrait of the Woman* (1974), a documentary on the life and career of Dr. Antonia Brico, a woman orchestra leader in her seventies, was the first feminist documentary nominated for an Academy Award; it opened the door to commercial distribution of feminist nonfiction films. Two years later, a woman director, Barbara Kopple, won the Academy Award for feature documentary with *Harlan County, U.S.A.* (1976), a film about a prolonged strike by Kentucky coal miners against the Duke Power Company.[16]

For a few brief years, Hollywood also experienced a revolution in its filmmaking. The old studio system had plummeted to its nadir and by the mid-sixties retained only its distribution function. Simultaneously, independent productions were rising as producers began to realize that, with the interest of the new American audience in "art" films and the auteur status of the director, such productions could make money if they were shot quickly on low budgets by inexpensive young directors, in the mode of the French and Italian New Waves. As the studios became open to distributing them, more producers and directors joined the independent ranks, including a group of young directors mostly from the golden age of live television in New York who had migrated in the early sixties to Hollywood to work for the studios and then moved into independent production in the mid– to late–1960s. With their increasing freedom and mobility, they were able to adapt the French and Italian New Wave techniques—location shooting, looser writing and acting, and deliberately cinematic camera movement and editing—to a more antiestablishment vision of American society that spoke to the concerns of the young audience. The director's decade began.[17]

Arthur Penn's *Bonnie and Clyde* (1967), Stanley Kubrick's *2001: A Space Odyssey* (1968), Sam Pekinpah's *The Wild Bunch*, (1969), Robert Altman's *M*A*S*H* (1970), and Penn's *Little Big Man* (1970) converted the clichés and formulas of the crime, science fiction, western, and war genres into condemnations of American institutions. Dennis

Hopper and Peter Fonda's *Easy Rider* in 1969 generated a brief cycle of "youth culture" movies about protest, drugs, and the generation gap, like Stuart Hagmann's *Strawberry Statement* (1970) and Arthur Penn's *Alice's Restaurant* (1969). A new kind of American cinema, soon dubbed the New Hollywood by the press, reflected the more permissive sexual values and rebellious attitudes of the baby boomer generation.[18]

Then, from 1972 to 1976, a coterie of even younger directors, baby boomers born during and after World War II and mostly trained in American film schools, ushered in a golden age of American cinema. It was "the last great time," Peter Bart, vice president of production at Paramount until the mid-seventies, was quoted in Peter Biskind's history of the period, *Easy Riders, Raging Bulls*, "for pictures that expanded the idea of what could be done with movies." A number of these directors began in Hollywood with the independent, low-budget, B-movie producer Roger Corman and went on to create in this four-year period films that were "character- rather than plot-driven," Biskind wrote, "that defied traditional narrative conventions, that challenged the tyranny of technical correctness, that broke the taboos of language and behavior, that dared to end unhappily." The year 1974 was perhaps the apex of this period with Francis Ford Coppola's Academy Award-winning *The Godfather Part II* and *The Conversation*; Roman Polanski's *Chinatown*, a neo-noir that ranks with the original noirs; John Cassavetes's *A Woman Under the Influence*, generally considered among the greatest of Cassavetes' films; and Martin Scorsese's *Alice Doesn't Live Here Anymore*, "perhaps the first feminist-oriented mainstream film."[19]

"It's well documented," wrote John Pierson in his memoir of the independent film movement in the seventies, "that the period in Hollywood from 1969's *Easy Rider* to the mid-seventies was a free-swinging, artistically inspired renaissance…. Graduates [of the Roger Corman school of filmmaking] like Bob Rafelson and Jack Nicholson teamed up for films like *Five Easy Pieces*, while Peter Bogdanovich left his film criticism behind to make *The Last Picture Show*."[20]

The movement was sustained in the United States by a vibrant film culture. An assemblage of critics—Andrew Sarris, Pauline Kael, John Simon, Stanley Kauffman, and Manny Farber—spearheaded the spread of "the new film gospel in reviews, books, talk shows, everywhere," *New York Times* film critic Manohla Dargis remarked in a look back at the era with her colleague A.O. Scott. Irving Howe observed in his 1973 *Times* article that "movie criticism in America seems livelier, more pungent than literary criticism. People who read any sort of criticism at all are more likely to care about Pauline Kael's opinion of a movie than what anyone in these pages says about a book." The skirmishes between auteurist Andrew Sarris and anti-auteurist Pauline Kael divided film buffs into Sarristes and Paulettes. In addition to movie criticism, thoughtful articles on directors and films were published by magazines like *Film Comment* and *The New York Film Bulletin*.[21]

New York was the center of this lively activity. The major critics were based in the city. The films of the American New Wave opened there. Revivals and independent films were ubiquitous on the mainstream as well as nonprofit screens. *Cue* critic William Wolf announced in 1971, that "New York has grown into a year-round film fest. Just about *everything* is available these days. What was once reserved for the film buff is now commercially viable." First-run theaters were now showing films that had once been relegated to marginal venues: the Paramount, Wolf pointed out, screened the 1927 silent film *Wings*; and a Broadway house, New Forum 47th Street, showed the esoteric *El Topo* (1970), with full-page ads in the *Times*. Interesting retrospectives were interspersed with first runs at the mainstream theaters. In 1971 Kips Bay screened a Roger Corman series and the rejuvenated 72nd Street Playhouse featured a Ruby Keeler festival.[22]

Along with the small, independent, nonprofit ventures in alternative exhibition, like Film Forum and Millennium Workshop, major New York cultural institutions were adding film programs to their principal missions. In 1970, the same year that Papp's Public Theater introduced Anthology Film Archives as a complement to its theatrical productions, the Whitney Museum of American Art established the New American Film Makers Series. Screening its first program in December 1970, the Whitney series, like the Film Forum but unlike Anthology Film Archives, embraced the wide array of independent films that had developed since the late sixties: abstract films; feature-length, low-budget narratives; political and feminist documentaries; the life-style film; animated films; student films; videos; and personal films. The Whitney's and Film Forum's broad approaches to independent film aroused the ire of Mekas, who accused them of ignoring the avant-garde. The Whitney's film curator, David Bienstock, responded in a February 1973 *Village Voice* article, that the Whitney's goal was to represent "as broad a spectrum of styles and approaches to the medium as possible ... from the uses of film as a means of social and political communication to the formal and structural approach." He faulted Mekas for limiting the avant-garde to the formal, structuralist school, even though the avant-garde, he wrote, consisted of all the approaches "that break the traditional concepts of the medium." Karen Cooper of the Film Forum made a similar argument in a letter to the *Voice*'s editor in 1974. Mekas also voiced his disapproval in several of his columns of the potpourri of different styles of independent films that characterized the programs of the Film Forum and the Whitney series. In his view, they were neglecting in-depth examinations of the work of avant-garde filmmakers.[23]

In 1978, Papp's Public Theater again added film to its offerings, after the departure of Anthology Film Archives. Unlike the restricted, avant-garde approach of Anthology, the goal of the new program, Film at the Public, was to nurture "lost" American films: undistributed, American independent films and studio films that had been shelved because the producers did not know what to do with them. Seven months later, under its new programmer, Fabiano Canosa, who had previously operated the innovative repertory theater, the First Avenue Screening Room, it expanded to "lost" foreign films, those from countries "whose cinematographies had received little visibility in the United States," as well as revivals of underrated classics and retrospectives of acclaimed directors. "So many unknown film makers," Canosa told the *New York Times*, "have been working for years that we haven't even begun to uncover. We need these specialized theaters to bring these films to the public."[24]

The Film Society of Lincoln Center, established in 1969, was not subordinate to but on an administrative par with the other constituent arts of the Lincoln Center for the Performing Arts, including the Metropolitan Opera, the New York Philharmonic, and the New York City Ballet. But it was not until December 9, 1991, when the state-of-the-art, 268-seat Walter Reade Theater opened in the Lincoln Center complex, that the film society acquired its own setting and achieved its goal of a year-round cinema. Prior to this, its only responsibility was to administer the New York Film Festival; hold annual galas honoring distinguished film artists (its first tribute in 1972 honored Charles Chaplin, who returned to the U.S. from twenty years of self-imposed exile especially for the occasion); and, in co-sponsorship with MoMA, carry out the annual New Directors/New Films.[25]

Begun in 1972, New Directors/New Films featured the works of emerging as well as distinguished, overlooked veterans whose work deserved wider attention. Filmmakers making their debuts included Steven Spielberg (*Sugarland Express*, 1974), John Sayles (*Return of the Secaucus Seven*, 1979), Wim Wenders (*The Goalie's Anxiety at Penalty Kick*, 1972), Hector Babenco (*Pixote*, 1981), and Wayne Wang (*Chan Is Missing*, 1982). The collaboration was a natural fit for the two organizations with their similar mission, the advocacy of film as art, and similar inclusive and eclectic visions of the art of film.[26]

Finally, in 1981 the inevitable progression to a full-fledged museum for film and the visual arts took place. The American Museum of the Moving Image (AMMI) was established in the former Paramount Studio East Coast production complex in Queens, which had been restored in 1980 as the Kaufman Astoria Studios, one of the largest film production centers in New York and on the East Coast. AMMI (later renamed the Museum of the Moving Image) at first presented film programs in temporary quarters in the Paramount complex before opening its own partially renovated building on the campus in September 1988, with a floor and a half of galleries, two screening rooms, and a museum bookstore/shop. Although operating repertory theaters comparable to those of MoMA and the Film Society of Lincoln Center, AMMI's principal mission as a museum, reported *New Yorker* magazine at its opening, was "to assemble not movies but the stuff of movies—the machines and ephemera of moving images, like Edison's kinetoscope and Clara Bow's hair ribbon and a Hopalong Cassidy lunchbox." Filling the entire second floor of the new, still uncompleted building, a permanent exhibition, "Behind the Screen: Producing, Promoting, and Exhibiting Motion Pictures and Television," comprising 7,200 square feet, presented important historical artifacts, such as costumes, fan magazines, posters, and a movie set, to illustrate who does what in motion pictures and television from inception to exhibition in movie houses and living rooms. As of 1993, the collection held over one thousand pieces of motion picture hardware from fin de siècle peepshows to the home video revolution.[27]

Along with this dynamic complex of nonprofit venues thrived its equally enterprising commercial counterpart, the repertory movie houses.

Chapter 8

The Second Wave of the Repertory Theater Movement

The first wave of repertory movie theaters had ended in 1973 with the closing of the Bleecker Street Cinema. Overlapping the first wave, the second one began in 1968 with the Elgin Theater and reached its zenith in the decades of the 1970s and 1980s. In 1971 McCandlish Phillips reported in the *New York Times* that the repertory houses had grown from three in 1966 to eleven and were flourishing while first-run theaters were having a bad time. Of the eleven theaters five were on the Upper West Side—the Symphony Theatre and the Thalia, both in the same building on Broadway at 95th Street; the New Yorker on Broadway between 88th and 89th streets; and the Olympia at Broadway and 107th Street. In Times Square, the Bijou on West 45th Street, an all-Japanese house, drew a largely black audience. Two were practically next door to each other in Greenwich Village, the Garrick and the Bleecker Street Cinema (in its final days under Lionel Rogosin), both on Bleecker Street between Thompson Street and Laguardia Place. The Elgin was located in the Puerto Rican neighborhood of Chelsea on Eighth Avenue (now the Joyce Theater); and the East Village was home to the St. Marks Cinema on Second Avenue and Theater 80 St. Marks on St. Marks Place.[1]

Nine more repertory houses opened between 1972 and 1988. The Quad opened in 1972 on West 13th Street in Greenwich Village as the first multiplex in Manhattan with four small auditoriums. The First Avenue Screening Room, one of the few alternative venues located on the Upper East Side, was launched in 1973. Four reopened under new ownerships between 1973 and 1982—the Carnegie Hall Cinema on Seventh Avenue near 57th Street in midtown and the Bleecker Street Cinema in the Village, both under Sidney Geffen; the Thalia under Richard Schwarz; and the Midtown, which became the Metro, under Dan Talbot. The Regency on Broadway between 67th and 68th streets and the Cinema Village in Greenwich Village on East 12th Street were converted from neighborhood theaters to repertory houses in 1975 and 1977, respectively; a later conversion in 1978 was the 8th Street Playhouse in Greenwich Village. The Thalia Soho on Vandam Street in Greenwich Village, the Biograph on West 57th Street in midtown, and the Gramercy on First Avenue on the Upper East Side were last-ditch efforts at the end of the 1980s to preserve the waning repertory house movement.

Paradoxically, while the art theaters were gradually closing after 1965, the repertory movie theaters were multiplying. They had two advantages over the art houses—more flexible programming and shoestring budgets. The mostly young entrepreneurs who operated these houses were risk-takers—but not for financial rewards. They were part of the fellowship of small mom-and-pop enterprises at that time willing to take chances on atypical, but important, films.

The following chapters focus on those major repertory houses whose owners/operators were still alive and available for interviews. Yet, the other repertory houses also contributed to the film culture of the period. The St. Marks Cinema in the East Village reopened in September 1971 as a repertory house, with plans to show "two strong features," its operator, Jay Fuchs, a 29-year-old Broadway producer, explained to a *New York Times* reporter, that will appeal to "two different audiences," and to sell organic candy for the young crowd. Closed down in February 1977 after a long decline as an affordable, clean repertory house for the neighborhood mixture of "students, artists, working-class ethnics, and middle-class professionals," it reopened under new ownership in May of that year, an *East Side Express* writer reported, with the same programming—a weekly double feature combining a second-run film with a less-recent release. Art films, ethnic festivals, and midnight screenings were the most popular ideas for shows. For eight years it remained a neighborhood staple, showing four-dollar double bills of recent films as well as at least six midnight movies a week, then closed permanently in September 1985, amidst rumors that it would make room for a shopping center.[2]

Like the St. Marks Cinema, the Olympia Theater had a troubled history over its thirty-one years. Reopening as a repertory theater in July 1971 with double bills through December of old MGM Technicolor musicals, it was an attempt, the owners, Robert Shaye and David Dretzin, told a *New York Times* reporter, to counter the competition with the "Gold Coast" East Side, which was hogging the good, first-run films. "That's why we go for interesting programming concepts," Shaye said, "instead of just being a third- or fourth-run neighborhood movie house." Shaye may have also been using the theater to screen films of his distribution company, New Line Cinema. In February 1972, janitors struck the Olympia over cuts in hours and layoffs, claiming in their strike flyer that the real reason for the theater's financial trouble was bad programming. From the mid–70s to the mid–80s, a new owner transformed it from a low-priced art house to a fourplex. The theater finally closed in 2002, with plans by the new owner to convert it to an apartment building.[3]

The Quad opened in October 1972 in Greenwich Village as the first multiplex in Manhattan. Its first program consisted of revivals—the least imaginative possible, Jonas Mekas complained in one of his Village Voice columns. From the beginning, it showed a mixture of Hollywood films, independent films, and revivals. In the late 1980s, when other multiplexes opened, the Quad survived by specializing in foreign and independent films. It prospered under this new policy as independents began having success at the box-office. By 2015, however, it closed for renovations under a new owner, Charles S. Cohen, a real estate mogul and owner of the Cohen Media Group, a film distribution company, with plans to reopen as a combination first-run and repertory theater, similar to Film Forum.[4]

The Upper East Side's First Avenue Screening Room was noted for its unique policy of booking only independent and foreign films ignored by distributors. The idea, analogous to the underlying concept of Dan Talbot's recent series at the New Yorker, "One

Dollar at All Times," was to provide an affordable New York opening for these neglected films. The theater's approach was a critical success, but financial failure. The New York Film Critics, Judith Crist had reported in the magazine *New York*, voted a special citation in 1974 for Fabiano Canosa, its programmer (who later went on to program the film series at the Public Theater), for his selection of neglected films that "has indeed done so much to enrich the film scene in the past year." *Variety* enthused over its innovative preview series of quality but little-known, neglected foreign product. It was virtually the only outlet for these films, *Variety* explained, since "[t]he surviving 'arty' situations (the Carnegie Hall Cinema, the Elgin, the Quad Cinema complex, Theatre 80 St. Marks and St. Marks Cinema, among others) operate on a re-run basis." Unfortunately, the New York "art film" audience did not share the critical enthusiasm, and the theater was sold in March 1975 after a two-year run.[5]

One feature set the 8th Street Playhouse in Greenwich Village apart from the other repertory houses—its thirteen-year run of *The Rocky Horror Picture Show* (1975) as a weekend midnight movie, a must-see for the young crowd. The theater specialized in retrospectives of American and foreign film classics and catered to a trendy audience with quiche Lorraine slices and specially prepared sandwiches on pizza dough. In an interview with the *Villager* in 1981, one of the owners, Steve Hirsch, said, "Believe it or not, there is a growing taxi and limo trade coming to 8th Street. Give people a clean, technically excellent place to watch a movie, and they'll keep coming back." His assessment did not hold up, though. In 1986, after his death, the challenge from the multiplex movie theaters that opened below 14th Street cycled the theater through several owners, who tried different formats, including first runs, to compete. In fall 1991, the theater switched back to repertory programming, but there was too much competition among revival and art houses downtown, such as the six-screen Angelika Film Center, the three-screen Film Forum, and the six-screen Village East Cinemas. The theater closed in October 1992.[6]

In 1982 Dan Talbot, in opening his new repertory movie theater, the Metro, explained to a *New York Post* reporter his reasons for returning to repertory programming: he had been bored by the New Yorker but was now refreshed and wanted to return to his roots. He renovated the dilapidated, art deco Midtown Theater on the Upper West Side, renamed it the Metro, and opened it as his second revival house, the largest in Manhattan with 535 seats. The initial idea, he told the reporter, "is to be eclectic, mixing old and new foreign and old and new Hollywood—until I get a feel for what the audiences are all about." By May 1985, Talbot once again abandoned revivals and converted the Metro to first runs with Columbia's John Travolta–Jamie Lee Curtis starrer *Perfect* (1985). Doing repertory had been fun at first, he told a *Westsider* reporter, "but when we began repeating bookings it was time to change."[7]

The repertory theaters presented a smorgasbord for film lovers to feast on, from rare old films to countercultural ones. "The Theatre 80 St. Marks," *Cue* film critic William Wolf wrote, "has made a full-fledged business enterprise out of showing old musicals," while "[s]pecial midnight showings of more esoteric films like…. *Viva La Muerte* have caught on at the Elgin and St. Marks Cinema." The midnight shows, forged by the old Charles Theater, were reintroduced and popularized by the Elgin Theater and then picked up by St. Marks Cinema, the Cinema Village, the Waverly, and the 8th Street Playhouse, among others. They were the rage among the young crowd. "Everybody's digging midnights," one young man with his girlfriend on his arm and plastic flowers in his hair told a *New York Times* reporter at a midnight screening at the Cinema Village. For film buffs, the repertory theaters held a special importance. "They [the Bleecker Street and Carnegie Hall Cinemas]," reminisced Pierson in his memoir on the independent film movement of the seventies, "along with the Elgin and Thalia (earlier), Regency, and Metro (later) were irreplaceable for cineastes before home video. The convivial, collective atmosphere and chance to see noir pairings of *Screaming Mimi* and *Bedlam* or prints of films like Howard Hawks's *Rio Bravo* made late-seventies pilgrimages to those theaters one of the brightest experiences I can remember."[8]

The actors in the small world of the repertory houses knew each other and sometimes circulated from one theater to another. Marty Rubin programmed for the New York Cultural Center before going to the Bleecker Street Cinema. Howard Mandelbaum worked at the Carnegie and Bleecker Street Cinemas after giving up the Thousand Eyes Film Society and later volunteered at the Thalia. Roger McNiven also worked at the Carnegie and Bleecker and afterwards wrote program notes for the Thalia. Greg Ford programmed at both the Thalia and Bleecker Street Cinema. After five years at the Bleecker, Bill Thompson took his Japanese series to the Thalia.

Recognizing the popularity and importance of the repertory houses to film culture in New York, the major New York newspapers and magazines, along with the smaller, neighborhood newspapers, all regularly covered these theaters. In addition to the weekly listings of the repertory house schedules in the newspapers, feature articles on the theaters appeared frequently, often motivated by upcoming series. *New York Times* film critic Guy Flatley, for example, drummed up interest in a major retrospective in January 1977 of "Columbia [Pictures] gems" at the Regency with an interview with Jean Arthur, "a one-of-a-kind star in a series of memorable comedy dramas during the 1930's and 40's by Columbia." Descriptions of the theaters and their specialties were another popular subject. *Village Voice* film critic Tom Allen devoted a whole page of the newspaper in 1978 to a description of the men (by 1978 the only female owner, Ursula Lewis, had retired) who operated the repertory theaters and their programming philosophies. Changing trends in the repertory houses' programming were also described; Janet Maslin reported for the *New York Times* on the addition to repertory calendars of recent films that had initially failed. Repertory theater closings warranted interviews with the departing owners and eulogies on their contributions to New York film culture. "It was hardly a comfortable theater," began the *Daily News*'s article on the passing of the New Yorker, "but you didn't go to the New Yorker for comfort, you went because you loved movies and because no other theater in the city provided such a never-ending feast of American classics, European masterworks and movies as yet undiscovered." Likewise, the opening of a new repertory house became a newsworthy event. "Long before New York was a summer festival," began the coverage in the *New York Times* of the "revival" of the Thalia, "there was the Thalia…. Now the Thalia, with most of its peculiarities intact, is returning to those golden days of yesteryear."[9]

In the early 1980s, hints of trouble threw a shadow over the otherwise robust repertory movement. The economics of running a single-screen, small, independent theater were changing. An early complaint was the increase in movie rentals and other costs. By 1987 a classic film that cost $50 in 1982 now cost a guarantee of $100 to $150 against a percentage of ticket sales. Added to film rentals were the increasing costs of labor, rent, printing and mailing a calendar, and shipping the films. In contrast to first-run theaters, whose advertising and overhead for a movie typically were paid by the distributor, who then took perhaps 90 percent of the gross, the repertory houses, explained Film Forum 2's Goldstein in an interview with the *New York Times*, had to pay all advertising and expenses plus pay the distributors a guarantee as well as some percentage of the gross. In addition, there was the aggravation of finding good prints. "And we have to publish the calendar," he concluded, "which is a crucial part of this business."[10]

By 1985 articles pondering the future of the revival house movement were appearing more often in newspapers and magazines as some theaters were closing or converting to first-run. In 1983 the Bleecker Street Cinema started showing first-run films like *Desperately Seeking Susan* (1985) in addition to its midnight runs of such cult classics as the *Rocky Horror Picture Show*; and in 1985 Dan Talbot's Metro converted to a first-run theater. Also in 1985 the Carnegie Hall Cinema was no longer showing revivals, and St. Marks Cinema closed. The repertory house managers were interviewed on strategies for survival. Programming, they agreed, was their principal strategy, but they argued over series versus random programming. Frank Rowley, the programmer at the Regency, and Goldstein were the chief spokespeople for the series approach. For Rowley, thematic series were the key to good programming, and good programming, he insisted in a 1987 *Newsweek* article, was the key to survival for repertory houses. Series, contended Goldstein, were a powerful marketing tool, which revival houses would need to depend on more than ever, while arbitrary programming will disappear. A great, rare film, he argued in a 1987 *New Manhattan Review* article, may not even be noticed if it is presented by itself in the middle of a randomly organized schedule; but as a part of a major, well-publicized series, the film was likely to be recognized. A similar argument was advanced by George Mansour, owner of the Images Cinema in Williamstown, Massachusetts, who proclaimed that theme bills were used more than ever by revival exhibitors, to pump new life into familiar films. "The *Harold and Maude, Casablanca, King of Hearts* thing is just passé," he told the *Newsweek* reporter in 1987. "But if you bring back *Harold and Maude* as part of an intergenerational sex film festival, you may have a hit." The principal, and perhaps sole, spokesman for the random approach was Howard Otway, owner of Theatre 80 St. Marks, who strongly felt that series-based repertory was a mistake. "So if you don't happen to like Joan Crawford, you don't go to the movies for six weeks?" he wondered.[11]

The closings continued despite experiments with programming, such as mixing first runs with revivals. In May 1987 the Thalia shut its doors, leaving four full-time, commercial repertory houses in New York: the Cinema Village, the Regency, Thalia Soho, and Theatre 80 St. Marks. These were complemented by the nonprofits: the Film Forum, Public Theater, and MoMA's Film Department. Four months later the Regency closed; and in 1990 the Cinema Village and Thalia Soho went dark. Of the full-time, commercial revival houses, only Theatre 80 St. Marks remained. With the death of Otway in 1994, Theatre 80 St. Marks closed; and the commercial, repertory movie theater movement in New York City came to an end.

Revival houses throughout the nation were undergoing a similar decline; in the seven years from 1980 to 1987 they had shrunk nationwide from 75 to 15. By 1980 the art houses, the other commercial sanctuary for film as art, had experienced a similar decline; those that regularly ran foreign films dropped to less than one hundred nationwide, most likely from the same causes.[12]

A number of changing conditions, in addition to escalating costs, spelled the doom of the movement, both locally and nationally. The two foremost changes were the rise of cable television and videocassettes and the jump in real estate values in the 1980s. Cable and videocassettes became formidable competitors to the repertory houses, offering the convenience of home for watching the same films that once could be seen only at the repertory theaters. Cult films like Stanley Kubrick's *A Clockwork Orange* (1971) or Ken Russell's *The Devils* (1971), which were once the exclusive domain of the repertory houses, were now features on cable television. Mainstream classics began showing up in video stores. "Whether or not people actually rent *Casablanca*, they know they can," observed Donald Krim, president of Kino International, in a *Newsweek* article.[13]

Some repertory managers challenged the conventional opinion about the effect of videocassettes on their business. Otway insisted that the revival houses had an advantage over videocassettes. "Well, you can't rent an audience to react to a picture," Otway said in a *New York Times* article. "And that's half the show. I think the VCR movie is competition for 'I Love Lucy' reruns." Rowley, interviewed for the same article, felt that a conservative programming policy was the insurance for survival. "What you have to make sure of," he said, "is that you have good pictures, popular stars and that you screen them in a nice setting.... And you can't be too adventurous. People come to see titles that they've heard about before. They might take a chance on a first-run movie, but they won't with a revival."[14]

While there were differences of opinion about the effect of videocassettes and cable television, there was consensus that the rise in real estate value in New York was the greater threat. By the 1980s the real estate of the theaters was worth more to the landlords than the repertory houses' leases. Developers were acquiring the properties and replacing the theaters with large multiplexes or other commercial chains. Talbot told a *New York Times* reporter in 2003 that he seethed every time he passed chains like Victoria's Secret that were "paying top dollar for space along a stretch of Broadway where nearly a score of theaters once stood." Since early 1986, a handful of large theater chains, or circuits, spent more than $1 billion buying smaller chains and independently owned theaters. One of the most voracious of these, the Toronto-based Cineplex Odeon chain, bought the Carnegie Hall Cinema in 1986 and the Regency in 1987. These chains were replacing the smaller theaters with megaplexes, which had an economic advantage: the higher grossing films ran in bigger rooms and the less popular ones in smaller spaces. The megaplexes were not gambling on one movie.[15]

Changes in Hollywood production and audience taste also spelled trouble for the repertory houses. The American renaissance in filmmaking, the Hollywood New Wave, was petering out and being replaced by blockbusters. The release of Steven Spielberg's *Jaws* in 1975 and George Lucas's *Star Wars* in 1977 signaled the start of the new Hollywood business model of blockbusters that were released in a blitz of nationwide releases. Simultaneously, the tastes of the incoming, post–baby-boomer student population, the *Chicago Tribune* reported, were shifting from the adventurous and countercultural bent of the previous generation to the safer blockbusters. They favored the kinetic style of these films over the more contemplative approach of the older films. In the 1960s, Toby Talbot observed in her memoir of the New Yorker, "[m]ise-en-scene superseded montage as a truer representation of continuity and respect for unity of space. In-depth shots, with foreground and background in full view, were favored." But, Lopate told this author, "film grammar was changing [in the late sixties on]. The integrity of the shot was breaking down and we began to get more of the slice and dice, MTV type of editing. Montage, quick editing came in more." Even the avant-garde had lost its creative edge. In reviewing the

"1985 Biennial Exhibition" at the Whitney Museum of American Art, P. Adams Sitney lamented the "weakness" of new avant-garde filmmakers. "The regular appearance of powerful new artists, which characterized the American avant-garde between 1943 and the early seventies, has petered out."[16]

The bread and butter of repertory—the classic films and the foreign language art films—no longer appealed to the young. The great films of film history, like Renoir's *Rules of the Game*, were replaced by cult films, what Lopate called the "newer, more truncated canons—film noir, pre-code, campy worst movies." Pierson summed it up when he wrote in his memoir, "I'm a member of the art-film brat generation ... the last generation to have a keen interest in our worldwide, century-long film history." The Eddie Murphy starrer *Beverly Hills Cop* (1984) or the fifth episode of the *Star Wars* series, *The Empire Strikes Back* (1980) now enthralled adolescents. "What had evaporated," author Louis Menand explained in his essay on Pauline Kael, "was the consensus that it all mattered." By the end of the 1970s, he wrote, the cultural authority of the movies had declined; they were no longer the dominant cultural force. These seismic changes in the interests of the young added up to the loss of a primary audience for the repertory houses.[17]

By 1994 with the closing of the last commercial repertory theater, Theatre 80 St. Marks, repertory programming had come full circle and was once again operating solely within the nonprofit sector, with its programming, pristine prints, and comfortable settings, which were better equipped to compete with home theater. The repertory scene was still vibrant, only now dressed in newer, more fashionable garments.

Chapter 9

The Elgin Theater: Midnight Movies and the Countercultural Craze

Among the second wave of repertory theaters, the Elgin Theater in Chelsea on Eighth Avenue at 19th Street was the countercultural standout. The theater's "All Night Show" (movies started at midnight and ended at dawn) and the "Midnight Movie" (a launching pad for offbeat films that became cult classics) gave it its hippie aura. "People were always getting stoned," Mandlebaum recalled, "and wandering around." Vivian Gornick described its atmosphere in a *Village Voice* article as "distinctly counterculture: Oroko Ambrosia is on sale at the candy counter, one cult movie or another plays at midnight on weekends, the street-smart audience is half the show, and every liberal cause in New York knows it can put the touch on the Elgin for a benefit showing."[1]

Ben Barenholtz, its owner and the architect of its ambiance, was born in Kovel, Poland, and migrated as a child with his mother and brother to New York from Nazi-held Poland. In 1952 he moved to Greenwich Village and its bustling arts scene. It was a creative, exciting time. "That whole generation that came out of the forties," Barenholtz said, "had a whole different attitude towards the arts. There was a certain kind of atmosphere, you had an idea, you could try it, nobody would say this can't work, that kind of freedom." Jose Quintero and Theodore Mann co-founded Circle in the Square Theatre and gave birth to the Off Broadway movement. Joe Cino created Off Off Broadway, staging the plays of such novice playwrights as Sam Shepard, John Guare, and Lanford Wilson in his tiny Greenwich Village coffeehouse, Café Cino. Aspiring young writers flocked to the Village and mingled with literary idols like Norman Mailer and James Baldwin at the White Horse Tavern on Hudson Street. Abstract expressionist painters Jackson Pollack and his contemporaries drank and caroused at the Cedar Bar on University Place. Barenholtz became part of the scene. "I hung out at Washington Square until I went into the army. Then from '59 to '66 my home was the old Cedar Bar, where I hung out and drank almost every night with Kline, de Kooning, all those people, about five years."[2]

He started in film exhibition in 1958 as a twenty-three-year-old assistant manager of the RKO Bushwick Theater in Brooklyn. Eight years later he was managing—and living in—the Village Theater, which he ran with his boss, Roger Euster, "a totally maniac, crazy, self-destructive, but brilliant man." The theater was described in *Midnight Movies* as "a sort of bargain-basement counterculture Carnegie Hall, which later became the Fillmore East." As a specialty and revival house that featured classic, independent, underground, cult, and experimental films, it became a home for the counterculture. "I never turned down anybody," Barenholtz said. "I had the first anti–Vietnam War meetings there. After Vietnam I gave the theater to Rap Brown, Stokeley Carmichael, Chinese opera, Yiddish vaudeville. I worked out deals, midnight shows, benefit shows. I had the first concert of The Who there, I had Nina Simone on a single concert, Ornette Coleman, [John] Coltrane, just before he died. It was never recorded." Timothy Leary also made an appearance.[3]

Barenholtz worked for Euster at the Village Theater for two years from 1966 to 1968, until they were evicted for nonpayment of rent. Euster, who owned one-third of the Elgin Theatre, made Barenholtz a proposal. The Elgin, located in the heavily Hispanic area of Chelsea, was in arrears because of its difficulty in getting popular Mexican films from the distributor Azteca Films. Euster wanted them out and offered Barenholtz the opportunity to run the theater. He proposed that Barenholtz round up some men to take over the theater in the middle of the night. "So we go over there at night," Barenholtz recalled, "and Euster knocks on the door, and the cleaners open the door, and he goes in and throws them out, and basically we camped in and locked the doors. By the morning there was a howling mob of local Puerto Ricans outside." The police came and evicted Euster, Barenholtz, and their crew. Eventually, the owners of the theater worked out a deal with the tenants, and the theater was available for Barenholtz to take over in May 1968.

The Elgin was a neighborhood movie house in a rundown building. "The Elgin, like Chelsea," Gornick wrote in the *Village Voice*, "is warm, rough, shabby, and completely open to the incredible human mix that walks the streets." The area contained a socioeconomic mix of middle-class residents on the side streets and a Puerto Rican population on Eighth Avenue, which was like "a Puerto Rican ghetto—bars, bodegas, Spanish bakeries, cheap luncheonettes, custard shops, open fruit and vegetable markets, clusters of men standing around day and night…. Music blares from open doorways, bottles smash on the sidewalks, arguments erupt and subside."[4]

With the theater's tacky exterior and marquee that lacked apostrophes, one might have expected an uncomfortable experience inside watching the movies. *Times* film critic Vincent Canby, however, noted that the large auditorium's dull, quiet, nondescript gray décor was well-suited for viewing. "Most important," Canby emphasized, "the projection and sound are first-rate, or, at least, as good as can be expected with some of the ancient prints they are given to show." The audience, he observed, were mostly young people who were a respectful audience, "except when *Caligari*, which has been fitted out with terrible 'oral' explanatory notes, is introduced by the voice of Conrad Nagel who says: 'The film you are about to see…' ('Oh, my God,' sighs a young man in the balcony) '…is a masterpiece of mounting whore….' 'Whore,' it turns out, was Nagel's way of pronouncing 'horror.'" Mandelbaum gave high marks to the management of the Elgin for operating it competently. "It was not falling apart like the others. It was a wide theater so widescreen movies could play there. I remember seeing *Mildred Pierce* there in 35mm and it was thrilling. They would get wonderful 35mm prints…. Of course, they didn't charge very much, and that was attractive."[5]

The Elgin boasted its own colorful cast of characters. Cigar-chomping, seventy-

9. The Elgin Theater

The shuttered Elgin Theater, ca. late 1970s. Courtesy Billy Rose Theatre Collection, The New York Public Library for the Performing Arts, Astor, Lenox and Tilden Foundations.

three-year-old Sam Clare, who was the projectionist at the Elgin for 23 years, had a fifty-three-year history as an operator [union word for *projectionist*] going back to the days of vaudeville. As a front-light operator at the RKO Palace on 47th and Broadway for thirty-seven years, he lit such names as Jack Benny, Paul Whiteman, Sophie Tucker, Eddie Cantor, Bill "Bojangles" Robinson, and Smith and Dale. Later, in 1951, while lighting Judy Garland's show at the Palace, he moonlighted at the Elgin, then a Spanish-language movie house, on Mondays, his days off—and he remained there. The Elgin also had its resident cat, the type of mascot that seemed to be indispensable to a number of the repertory houses. Mama Cat was a clamdigger cat with a very wide paw, who was the subject of an article in *New York* magazine. "Everybody loved Mama Cat," said Steve Gould, one of Barenholtz's later assistants. "Mama ruled the theater. Everybody'd say, 'Where's Mama Cat?' And she'd sit upstairs and watch when people were coming in; and when we showed Samurai movies, we would see her sitting on stage making noises, I guess because the atonal aspects of some of the instruments in the sound track hurt her ears. And everybody'd say, 'Oh, yeah, that's her favorite movie, the samurai movie.'"[6]

Barenholtz began at the Elgin with a major handicap: totally broke, he was unable to rent films. He approached Mekas's Film-Makers' Cooperative, the distributor of avant-garde films, with the sales pitch that the Elgin would be a great theater for their films. At first the Cooperative refused, but he was finally able to convince it to try the theater out. "So they gave me *Chelsea Girls* on second run, it had already played," he remembered.

"Then as I was walking out, I realized I don't have any money. So they gave me like $48. That's what I started the theater with." Euster and his partners paid the first month's rent, and Barenholtz did all the work preparing the theater for its opening. He also made a deal with the projectionists' union's chief officer, Steve D'Inzillo, for a break on the projectionists' salaries. "Steve was a great guy so I could make the deal.... He was head of the projectionists' union and could never become president of the national union because he had been a veteran of the Lincoln Brigade. So they always smeared him as a commie."[7]

After the first month the Film-Makers' Cooperative pulled out and Barenholtz took over the programming, but attendance was poor. He was on a month-to-month lease, and the treacherous Euster was surreptitiously trying to lease the theater to others. Every other day he was bringing people to inspect the theater. Meanwhile, Barenholtz was struggling to keep up the monthly payments and pay the projectionist and a couple of young helpers. Then, in the fall of 1968, his fortunes changed when he met Bill Pence, who was working for Janus Films. Although Pence refused his request to book the Janus Film Festival, which was then an annual event at the New Yorker, he offered him, instead, a double feature of his choice. Barenholtz selected François Truffaut's *Jules and Jim* (1962) and *Shoot the Piano Player* (1960). The double feature opened on New Year's Eve Day 1969, and, despite the snowstorm that morning, there was a line around the corner. "From then on," he said, "things started really improving."

Phillip Lopate described the early programming at the Elgin as an educational resource. "For a while," he said, "the Elgin was indispensable ... doing the important service of showing classics and recent classics. They were not doing the marginal cinema thing [showing mostly cult films]; a lot of young people hadn't seen *Shoot the Piano Player*, so that would be the place you would go to see it. And they would show American movies, too."

Barenholtz devoted much of his programming to festivals rather than to the random approach. Early festivals included "The French Cinema," double features devoted to both older and contemporary French directors, and "A Tribute to ... Bergman, Fellini, Welles, Truffaut." He soon obtained the gold standard of festivals, the Janus Film Festival. "Janus at the Elgin" was a summer highlight for three years from 1969 to 1971. Featuring mostly foreign classics, these festivals ran double bills like *The Magician* (1958) and *Smiles of a Summer Night* (1955), *Citizen Kane* (1941) with *The Lady Vanishes* (1938), *The Blue Angel* (1930) with *M* (1931), *Grand Illusion* (1937) and *Forbidden Games* (1952), *Black Orpheus* (1959) and *Shadows of Forgotten Ancestors* (1965), and *Potemkin* (1925) with *Alexander Nevsky* (1938). Barenholtz claimed he took the Janus Festival, the Holy Grail for repertory houses, away from Dan Talbot at the New Yorker, by paying the higher rate of percentages instead of the flat rate. Talbot, however, denied that he had any special claim on the Janus Film Festival or that he paid low fees to the distributor. "They [Janus] were tough hombres to deal with," he wrote in an email. "Since I wanted very much to play their films, I had to pay top dollar to get them. This would also have applied to the Elgin." Lionel Rogosin at the Bleecker Street Cinema had blamed Barenholtz for adversely affecting his business by taking the Janus films away from him. The circle eventually closed when, by 1975, the summer Janus Film Festival returned as an annual event to the Bleecker Street Cinema, now owned by Sid Geffen.[8]

Barenholtz's growing success ironically put him in a vulnerable position since he had no long-term lease to prevent Euster from leasing to other exhibitors who were now interested in the theater. He met with Euster's two partners, who controlled the theater with their combined two-thirds shares. "They were just two old guys," he said. "I took them aside and said, 'You think you're going to take advantage of what I did, worked my ass off, twenty-four-hour days, to put this theater on the map? You're going to sell it to me, or else you're never going to live to enjoy it.'" They were persuaded to give him a year's lease. Eventually Euster worked out a deal with his partners and became the sole owner of it. In turn, he gave Barenholtz a mortgage on it. "The kind of deal I made with the mortgage," Barenholtz said, "was a bad deal. It would even be high today."

Barenholtz had no special programming predilections. Replicating his programming philosophy at the Village Theater, he was receptive to all kinds of films and special events and willing to take risks with unusual ideas if he thought they had economic possibilities. "I wasn't interested in cinema art," Barenholtz said. "I'm not an academic…. A lot of the people who took courses in film, they had all these ideas of what is good film, bad film, but I didn't care. So I had a little bit more freedom to experiment." When *King Kong* (1933) was playing, someone contacted him with outtakes from the film, in which King Kong undresses Fay Wray. Barenholtz loved it and told the man that he would advertise it as the uncut version. "This guy would come every day," remembered Barenholtz, "bring the outtakes, splice them in, and then we'd have to take them out every night because he would not leave them there. So this went on for the whole showing, but it was the original, uncut version." One Friday night, Barenholtz recalled, he was standing in front of the theater, listening to the laughter from the full house inside, when a young man came up to him and said, "My mother was very upset about people laughing." Barenholtz asked him who was his mother, and the young man replied, "Fay Wray."

His wide-open method led to the theater's eventual countercultural reputation. Some of the earliest happenings took place in 1969 in an effort to use the theater during its dark hours. "The mortgage and the expenses were so high," Barenholtz recalled, "I started thinking, how can I utilize more time? So I started booking in morning shows, made a deal with Film-Makers' Cooperative; they used to come in on a Sunday or a Saturday morning, and show their avant-garde films. I also started screening dance films, psychology films, not an original concept since Ursula Lewis had done those things at the Thalia way before me, but I was doing it in a different form. I just did it in the mornings at 11 o'clock while she would do a series of dance or opera films."

Similar considerations led to the midnight shows in 1970. Barenholtz wanted to expand the schedule to the dark hours with the cult films that would appeal to the younger crowd. His problem was how to inexpensively reach this special audience. "I had done midnight shows at the Village Theater," Barenholtz said, "and I just started thinking of combining my need to utilize as much time as possible and [ways] to reach an audience economically at the underutilized hours. I realized that there were certain kinds of films that had a very strong, but limited, audience. The trick was, and still is, how you reach that audience economically." It was the same dilemma that Talbot had struggled with at the New Yorker. His answer came to him in thinking about the Broadway practice of previewing plays before the critics' reviews on opening night. "I noticed," he said, "how many shows you see that have previews and sell out the previews and as soon as they open and get a bad review, they're gone." Midnight shows would serve the same purpose—a chance to premiere unconventional films without expensive advertising and without risking critics' negative reviews.

The first midnight show at the Elgin, *El Topo* (*The Mole*), a surreal, symbolic, Mexican western directed by and starring Alejandro Jodorowsky, gave him the opportunity to test his theory since it had not yet screened theatrically. He had discovered the film—a weird story about the eponymous character, a violent, black-clad gunfighter, who is seeking enlightenment and, during his quest, meets bizarre characters, such as maimed and dwarf performers—at a screening at MoMA. "I was actually with Jonas Mekas and we came out and we went to the Greek coffee shop across from the Elgin and I said to Jonas, 'How did you like the film?' And Jonas said, 'Vell, I don't think it's a good film.' And I said, 'Okay Jonas.' I just ran across the street and got on the phone—I used to use Jonas as my sounding board; if he didn't like a film, there must be some commercial value to it—and called the distributor; they said the film had been sold to a guy named Alan Douglas, who ran Douglas Films." Barenholtz forgot about the film until two weeks later when he received a call from Douglas, who wanted to open the film at the Elgin. Barenholtz pushed for a midnight opening because the critics would kill it if it got a regular opening. Douglas, who, Barenholtz said, "was a genius in his own way but was stoned most of the time," agreed. "I had one of the kids do a hand-drawn sign, which was crooked, and he put it in the window, and all it said was '*El Topo* at midnight.'"[9]

Opening on December 18, 1970, it was an instant hit despite the lack of advertising, running seven nights a week at midnight for six months to sold-out audiences. "We were going to call it previews," Barenholtz said. "If the critics came, let them come at midnight, see it with the audience. Of course people were saying, 'Who's going to come to see a film at midnight?' The experts were telling me it can't be done. But I was too dumb to listen to them." The mostly young audience at the regular show on the night of the first midnight screening was invited to stay for the midnight show. It was what Chuck Zlatkin, the Elgin's manager at the time, called an invitational opening, an underground opening, only for the counterculture people. "That was an extraordinary night," recalled Zlatkin. "And it was pretty innovative, because we didn't have a separate admissions policy for the film; it was there to be discovered. So you came to see the regular double bill and you could just stay over." The strategy worked. Within two weeks, based mostly on word of mouth, they were selling out the six-hundred-seat theater every night of the week. "The secret," Zlatkin once explained to a *New York Times* reporter, "is to find a film that people can feel they've discovered themselves—a film that lets them say, 'Hey, let me tell my friends about it.'" Vincent Canby of the *New York Times* wrote that "there has become attached to *El Topo* the sort of multi-leveled chic that makes it a required experience for the experience-collecting young." Roger Greenspun, in another *Times* article, described its audience as the "kids in capes and wide-brimmed hats, the 'El Topo' freaks." Not everyone, however, found the film exciting. "I remember falling asleep during *El Topo*," said the middle-aged Ed Maguire.[10]

Barenholtz's innovation was to use the midnight movie as a first-run venue for movies that, he explained, had "a certain kind of far-out originality," which made them unsuited for the usual theatrical release. "They were not art films in the narrow sense," Barenholtz said, "but totally new and different, and appealing to a younger audience." *El Topo* was the start of the midnight craze that soon spread to other New York theaters and eventually became a national and international phenomenon.[11]

The film ran until June 1971, when John Lennon and Yoko Ono, who had seen it a number of times, persuaded Allen Klein, the manager of the Beatles, to buy the film for a mainstream run at a Broadway theater. Zlatkin felt the film could have continued its run, but, he said with a sense of betrayal by his idols, "they stole *El Topo* from us." The film lasted only a week at the Broadway theater, even though, or probably because, they had treated it as a major opening with television spots and extensive newspaper space. "It was not the way," said Zlatkin, "to handle something like that." After that, the film played repeatedly in the all-night programs that Barenholtz later developed, as well as in midnight shows at other theaters locally and nationally.[12]

Other midnight shows on Wednesdays through Fridays followed, mostly non-premieres, such as the double feature *Reefer Madness* (1936) and Betty Boop cartoons in November 1972. The next midnight hit that ran for over a year was the New York premiere of John Waters's bad-taste comedy *Pink Flamingos* (1972), a film about the 300-pound drag queen Divine, who wants to clinch her title as "The Filthiest Person Alive" and who, in the infamous, final scene, tastes a dog's feces, then looks at the camera with a "shit-eating" grin. This midnight show established the reputation of the film and its director. *Pink Flamingos* was brought to Barenholtz's attention by Bob Shaye, founder of the distribution company New Line Cinema (and owner at one time of the Olympia theater), who told him on a visit to his office that he had "this piece of shit" that he wanted him to take a look at. Barenholtz watched half of it and then asked Shaye to send it over to the theater, where he showed it to Gould and Zlatkin. "We kind of stared at each other wide-eyed when we screened it," Gould remembered, "and said, 'Well, let's run it up the flagpole. Give the people what they want.' So, we put it on at midnight on a handshake deal with Bob Shaye, and maybe two years it played midnights at the Elgin."

The first screening was a trial run on a freezing Tuesday night, February 16, 1973, replacing *Marijuana: The Weed with Roots in Hell* (1936) and *Child Bride* (1938). About two hundred people showed up. After a break the following week for an all-night Marx Brothers festival, the film returned on March 2; and through word of mouth, it soon gained a cult following, Barenholtz said, of "downtown gay people, more of the hipper set." Many of its fans began reciting lines from the film at the screenings, a phenomenon later to become associated with another popular midnight movie of the seventies, *The Rocky Horror Picture Show*.[13]

John Waters, the director, grateful for the boost that the Elgin had given his film, sometimes visited the theater with his cast. Gould and Zlatkin reminisced about some of these visits in an interview in *Film Quarterly*.

> STEVE: John Waters never forgot that [the Elgin's role in promoting the film]. He's a very honorable man—and always fun, because he'd bring that tribe down. Edie the Egg Lady showed up all the time. The best was when Divine was throwing dead mackerel from his brassiere.
> CHUCK: Between his legs.
> STEVE: And then poppers from his brassiere. And that was the worst. Because when the amyl nitrate was caught on the floor, people stepped on it. And the smell was just like old socks. And scrubbing the floor. That was pretty rank.[14]

Pink Flamingos began as a midnight show on Fridays, but around April 1973, its schedule was increased to six midnights a week from Sundays through Fridays until the end of its run. "Maybe *Pink Flamingos* was the last one to run every day," said Zlatkin. "After that the times changed, and it was a little different in terms of people coming out. So midnight shows afterwards were primarily on Fridays and Saturdays." The film ran approximately 48 weeks starting from early March 1973. Eventually, Barenholtz felt that it had run its course, since it now drew an audience of Jersey and Brooklyn gangs that came to see "the fag eat shit" and throw things at the screen. It was no longer fun, he remembered.[15]

The most popular of the midnight shows, and the Elgin's final one, was Perry Henzell's *The Harder They Come*, a 1972 Jamaican crime film, which starred reggae singer Jimmy Cliff, who plays a singer turned outlaw turned hero, and that introduced reggae music to an international audience. "*The Harder They Come*," said Zlatkin, "had a lot of good elements to it. We threw it on a Sunday one-day showing, and the thing went through the roof. And that's when we turned it into a midnight show that ran forever." The first feature shot by Jamaicans in Jamaica, *The Harder They Come* was released in February 1973 in New York City by Roger Corman's New World Pictures to good reviews but little attendance.

The Elgin's midnight screening of the film was not the first for this film, nor did Jimmy Cliff's popularity initially begin in New York. A *Boston Phoenix* article on the history of the film in the Boston area reported that after its flop in Manhattan, the Orson Welles Cinema in Cambridge, Massachusetts, had successfully revived it in April 1973, over a year before the Elgin's opening. It ran for six months before moving to weekend midnight shows for another five-and-a-half years. An album of the film's music was a best seller locally, "and Cambridge became the country's first and most enduring stronghold of reggae fans." Jimmy Cliff visited the theater in 1974 while in town for a concert and "was kind of awed by the whole thing…. Here was this one city in America where he was a legend."[16]

The Harder They Come repeated its Cambridge success at the Elgin, where it became "a giant of a midnight film," according to Zlatkin. It maintained a healthy run for about two years and five months, from October 1974 until March 1977, attracting 150 to two hundred people for each screening, unlike *El Topo* and *Pink Flamingos*, both of which started strong but eventually wound down. The film appealed to a much broader audience than did the two previous midnight hits: people who came to hear the music, film buffs who were interested in seeing a Jamaican film, and straighter, more middle-class types who had never been to a midnight show. "It's a film," Zlatkin told a *Daily News* reporter, "that can appeal to people for all different reasons. It has reggae music. It makes a political statement, it gives a realistic look into another culture. It's not the Jamaica you see in travel brochures. And it's basically done like an old James Cagney film." It was also a classy exception to the typical midnight film, which was described by a *Times* reporter as usually "crummy kink, banal camp, bad sex"; but, because it was too low budget and too rough, it was unmarketable in a mainstream theater. The midnight screenings, Zlatkin and Gould claimed, made it a cult hit that soon moved to other cities and began a successful, nationwide career for its star, Jimmy Cliff.[17]

The core audience of the midnight shows consisted of a collection of faithful, who, Gould said, "became almost like six hundred regulars, old home week." Health food was a big seller at the counter. "We would sell sandwiches with bean sprouts," Gould recalled, "and everything on it at the candy stand. Of course, people had been maybe having some drinks or a smoke before they went in, so that their appetites were a little more voracious—you'd have people spending maybe $10 or $12 at a candy stand, which, in 1972, was a lot of money." Many of these regulars matched the bizarreness of the films they were coming to see. "People would dress in costume," said Zlatkin, "to complement the film they were watching. At times I would have to stop people in the waiting room downstairs because they came to see *El Topo* and brought cap pistols that they were shooting; and upstairs it sounded like gunshots. People were spaced out, there were various levels of consciousness."

In 1972 Barenholtz began another favorite program of the young, counterculture crowd. This one resulted from a suggestion of Zlatkin and Gould's. "If the kids [Zlatkin and Gould] came in and wanted to try something," he explained, "I'd say, 'Sure let's try it.'" The two presented him with the idea of all-night shows on the weekends. The hours from Saturday midnight until early Sunday morning, they pointed out, were lying fallow and could be filled with programming that would attract the younger crowd. The idea appealed to Barenholtz, who then acquired Louis Malle's six-hour, European miniseries *Phantom India* (1969) from Dan Talbot's New Yorker Films. *Phantom India* screened in November 1972, from Saturday midnight to 6:00 a.m. on Sunday morning. "We had a good turnout for that one," said Gould, "and we saw that people were willing to stay six hours." The all-night shows became a regular feature on Saturdays from midnight to any time between six and eight on Sunday mornings. Generally, there were four movies for the price of one. "I used to book two Marx Brothers films for a Saturday," said Gould, "and two Marx Brothers films for a Sunday, but overnight I would run four of them together, so people could come in at midnight and get out at sunrise. I also did that with four Clint Eastwood films."

An all-night show might have a directorial theme (four Howard Hawks films) or a genre theme (Gordon Parks, Jr.'s blaxploitation film *Super Fly*, 1972; Sam Peckinpah's western *The Wild Bunch*, 1969; and Roger Corman's gangster film *Bloody Mama*, 1970). In March 1973, one all-night, Saturday program featured the twelve chapters of the serial *The Return of Captain Marvel* (1941), plus twenty cartoons. Another showed three Warner Bros. films—*Casablanca* (1942), *The Maltese Falcon* (1941), and *Little Caesar* (1931). Other all-night shows featured a program of Woody Allen double features; another, of the Bangladesh and Fillmore filmed concerts; and still another, of four countercultural films—*El Topo*, Roger Vadim's *Barbarella* (1968) with Jane Fonda, the Maysles brothers's documentary of the Rolling Stones's 1969 U.S. tour, *Gimme Shelter* (1970), and *Putney Swope* (1969).[18]

One of the all-night, Marx Brothers screenings almost ended in bedlam. The movies were scheduled to start at midnight, but more people had showed up than could fit in the theater, leaving a lot of unhappy people outside. A short time later, Zlatkin and Gould got a call from the police that there was a bomb threat. The police came and told Zlatkin that they were going to evacuate the theater. "I'm thinking to myself," Zlatkin remembered, "that it's going to be total chaos." About six hundred people had been squeezed into the theater, and another couple hundred were still milling around outside. "There'd be no way," thought Zlatkin, "to separate the hundreds who were out there from the people inside. And I just thought it was some disgruntled fan, so I said, 'Is there any way I could take responsibility for this?' I would not do this today, but it was a different time then." The police agreed, and Zlatkin and Gould went through the night holding their breath. There was no incident.

While the young, hip crowd, who favored the cult, marginal films, flocked to the midnight and all-night shows, the more serious fans of film, who esteemed the classic Hollywood and foreign films, were excited by the September 1970 premiere of the landmark Buster Keaton program assembled by the film collector Raymond Rohauer. Rohauer's Keaton series was a major theatrical event since most of Keaton's silent features and shorts had been unseen for years; they had either been unavailable or existed for a long time only in shabby, incomplete prints. Only in the 1960s did film historians begin to assemble and restore Keaton's lifework. Film buffs prized the opportunity to see these rare films. "They started showing them at the Elgin every day," said Ed Maguire. "I saw every program three or four times, figuring they would disappear, but of course they showed up a lot later." While the Elgin, wrote John Pierson in his history of the independent movement in the seventies, was the birthplace of the midnight show, "it was even better to have a yearly opportunity (normally in February) to see the complete silent works of Buster Keaton, the greatest and most original filmmaker in history."[19]

Barenholtz saw the possibilities when Rohauer contacted him about screening his Keaton films. The film collector proposed to give him exclusive rights to show these films if Barenholtz would give him the money to make new prints of his negatives. It was risky to partner with Rohauer, who had an infamous reputation for making questionable claims of owning rights to films and for duplicating prints without permission from the owners of the film rights. But the importance of the series tilted Barenholtz in favor of the proposition. "I got him ten thousand dollars," said Barenholtz, "which was very hard for me to get. When I saw the brand-new prints, they were so beautiful. Every time I think about them I don't think about them in black and white, I think of them in color."

Rohauer was one of the more important, albeit controversial, collectors of Keaton's silent films. The core of his Keaton collection came from a surprising source. The actor James Mason had bought the old Keaton home in 1955 and discovered, around the side of the house, a small vault by the site of Keaton's old editing shed, in which he had stored the prints after editing them; he apparently forgot about the vault and its contents when he moved. The combined value of the found films exceeded the worth of the estate at that time. They included a superior print of *The General* (1926) and one of *Parlor, Bedroom and Bath* (1931), which was shot on the property. Mason, who was considered the owner of the prints (Keaton made no claims to title or rights to them), eventually donated them to the Academy of Motion Pictures Arts and Sciences. Somehow, Rohauer obtained duplicates, set up a partnership, Buster Keaton Productions, Inc., with Keaton, then proceeded to sue, or threaten to sue, a variety of theaters and nonprofit institutions for screening Keaton silent films to which, he claimed, Buster Keaton Productions, Inc., owned all the rights in all outstanding prints. It was a disputed claim since a number of the films were in the public domain and the rights to others were uncertain. The tables were turned on him when MGM and Loews, Inc., sued him for showing Keaton's *The Navigator* (1924), which they claimed rights to; he lost the case.[20]

In 1962 there was a pending Federal trial against him. "They basically shut him down in L.A.," said Barenholtz, "forbade him to show films in California because he was doing it illegally, particularly the old films." Later, Rohauer staged film festivals of his Keaton films in Europe and America, outside Los Angeles. Those screenings were credited with sparking renewed interest in the filmmaker. "He did arrange for a tribute to Keaton in Venice," Barenholtz said. "Keaton was brought out on stage, he was actually crying." The Keaton prints also became the foundation of the Buster Keaton Archives, which opened in 1989 in Columbus, Ohio. In the 1960s Rohauer returned to New York (he had been born there), where he became film curator of the Huntington Hartford Gallery of Modern Art on Columbus Circle. It was then he approached Barenholtz.[21]

Rohauer, so ready to steal from others, was obsessed about guarding his films from theft. "Being the film pirate," surmised Barenholtz, "he was afraid someone else would do the same thing." He kept prints under the bed at his apartment on 65th Street. For this and subsequent programs at the Elgin, he made sure that the films were taken out of the projection room every night and locked in the office. "I would have to lug them down from the projection room to the office," said Barenholtz, "and he would stay, making sure they were locked in the office. He was a strange, strange bird, creepy guy, too."

Barenholtz had modifications made in the projectors to enhance the screening of the films. He had the aperture plates cut so that the films covered the whole screen while still maintaining the 1.33:1 projection ratio. He also had the speed adjusted to its proper speed of close to 18 frames per second. "One of the kids working for me that I got into the projectionists' union," he said, "told me that we could get a motor and attach it to the projector and show it at its proper speed. It was a ten-dollar motor, and we attached it to the projector. So not only were the films showing on a huge screen but also at its proper speed, so it wasn't jumpy. It screwed up our scheduling because it [the scheduling] was based on the faster speed." (The schedule was similarly disrupted when he later showed D.W. Griffith's *Intolerance*, 1916, which ran four hours instead of the usual three hours.) A local pianist, who was Sarah Vaughan's accompanist, provided music. "Around the middle of the run," Barenholtz remembered, "the kid came to me and said, 'Sarah called me and I have to go out on tour.' So I went up to the projection booth where we had some old records and threw some on; it didn't make any difference."

Zlatkin, who had begun working for Barenholtz around this time, immediately saw the marketing potential of the series. "Barenholtz was open to ideas, and at that time I remember they had some press thing, and they had about twenty people invited, and I said, 'This is crazy, this is fabulous stuff that we're doing here,' and that's when I started doing the media work and the press, before I got into programming or management there." Advertised in the Elgin calendar as "Raymond Rohauer presents the first theatrical showing in the United States of the internationally successful cinema series.... Buster Keaton Film Festival at Elgin," the festival showcased ten features and twenty-one two-reel shorts "produced & directed by, and starring Buster Keaton in the golden era, 1917–1927." The ten features ran from September 22, 1970, to October 26, 1970: *The Three Ages* (1923), *Our Hospitality* (1923), *Sherlock, Jr.* (1924), *The Navigator* (1924), *Go West* (1925), *Seven Chances* (1925), *Battling Butler* (1926), *The General* (1926), *College* (1927), and *Steamboat Bill, Jr.* (1927).[22]

Other Rohauer festivals gleaned from his collection followed. The next major one, from February 8, 1971, to May 2, 1971, paying tribute "to Raymond Rohauer whose perseverance made these programs possible," included a D.W. Griffith festival. Like the Keaton films, Griffith's films had not been seen theatrically for many years. "If you weren't near a museum," said Gould, "or weren't a member of a museum, or weren't in college where they would have a college film society's access to these films, you might not have seen them all." Twelve Griffith films were in the series: single features such as *The Birth of a Nation* (1915), *Hearts of the World* (1918), and *Intolerance*; two double features *Broken Blossoms* (1919) with *Dream Street* (1921) and *Way Down East* (1920) with *Orphans of the Storm* (1921); and a double feature of his sound films *Abraham Lincoln* (1930) with *The Struggle* (1931).[23]

Birth of a Nation naturally generated controversy in this era of black power. "Of course we showed *Birth of a Nation*," recalled Zlatkin. "And the next thing you know there's a demonstration in front of the theater, showing this racist film." Zlatkin negotiated with the demonstrators, who numbered about twenty. "We explained who we were, what our credentials were, what the rationale was behind it. And then I asked if any of them had ever seen this film. And of course none of them had." He let them in for free to see the picture, on the condition that afterwards they would tell him if they thought there was any value in screening the film. "And it worked. Sure enough, afterwards, they came out, and we discussed it. At that point they had called some other people and found out the radical credentials that we had and went away. That was it."

In addition to the Griffith festival, the public also saw Rohauer's collection of all of W.C. Fields's two-reelers, "presented for the first time on one program" (the program was later repeated under the clever heading "W.C. Fields Lurches Back to the Elgin"); a rerun, "by popular demand," of the Buster Keaton Film Festival; and "A Theatrical First. Harry Langdon at Elgin." Future Rohauer festivals included a program of rare silent films, including early French avant-garde films, in 1972, and a repeat of the Keaton Festival in 1974.

In 1972 Barenholtz began thinking of going into film distribution, much as Talbot had done a few years earlier. "I was doing all the work and the distributors were getting the benefit of my work," he said. His first venture into distribution was as a subdistributor of Phillipe de Broca's *King of Hearts*, which had already had a brief, successful run at the Elgin. He had learned that an exhibitor in Seattle, Randy Finley, had bought the U.S. rights to the film for a "ridiculous amount" from United Artists. "It started Ben thinking," said Gould, "and he really loved that idea. So he got into distribution through that." Barenholtz made a deal with Finley for the rights for New York State only and opened it at a theater in the Lincoln Center area. Eventually, he formed a distribution company, Libra Films.[24]

His involvement in distribution progressed gradually, as he began handing over more of the daily responsibilities to Zlatkin and Gould while keeping final control. All major decisions continued to need his approval, even the candy. Since he lived two doors down from the Elgin, he was still there every day, working with the two on the calendars, approving business decisions, such as the rental fees that Gould negotiated for films, approving their ideas of publishing a newspaper or instituting a new, senior-citizen policy, and handling budget and financial concerns.

Zlatkin, who had been the first to be hired by Barenholtz, probably in 1970, felt he had connected with the Elgin at a time that was right for the theater and for him. "It gave me a lot of chances for expression of my views and interests. We got to indulge ourselves a lot of times by showing films that we believed in. Our last U.S. premiere was *Union Maids* (1976), a documentary on the Rosie Riveters of World War II. It was nominated that year [1976] for an Academy Award as best documentary." A Bronx native, he had dropped out of City College "because it was the sixties," married and lived with his wife for a while in Woodstock. Back in New York City, he was an active, grassroots organizer in the antiwar movement while also trying "some things in radio in New Jersey, documentary stuff that didn't fly," to earn a living. A colleague told him that the Elgin was hiring. "I got a job as an usher at the Elgin, at $1.85 an hour. That was my big break in the movies."[25]

Gould, a native of Brooklyn and Queens, had a bachelor degree from Syracuse University and a master's degree in arts management from New York University when he was hired to manage two of Barenholtz's theaters—the Orpheum, an East Village movie house, and the Garrick, the next-door neighbor of the Bleecker Street Cinema in the Village. Barenholtz also had Gould oversee his movie theater, TLA, in Philadelphia, formerly a legitimate theater, Theater of the Living Arts, which had been operated by the director, André Gregory. Gould, however, wanted to return to New York, and another of Barenholtz's employees, Al Malmfelt, took over the theater. Eventually, Barenholtz gave up the Orpheum, Garrick, and TLA. Around 1971 Barenholtz moved Gould to the Elgin, where, he said, "I started working with my once and future partner, Chuck Zlatkin."[26]

Zlatkin, a burly, serious man, was the showman, specializing in marketing (the Keaton series was probably his first effort). "That was my specialty," he said. "I enjoyed doing that. My contributions to the theater had to do with getting it more known, with my more aggressive approach to publicizing that it was a tremendous institution. So we sent out press releases to everybody in New York. The media was pretty kind to us. We got a lot of coverage." Their newspaper, the *Elgin Marble Film News and Comment*, which Zlatkin thought up and Barenholtz approved in 1973, was another important marketing tool for the theater, but also a vehicle to educate the public about films. Film students and others interested in expressing their ideas on film were invited to write for the newspaper.

Chuck Zlatkin, left, and Steve Gould posing in front of the Joyce Theater in 2000 for the *Film Quarterly* interview with the author. Photo by Lynn Padwe.

Gould, a colorful, inveterate New Yorker who spun out stories in a vivid style, helped Barenholtz negotiate with distributors. "Ben found out that I liked to hondle," said Gould, "a Yiddish term for bargaining, so I was the one that tried to beat the shit out of the theater distributors, to get the best deal possible." While Barenholtz dealt with Rohauer and distributors he knew, like Talbot and Pence, Gould worked with the smaller distributors and the major studios.

Like Barenholtz, the two were receptive to innovative ideas. "If someone came to us with a good idea, and it was possible to do it," Zlatkin recalled, "we did it." As Barenholtz's managers and later when they took over the lease from Barenholtz, they carried out the groundwork that Barenholtz had built: the Janus Film Festival in the summer, the yearly Rohauer festivals, the ballet and opera films on Sunday mornings, the midnight shows, and the all-night, weekend shows. The festival approach continued; Gould and

Zlatkin understood its value. "Part of the enjoyment in viewing film," Zlatkin wrote in an issue of the *Elgin Marble*, "is the context in which it's presented.... For this reason, the Elgin attempts to present film in context. The presentation of films in festival format, or in related double, triple or quadruple bills can only add to the enjoyment of the films we present as an art form and as entertainment."[27]

Benefits "for every cause under the sun" were scheduled. Some were for community causes. Barenholtz had loaned neighborhood groups the theater for benefits, and the two maintained the practice. "We made the theater available for free," said Gould, "and then we paid for the projectionist. We really felt that we had a responsibility to be a part of the community, because so many of the people that were coming were from the immediate Chelsea community at that time." Gould remembered when one of the charity benefits turned into a mini-crisis. They had lent the theater to United Cerebral Palsy of New York City, whose new director, thinking that the Elgin served the handicapped, brought seventy people in wheelchairs instead of the usual twenty-five. "Chuck called me at home that evening around six because it was his day to work," Gould said, "and says, 'You son of a bitch, you did this, didn't you?' I says, 'What are you talking about?' He said, 'Cerebral Palsy sent a group here, two busloads. I have seventy people in wheelchairs. Where am I supposed to put 'em?'" Zlatkin managed to fit them all in, with wheelchairs along the sides and aisles. Later over a peace-making coffee, they laughed over the source of the mishap: the cashier on duty, when told by the Cerebral Palsy director that they weren't ambulatory, said it was okay. "I didn't think," he later explained to Gould, "that you would want ambulances there."

Other benefits were for social or political causes. "Chuck and I were obviously interested in making the world a better place. If that meant politically, environmentally, peace issues, whatever, we would have town hall meetings there sometimes on weeknights. We offered the theater to organizations that we thought should be supported. We didn't charge, it was almost like a gift to them where they could show a film that was made by one of their group or one that was donated to them." One such controversial town hall meeting revisited the Kennedy assassination with a screening of the Zapruder film of the tragic national event. That was the occasion for another bomb threat. This time, however, they cleared the theater. "This was a little more controversial than the Marx Brothers," said Zlatkin, "and maybe there were some people who didn't want this to be shown." Another time they featured Mae Brussell, a noted conspiracy theorist. "She was a modest housewife," said Gould, "who started checking facts and realized that some things hadn't added up. People came down for that. Besides some strange, paranoid people, we had working-class men and women who felt that we weren't getting the whole story and college students who were fascinated that people were examining it again."

Another type of event was off-the-wall, live performances by the likes of C.S. Haywood, "who did a modern dance," recalled Zlatkin, "and played the saxophone to the Knapp Commission hearings. He had developed an incredible following, and he did a half-hour show before our midnight movie." Then there was Larry Estridge, a folk singer who would come on at the end of the all-night shows to do a set, and a theater company, the Intense Family Theater Company, which performed short skits on Friday nights before the midnight show. Another act that sometimes preceded the midnight show was an abbreviated version of a drag *Swan Lake*. "Not everything was a tremendous success," said Zlatkin. "But that didn't deter us from having some magnificent failures."

In addition to carrying on Barenholtz's legacy, Gould and Zlatkin moved in new directions. They wanted to promote worthwhile, unconventional films that had failed in their initial releases because the studios were obtuse about them. "It was only a few distributors like Dan Talbot," explained Gould, "that could handle those films well." Not knowing the goldmine they had, the studios would rent these films to Gould for a minimal price. "We were able to go in and say to the studios' representative, 'You see those old things over there?' He'd say, 'What, those clunkers?' 'Yeah,' I says, 'throw them in a bag, we'll take them, we can do something with them.' There were many, many times that a movie played at the Elgin, and it was because of that that major studios or the person who owned the film got a new lease on life for the film."[28]

Hal Ashby's *Harold and Maude* (1971) was one of their successful "failures." "We had seen it," Gould remembered, "and said, 'It's not that bad, it's kind of strange, probably something that our audience would really like. We thought it would make a great double bill with *King of Hearts* because they were both very bizarre.'" Other resurrected, failed first-runs were George Lucas's first film, *THX 1138* (1971), which they paired with Tom Laughlin's *Billy Jack* (1971), and Martin Scorsese's 1967 student film, *Who's That Knocking at My Door*. Many of the films that they unearthed came by word of mouth. The first film that Tommy Lee Jones ever made, a Canadian film entitled *Eliza's Horoscope* (1975), was brought to their attention through a friend, who sent Gould a copy of the *Toronto Star* containing an article mentioning the film. "It was a lovely little film," said Gould. "We called the woman who directed it, and the guy who produced it, and they came down with it."

Promoting younger American filmmakers like Woody Allen and Bob Rafelson was another initiative. "I think very honestly that we had the first retrospective of Woody Allen films," Gould recalled. In order to make the Woody Allen retrospective complete, he had to find a copy of Allen's first produced script, *What's New, Pussycat?* (1965), which the owner, United Artists, claimed had been taken out of service for an unknown reason. Knowing that Allen frequently visited the Elgin and counting on his fondness for the theater, Gould telephoned his producers, Jack Rollins and Charles Joffe, to find a print; he spoke to Rollins, who promised to help. "So the next day," said Gould, "I get a call from my cashier because I was on duty, who told me that David Picker [United Artists president at the time] was on the phone. I said, 'Get the fuck out of here. What are you talking about, David Picker's on the phone?' So I went downstairs, took the phone, he says, 'This is Dave Picker here.' I figured, 'Hell, Christ, this is a lawsuit coming.' He says, 'Jesus Christ, did you have to get Woody Allen on us to get this print of *What's New, Pussycat?* You've got it, but please, don't shake the trees like that. If you've got a problem, call my office first.'" The complete Woody Allen series, with three sets of double features, including *What's New, Pussycat?*, played from May 27 through June 12, 1973.

Similar difficulties were encountered in booking Bob Rafelson's film *Head* (1968), starring The Monkees, for a retrospective on the director. The film had already been booked and advertised when Gould and Zlatkin got a call from Columbia that it did not have a print. Gould was incensed. Once again the director came to their rescue. "We got a call at the theater from Bob Rafelson, who had his own print, and he said, 'It's with hesitation that I do this because it's my only print, and I'll come out and kill you if something happens to it. But I'll send it to you if you promise to treat it with tender, loving care.'" Gould related with pride that Rafelson had heard, even out in Los Angeles, that a theater in New York was doing a retrospective of his work.

Zlatkin and Gould later initiated a vertical-series policy, which they felt made an effective marketing tool. They devoted Tuesdays to French films, Wednesdays to Italian films, and Thursdays, to Japanese films. "We decided," said Gould, "that there were a lot of Italians in New York who still spoke Italian, French people, French, and Japanese people, Japanese; so that if they wanted to catch a film in their native language, they would know which day to come." Zlatkin promoted the assorted vertical series through the *Elgin Marble News*. "For French Tuesdays," said Zlatkin, "we would take the paper to Alliance Française; Italian Wednesdays, to the Italian churches in the area; and Japanese Thursdays, to the Japan Society." Zlatkin remembered that a director of samurai movies, having heard of the number of people coming to see these films, showed up one Thursday and was amazed to see about four hundred people watching a double bill of samurai films. One-third of the audience, Zlatkin estimated, was Asian; one-third, students; and one-third, a mixture of young, old, and different ethnicities. At the end they stayed, they saw the credits, they applauded.

The remainder of the week had its own identity. On Fridays and Saturdays, the two would show "money films," according to Gould, "maybe some first-run movie that became available, like Mick Jagger in *Performance* (1970), or *Clockwork Orange* (1971). *Harold and Maude* was also an example of a Friday/Saturday film. The Friday and Saturday crowd was the younger crowd, the more hip crowd." The regular features on Sundays and Mondays were the literary types, such as George Cukor's *Travels with My Aunt* (1972) paired with William Friedkin's *Boys in the Band* (1970), based on Mart Crowley's Off-Broadway play about a group of gay characters and a milestone in queer cinema. Sunday mornings before the regular features were allocated to films on the arts. "The first time we showed *An Evening with the Royal Ballet*," said Zlatkin, "limousines pulled up with women in mink coats. That's the movie that has the encore, so the audience applauds at the end and then the dancers come back on and dance again, and the audience went crazy, a standing ovation, on Sunday morning." A *Times* film critic wrote that "[t]he Elgin Cinema seems never to run out of ideas about keeping its premises profitably dark."[29]

Gould and Zlatkin, with Barenholtz, put together most of their double bills much as the other repertory houses did—pairing films with similar or contrasting points of view or with the same star or by the same director. A few were combined simply because they were special deals from the same distributor. "Surprisingly, we would sometimes get kudos for these double bills," said Gould. The two would do playful billings, such as the week they played Phillipe de Broca's *King of Hearts* (1966) with a different co-feature each day. "So it would be *King of Hearts* and *Fellini Satyricon*," said Zlatkin, "*King of Hearts* and *200 Motels*."

Keeping books for patrons to write in their comments seemed to have become standard practice for a number of the repertory houses, including the Elgin, whose books were located in the basement lounge. "I might pull the book towards the end of the day," said Gould, "thumb through it, see what people put down. They might mention a film by Fellini, for example, that I didn't realize he did, this would be great. Sometimes, it was just dumb luck."

Another of their initiatives garnered considerable press: their senior policy of twenty-five cents for all persons sixty-two years old and over at all times, which they began in November 1974 with Barenholtz's approval. Both young men felt a deep sympathy for the elderly, many of whom were poor and alone. "It was the nursing home scandal that did it," Zlatkin told Gornick. "For the first time I began thinking about how lousy it was to be old in this country. Then I thought—Jesus, we do things for everybody from the farm workers to Ramsey Clark, why not do something for the old people in Chelsea?" Even though the new policy represented no real economic loss for either the theater or distributors since the elderly patronized the theater mostly during the day when it was empty, it made the film distributors absolutely crazed, according to Gould. But they did it, anyway. Zlatkin sent out a press release, which generated tremendous coverage. "Television crews," he said, "came down for the whole thing." A year later, on the anniversary of the senior citizen policy, the two put on a celebration for the elderly with coffee and cake and screened the surprising double feature that had the highest attendance of seniors during the year: Joseph Strick's *Ulysses* (1967), the first film adapted from James Joyce's novel, and *Tropic of Cancer* (1970), based on Henry Miller's autobiography. "We got a lot of press for that, too," said Zlatkin.[30]

By 1974, Barenholtz was disengaging more from the Elgin; and in 1975, he pulled out of the theater completely. "It was at that time," he said, "that I went into distribution full time." He was also having problems with the theater. It was not doing well financially, and Euster was making trouble. "There was a period of about two or three years where it was going well," Barenholtz said, "and then came the struggles again because—I don't know—Roger was starting some problems." Euster had instituted a lawsuit against him concerning payments on the mortgage. Barenholtz believed he wanted to take over the Elgin. His lawyers advised him to give the theater back to Euster; instead, he made an offer to Zlatkin and Gould. "I said to Chuck and Steve, 'Here is the situation. If you can make a go of it, the theater is yours, I don't want anything. See if you can work out a deal with Roger.'" They accepted. Barenholtz paid the staff and all the bills before he left. Zlatkin and Gould's tenure as the sole leaseholders and independent operators of the theater lasted about two years.

Business continued to do poorly. Competition was increasing with the advent of the Betamax and college film courses that were showing films as part of their programs. People were becoming less interested in the types of specialties that the Elgin offered, like the opera and ballet series and the town hall meetings. The all-night shows were also suffering because "it was getting dicey," said Gould, "to be out late at night." In late 1976 Zlatkin and Gould established a production company, which produced a cable show, *Movie Watch*, as a marketing tool for the Elgin. "We were seeing the handwriting on the wall," said Zlatkin. "We weren't giving up on the Elgin, but we figured that if it [the cable show] takes off, we could plug the Elgin and maybe do a subscription series with cable subscribers to come down to the Elgin." They were moving towards a setup similar to the old Cinema 16's. The cable show, however, was undercapitalized, and the two were unable to attract sponsors.

Euster, meanwhile, refused to renegotiate the lease. "Euster wasn't interested in the well-being of the theater," Zlatkin said, "or in helping us out." Gould was trying to obtain a Title IV arrangement with the City of New York where it would pay to bring in youngsters during the day for special films, and the theater would return to regular screenings during the weekday evenings. He had to negotiate certain concessions from the union to do this. "All of this was in the works," said Gould, "but it was taking a lot of time, we were behind in rent, and Euster was impatient." The landlord did not strike Gornick as a man who would have much sympathy for the two. "Roger Euster, clearly the real power in this whole business," she wrote, "is a small man in his mid-forties with intelligent eyes behind mod glasses, a paunch beneath a camel-colored jacket, and the personality of a Hollywood press agent. Neither cordial nor sinister, Euster was simply all business."[31]

Attendance was down, and their cash flow was not covering their expenses. They found themselves putting their own money into the theater to pay staff and other expenses, including the payments to the projectionists' union pension fund, the seven percent occupancy tax on the rent, and payoffs to the trash collectors. They couldn't staunch the bleeding. The crisis eventually climaxed in March 1977, when, with their rent $21,000 in arrears (four months nonpayment of rent), Euster evicted them. On Monday, March 21, 1977, at noon, the Elgin closed. The sign on the marquee read "Evicted by the Landlord/Gone with the Wind/RIP."

The two co-proprietors attributed a variety of causes to the closing. "It was a whole confluence of issues," Gould said. Zlatkin blamed the industry, which raised the rental price of prints as the repertory theaters developed into successes. After the Elgin had popularized formerly marginal films like *El Topo*, they became unaffordable. "We would get a film going," Zlatkin said, "and then price ourselves out of it after that. It happened to us over and over again. When they came out with *Holy Mountain*, the sequel to *El Topo*, we weren't even in the running to get that." The increase in operating costs also hurt them. Finally, attendance plummeted. "[T]his winter," Zlatkin told Gornick, "was the worst we ever experienced. People just didn't come to the movies. That crippled us." They had also overextended themselves, dealing simultaneously with the theater, the newspaper, and two weekly television shows. "Chuck and I got really, really burned out," Gould admitted.[32]

Finally, their lack of business experience hampered them. "All of this happened so quickly," said Gould. "Neither of us had an MBA, it was kind of scary running these things. We looked for some investors, but because we didn't have a solid business plan, it wasn't like they thought this was going to be a great investment." Euster laid the blame on them. "[T]hese boys were ... academicians," he told Gornick. "They may have loved the movies but they didn't have the quickness or the chutzpah a true showman must have.... It's a cutthroat business, running an independent theatre, and you've got to know how to deal in it. They didn't."[33]

As novice entrepreneurs, Gould and Zlatkin had an uncanny resemblance to Walter Langsford and Edwin Stein, the young partners who ran the Charles in the previous decade. Like them, the unsophisticated Elgin proprietors had idealistic aspirations that shattered against economic realities. "The Elgin was my life," said Zlatkin. "I believed in it, and so did Steve. We replaced the screen with a Cinemascope screen from some theater when someone threw eggs at the screen; eggs are the worst thing. Outside of the Ziegfeld, it had the largest screen in Manhattan, over forty feet wide and twenty feet high. We got all new seats. We had old air conditioning that we kept going. The heating was good. The sound system was great, always. I remember, before the midnight show, we put on some old cartoons without the sound and played rock music, and people would get up and dance on the stage." They loved the theater, but they did not have the capital, the business experience, or the support to save it.

Ironically, Euster himself was not a savvy businessman either, at least in his next deal on the Elgin, leasing the theater to a producer of gay pornographic movies, William Perry of Tel-A-Gay Corporation. He had not counted on intense community opposition. Describing the community reaction, Gornick wrote that "[t]he landlord attempted to reason with them about the 'economic realities' of life. They would have none of it. Euster was not talking about the economic realities of life, they felt, so much as the economic realities of profit." He lost this battle and had to cancel the new lease. But it was too late for the Elgin of Zlatkin and Gould. In late 1977 the theater shut down for good until the Feld Ballet took over the building, renovated it, and opened it in 1982 as a dance theater, the Joyce Theater.[34]

"There was a little bit of antagonism at the end," Barenholtz admitted. "They felt that I had let them down." But, he insisted, there was nothing he could do at the time. Zlatkin was especially bitter about Barenholtz. "It took me a long time to even look at a film that had Barenholtz's name on it. I don't know what the particulars were in the relationship between Barenholtz and Euster and their dealings. But he needed to not have liability, so he could free himself from entanglements."

After leaving the Elgin, Barenholtz continued to work in the film industry as a distributor; his Libra Films re-released a variety of foreign films as well as new films, including David Lynch's first feature *Eraserhead* (1977). Later he moved into production, producing the early films of the Coen brothers—*Blood Simple* (1984); Barton *Fink* (1991), awarded the Oscar at the Academy Awards and the Golden Palm and Best Director Awards at the Cannes Film Festival; and *Miller's Crossing* (1990), San Sebastián International Film's Best Director Award—as well as the early ones of George A. Romero (*Martin*, 1977) and Darren Aronofsky (*Requiem for a Dream*, 2000). More recently, he has directed his first feature, *Music Inn* (2005), a documentary about the famed eponymous jazz venue; produced Suzuya Bobo's first feature, *Family Games* (2012); and directed and produced *Wakaliwood: The Documentary* (2012), on the Ugandan filmmaker Isaac G.G. Nabwana.[35]

Zlatkin worked in publicity for a while; but in need of a steady income with a wife and child to support, he worked for the post office until 2014 when he was hired by his union to be its representative in Washington, D.C. Gould, who continues to live with his wife in the same apartment on Christopher Street in Greenwich Village, worked as a freelance publicity and marketing agent for movie theaters and distributors and is now employed by a nonprofit social service agency for the elderly. The two have remained close friends. "I wouldn't have missed it for the world," said Gould. "I must say that there were very, very hard times, and Chuck and I had one or two yelling matches. But as Chuck said to me on the subway ride up to the lawyer's office one time, 'Well, if we can stay friends and get through this, we'll know we did something right.' And to this day, we're friends, we see each other, families, and share good times, and if anything came out of this, it was knowing that I had a partner like Chuck."

Barenholtz had created an eclectic theater for an assortment of audiences. There were about fifteen different core audiences, Zlatkin estimated. "You'd have rock stars showing up in limos on Saturday midnight to see what was going on, and maybe have some limo showing up on Tuesday evening for French Tuesday. Women with the minks coming in to see *An Evening with the Royal Ballet*, at 10 o'clock in the morning; and just a few hours before, people had exited from some all-night, manic-depression festival, spaced out of their minds. And to each of them the Elgin was the theater for that." Rarely did those audiences mix, except for the marijuana smells from the Saturday, all-night movies that frequently lingered into the Sunday morning ballet series. "The Elgin," laughed Mary Maguire, "was a fascinating place because you'd go there on a Sunday morning to see a ballet film, and you'd practically pass out from the marijuana smoke."

There were the eccentrics like the "Piss Man," a senior citizen who was incontinent. "People would complain there was some guy next to them who reeked of urine," Zlatkin recalled. He had to be forbidden to return, but the two soft-hearted, young men felt bad about telling him. They drew straws and Zlatkin lost. When Zlatkin told him, his response was unexpected. "He said, 'I'm surprised it took you so long,'" Zlatkin laughed. "This guy had been thrown out of every place in the world, like right away, and he'd been coming to the Elgin for weeks." Another regular patron that the two sympathetic proprietors took care of was the developmentally challenged young man, whose mother, Gould remembered, would call up and say, "You're always so good to my son. I'm letting him come to the theater today because he loves the Marx Brothers. Can you make certain that he gets in all right, and he gets back to the subway?"

The theater, Zlatkin's press release on the closing summarized, was also "the court of last resort for independent films, a place for films that the critics hated and for films the critics loved but people needed a second chance to see," a place where people could see "a million other things from Cat Film Festivals to guest speakers that made the Elgin one of a kind.... The infamous Mama Cat, the Elgin's mascot for all the years," it concluded, "will now reside in Milton's Store located one block north of the Elgin."[36]

The Elgin meant many things to all kinds of people. Gould remembered the stranger who ran up to him at a wedding in California, shook his hand, hugged him, and said, "Thanks to you, I'm in this business. Even when I was underage, you let me come into the all-night shows to see the movies. I lived on those movies. That's why I write screenplays now." There was the young woman, featured in a *Village Voice* article, who would "play hooky from work in the afternoon, sit through a Preston Sturges double, nip out for a quickie dinner at Asia de Cuba—which looks like you're taking your life in your hands to eat there but has great food—and head back for the evening show.... I got my film education at the Elgin," she declared.[37]

And there were the elderly who found relief from their loneliness and isolation at the Elgin because of the twenty-five-cent-at-all-times policy. Gornick's mother, who lived near the theater, went there all the time. "Sometimes I go to see a particular movie," she was quoted in the article, "sometimes I don't know what I'm watching. Sometimes I go alone, sometimes with a friend. I go to forget myself, and sometimes I meet people there. For 25 cents I can take a big chance, no?" The regulars, Gould told Gornick, were always paying them back with gifts, like the scarves that the lady from the Bronx knit for them, or the coffee that others brought for the cashier, or the neatly tied stacks of photography magazines that one man brought for an Elgin employee who was a photographer. "I laughed to myself," wrote Gornick, "and thought: My God. People like my mother knitting scarves for two guys running a counterculture movie house in the middle of a Puerto Rican ghetto. What a city."[38]

Chapter 10

Theatre 80 St. Marks: Joan Crawford, Grauman's Chinese Theater and Other Memorabilia of Hollywood's Golden Age

Howard Otway was a showman, and Theatre 80 St. Marks in the East Village on St. Marks Place was his showplace, an homage to the classic Hollywood films and stars that graced its screen. Newspapers of the time painted the theater as a reincarnation of old-time movie glamour. A *Villager* reporter described the small, intimate lobby festooned with large autographed blowups of Myrna Loy, Katharine Hepburn, Gloria Swanson, Bette Davis, Tallulah Bankhead, Brian Aherne, and Henry Fonda. A spotlight shone on an oil portrait of Joan Crawford, a leftover from *Forsaking All Others* (1934) and *Whatever Happened to Baby Jane* (1962) and a gift from the actress shortly before her death. The old-style snack bar, contiguous with the lobby, was lit, he wrote, with moody *Blue Dahlia* lighting. In the background the songbooks of Ella Fitzgerald and records of Blossom Dearie, two of Otway's favorites, played softly. The setting had "the stylized look of a 1930s movie set complete with the fresh flowers that Otway insisted upon over the objections of his accountant." An elegantly dressed impresario, the trim, energetic Otway would often greet and chat with his audience as they entered the lobby. "I believe in the total show," he told the reporter. "The lobby, intermission are all part of it, all part of a personality." The personality was all Otway's.[1]

Otway was charismatic. Paul Power, one of his former staff, described him as a very forceful personality. "He was the kind of person," he remembered, "who would walk into a room and command it, even at the stage when he was ailing physically and his emphysema was quite strong." He was also a delightful storyteller "with a great sense of humor, and enough devilishness to be truly interesting," William Reiss, a literary agent and friend of Otway's, remembered in a letter to Mrs. Otway on his death. He described him as a kind man "who stuck by his friends and enjoyed life a great deal," but one who could also be vindictive and bitter. "I think it [Reiss' failure to place his manuscript, *Young Man of Promise/Who the Hell Is Howard Otway?*, with a publisher] confirmed his suspicion that people in publishing in general and literary agents in particular were more inept than members of the federal government, and about as intelligent."[2]

Otway was born in 1922 in Moose Jaw, Saskatchewan, to Salvation Army parents who were on their way from Scotland to their post in the Midwest. His father had been the provincial commander for the Salvation Army for all of Ireland, "which is about the level of cardinal," Otway's son Lorcan explained. Pieces of his early life are scattered in interviews he gave to various newspapers over the years. In an interview with a *New York Newsday* reporter in 1994, he said that, drawn to the stage and to writing, he left home at an early age and was hired as a scriptwriter at a local radio station in the Midwest, where he was soon promoted to sing and perform as the radio "Voice of the Iowa Grain Exchange." The Salvation Army strongly disapproved of the theater, but Lorcan credited his father's genes, passed down from his maternal grandmother, who had been a successful music hall performer, for his love of theater. From the Midwest he moved to New York at age 19, where, he told a *New York Post* reporter, one of his first jobs was as a bellboy at the Plaza; soon, though, he graduated to holding the rope at the Persian Room. His first job as an actor was with Gloria Swanson in the road company of *Let Us Be Gay* in 1943. He remained lifelong friends with her. His next engagement was in the Broadway revival of *The Barretts of Wimpole Street* in 1945 with Katharine Cornell. (A large publicity photograph of him as he appeared in the play also hung in the lobby of Theatre 80.) Lorcan recalled a story about a visit his father's mother made to New York to see him in the play. After the performance, he introduced her to Cornell. "They became dear friends," Lorcan said, "and had a correspondence for years."[3]

Around 1947, Otway married Florence Kirschen, who was a designer of women's shoes—and a supporter of progressive causes. She was part of a "welcome home" rally for the Abraham Lincoln Brigade at the end of the Spanish Civil War and, during the Second World War, volunteered at the U.S.O., a social and entertainment agency for the armed services. The couple moved to Jane Street in Greenwich Village, then around 1950 bought and moved to a rural retreat in Westchester County. They had two sons, Lawrence (who later changed his name to its Irish version, Lorcan) and Thomas. During the fifties Otway worked as a salesman and wrote two novels—*The Evangelist* (1954) and *The Paradise Bird* (1956)—as well as several plays for Off Broadway, which was in its early phase. Looking for a producer for one of his plays, he decided, on the suggestion of a friend, to become one himself and went on to produce his plays as well as those of other playwrights. He originally opened Theatre 80 as an Off Broadway theater for his productions; it soon became the site for a successful, four-year run of *You're a Good Man, Charlie Brown*.[4]

With his own theater occupied, he used other Off Broadway houses for other productions, including the Actors' Playhouse in Greenwich Village on Seventh Avenue for *One Night Stands of a Noisy Passenger*, a trio of one-act plays written by the actress Shelley Winters, which opened on December 30, 1970, closed four days later on January 3, 1971, and featured the still-unknown, young actors Robert De Niro, Diane Ladd, Richard Lynch, and Sally Kirkland. Lorcan and his mother had fond memories of the play and its actors. "My headmaster at the prep school on the East Side I went to for a year," Lorcan recalled, "told me to shave my mustache. Shelley Winters called him up and yelled at him." Mrs. Otway described de Niro as very good-looking and thoughtful. "One night they [the cast] were rehearsing here [in Theatre 80]," she said, "and I was mad, because I had cooked a special dinner for two of my work colleagues, and I had to add all this stuff to make it go that far. And Bobby was the only one who helped. He helped clear the table, he helped with the dishes, he was just delightful."[5]

In the mid-sixties Otway purchased the two five-story buildings at 78 and 80 St. Marks Place in the East Village that became Theatre 80 St. Marks. "I was looking for a theater for a new play," he told the *New York Post* reporter, "when I happened to pass this closed coffeehouse that had been called The Ski Lodge. I just had a feeling that in the back there, there was a hole large enough to put a theater. I got the super to open the door. It was pitch black, but I knew this was it." The buildings had been the site of a famous speakeasy during Prohibition, then a jazz nightclub, and finally a coffee house.[6]

Unbeknownst to him, he was walking into a trap. It was another story from his father's colorful background that Lorcan delighted in relating. Otway bought the buildings from a Walter Scheib, who had worked for a mob boss, Frank Hoffman, until

Howard Otway, sitting in front of a studio portrait of Tallulah Bankhead. Theatre 80 St. Marks Collection (T80SM), the Museum of Modern Art Department of Film Special Collections, New York.

Hoffman disappeared in 1945; but as far as Scheib knew he could still be alive. In the basement of one of the buildings was a safe that contained about $12,000,000, which Scheib was afraid to open because the money belonged to his boss, an extremely dangerous man, "not the kind of guy you would open up the safe without asking," Lorcan explained. Scheib devised a complicated scheme, according to Lorcan, that would allow him to open the safe without any risk and take the money. He needed a patsy, someone without much income to take out a mortgage on the building that he could not afford and would eventually default on, so that Scheib, who gave him the mortgage, could take back the building and safely open the safes. "If Hoffman ever returned," Lorcan said, "Scheib could say, 'I don't have the money, ask the guy I sold the building to.'"

When Otway came along, Scheib just asked for a reasonable down payment with the mortgage. Otway found the safes but was too wary to open them himself. "He told Scheib," Lorcan said, "that he was too curious to leave the safes closed and too cautious to open them without him there." That saved his life, according to Lorcan. Scheib opened the safes and found two million, instead of $12,000,000, in expired gold certificates. "I think he was going to use them in Europe," Mrs. Otway said. "You couldn't spend it here." It turned out, according to later, discovered evidence, that Hoffman and his girlfriend had been murdered the night of November 7, 1945, by his bodyguard while he was in the process of emptying the safes of the money that he should have split with his gang; the bodyguard took ten million of the $12,000,000 after he killed the two.[7]

Otway now had his mortgage and, without any previous building experience, began constructing the theater himself. He combined the two houses into one, built a triplex upstairs for his family (one floor was reserved for tenants, the most famous of whom was the Abstract Expressionist Joan Mitchell, who left behind one of her paintings when she moved), and even taught himself to cast the apartment's decorative moldings. In the initial stages of construction, he stayed alone in the theater while his family continued to live in Westchester; but eventually he ran out of money because of delays in getting various permits, and the family had to move into the unfinished building. "I had to sell the house in Westchester and move down to absolute squalor," Mrs. Otway remembered. "I cannot tell you what it was like. I had a tent for the children over there for them to sleep in until I could clean up the place. I was crying, I felt so awful, sleeping on the stage and living in this filth. But the kids said, 'What are you upset about? We're the only kids in the school who sleep on a stage.'"

There were several serious mishaps during the construction. "Dad was one of the strongest fellows I ever met," Lorcan said. "When he was building the theater, he had the floor opened; and alone one night, he fell between the beams and landed on a board with nails in it. He was literally nailed to the board. He had a crowbar with him and he actually pried himself off the board." Another time he was stabbed and tied up by someone in the theater late at night. "It was his own fault," Mrs. Otway said. "Someone knocked on the door and he opened it." He knew that if he lost consciousness, he would die, so he dragged himself with his chin (he was still tied up) to the front door and banged his head against the door until some passersby called the police. "This was a time when the city was dangerous," Mrs. Otway remembered.

The design of the theater was his. He built a 38-by-21-foot stage and 199 seats whose legroom was sized to suit his own smallish build; this was a mistake he later corrected by removing seats. "When he was building it," Mrs. Otway explained, "he said, 'Florence, come sit down, tell me if you have enough room.' I'm 5 foot, so I said, 'Yeah, everything's okay.' But at opening night we looked and saw Walter Kerr [then *New York Times* theater critic], who was over six feet, sitting with his knees tucked into his chin. So he took out a whole row and got wider seats so that his audience would be comfortable." The Off Broadway theater went from 199 seats to 175.

Theatre 80 St. Marks opened in November 1966 with Otway's play, *This Here Nice Place*, which received lukewarm reviews in the *New York Times*. Still owing Scheib $65,000 on the mortgage, Otway was bankrupt and went into hiding for six months, afraid that "Scheib would break his legs if he fell behind on the payments," Lorcan said. Because he had already found the safe, Scheib did not come after him; and before he could take any action against Otway, the next play, *You're a Good Man, Charlie Brown*, opened on March 7, 1967, to a decisive critical and popular success, enabling Otway to pay off the mortgage.[8]

Otway had a co-producer on *Charlie Brown*, Arthur Whitelaw. "They had the music," Mrs. Otway remembered, "but they didn't have a script or anything. What they did was just have the actors bring in their favorite comic strips, and they built it like that." The play ran successfully for over four years and then transferred to Broadway's Golden

Theater in February 1971 because of the first Off Broadway actors' and managers' strike, which began in November 1970. There were picket lines at ten of the seventeen theaters, including Theatre 80 St. Marks and Actors' Playhouse, where Otway's other production, *One Night Stands of a Noisy Passenger*, was playing. "The demands were completely ludicrous for a small theater," Lorcan said. "You had to have showers backstage, things that most Off Broadway theaters couldn't maintain." The Actors Equity Association's major demand was an increase in wages. An Equity member his entire professional life and a strong union supporter, Otway closed Theatre 80 rather than turn it into an Off Off Broadway, nonunion theater. He was thinking that there would eventually be a balance again and he would be able to go back to legitimate theater.[9]

What to do with the theater was now the question challenging Otway and Whitelaw. Whitelaw presented Otway with a solution. Inspired by the popularity and large crowds for the movie musical revivals at MoMA, he dreamed up the idea of a revival house of musicals. "After I had thought about the idea for a few days," Whitelaw told the magazine *Show*, "I called Howard Otway, my co-producer, and told him. He was very enthusiastic and agreed to join me in the venture." However, according to Mrs. Otway, her husband had some reservations because there was no place for a projection booth. Whitelaw's solution was rear projection of 16mm prints. Theater 80 St. Marks was reborn in 1971 under the corporate title of the Musical Film Co.[10]

The two impresarios dressed up Theatre 80 as an old-fashioned movie theater, with a uniformed usher greeting customers at the door, another one tending a mahogany bar loaded with Jujubes, and others ushering patrons to their seats. The opening night on August 22, 1971, featuring Jerome Kern's *Sunny* (1930), starring legendary Broadway star Marilyn Miller, and *Look for the Silver Lining* (1949), a musical biography of Miller, brought limousines crowding the street and klieg lights orbiting the sky. "Just about every star in New York was there," Otway proudly pointed out to the *New York Post* reporter years later.[11]

Gloria Swanson, who hosted the event, had sent out invitations to a number of Broadway and Hollywood stars. Among the gathering of contemporary and older celebrities were Alexis Smith and her husband Craig Stevens, Gene Nelson, and Yvonne De Carlo, all of whom were then starring in Stephen Sondheim's *Follies* on Broadway; Warner Bros. stars of the thirties, Ruby Keeler and Joan Blondell; superstar Jane Russell; Broadway stars Eileen Heckart and Maureen Stapleton; television and Broadway star Imogene Coca; Wini Shaw of "Lullaby of Broadway" fame from *Golddiggers of 1935*; Lillian Roth, singer, movie and Broadway actress, and subject of the film, *I'll Cry Tomorrow* (1955); singer and actress Fifi D'Orsay; Rita Gam, film and television actress and documentary filmmaker; and theater and film director Morton Da Costa, among others. Otway's pal, Joan Crawford, though, refused to come while Swanson was there. It was an emotional experience for a number of the older celebrities. At two in the morning after the last film played, Fifi D'Orsay came out from the dark into the klieg lights, muttering "Dead ... dead ... they're all dead."[12]

That night many of the stars signed their names and pressed their foot or handprints into wet cement on the sidewalk in front of Theatre 80, inaugurating the Lower East Side version of Grauman's Chinese Theater. Otway gave a detailed account of the opening night to the *New York Post* reporter. When somebody had suggested making the theater into an "itty-bitty Radio City Music Hall," he had countered with the idea of making it an "itty-bitty Grauman's Chinese." An area was roped around wet cement forms so the

Gloria Swanson and Arthur Whitelaw at the opening night of Musical Film Co., Theatre 80 St. Marks, August 1971. Photo by Zodiac Photographers. Photofest.

stars could sign their names into the sidewalk. "Fifi D'Orsay wanted to sit in the cement," he told the reporter. "She said that was the best part of her act." Gloria Swanson, Lillian Roth, and Wini Shaw also left their imprints. Those of Maureen Stapleton and Eileen Heckart were unfortunately lost later on. Crawford came another night to inscribe her name in the cement. Arriving in "a long, long double-stretch limousine" that had Pepsi-Cola pillows and a rug with the Pepsi-Cola labels printed on it, she exited the car and knelt to write a big "Craw" that left no room for the "ford." "I told her she should let me wipe it out so she could do it over again," Otway remembered, "but she said, 'No, let 'em know I don't plan ahead.'" This may have been the memorable night when one of her early films, *Dancing Lady* (1933), was playing. People who were there remembered her appearance. "[T]he audience went respectfully 'wild' with applause," wrote one fan to the *New York Times*. "[T]here we were in legion, applauding and cheering as Miss Crawford graciously accepted her welcome with tears on the surface of her ever beautiful eyes."[13]

Myrna Loy was the last one to put her print on the sidewalk. One of the press asked to photograph her in front of a forties publicity blowup of her at her peak. "Now nobody at her age wants herself photographed," Otway said, in recounting the incident to the *Post* reporter, "but she smiled through gritted teeth and said, 'Of course you realize this is the meanest thing anybody has ever done to me, don't you?'" Other actors who were memorialized in cement included Joan Blondell; Allan Jones, who left his right handprint; Kitty Carlisle, who just signed her name; Dom Deluise and his right handprint; Hildegarde with her left handprint; and Ruby Keeler. In the late 1990s, the city department for street and arterial maintenance was threatening to destroy the sidewalk, claiming it was defacing property. After a hard-fought fight by Mrs. Otway, the city finally relented in 1999. Then Mrs. Otway thought of moving her collectible concrete closer to her building, out of the way of pedestrians.[14]

The theater showed Hollywood song-and-dance films from the late twenties to the early fifties. Whitelaw seemed to be the spokesman for the theater in the early days. He told the *Show* reporter that he had never been a movie exhibitor before, but was quickly learning. Concentrating on movie musicals seldom revived or seen on television, he bragged, allowed them to present "some dandies that hadn't been seen publicly for 10 or 15 years."

Ruby Keeler impressing her footprint into the wet cement, helped by Arthur Whitelaw at left and Howard Otway at right. MoMA Dept. of Film Archives, New York.

The early double features, which were paired thematically for three-day runs, included the Broadway-to-film musicals *Anything Goes* (1936) and *Lady in the Dark* (1944); Cole Porter's *Fifty Million Frenchmen* (1931) and *Wonder Bar* (1934); the biographies of Broadway composers George Gershwin (*Rhapsody in Blue,* 1945) and Cole Porter (*Night and Day,* 1946); the Fred Astaire films *Dancing Lady* (his first film) and *Easter Parade* (1948); and the early all-black musicals *Cabin in the Sky* (1943) with Ethel Waters and *Hallelujah* (1929), the director King Vidor's first sound film.[15]

The impressively attired ushers greeted patrons, the lobby decorated with movie memorabilia accommodated them as they waited for the feature to begin, and free penny candy lay at their fingertips. These were Whitelaw's ideas, but they were impractical. "Arthur had everyone in Roxy uniforms," Lorcan explained, "and running every film for a week at a time. It almost ran us bankrupt." Mrs. Otway confirmed the problems with Whitelaw's concept. "They were running something like $19,000 a month," she said, "and we couldn't go on like that. I think they were charging $2.50 a ticket and all the free coffee, free candy, and the ushers in uniform. And three union projectionists." Even allowing for some leeway in Mrs. Otway's memory of the actual monthly expenses, the theater must have been running a considerable deficit in the beginning since its average monthly grosses in the first full year of 1972 amounted to $9,347 and in 1973 to $10,882.[16]

At some point between May 1972 and June 1973 Whitelaw withdrew from the partnership and Otway took over the debt. "My dad then came up with a formula," Lorcan said, "of dividing up the weekend in half and then dividing the week in half. So that if you had a really horrendous double bill, the most you'd lose is three or four days. And then he joined the projectionists' union and took over one of the shifts, so that he was able to cut down the running costs." Three years later, in 1976, the theater experienced a sharp drop of nine percent in annual grosses and another two percent decline in 1977. Otway's solution was a switch in late October 1977 to daily changes of double features during the week and a two-day run of one twin bill on weekends. Almost immediately, the box office improved. The annual gross for 1978 rose almost 14 percent over the previous year to $150,336.50 and continued to rise each year until in 1982 it passed the $200,000 milestone for the first time and stayed above it until the theater's closing (except for two years—1992, when it dipped to slightly over $191,000, and 1994, when the theater closed halfway through the year).[17]

Otway stayed with the formula of daily weekday changes to the end. He never programmed series or festivals. His rationale, he told the *West Side Spirit*, a community newspaper, was that he did not think one should have to wait through six weeks of mysteries if they wanted to see a comedy. Another reason was economic, as Lorcan explained; a festival that bombed could put you in the red for the length of the series, whereas one weak double feature could be followed the next day by a strong, dependable one that "would put food on the table."[18]

Accompanying the new scheduling came some inexplicable coincidences. "This was the strangest thing in our case," Mrs. Otway recalled. "Nobody could ever figure this out. Practically every well-known star who died during that time would die on a day we were showing their film, or the day before, or the day after. Since we had to do our programming at least six weeks in advance, it was absolutely the strangest thing. We had television people coming down and asking, 'How did you know?'"

A uniformed staff tending the snack bar of Theatre 80. T80SM, MoMA Dept. of Film Archives, New York.

As a programmer, "Howard was very knowledgeable about his movies," Power remembered, "even those he hadn't seen; he was aware of the actors and director. He had a very good sense of what worked together." But he was not interested in the current intellectual trends in film discourse. The auteurist theory had no relevance for him, and he preferred the term *movie* to *film*. "To call *Camille* George Cukor's *Camille* is stupid," he told *The Villager* reporter. "It's Garbo's *Camille*." Programming for him was a matter of "show biz," not educating or propounding great art. As at the Regency, the other great shrine to vintage Hollywood films, Lopate remembered having a good time at Theatre 80. "They were encouraging a kind of pleasure-loving, watching movies. You weren't supposed to take them that seriously but there was the pleasure of the well-made film, so you could see Mitchell Leisen films, that kind of thing. That was great, they really fulfilled a need."[19]

Otway concentrated on the integrity of the double bills, according to Power. They were carefully curated, always linked by a theme—star, director, studio, genre, content. Power described his curating as intelligently eclectic. In the early years he brought in less well-known musicals, in addition to the big hits like *Harvey Girls* (1946), with Judy Garland and *Love Me or Leave Me* (1955), a biopic of singer Ruth Etting, starring James Cagney and Doris Day. In 1972, for example, Theatre 80 screened a number of rare musicals: opera singer Grace Moore's first film, *A Lady's Morals* (1930), and *Marianne*, a 1929 Marion Davies vehicle; 20th Century-Fox's 1931 musical, *Delicious*, with Janet Gaynor and Charles Farrell, and songs by Ira and George Gershwin; and a double bill of two almost unknown 1933 Maurice Chevalier musicals from Paramount, *Innocents of Paris*, the first musical produced by the studio, and *A Bedtime Story* (1933). In its leanings towards the lesser known, bread-and-butter films of the thirties, Theatre 80 resembled the programming approach of Everson's Theodore Huff Memorial Film Society. These rare musicals seemed to do respectable business; the twin bills featuring *A Lady's Morals* and *Marianne*, for instance, each sold over 300 tickets in their respective three-day runs.[20]

In the winter 1971–1972 program, Otway presented the first of his resurrections of important films from Hollywood's past—the first screening in thirty years of the 1936 version of Jerome Kern's *Show Boat*, featuring Irene Dunne, Allan Jones, Helen Morgan, and Paul Robeson, on a double bill with Kern's biography, *Till the Clouds Roll By* (1946, in color). "Starts Today Thru Jan. 1," the calendar announced, "Not Seen in 30 Years!" Otway had never seen the 1936 *Show Boat*, but he had learned of it by reading and talking to people in the business. He particularly wanted that film, Lorcan thought, because of the cast, including Paul Robeson, whom he greatly respected. "The *Show Boat* of the 1950s offended him when he showed it," Lorcan remembered. "He had a certain sense of outrage that you would replace this wonderful cast from the original film with the mediocre cast from the second film. So a lot of it was a matter that it hadn't been seen, and he realized the value of the original cast." Running from December 19, 1971, to January 1, 1972, the film was a success, grossing $7,413.50 with the sale of 2,989 tickets, and was repeated two months later in March.[21]

Years later, in a *Village Voice* article, Otway described how the restoration of the film came about. "M-G-M had brought [*sic*] the rights from Universal [Universal Studios had produced the 1936 version]; and, on the theory that nobody would ever want to see Helen Morgan when they could see Ava Gardner in color, made no effort to preserve the original. Having sold the property, Universal had no vested interest. We found a print in the Library of Congress [according to another *Voice* writer, Otway was assisted by film

Joan Crawford, Howard Otway, and Arthur Whitelaw viewing the still from *Show Boat* (1936), ca. 1972. T80SM, MoMA Dept. of Film Archives, New York.

producer Jack Haley, Jr.], and M-G-M consented to make a new negative and reduction to 16mm." This was typical of Otway's doggedness in uncovering films he was interested in. "He was a digger," Lorcan remembered. "If there was something that he wanted to see, if he thought it was valuable, he'd call the original distributor; and if they'd say, 'I can't do it,' instead of just hanging up, he'd say, 'Why can't we do it?'"[22]

Other restorations followed *Show Boat*. The March 1972 calendar announced the screening for the Easter holiday of *Roberta*, "the most often requested 'lost' film we have managed to resurrect." *Roberta* was the 1935 production of the Jerome Kern musical starring Irene Dunne, with Fred Astaire and Ginger Rogers in their first musical together. The calendar's announcement ended with a summing up of the theater's restorations to that point: "This is the third restored film we have shown, the first being *SHOW BOAT* (1936), followed by *MUSIC IN THE AIR* [1934, it showed for two days in February, starring Gloria Swanson and John Boles]." *Roberta* was repeated in August 1972 in a double bill with *Show Boat* for a week's run.[23]

Roberta, along with three Fred Astaire–Ginger Rogers films, *Follow the Fleet* (1936), *Carefree* (1938), and *Flying Down to Rio* (1933), had legal problems because the music rights had reverted back to the composers. "We were able to clear our showings," Otway told a *Village Voice* reporter, "which in turn led to negotiations that restored the music rights to the companies holding the picture rights, thus bringing the films back to the catalogues." For *Flying Down to Rio*, Otway was able to convince the family of Vincent Youmans, the composer, to permit him to screen the film, which, with *Swing Time*, became a regular repeat.[24]

The route through which he obtained permission to show *Follow the Fleet* and *Carefree* was circuitous. "Irving Berlin [the owner of the music rights to both films] refused to allow them to be shown," Mrs. Otway recalled. "They hadn't been seen in thirty years, and nobody could get him to release them." Otway enlisted the help of his friend and former co-producer of *One Night Stands of a Noisy Passenger*, Larry Goossen, who had hired Irving Berlin's granddaughter for one of his shows. Otway asked him to arrange a meeting with her. Through Goossen's intervention, Otway was able to speak to her and promised her that he would only show them for a week. In turn, "she got to grandpa," Mrs. Otway related, "and grandpa said, 'Okay, we'd do it this time.'" The films played in June 1974. "Howard advertised them," Mrs. Otway remembered, "and we had lines down the block for the full week. We were sold out for every single show."

Because of their popularity, the double feature was repeated in August of the same year, Otway told *The Villager* reporter, after Berlin made the films available exclusively to him for a year. One small incident from the first outing particularly stayed in Mrs. Otway's memory. "One morning we had opened early to get everything ready, and there was [Richard] Avedon and somebody else in the coffee bar having coffee; and he was singing and dancing. He said, 'Hi, Howard, I was just talking to Fred Astaire and telling him when Howard shows the Fred Astaire films, how the young people come and sit on the steps and all that.' I wanted him so badly to come and see this, but he said, 'No, I'm too old.'"[25]

One time the question of legal rights over a restored film led to a court battle. Otway had rented two World War I films, the silent film *Wings* (1927), the first to win the Oscar for Best Picture, and the early sound film *Hell's Angels* (1930), both of which had not been seen since their original release. "He had advertised that he was showing them on the weekend," Mrs. Otway recalled, "and I can't tell you the excitement; there were lines down the block." But, before he could show them, lawyers representing Howard Hughes, the producer of the two films, stopped the screening, claiming that Hughes owned the rights and Otway had no right to show them, even though he had proof that he had bought them legitimately. Otway and Hughes took the battle over the rights to trial, which took place in New England. "Hughes's lawyers wanted to get it out of New York and away from California," Mrs. Otway said. The two-day trial ended in a stalemate with no resolution, so the judge, in frustration, gave Otway the rights to one of the films and Hughes the rights to the other.

Over the years, Otway continued to pressure and coax studios to have new 16mm prints struck from originals decomposing in their vaults. "Many times," he told the *Village Voice* reporter in 1978, "it is just a matter of getting the studios interested in opening up their vaults and seeing what they have." The year before, he noted that Columbia found two pre–Code Barbara Stanwyck films, *Ten Cents a Dance* (1931) and *Miracle Woman* (1931), plus one of the best newspaper comedies, *Platinum Blonde* (1931), with Jean Harlow. His most recent find was Paramount's 1929 *Canary Murder Case*, a Philo Vance mystery starring William Powell and Jean Arthur, which he showed theatrically for the first time in over 30 years. "Each time I start a program," he said, "I think we must run out of the rich past—but somehow great treasures keep turning up"—treasures like F.W. Murnau's

1922 *Nosferatu* and G. W. Pabst's 1931 *Threepenny Opera*. "Now everyone does it, everyone has better prints," Mrs. Otway remarked. "But he was the first one to put it together."[26]

In its first year or so of operation, the theater was devoted exclusively to movie musicals, drawing in the nostalgic "Jeanette MacDonald–Nelson Eddy crowd." Around the beginning of 1973, shortly before he took over the theater from Whitelaw, Otway began to open up his programming to dramas, screwball comedies, and other nonmusical genres. This came about, he told *The Villager* reporter, after a dinner conversation with his friend, the actress Eileen Heckart, who was thinking of appearing in a Broadway revival of *The Women*. He mentioned to her that he had never seen *Dinner at Eight* (1933); and in the course of the conversation, he came up with an inspiration—pairing that film with the 1939 film version of *The Women* on New Year's Eve and inviting the audience for champagne at midnight. (Both films were highly successful thirties MGM ensemble films, directed by George Cukor, which had been based on Broadway plays.) The event proved so successful that not only did he continue with nonmusical films, but he also made the New Year's Eve champagne party an annual tradition, one that he threw himself into with enthusiasm each year, directing his family and staff, Lorcan remembered, "like an eighteenth century ship's captain," in all the preparations. (At the end of the party, the leftovers would be handed out to the homeless on the street.)[27]

Another factor that probably contributed to broadening the programs was the dwindling interest in the Jeanette MacDonald–type nostalgic films. By September 1973 Otway was programming more non-musicals of the thirties and forties, including both obscure ones like *Stand In*, a 1937 United Artists comedy, with Humphrey Bogart and Leslie Howard, and better known ones like *Imitation of Life*, a 1934 Universal drama, with Claudette Colbert and Louise Beavers. In January 1977 in recognition of the new direction, the headings of the calendars changed from "Theatre 80/*The Movie Musical*…" to "Theatre 80/*The Movie*…." The expansion brought in a new, younger audience, like the one in 1994 that included, the *New York Newsday* reporter noted, "cult fans enjoying hokum siren Maria Montez's *Cobra Woman* (1944), and NYU students filling all 160 seats for the gross-out orgy of *Blue Velvet* (1986) and *A Clockwork Orange*."[28]

The expansion was a gradual process. By the late 1970s, Otway was featuring more fifties films and a few from the sixties, like *Cat on a Hot Tin Roof* (1958), with Elizabeth Taylor and Paul Newman, and *Breakfast at Tiffany's* (1961), starring Audrey Hepburn. The genres ranged from the musicals to the dramas of the Big Five studios as well as those of the Poverty Row studios. By 1981 he was adding foreign art-house titles, like Jean Cocteau's *Testament of Orpheus* (1959), and *Blood of the Poet* (1932), which screened twenty-two times between 1981 and 1994, and Ingmar Bergman's *Shame* (1968) with *Wild Strawberries* (1957), which was shown eighteen times between 1982 and 1993. With this expansion of his repertoire, his tastes began to change. He told *The Villager* that he found some contemporary films, like Francis Ford Coppola's *Godfather I* (1972), "infinitely superior" to Howard Hawks's *Scarface* (1932) and several contemporary stars, like Cicely Tyson and Jane Fonda, as luminous as those of the thirties and forties.[29]

Otway continued to find "lost" films that he thought deserved a new life. A later example was *North Star*, a 1943 RKO film scripted by Lillian Hellman and produced at the height of the Second World War when the Soviets were our allies. The film presented Soviet collective farms in a favorable light; but in the anti-Communist fever of the 1950s, it had been withdrawn by RKO and recut to delete pro-Soviet scenes and to add anti-Soviet content. It was re-released under the title *Armored Attack*. Somehow, Otway located a print of the original version in the possession of a private collector. These private collectors, he told a *Staten Island Register* reporter, often acquired rare films like *North Star*. "If it weren't for these people," he said, "many of the films would have turned to dust years ago." *North Star* played at Theatre 80 in August 1977.[30]

Theatre 80 was famous (or infamous, depending on one's viewpoint) as the only rep movie house to use rear projection as well as the only one to screen only 16mm prints. Although rear projection would make even a pristine print look fuzzy, Whitelaw and Otway had no other option, since there was no space at the back of the auditorium for a projection booth. Their deep stage, however, could accommodate projectors at a sufficient distance from the screen at the edge of the stage, to make rear projection a viable alternative to conventional projection. "You're shooting from a mirror with a ninety-degree-angle lens," Lorcan explained, "onto a screen that is translucent, so the images are reversed and go through the screen, almost like a television set. In fact, with the first rear screen, we had a standard 16mm projector with literally a mirror; we would shoot into the mirror and onto the screen. We then developed a lens that had a built-in mirror so that it was a ninety-degree-angle lens."

One thing that rear projection did not permit Otway to show in their true ratio was Cinemascope films, despite some attempts to improvise a method. "My father and a Korean technician, who worked for us for years, at one point had a huge nine-foot by sixteen-foot mirror made out of optical glass, which I rigged so that you could set it at different angles," Lorcan said, "but the light loss was too much. For the entire run of the movies, my dad tried to find a way of showing Cinemascope; we came really close." This created problems in showing widescreen films. When Otway showed the MGM musical *It's Always Fair Weather* (1955) in 16mm, for example, one patron complained to the *New York Times* that it "included two-thirds of the picture at any one time, wreaking havoc with compositions, and in the case of a pas de trois in split screen, totally destroying the sense of the sequence." Otway received the brunt of the blame for being insensitive or indifferent to the quality of the film image. "They had no respect for the ratio of the films," recalled Mandelbaum. "I remember calling up when they were showing *Les Girls*. I asked if it was going to be 'scope prints, because in 16mm, rather than the hateful pan-and-scan technique, there was letter boxing. The owner said 'We have a much better way, the important images are selected for you,' which meant you were losing half. Sometimes I would complain about the bad projection, and the owner, who was also the projectionist, would say, 'What do you expect? It's an old movie.' I tried not to go there. They had enthusiasm but they didn't seem to care what the image looked like."[31]

Complaints were also common about the distorted colors in prints. "The two main problems [with prints]," Power explained, "were the physical and the chemical ones. The chemical problem was mostly in evidence on color prints where, after a lot of use, they seem to get very red. I know from speaking to [Ron Magliozzi] at MoMA, that reddening of older color prints is an occupational hazard." Another complaint to the *Times* criticized the reddish tint in *It's Always Fair Weather* and the orange-y monochromatic and grainy print of the second film on the double bill, *Les Girls*, which sometimes "shifted into deep sepia, then oozed into the crimson family and back to orange." The physical problem was torn or broken sprockets. "What often happened," Power clarified, "was that when prints were used in other places, projectionists might not have been as careful with the final frames of a reel, and kept chopping off one or two frames every time it's shown [because of broken sprockets]; very soon you lose seconds or minutes. A lot of that happened. There were quite a lot of jumps."[32]

Otway and his staff tried to prescreen the films the day before the scheduled screening. If there was a problem with the film—such as a dubbed soundtrack, mistranslated subtitles, poor picture quality, or too much gum or glue damaging the print—it was still time to put in a call to the distributor for another print to be sent overnight. If this was not possible, an announcement would be made before the film; or patrons would be warned at the box office that this was not the print they were expecting. Storing the cans of film in a small theater could be a headache. They would be stacked on top of and behind each other. "I cannot tell you how many times they'd call me from back stage," Mrs. Otway recalled, "because they had to get the film ready and they couldn't find it. So I would have them take the box office and I'd go in. I always found it."

Otway rented prints from a variety of sources, including Films, Inc., Columbia Films, MGM, Janus Films, and even Rohauer, his archrival. "Rohauer was his great nemesis," Lorcan remembered. "He bought up parts of the rights, part of the package of film rights to films. For example, if the book was available, he'd buy the rights to the book, and that way he was able to limit the showing of films that had been in public domain." Like some other rep house owners, Otway also had his own library of films in the public domain. "He had friends," Mrs. Otway remembered, "who let him know when a film was now in the public domain and who had a copy to sell." His prints included many from the 1930s and 1940s, such as early Hitchcocks from England (*Secret Agent*, 1936, and *The Man Who Knew Too Much*, 1934), German Expressionist films (*The Cabinet of Dr. Caligari*, 1920), and Eisenstein films (*Battleship Potemkin*, 1925, and *October: Ten Days That Shook the World*, 1928) as well as the Bulldog Drummond, Sherlock Holmes, and Charlie Chan series.[33]

The Otways also had their stories about last-minute crises, a common feature of running a rep house. One such crisis involved a rescue by Gloria Swanson. "One night we were going to show *Sunset Boulevard*," Mrs. Otway remembered, "but the film didn't come the night before, and we had sold out for it. Howard called Gloria Swanson in Rome, where she was publicizing her book; she got the message and called back. Howard told her that the film hadn't arrived and we had to show it the next day. She said, 'Don't worry. I have a copy in my apartment, and I'll call one of my staff.' This young woman called the next day and brought the film to us an hour before the screening. Gloria Swanson was wonderful to us."

Competition from other theaters was a constant worry for Otway, especially as Theatre 80 became more popular. A number of the movie houses, according to Mrs. Otway, would learn of an upcoming program and book the same films a week or so before. The New York public television station, PBS, Lorcan claimed, did the same thing. "PBS was picking up his program," Lorcan said, "and showing it a week before he did. And it just got to the point where it wasn't coincidental." Sometimes, his booking agent would tip off other theaters to films that were in the offing. Furthermore, Mrs. Otway added, "when the big chains opened, and we'd go to book our films that we'd been booking for years, they'd say, 'We can't release it for another two months, it's been booked.' The distributors would give the chains a guarantee that they wouldn't let anyone else book it for two months."

Competition from the nonprofit venues was especially irksome to Otway. Ed Maguire, who did some work for him, remembered him complaining about the Film Forum and the Public Theater because of their tax-exempt status. But he was particularly angry at the museums for including in their repertoire the revivals that the for-profit rep houses also screened. "The only thing that would get him crazier than Rohauer," Lorcan said, "were museums who were cutting into the commercial enterprises. He'd absolutely go crazy when they were showing something that was commercial. He felt that because they were not dependent on the bottom line, let them show art films, let them show the kind of things that people are fighting Mayor Giuliani over today."

The public was divided in its sentiments towards the theater. There were the film "purists" who complained about the rear projection and poor quality of the 16mm films and who consequently often refused to go there. The late historian Carlos Clarens, Elliott Stein remembered in a *Village Voice* article, used to say he would not set foot in Theatre 80 even if they were showing outtakes from Erich von Stroheim's *Greed* (1924). Stein had similar thoughts. "A few days ago," he wrote, "I [went to see] one of my favorite black-and-white movies. On screen there was no black or white; the movie was all muzzy, fuzzy, skuzzy, tattletale gray. I left after one reel. Complaining does no good. Staying away might—a number of the films so badly shown at Theatre 80 can be quite adequately viewed at the Biograph uptown."[34]

In contrast to the purists, the theater's loyal clientele and the more than 4,000 people on its mailing list found that its strengths—its wide range of presentations and its unique atmosphere—rendered its liabilities insignificant. "The theatre has been one of my favorite haunts," wrote one patron to Mrs. Otway on the closing of the theater. "[I]t had the best sightlines, the best programming, (what a range!), even the best candy counter. [It] was so much more than just a place to see old movies.... The theatre had an indescribable atmosphere, an aura about it, a richness of presence that came from the many personal and loving touches." Another patron wrote on the *Cinema Treasures* website that "[i]t was, without a doubt, the most special theatre in which to see a movie. How can you beat eating a homemade brownie to Billie [Holliday] while waiting to see Bergman in *Notorious* [1946] ... but it was much more than the movie that drew me there. Sitting in that small room, intimate and seemingly carved out of stone, with a group of like-minded enthusiasts, and preferably on a date, was electric."[35]

Interviewed by a *New York Times* reporter at the closing of the theater, Mrs. Otway remembered "when people lined up down to Second Avenue." Large crowds, *Variety* noted in 1980, surprisingly turned out for the obscure pictures in the 1929–35 Hollywood era that were his specialty, forgotten films of such stars as William Powell, Kay Francis, and Marilyn Miller. The shopping bags of letters from different patrons that Mrs. Otway saved over the years attested to the affection of so many for the theater. "Some of them are so charming," she said, "like from this one couple, who used to come from the West Village; they would take the 8th Street route to the theater, and they called it the Theatre 80 express. They met in the theater, they got married after meeting here, and she wrote the most charming letter about it." The New Year's Eve parties were a favorite of the patrons. "*New York Magazine*," Mrs. Otway reminisced, "did an end-of-the-year story on the best things in New York, and ours was the only theater they wrote up. They said it was the most personal theater in New York and they mentioned the New Year's Eve party. We must have turned away 2,000 people, and we sold out every New Year's Eve."[36]

Establishing a rapport with his audience, which had been variously described as local couples and loners, cultural historians, students, shopping bag ladies, middle-aged devotees of Astaire/Rogers films, and young people mostly under the age of thirty, was important to Otway. In addition to greeting and chatting with patrons in the lobby before the films began, he would also address the audience when there was something special about the movie. "When he was the first one to show *Nosferatu*," Lorcan remembered, "he talked about how he got it and put it together."

"He was awfully nice to his audience," Mrs. Otway remembered. "Everyone was treated equally, but he reacted with anger if anyone betrayed his hospitality." Lorcan related an incident where someone tried to steal stills and he threw him out. "He was so angry," Lorcan said, "he hardly knew what to say." He could also be defensive when someone criticized the quality of the film, even when it was justified, as it was in Mandelbaum's experience. One time a patron walked out of the theater during a screening of *Show Boat* because "it was just too unbearable" to watch and asked for his money back. Otway rudely told him he knew nothing about movies, but later apologized after receiving an angry letter from him. Another patron remembered how cantankerous he was. "I asked him once if I could make a request and he told me he didn't take requests, but I could make a suggestion for a film to show."[37]

He was also generous. Mrs. Otway told the story of a little old lady who was suffering from Alzheimer's. "She lived down the block and came in one night and said, 'I'm lost, I don't know how to get home.' And then she said, 'Could I have something?'" Otway gave her hot chocolate and cookies, then found out where she lived, and had one of the staff direct her home. "It became every night," Mrs. Otway said, "which was alright, we didn't mind. But she came for her hot chocolate and cookies and someone to show her how to get home." The single fondest memory of one out-of-town patron was the time Otway delayed the scheduled screening of *Sudden Fear* (1952) for his benefit after learning he would be coming to New York from Pittsburgh the day after the scheduled screening.[38]

Otway died on April 18, 1994, from emphysema; he had been a heavy smoker. He was seventy-two years old. On July 31, 1994, his wife and two sons closed Theatre 80 as a revival house with the final double feature of *Shane* (1953) and *High Noon* (1952) and rented it to the Pearl Theater, a classical theater company. It was his wish to return it to its origins, Lorcan announced in an open letter on behalf of the family. The movie house had been his father's personal undertaking and reflected his personal tastes; "if we endeavored," he explained in the letter, "to carry this program [the movie theater] into the future, his mark on the program would be lost."[39] (Fifteen years later, Lorcan reclaimed the theater and turned it into a mixed media center, featuring both film and live theater.)

Lorcan and his mother also discussed the other factors involved in the decision to close. Poor box-office receipts were not an issue. Paradoxically, if Theatre 80 had completed the year, the final year's gross would probably have been a close second to the theater's most profitable year, 1987. The highlight of that last year was the sale of its one millionth ticket on January 3, 1994, over seven months before the closing. But, like Sommer's assessment of the future of the still-profitable Regency, Lorcan and Mrs. Otway felt that the future of Theatre 80 was uncertain. "Several months before he died," Lorcan said, "we discussed going back to legitimate theater because it [legitimate theater] was now maintained by subscription and by grants [unlike the insecure financial base of the commercial revival houses]."[40]

Mrs. Otway added another problem with continuing as a revival house. "Even if he hadn't got sick," she said, "we probably would have had to go out of business. One thing was 16mm. Howard was able to repair any film of his that was damaged; but distributors wouldn't repair their films. So the product was becoming obsolete. And then the royalties were going up." In addition, 16mm films were becoming rarer as college film societies were turning to videotapes, and distributors were responding by building their videotape libraries and paying less attention to their 16mm ones. Related to the problems with 16mm films was the difficulty in having 16mm projectors repaired. In Lorcan's estimation, videotape did not cut into the revival business, as many thought, but rather into the number of companies that maintained 16mm machinery. They were turning to exclusively maintaining video equipment, and consequently technicians for 16mm equipment were no longer easy to find.

The eulogies to Theatre 80's demise in a number of newspapers and magazines mourned especially the loss of Otway. "It's almost appropriate," wrote the *Columbia Summer Spectator*, "that the last double feature ever to unspool at the Theatre 80 will consist of *High Noon* and *Shane*.... [T]he two films also center around one valiant, honorable man ... duking it out against the corporate goons and blowhards. (What the hell is an Odeon, anyway?)." The *New York Newsday* reporter, in enumerating the attractions of Theatre 80, wrote that the most irreplaceable of these attractions for many patrons was "the theater's founder and guiding extrovert, one-time stage actor Howard Otway, whose young sons slept onstage after he hocked his house to fashion a theater out of an old speakeasy in the 1960s, and who died April 18 at age 72 as a result of cigarette smoking."[41]

Even in foreign countries the theater had had a presence. "I did a lot of work in Italy," Mrs. Otway said, "and once I went into the office of the president of the factory where I was working, and on the wall was this big poster of Manhattan with the names of all the places of interest, and there was Theater 80, in Italy, on this poster. Another time I was in Florence and looked into the newspaper and there, in this Italian newspaper, was a picture of Theater 80 and a picture of Howard and this long interview with Howard." Recalling yet another memory of foreign fandom, she was in front of the theater one day "and there was this group of three people with a camera and one of them was very upset. They were Russians who had come to the States and their main thing was to photograph Theater 80 and do interviews. And we were all closed. They didn't know that."

Otway accomplished two things with his movie theater: he rescued some important films that had been in limbo, and he created a theater with a personal, intimate, yet glamorous ambiance that was so special to so many. He loved his audience. For him it was a critical component in watching a movie. "I own a lot of films," he told the *New York Post* reporter, "but I've never sat down to watch one of them by myself. See, to me an audience is as much a part of the performance as what's on the screen. I don't think seeing a picture on television is anything like seeing it in a theater. I think the person next to you is important. In a sad scene you might hear a sniffle a couple of seats away and it turns you on. A scene that you would smile at in your own home, you laugh out loud in a theater. That's why we still draw such a great audience."[42]

Chapter 11

The Regency: MGM Reigns Supreme

The Regency on the Upper West Side at Broadway between 67th and 68th streets was one of the most popular and commercially successful of the repertory movie theaters—so popular, in fact, that when it was supplanted by a Cineplex Odeon theater, the outpouring of public outrage from politicians and celebrities as well as the general public forced the theater chain to find a replacement theater for the Regency's long-time manager and programmer, Frank Rowley. For eleven years, Rowley had run a succession of well-liked festivals of mainly Hollywood films from the thirties through the fifties, festivals that were distinguished for featuring mostly pristine, 35mm prints. Van Sommer, the owner of the theater and Rowley's employer (Rowley was the only one of the major repertory managers in this book who was not the owner of the lease), attributed the theater's popularity to Rowley's perfectionism. "One of Frank's greatest strengths," he remembered, "was that he was a stickler for everything. He wanted perfection, from his programming to all the little details, making sure the curtains opened and closed (how many theaters had curtains open and close?), the masking was perfect, and the aperture plates were filed all the time. And these little things went a long way towards the audience appreciating it and wanting to come back."[1]

Rowley's background was in theater management. Born and raised in Los Angeles, where his father handled the insurance for a number of movie stars, Rowley moved to New York in 1959 and settled on the Upper West Side. He was hired soon after as stage manager by the producer Alexander Cohen for several of his Broadway shows, including *Ken Murray's Hollywood* and *The Devils* with Jason Robards and Anne Bancroft. When the latter show closed because of a transit strike, he went to work for the puppeteers Bil and Cora Baird at their theater on Barrow Street in Greenwich Village, managing the theater and fundraising for five years. Leaving there and looking for work after his unemployment insurance ran out, he was walking around his Upper West Side neighborhood and decided to check out the neighborhood movie theater, the Regency, for any job openings. "I went by the Regency," he remembered, "and I asked 'Are you looking for anybody?' and they said 'Yes' and I was hired as an assistant manager."[2]

The 560-seat Regency (460 seats on the main level and one hundred in the balcony) was larger than most of the other repertory houses. A Sommer family business for three generations, it was going through major changes when Rowley was hired. It had been an Upper West Side neighborhood theater, the Alden, from its opening in 1931until the mid-sixties when Sommer's father refurbished it and changed its name to the Regency "to show people it was a new theater," Sommer explained. (But he did not remember why his father selected *Regency* for its new name.)[3]

With the refurbishing and name change came a change in its programming. Sommer's father tried to operate it as an art house. "At one point he ran [Andy Warhol's] *Chelsea Girls* [1966, the film screened at the Regency in December 1966]," Sommer remembered, "the raw thing. He could have played it for months and months, but he yanked it out because it was shot sort of funny and looked sort of funny on screen. I don't know how much of it was intentional, how much of it was bad equipment, but there were problems with it: some of it would break down, and it ran at different speeds. My dad thought the theater would get a bad reputation, because the performances were so bad. Then another theater picked it up, and it ran for months and months. He was kicking himself afterwards." According to Hoberman and Rosenbaum in their book *Midnight Movies*, *Chelsea Girls* ran seven weeks at the Regency before moving to the York on First Avenue. Warhol reportedly complained about its being in "that tacky little house" and refused to see it there.[4]

Sommer's father continued booking art films on his own until the late sixties or early seventies when two different programmers rented the theater to put on film festivals. One of them was Sid Geffen, who had not yet opened his own theater. Geffen screened a month-long festival of Janus films while the other programmer ran a Japanese festival. Both did very well. The success of these events gave Sommer and his father the idea of bringing in their own programmer; they hired Russell Schwartz. "I don't know where my dad got Russell from," Sommer said. "Obviously somebody recommended him, and he was great." One of Schwartz's early programming successes for the theater was *Belle de jour* (1967), which ran several weeks.

In 1975, Schwartz expanded the bookings to what Sommer called "the first big thing we did," a festival of MGM revivals. In 1974 MGM had released a compilation film of their musicals, entitled *That's Entertainment!*, in celebration of the studio's fiftieth anniversary. United Artists, which owned the MGM catalogue, was making new prints of some of the films with the intent of showcasing them around the country. Sommer and Schwartz visited Donald Krim, then head of the classics division at United Artists, at his office to discuss booking an MGM festival at the Regency. "This was right down Don's alley," Sommer said. "He was excited about doing this. If we did well with this festival, they could sell it to theaters around the country." The Sommers proposed financing an advertising campaign themselves, a tremendous risk for them. "If the festival didn't do well, it would be a big bath for us," Sommer said. "It was a risk, but if it worked, we would get a lot of the upside of the thing." The series turned out to be a great success. "It got a lot of ink," Sommer said, "because this was the first big MGM festival."

The success of the MGM series, which ran in the summer of 1975, convinced Sommer and his father of the value of the festival format. Nevertheless, throughout the remainder of the year, Schwartz continued to premiere new films along with scheduling revivals. Rowley, whom Schwartz had hired by this time, had taken over the programming of the revival festivals while Schwartz concentrated on the new films. In June 1976 the theater booked another series through Krim and United Artists Classics, "Salute to Warners," for which the distribution company imported Olivia de Havilland to be the guest speaker on opening night. She introduced two of her films, *Adventures of Robin Hood* (1938) and *Captain Blood* (1935), and talked about her experiences at Warners and working with Errol Flynn. It was another successful series, as was a subsequent festival of Katharine Hepburn films, the first in New York devoted to her work. As the theater began to focus more on festivals of revivals, Schwartz lost interest. "I don't think he was interested in old films," Rowley recalled. He finally left to work for several first-run companies, although he continued to consult with Rowley and Sommer. Rowley was put in charge of the programming by late 1976.

The theater was now a full-time revival movie theater, committed entirely to the horizontal series approach. Sommer, a savvy businessman and experienced theater owner, had set the theater's overall direction, persuaded that the horizontally scheduled festivals could best ensure a repertory theater's profitability. It was the antithesis to Otway's approach at the other temple to the classic Hollywood film, Theatre 80 St. Marks. Foreshadowing the argument later expounded by Goldstein, Sommer explained that following the first MGM festival, "we decided that we could get good press, good articles with this format." The length of the festivals, he and his father believed, would also allow time for word-of-mouth to spread, an advantage a theater like Theatre 80, with its daily, unconnected changes in schedule, did not have. "Our format just focused like a laser," Sommer said, "a spotlight on what we were doing." The horizontal series, generally lasting four to six weeks, some even longer, became their modus operandi, generating the press that Sommer considered critical to their commercial success.

Within the direction laid down by Sommer, Rowley was the face and driving force of the theater. The programming was in his hands, although Sommer had final approval. But he generally rubber-stamped Rowley's choices. "Frank had a really free hand in the programming," Sommer said. "I left it up to him. This was his life and I wanted him to be happy." He would seem to have been a peculiar choice as sole programmer, though, since he did not have a background in film. "I didn't really know much about old films at that time [when he began at the Regency]," Rowley said. "As a matter of fact, I thought that people wouldn't want to see the old movies twenty years later, but I was proven wrong." To fill the gap in his knowledge, he educated himself. He read books, especially on the stars, and continued to consult with Schwartz. He also listened to suggestions from various people. "My roommate, Miller Lide," Rowley said, "worked as an actor and knew a lot about movies. He would talk about certain ideas for series and would sometimes look at the synopses I'd written and make them more concise." His co-manager, Morton Tankus, also made recommendations. "I'd come up with ideas for series and for pairings, which he would take or leave," Tankus remembered. Other staff would also contribute. "I had some help from George Morris," Rowley recalled. "He wrote a book on Doris Day and several on theory, and he wanted to know if he could help in any way. He worked in my office and once in a while he mentioned a movie." Periodically, Columbia or another studio would approach him with films that they wanted the Regency to show.[5]

Each series was based on a topic. It could be films from a particular studio ("RKO at the Regency"); a star ("'The Fondas,' Thirty films starring Henry, Jane and Peter Fonda"); a director ("Directed for Comedy," comedies of auteur directors like Billy Wilder and studio directors like Melvin Frank); a theme ("Murder, Mystery, Mayhem"); or a country ("England at Home and Abroad"). The lion's share of the various series was devoted to Hollywood films of the thirties through the fifties. "The Regency would show screwball

The RKO Goldwyn festival at the Regency, 1982. Photofest.

comedies, Jeanette MacDonald and Nelson Eddy movies, Maurice Chevalier," Lopate, who included the Regency in his circuit of indispensable film venues, remembered. "That would be the place to see classic American movies in a slightly indulgent mood. The audience was primed for that. They weren't expecting deep thought when they went to the Regency." The *New York Times* reported in November 1977 that the "Regency was jamming its aisles with fans of early Hepburn, Crawford, and Davis and—starting December 4—MacDonald and Eddy."[6]

The festivals of stars were especially popular. One well-received series in the fall of 1977, "Bette & Joan: The Best of Bette Davis and Joan Crawford," paired the films of the two often feuding divas. "I remember in 1977," a fan posted on *Cinema Treasures* web site, "they featured a Bette Davis/Joan Crawford film festival that lasted several weeks. Opening night was a double feature of *The Old Maid* [1939] and *Mildred Pierce* [1945]. The line was down the block. It was so exciting." Featured actors in the various series often responded positively to Rowley's requests to send him their signed photograph; Katharine Hepburn, however, was a holdout, also refusing to make an appearance for any of her films. Lide, who had toured with Hepburn in Enid Bagnold's *A Matter of Gravity*, had showed her a list of the films in one of her series; her comment with a grin was, "Well, he's certainly got all the stinkers in here!"[7]

Particularly memorable was the opening night of the "Barrymores" series featuring the films of the three Barrymores—Ethel, Lionel, and John. "Joan Bennett was introduced by Rowley," Lide remembered, "and she moved forward with difficulty to the front of the theater to speak on the mike. She told the audience that her main memory in making *Moby Dick* in 1930 with John Barrymore was running around the set trying to escape his advances and pinches." Then, Lide related, came the surprise announcement from Rowley—there was one actress in the house who had worked not only with all three Barrymores, but also with their father, Maurice. Gasps of disbelief came from the audience. It was Blanche Sweet, the silent film star. She was seated in the last row of the orchestra underneath the balcony overhang. "As Rowley beckoned to her to come down to the microphone," Lide continued, "she boomed out in a loud voice, 'I don't need those things!'" To the audience's laughter and applause she rose and proceeded to speak clearly and with great energy. "'Well, I certainly don't remember Maurice Barrymore,'" Lide remembered her telling the audience. "'I was an infant in a baby carriage and travelled with him in a play touring the country in the late 1800s. But I sure knew the other three.'"

Festivals highlighting dance also drew in the public. The "Dancing Ladies" retrospective, the *New York Times* reported in 1980, was "packing the Regency" with not only the Hollywood musicals but also Michael Powell's *Red Shoes* (1948) and some films with Martha Graham, as well as a Spanish gypsy version of *Romeo and Juliet*, *Los Tarantos* (1963), "which first opened here," wrote a Times reporter, "to rave reviews and promptly slid into limbo."[8]

The Academy Award series was a smash hit. "We played all the best pictures we could get," Rowley said, "from the beginning up to the time that the series took place." Unfortunately, three of the "Best Picture" films were unavailable to Rowley. Two were held back because plans for remakes were underway. Elizabeth Taylor, who held the rights to *Around the World in Eighty Days* (1956) as the widow of the film's producer, Mike Todd, was considering a musical version of the film; and MGM/UA had plans to remake *Annie Get Your Gun* with Barbra Streisand. The third film, *All Quiet on the Western Front* (1930), could only be had in a 16mm print, which Rowley rarely, if ever, used, from Universal Studios.

As usual with the repertory theaters, many films were repeated in different series (playing daily or two-day double features necessitated repeats of individual films, although series at the Regency were never repeated). "We could put *Philadelphia Story* in a Katherine Hepburn series," Rowley said, "and then repeat it in a comedy series or an Academy Award series or a James Stewart series—he won an Academy Award for that." First-time appearances of films were duly noted in the calendars with "First performance at the Regency."

Some series were dreamed up by Rowley to fit current events, in an effort to get publicity from the *New York Times*. One of the theater's most successful in its eleven years was "The Three Rebels," which was tied into Patricia Bosworth's new biography on Montgomery Clift. "She wanted us to do some of his movies," Rowley said. "We decided to do not just Montgomery Clift, but also James Dean and Marlon Brando in the same series." Another festival, "Americana: Four Centuries of America on Film," was programmed during the bicentennial year. This one was less successful. "It was a good series for film buffs," Tankus said, "but not for the mass audience. It had the most rarities, but it was the worst attended that we had. People didn't necessarily want to see obscure historical films, and there were a number of clunkers in it."

At least twice, Rowley jettisoned the series format to screen single, stand-alone features: once with the German director G.W. Pabst's *Pandora's Box* (1929), starring the legendary American silent screen star Louise Brooks and the second time with David O. Selznick's *Gone with the Wind* (1939). Brooks was by then a cult figure who had been rediscovered by Henri Langlois, the proprietor of the renowned Cinémathèque Française in Paris. Her memoir, *Lulu in Hollywood*, was coming out, and Krim, who now headed his own distribution company, Kino, wanted to show the film, one of the two with which she was particularly identified (the other being another Pabst film, *Diary of a Lost Girl*, 1929). "We had a big splash showing *Pandora's Box*," Tankus recalled. "We showed it every day for a few weeks as a stand-alone feature, not as part of a series, which was unusual for us, and it actually did extraordinary business. We were selling out for two weeks." For *Gone with the Wind*, which had only been shown theatrically in recent years in poor prints, Rowley screened a beautiful, new Technicolor print. "They had some terrible, blown-up, 70mm version," Tankus said, "that they came out with in the mid-seventies and it was horrible looking. We brought *Gone with the Wind* back in a pristine print, and initially showed it on the schedule for ten days. It just sold out, sold out, sold out; and later we brought it back because people really wanted to see the film on the screen in that beautiful print."

The MGM catalogue was Rowley's principal source for films. "If it weren't for MGM and all the films they had," Rowley said, "we could never have done these kinds of series. They were the nucleus of all the pictures we played." MGM and, later, Ted Turner, who bought the MGM catalogue, were on good terms with Rowley. Other studios, like Columbia Pictures and RKO, seeing the success of MGM's *That's Entertainment!*, followed suit with their libraries. "Many of our films came from the movie studios themselves," Tankus recalled. "Because we had a good reputation and treated the films well, we'd sometimes be able to get films from the studio archives that weren't in normal distribution and hadn't been seen for a while." There were, however, uncooperative studios, like Universal, whose owner, MCA, had bought the pre–1950 Paramount films for television. Consequently, many good titles from both Paramount and Universal were unobtainable. "On occasion," Rowley said, "we couldn't do a series on a particular star because they made pictures at studios that weren't interested in the classics." Dan Talbot had experienced the same problems with MCA.[9]

The theater was treasured by the public for screening only 35mm prints. The difference in quality between 35mm and 16mm was noticeable. "It was 35mm prints that made the films at the Regency look fresh and vibrant," a *Village Voice* reporter wrote. "The alternative, 16mm, costs only $300 per print, but produces a darker, grainier, less detailed image." The quality of the 35mm prints was generally good. "Frank made sure the prints were complete [no scenes or shots were missing]," Sommer recalled. "A lot of times he checked where the films were coming from, making sure they had a good experience elsewhere." The films were also properly screened. "Framing of the picture, a key factor in proper film projection," *Variety* reported on the Regency, "is good, with the old films in 1.33:1 ratio not bleeding beyond the squared off screen. New and 'Scope ratio films are shown complete with masking at top and bottom, rather than forcefitting all pictures into a standard rectangle."[10]

Unlike the other repertory houses, the Regency could often persuade its major distributors to provide it with newly minted prints. "They made good money with us," Rowley explained. Because of the Regency's size and drawing power, the studios could quickly recoup the costs of new prints and make a profit. In addition, the success of a new print at the Regency was a selling point for the distributor. "So they didn't just recoup their money from a run at the Regency," Tankus explained, "but then they would tell the Castro in San Francisco that the Regency did really well with this double bill and you should play it. They probably did it with other theaters as well." From time to time, a new print came from one of the smaller distributors, like Kino, who gave the theater its smash hit, *Pandora's Box*. "Kino would give us good prints because he [Don Krim] knew what kind of business we would do for them," Rowley remembered. "If they couldn't make a good print from a bad one, then they would withdraw it from their catalogue."

On occasion, though, the film companies were uncooperative. Warner Bros., for instance, refused to make new prints of their more recent films from the fifties on. As a result, for the "The Three Rebels" series, the prints of the two James Dean movies, *East of Eden* (1955) and *Rebel without a Cause* (1955), were in bad shape. "*Rebel without a Cause*," Rowley said, "was faded, the color was all gone; and *East of Eden* was trash and junk." Ironically, this double bill grossed an extraordinary amount of money despite the poor print quality, and Warner Bros tried to raise the fee. The Regency sued, and after a long court battle, won the suit. The whole series ended up doing exceptional business. In another instance, Columbia tried to foist a poor print on Rowley. "We were showing *Twentieth Century* with Carol Lombard and John Barrymore," he remembered, "and Columbia had a print that was a dupe; it was very soft focus, nothing very sharp. They said, 'That's all we can do with it,' but that wasn't the truth. We insisted on it and they finally made good prints of it."

Infrequently, the Regency would play a nitrate film. This was a special treat for film buffs since the quality of the original nitrate film was superb. "The black and white of nitrate films was glistening, sparkling," Thalia programmer James Harvey rhapsodized. "This was the kind of visual magic that I regularly saw as a child. But now it was all gone. Only at the Regency could you see it again." Because of the combustibility of nitrate, distributors refused to be responsible for safety in interstate shipments, making such films difficult to get. By the late seventies, fewer of these films existed since most studios had transferred their nitrate to safety films. Rowley claimed he had only shown four or five nitrate films once, for the Warner Bros series, although Jim Harvey believed more were shown there. After that the projectionists refused to handle them again, and the union would not allow it. But there would have been no problem, Rowley insisted, because the projection room had an iron shutter at the glass that would come down if there was ever a fire.[11]

Rowley was not interested in providing program notes—as Lopate noted, the Regency was not known for its intellectual aura—but he enjoyed setting up a different bonus for the audience: guest appearances of Hollywood actors and directors who were featured in his series. Blanche Sweet's appearance for the Barrymore series was among the more memorable ones. Celeste Holm, who lived in Manhattan, made several appearances. "Eric Rhodes from the Fred Astaire movies was here," Rowley remembered, "and Irving Rapper [Warner Brothers film director] and Geraldine Fitzgerald [a Warners' contract actor of the thirties and forties] came during the Bette Davis series." Douglas Fairbanks, Jr., read a telegram from Laurence Olivier on opening night of the series on Olivier, "Knights and Dames," which took place during his birthday. Allan Jones, who lived nearby, spoke before the screening of the 1936 version of *Show Boat*, in which he had starred. On one occasion, a scheduled personal appearance by Frank Capra for the series "Directed by Frank Capra" fell through. No one had informed Capra of the arrangement. "Capra was

Frank Rowley, left, and director Robert Wise, during Wise's personal appearance at the opening of his film *Star!* at the Regency, January 14, 1986. Courtesy Frank Rowley.

getting an award from the Kennedy Center," Rowley recalled, "and Columbia Pictures asked me if I would do a series about his pictures and they would guarantee that he would be there for the opening night. But they didn't tell him that and he didn't show up." Andrew Sarris saved the day by agreeing to speak in Capra's place.

Befitting the old-style personality of the theater, Rowley maintained cast boards in the lobby, listing each film's players and its characters' names, as well as technical credits. "We used a lot of large blowups," Rowley remembered, "to put on the doors, and we changed them each time we did a series. For the series about famous locations around the United States, we had maps, on which we pinpointed where the films took place." Rowley also insisted on using original one-sheets, called posters, to put outside the theater as advertisements for the films. Rounding out the nostalgic feel of the theater was an old-fashioned ticket booth, with rounded glass, which was big enough for only one cashier, a drawback during busy times. The Regency was also one of the last theaters to use its original, carbon arc projector. "These projectors threw a warmer light on the screen," Tankus explained, "that was part of the attraction for people coming to the theater, whether they knew it or not."[12]

Working the old-time carbon arc projector was the aged projectionist, Sal Bevilacqua, who had been there since the days of Sommers' grandfather. The theater was his whole life, Rowley recalled. "He worked six days a week from opening to closing each day and had Sunday off. We had to retire him because he was getting forgetful." Other long-time employees were two elderly ladies, Edie and Vartoohi Kaloostian, whom everyone called Kay. "Edie had a shrieking voice," Tankus remembered. "I'd be in the theater and Edie'd be shrieking 'Morton, Morton,' and I'd run out, thinking someone's attacking her; and she'd say, 'I counted the money and everything worked out.'"

Not all the staff were old-timers. The twenty-five-year-old Tankus, a graduate of New York University with a Bachelor of Fine Arts and major in Cinema Studies, was a typical film buff of the era, spending his free hours haunting the revival houses in the city; Rowley hired him on a part-time basis in July 1979. His responsibilities included researching the cast listings for each film at the Lincoln Center Library for the Performing Arts. A year later Sommer made him a full-time co-manager, to split the shifts with Rowley.[13]

Rowley was not only a meticulous programmer but also a meticulous manager. Under his direction, the theater ran with machinelike precision. In order to have as many showings as possible, he scheduled short intermissions and arranged for people to be herded in and out as quickly as possible. "We didn't have a big lobby," Tankus said, "so we'd fill up the lobby, one set of doors for the audience to leave and another to bring in the people from the lobby. Some people didn't like that cattle-herding mentality, but we had to get them out and then in as quickly as possible." The two co-managers did not countenance anything disturbing the audience, whether it was eating and "stinking up the joint," talking, or any inappropriate activity. "I would tour around the theater," Tankus said, "and see that everything was all right." Henry Fera, a regular patron of the Regency, remembered that it was a good place to see movies. "He [Rowley] ran it so well. He wouldn't tolerate talking. He ran it professionally."[14]

Sommer appreciated Rowley's work, but in one area they disagreed, reflecting their differing slants on programming. "If there was one thing that Frank and I went back and forth a lot on," Sommer said, "was that I was pushing for what would be more commercial and Frank was more like a curator. He would want to bring in obscure films to complete a festival, films that people wouldn't want to see, whatever. I said to him, 'You're doing this like it's nonprofit, but we are not nonprofit, it's not our object to do what a museum does.'" While recognizing the need for the popular films, Rowley, nevertheless, wanted the festivals to illustrate the full range of work of a director or star. "If you did a series on Bette Davis," he said, "people wanted to see more than *All about Eve* and *Jezebel* (1938). They wanted to see some of the earlier ones and some of the later ones." The series celebrating MGM's sixtieth birthday, reported the *New York Times*, included films that "don't usually make the circuit of revival pictures." Still, Sommer usually let Rowley get his way, even when he resisted certain commercially viable concepts, such as Japanese festivals. "Japanese festivals always did well," Sommer recalled. "I asked Russell what Frank had against Japanese films, and Russell said, 'A lot of guys would come in dressed as samurai. Maybe he felt it would turn off part of our regular audience.'" Nevertheless, he did curate an eleven-week Japanese series in April 1977, which opened with the American premiere of a pair of "Kung-Fu diversions," *Zatoichi's Fire Festival* (1970) and *Zatoichi Meets His Equal* (1971).[15]

Foreign films in general were not his forte. His employee, George Morris, who was a protégé of Andrew Sarris's and a contributing writer to Sid Geffen's *Thousand Eyes* magazine, tried to interest him in the foreign auteur directors, but Rowley insisted that their films did not appeal to his audience. "He and Sarris tried to get us to play some Rossellini," Rowley remembered, "some Godard, that kind of stuff. But that cleared the house. We did a Renoir series once, we did Truffaut, but not too much of the others." In Tankus's assessment, Rowley was more comfortable with the Hollywood films and did not know much about the foreign films. Yet he was not rigid; he did put on some foreign language series (the winter 1977 series, for example, "The Regency Presents Europe," featured films mostly from England, France, and Italy) and included foreign language films in other series when they were appropriate.

At the end of each year, Rowley would put on two special events. One was the annual "Best of the Year" series each December, the slow time for revival houses, featuring the best attended films of the year. "Best of the Year" was a special favorite of Sommer's. "I was happy," he said, "because these were more commercially acceptable films that people would come to see." The other elite event was a champagne gathering of the audience after the last show on New Year's Eve, similar to Theatre 80 St. Marks's annual New Year's Eve gala. "Frank asked me one year if we could do that," Sommer said, "and it became a tradition. We didn't advertise or push it, but regulars who had been there previously would know about it. People really appreciated it. It gave them a sense of belonging, that they were part of something if they came on New Year's Eve. People would mill around and talk and discuss films, whatever. It was fun, a nice touch. I was glad Frank thought of it."

Who came to the Regency for its Hollywood classics? There was no one type. Different audiences were attracted to different series. "A musical crowd," Tankus said, "was a little bit different from a film noir crowd." The music series had an older audience—senior citizens preferred the more genteel, nostalgic films of Grace Moore, Jeanette Mac-Donald, and Nelson Eddy—while a series like "The Three Rebels" attracted a younger one. The dance series, which mixed ballet films with Gene Kelly and Fred Astaire starrers, brought in the Lincoln Center dancers in droves, while the opera series were seen by opera lovers and opera professionals like Beverly Sills and Leontyne Price, who came to see Bernardo Bertolucci's *Luna*, in which her recording of an aria was on the soundtrack. Vladimir Horowitz and older members of the Carnegie Hall orchestra came to see the "Looking at Music" series with a classical music theme. Film buffs came to see the classics in good prints. "I went to the Regency," Lopate recalled, "because I wanted to see, for example, Cukor's *Keeper of the Flame*, which would be a typical example of a Cukor film with Hepburn. I wanted to find out what it was like. It turned out not to be so good, but it was a good print."

People throughout the metropolitan area would frequent the Regency. "All types of people came from all over the city and other parts of the area," Rowley recalled, "not just Manhattan, but Brooklyn and Connecticut and New Jersey." Gays made up a certain portion of the audience, and the afternoon crowd of seniors who took advantage of the senior price, another sector. The latter crowd often included some celebrities of an earlier era, such as Geraldine Fitzgerald and Lincoln Kirstein, founder of the New York City Ballet. Ingrid Bergman's young grandchildren first saw their grandmother on the screen at the Regency when their mother, Pia Lindstrom, Bergman's daughter by her first marriage, brought them to see *The Bells of St. Mary's* (1945). Woody Allen would sometimes come alone in the afternoons, often after the movie started, and would leave before it ended in order not to be bothered by fans. When he was courting Mia Farrow before their relationship became a news item, they frequently came together to the theater and sat in the back row. "Before anyone knew," Tankus recalled, "we knew. What's funny was that, once or twice, Mia Farrow would come out and in her little voice would say, 'I think the film is a little out of focus.' You knew that he sent her out; he didn't want to come out himself."

Some of the celebrities brought back pleasant memories for the two managers: Bernadette Peters sweetly asking Tankus to help a young girl find her grandmother in the theater; William Hurt, on a return to New York after his success on the West Coast, acknowledging Tankus's greeting of welcome as he walked past the theater; Bill Murray engaging in friendly chats with Tankus on the days when he was attending a Renoir series. Other celebrities, though, evoked less pleasant memories. Dustin Hoffman was one. Tankus remembered him bypassing the cashier once and walking into the lobby without identifying himself and telling Tankus that he was "only staying twenty minutes" as he entered the theater.

In the evenings people came after work, and the weekends saw the dating and married couples. Making up a significant part of the audience were the regulars—not the film buffs or the ones with specialized interests, but the average moviegoer, who came to see mostly everything and discovered in the process that they were receiving a film education. "I've been coming here," a patron told Rowley in a letter at the time of the theater's closing, "since its start as a revival house in 1976 when I was 17.... I've always thought the Regency's programs were outstanding. I've lost count of how many films I had the privilege of seeing for the first time in this theatre."[16]

By the late eighties, the future of the repertory houses was looking bleak, but Rowley, one of the last die-hard defenders of the old ways, adamantly continued as usual. In the earlier years, in the seventies and eighties, the programs of the Regency sold themselves. Rowley would send out a press release for an upcoming series, and the papers would write articles in the Friday or even Sunday editions on the stars or directors that the series featured. The *Times* was especially supportive of the theater, Sommer remembered, particularly its film critics Peter Flint and Howard Thompson. Rowley also mentioned Janet Maslin. Flint and Guy Flatley, another *Times* critic, did the last interview with Irving Berlin that he ever gave, for a Fred Astaire–Ginger Rogers series at the Regency. Not all reviews or articles were positive. When Kael wrote a negative review in the *New Yorker* of a Bette Davis film, Rowley complained in a letter to her. "She printed a damning review of one of the pictures we opened with in the Bette Davis series, and I didn't like it. So I wrote her a letter. She called me on the phone. She was angry with me writing her a letter and said that Bette Davis had made only two good pictures in her life or something like that. I said that we were trying to open a series and when they see a bad review of one of her pictures, they may stay away. I said, 'It's been a long time since you've probably seen her movies.' She didn't like that."

Later in the eighties, though, the newspapers were giving less coverage to the Regency series and more, Rowley complained, to the Film Forum. He believed that the *New York Times*, for example, was favoring the Film Forum because it was newer and needed the support; but Tankus thought Rowley's attitude toward publicity was the problem. He pointed out that Goldstein, who was the repertory programmer for the Film Forum, was aggressive in selling the theater's series to the newspapers while Rowley, with his atypical attitude for a theater manager, refused to plug his films. The calendars, for example, consisted only of one-sentence synopses of the plots. "I didn't think it was good to say, 'This is a good example of film noir,'" Rowley said, "and give a quote from Pauline Kael or somebody like that. People should decide on their own." The only comment he would add to a plot synopsis would be mention of an Academy Award if the film had won one. Otherwise, even if it was a great film but without an Academy Award to its credit, he would not promote the film. "If *It Happened One Night* hadn't won four Academy Awards," Tankus said, "the blurb would have read 'Newspaperman meets an heiress and complications ensue.' He was not a Bruce Goldstein, who could make something out of nothing."

In the changing times, however, the shaky situation of the repertory houses required a more aggressive publicity approach. The Regency's audience was getting smaller, and the income had to support growing rental fees and the extra costs that were peculiar to repertory houses, but not to mainstream theaters, like advertising. "We had a big advertising budget," Sommer said, "which I always thought was worthwhile, at least in the *New York Times*. And our flyers were beautiful, they were fun, but they were expensive to print." He found the *Village Voice*, however, less cooperative. "I had a running battle over the years with the *Village Voice*,

Geraldine Fitzgerald and Frank Rowley in front of the Regency, April 1986. Photograph by Robin Holland. Courtesy Frank Rowley.

which wasn't giving us what I thought was our fair share of articles and write-ups." At some point he reduced his advertising in that newspaper.

There was another element whose full significance Rowley seemed blind to—the real estate revolution. "Small, independent theaters—those with one or two screens that aren't part of a chain," *Newsday* reported in late 1985, "are finding it increasingly difficult to survive in the face of tremendous obstacles…." But because the Regency was one of the few New York repertory houses in the mid-eighties to maintain its profitability, Rowley thought it was invulnerable to the real estate onslaught. The last two years of the theater's existence continued to show a healthy box office; all its series during this period topped the theater's break-even point of $8,000 a week. Ten reached gross weekly averages ranging from $15,610 ("Films of Woody Allen, Charlie Chaplin and Buster Keaton") to $22,201 ("Orson Welles" series), with four in the $17,000 range ("François Truffaut and Friends," "Fred and Ginger," "Sixty Years of Comedy," and "The Films of James Stewart"); the remaining series ranged from a low of $11,180 ("Raoul Walsh Retrospective") to a high of $14,437 ("Jean Renoir Retrospective"). The penultimate series before the Regency's close in September 1987—"Three Beauties," the films of Jean Harlow, Vivien Leigh, and Marilyn Monroe—averaged a weekly gross of $20,112 in its seven-week run. "We were successful all the time at that location," Rowley told a *Newsday* reporter in 1987. "Although attendance had dropped off, we were still doing respectable business." But the changing economics of film exhibition trumped the continuing profitability of the theater. What led to the closing was the offer by Cineplex Odeon for the theater's lease. "Cineplex Odeon came into the picture," Rowley said, "and he [Sommer] told me he got such a good offer that he couldn't resist it."[17]

From Sommer's perspective, he had no option; the economics of running a single screen theater no longer made sense. "I could have stayed there," he said. "I didn't have to get out. But the costs were going up. There was no question that video and then cable were cutting in to what we were doing. Granted there were people who wanted to see it on the big screen, but you did lose some audience to those other outlets." Equally important, he anticipated being forced out soon by his landlord. "The landlord, like all landlords," he said, "was looking for the best use of his property." The lease was coming to an end, and the landlord would most likely sell the lease to Cineplex Odeon, which was buying theaters in the area. Sommer finally decided to sell the remainder of his lease to the theater chain. "The handwriting was on the wall. Cineplex presented an opportunity to get out and salvage something, because the trend was getting worse and worse. So for the time I had left, at least I would salvage something for the business and for the other owners [family members jointly owned the lease with him]."

On September 2, 1987, the Regency abruptly closed midway through a seventy-fifth anniversary tribute to Paramount Pictures, almost four months after the closing of the Thalia. The announced closing triggered an avalanche of condemnation from different segments of the New York community. Letters of protest from the general public were written to Cineplex Odeon as well as notes of condolence and sadness to the theater and Rowley; New York politicians on all three levels of government—such as Congressman Ted Weiss, State Assemblyman Jerrold Nadler, and the mayor's director of the Office of Film, Theatre and Broadcasting, Patricia Reed Scott—urged Cineplex Odeon to reconsider their decision; and Community Board 8, the *Village Voice* reported, passed a resolution supporting the continuation of the Regency as a revival theater. Most of the major New York City newspapers and magazines, as well as the Upper West Side newspapers, carried prominent articles on the closing, some urging letter-writing campaigns. Reporters reported on the sorrow and anger of average New Yorkers: "'How could you do this to us?'" a *Times* article quoted a woman futilely asking the only theater representative present, the ticket taker. Many of the complaints lamented the decimation of cultural life on the Upper West Side as well as in the whole city.[18]

The biggest event became a September 3 rally in front of the Regency, arranged by ROAR (Revivals Only at the Regency), a coalition of actors, directors, and filmgoers. The *Village Voice* reported that more than 200 protestors listened to Isaac Asimov, Councilwoman Ruth Messinger, State Senator Franz Leichter, the songwriting team Betty Comden and Adolph Green, and actors Celeste Holm, Tony Randall, and Phyllis Newman, among others, condemn the Regency's closing, "this city's finest revival house." Betty Comden, articulating the feelings of many, told the crowd, as reported by the *Westsider*, that "[a]nything that takes away from the color and diversity of New York diminishes our city." Tony Randall remembered the standing ovation that Laurence Olivier's *Henry V* received at the Regency: "...the audience stood and cheered! It was more than a movie; it was a genuine theater experience. You don't get that on cassette." The rally drew surprising coverage, the *Village Voice* reported, not only from local radio, TV, and press, but also from national and foreign media—Canadian Broadcasting, *The Toronto Globe and Mall*, National Public Radio, Cable News Network, and *Entertainment Tonight*. The *International Herald Tribune*'s story went to 164 countries.[19]

This entire public outcry produced results, at least for a time. "He [Garth Drabinsky, the Cineplex Odeon chairman] got such a bad press," Rowley said, "that it affected his other theaters in the city, so he agreed to let us use one of his other theaters." Of the movie theaters he offered, Rowley chose the New Carnegie on West 57th Street, which was refurnished and renamed the Biograph Theater. Almost six months after the closing of the Regency, in February 1988, the Biograph opened. But, wrote the *New York Post*, "[t]he 'antiseptic' Biograph lacks the Regency's 'old-time ambiance,' which added to the enjoyment of vintage films." Rowley ran it for several years before Cineplex Odeon closed it. "The lease was coming up," Rowley said, "and they [Cineplex Odeon] didn't renew it, I guess they didn't think it was worth their effort."[20]

Rowley approached Sommer about taking over the lease and converting the theater into two screens; Sommer was interested, but the costs of renovating the theater, including installing an elevator, was too high. Cineplex Odeon offered Rowley the programming position at the Worldwide Theater on 50th Street, which it had recently opened, but he did not like the location. "It would have been mixed with everything else and it wouldn't work." Rowley, instead, eventually ran another revival theater, the Gramercy, on East 23rd Street, which was rented by a nonprofit organization from the Samuel Goldwyn Company. But that failed. "It didn't work because of the location," Rowley said. "We didn't have enough money to run it. We started off pretty well, but it didn't last very long." He was about to retire when Dan Talbot asked him to work for him at his Lincoln Plaza Theaters.

The demise of the Regency had concrete repercussions for the revival movement. Without the Regency, Krim, president of Kino International, told the *Newsday* reporter at the Regency's closing, it would be harder for Kino and other distributors to make or keep 35mm prints. As he explained, "It can cost up to $3,000 to strike a new 35mm print, and no one will do that if they can't recoup the cost quickly. In the past, a booking at the Regency would almost justify making a new 35 [sic], if we didn't have one, because of the size of the audience there. Ultimately the closing of the Regency will mean more use of 16mm, because we won't be able to replace our 35s as they wear out."[21]

"We did it right," Sommer reminisced. "Everyone—Frank and Morty and the rest—were the best, they made it work, that's why we were able to do it so long. The people that came felt part of the Regency. One of the best things, from the very early days, was when Russell suggested that, if it was a musical, he and I stand at the right and left sides of the theater at back and applaud when the dance number finishes, and let's see if we can get the audience to applaud. We did that and a couple of people applauded, and then some more did it. We did it at particular numbers, a musical or dance number, and eventually it became automatic. The audience became accustomed to applauding and it was great. Wow, that doesn't happen in too many places. I guess it gave people a special feeling to go there." Mandelbaum remembered the applause. "When the Regency audience applauded musical numbers, it was a theatrical experience. I'd see films like *Bells Are Ringing* and it was like going to a theater."

It was the testimonials, though, of the average Regency patrons and the scholars and film critics that expressed the special quality of the Regency. Patrons remembered the personal touches from the staff. "You know me by sight," wrote one patron to Rowley when she heard of the closing, "but this is the first time you're learning my name. I'm the woman about whom you so kindly inquired many years ago of my husband, when you hadn't seen me for a long time.... I was deeply touched by your interest in one of your customers." Patrons wrote to Rowley about the influence the Regency had on their film education. "I was both saddened and dismayed to read of the Regency's imminent demise," another patron wrote to Rowley, describing vividly the beginnings of her film education at the Regency. "I first visited the Regency in February of '77. It was a very cold night, and I don't think there were a dozen people in the theatre. I was a budding Bogey fan, and you were showing *In a Lonely Place* and *Knock on Any Door,* 2 [sic] Bogeys I'd never seen. Well, Mr. Rowley, I fell in love with your theatre that night, and have since returned literally hundreds of times.... I had my introduction to dozens upon dozens of classic pictures, stars and talents, not to mention many obscurer films and personalities I'd never heard of before." Still another patron unintentionally validated Rowley's insistence on complete retrospectives. "You have educated New Yorkers to unknown films as well as classics.... How will we [now] become aware of the lesser films as well as the major films of Bogart, Cagney, Grant, Gable, Davis, Brando, Clift, Dean, and all the many, many stars you introduced us to in your wonderful, well thought out, in depth retrospectives."[22]

Richard Schickel, film critic for *Time,* spoke for the many film critics and scholars who treasured the Regency. "To put it simply," he wrote in a Letter to the Editor in the *New York Times,* "the Regency was the only revival house that made a serious and imaginative effort to reach beyond the standard 'classic' American film repertory and bring to a modern audience films that have been lost in the historical shuffle, films that helped one perceive new dimensions in the careers of the great stars and directors of the past, films that added to our general sense of the industry that produced them and the culture that absorbed them." Summing up his tribute to the Regency, Schickel drew a striking analogy to what the loss of the Regency meant to most. "[T]he feelings generated by the loss of this institution are akin to those opera lovers would feel if it were suddenly announced that the Metropolitan was being shuttered and that henceforth they would have to stay in touch with their repertory exclusively on compact disk."[23]

Chapter 12

The Thalia: A Temple to B Films, Trashy Films and Other Critical Rejects

The venerable, beloved Thalia, inactive since 1973 as a repertory movie house, was restored to its former life four years later in January 1977 by an eccentric, obsessive film nerd, the 26-year-old Richard Schwarz; and for the next ten years, he indulged his passion for the noncanonical segments of film history—rarely seen films, the belittled B films of the 1950s, the trashy films of Edward Wood, Jr. His theater was influential in popularizing the postwar film genre, film noir, and resurrecting the work of non–Disney cartoonists. Andrew Sarris told a *Daily News* reporter in the final days of the theater that the classics and cult films that few other theaters featured made the Thalia unusual and important to the world of cinema. "The Thalia always showed films unavailable elsewhere," he explained, "such as the 1950s [*Little*] *Shop of Horrors* and obscure films by Chabrol, Fassbinder, and Coppola. Those of us interested in arty and obscure films treasure it. It has uncomfortable seats and terrible sightlines, but it made up for that by its adventurous programming."[1]

Schwarz was born in Middletown, Connecticut, on May 2, 1951, and spent his early years in boarding schools. He majored in film as an undergraduate at Emerson College in Boston and graduated in 1974. While an undergraduate, he also became an expert in repairing movie projectors, and put himself through college buying and selling the seats and projection equipment of the movie theaters in the Northeast and other sections of the U.S. that were closing in droves in the sixties and seventies. "His idea of a holiday was to put the dog in the car and go out and visit old theaters," Ralph McKay, an independent curator, related in an obituary for Schwarz for the Upper West Side's local newspaper, *The West Side Spirit*. "He leafed through back issues of *Photoplay* in order to find out where the theaters were located. Sometimes they were gutted, but maybe the booth was still there." Schwarz had a large collection of carbon arc projectors, his sister, Gail Aronow, recalled. "I remember so well," she said, "he would be driving around with all this equipment in the back of his car, he would fix it, and sell the equipment, shipping a lot to South America." His little business often took more of his time than his studies.

"He was loosey goosey," she said, "about going to undergraduate classes because he was so busy."[2]

In addition to his equipment business, he also worked in movie theaters, mostly during the summers. One job following graduation, he had once told his sister, was at a blaxploitation movie theater in Hartford, Connecticut. A part-time job while he was still in college had him screening films for obscenity for the Boston district attorney. His sister also remembered him talking about doing lighting in Boston's "Combat Zone" for a well-known stripper named Chesty Morgan. After graduating he operated a series of summer repertory cinemas in the New England area, including Toad Hall at the famed Music Inn in Stockbridge. His first full-time theater was the Bijou in Cold Spring, New York. "It was a tough town in those days," Aronow, who helped him, recollected. "We opened with *Patton* and soon thereafter played *Gone with the Wind*. We spent a great deal of time cleaning up popcorn thrown all over the theater by the very rowdy local audience." In these early years he made frequent visits to experienced theater owners around New England to understand their operations; probably his most influential mentor was an aged member of the well-known Loew family who lived in or near Worcester, Massachusetts.

During his final days at the Bijou, he bought the Thalia's lease. Since its demise as a repertory movie theater in 1973, the Thalia had become an undistinguished movie house, showing a random selection of first runs and reruns of relatively recent releases, until it closed in the summer of 1976. But its past still resonated with Schwarz. "It was the Thalia," McKay recounted for the *West Side Spirit* obituary, "that always attracted Schwarz more than any other movie house. He would come to the Thalia and admire its wonderful, dilapidated state." He leased the Thalia on a ten-year basis in December 1976.[3]

After acquiring the Thalia, Schwarz later told a *New York Post* reporter, he spent almost his entire savings of $10,000 to repair the equipment and physical space. "When I took over here," he said, "the equipment was in bad shape, so I replaced that, and redid the seats and put in a new screen." His sister remembered his description of the theater as having been largely stripped of equipment when he took it over. Proud of the state-of-the-art projection equipment that he installed, he boasted to the reporter that his was the only theater in New York that could show 3-D properly, as well as other formats. "We can show the old sound film ratio, the European widescreen, and the American widescreen. Vistavision, too. And silents."[4]

Despite his claim that he made physical improvements, including redoing the seats, the staff who were interviewed had different recollections of the physical condition. James Harvey, who became one of his first programmers, remembered telling him, "'Richard why don't you fix this or that?' But he would answer, 'No, no. The theater was okay.'" Howard Mandelbaum, who later created some of the programs and film notes, similarly remembered that "[p]eople got restless with seats that were falling apart and also with the poor insulation, so that if you were inside the theater you could hear people arguing in the lobby." Schwarz's modus operandi, he claimed, was "to go cheap." He most likely had spent the greater part of his savings on his projection equipment, which meant most to him. There were other factors as well, whether he considered them or not, that may have hampered any serious attempts at physical improvements. Replacing the smaller seats, which were no longer being made, for larger ones, for instance, would have meant a loss in patronage capacity and therefore a financial loss for the already financially strapped theater, as Ursula Lewis had previously realized. Furthermore, while acknowledging that the theater was run on a shoestring, Aronow pointed out that the meager profits barely, if at all, covered the expenses; and her brother rejected going the nonprofit route, which he thought was dishonest. "This discussion I recall quite clearly," she wrote in an e-mail. "He was trying hard to be self-sufficient, a central aspect of his character."⁵

Greg Ford, who curated the annual animation series, however, liked its funkiness. "I loved the setup," he said. "The Thalia was interestingly tacky, and Richard had something to do with this. He had a following, a dedicated audience, who was there for the movies, not for coffee or candy." And it did have its charms. One charming feature of the theater was its mascot, Schwarz's dog Carol, who, Mary Maguire remembered, "saw every movie, and if she liked you, she sat next to you. She was adorable."⁶

Richard Schwarz. Courtesy Gail Aronow.

His dedicated audience included students from Columbia University and other New York colleges, neighborhood patrons, film buffs outside the neighborhood like Maguire, and offbeat patrons like Butterfly McQueen, the actress whose first, and most famous, film role was Prissy in *Gone with the Wind* (1939). "Butterfly McQueen was this eccentric woman living very modestly in Harlem," Mandelbaum remembered, "who would come down to the Thalia, and because she had no money, she would give the ticket taker a piece of fruit. I was there when she paid a visit, and there was a black couple in the lobby, and the man said to his wife, 'Can you imagine, a big star like that chooses to live with her people.' His impression must have been that she could have lived in Beverly Hills, this woman who couldn't even pay the eighty-five cents for the ticket."

Schwarz was himself eccentric. "He liked to play movie mogul, to talk in the voice of a hard-nosed businessman," Bruce Goldstein, who later worked for him, recollected. "He was a little meshugah [crazy]." He could be explosive towards his staff, even at inappropriate times. "He would yell at me and others," Ford said, "when we were in the booth editing the cartoon series; and of course the whole audience could listen. But to him it was like they were in his living room." Sometimes, his provocativeness had a masochistic edge. Once he so exasperated the normally placid Ford, who had never struck anyone, that he hit him and knocked him to the floor.⁷

His dealings with the public could be equally abrasive. Goldstein related an incident when Schwarz came out of his office to talk to the movie director Garson Kanin and his wife, the actress Ruth Gordon, who had come to see that day's program; he asked Kanin if it was true that he stole his film *The Marrying Kind* (1952) from *The Crowd* (King Vidor's silent 1928 film). "He didn't care who he offended," Harvey said. "He drove everyone crazy, but he didn't care." Harvey called him the Andy Kaufman of the repertory scene.

Yet positive aspects to his personality counterbalanced to some extent the disconcerting ones. Ford found him funny and at times gracious, such as the time he complimented Ford's girlfriend, who sometimes played piano at a jazz club, on her skill with jazz. "I could tell he was sincere," Ford remembered. "He knew jazz." Michael Silberman, another former employee, remembered him as "absolutely maddening, combative, self-absorbed and self-destructive, but he was also very generous to people he considered his friends. He would buy lunches and dinners, lend his car, etc. He had a soft spot for the crazies, which isn't a bad thing. Quirky guy. But I miss him." So does Harvey. "He was a pain in the ass to customers and staff," he said, "yet when he wasn't there, you missed the energy. The place was dead." Mandelbaum similarly recognized "his manic energy that was incredible."[8]

It was his passion for film that energized the theater. "He lived and breathed movies," said Aronow. "The Thalia was his own world." This world could be endless, all-night sessions watching films with others, arguing about them, editing the Hollywood outtakes that he had scavenged from the trash cans of the distribution centers or had traded with film collectors. "[P]robably there was no other revival house where the act of programming was so impassioned," Harvey wrote in his tribute to Schwarz for the Anthology Film Archives, which launched a film noir series and other annual programs in his memory. "He liked to stay up all night—preferably inside the Thalia, surrounded by the highly variegated types who constituted his staff, more or less, as well as invited outsiders who could be encouraged to engage in round-voiced controversy about a movie, or to watch a two a.m. screening of another one, or to look at yet another edition of his *Hollywood Out-Takes* movie with the new footage he'd just found—when some of us who had seen it too often were trying to slip out the door and go home to bed. 'Don't you want to have coffee afterwards?!' Richard would say if he spotted you leaving—with real disappointment."[9]

His passion for the rare film gave the theater its cult reputation. Shortly after opening the Thalia, Schwarz was already considered by the *New York Times* film critic Vincent Canby as one of the most adventurous revival house programmers in the city. In a review of the "new" Thalia, Canby praised the management for "maintaining one of the most original, unusual, and, sometimes, odd programming policies of any theater in New York.... When you drop into the Thalia, ... you'll find ... a film that isn't likely to turn up in any circuit house. It might not be great or even good, but it will be rare." According to Harvey, he loved ferreting out and screening films that had never been released in New York, especially B films and other minor films that no one else had discovered.[10]

The theater's adventurous reputation, however, was also partly rooted in another one of Schwarz's idiosyncrasies—his refusal to pay percentages, a sliding attendance scale, for rentals. He would only pay flat rates, even when a percentage basis was more economical. As a result, the big studios like MGM and Universal would not do business with him, leaving as his only options the B movies from minor studios like Eagle-Lion and Allied Artists, films from small distributors, ones in the public domain, and prints from his extensive private collection. "It drove the rest of us crazy, his insistence on the flat rate," Harvey remembered. "A lot of the things that the Regency or the other places could get we could never get." Ford remembered that his attachment to public domain films became a running joke. "He would ask, 'Is it pd [public domain]? Is it pd?' It became a joke with him and us. 'Gee, *Raiders of the Lost Ark* is doing great. Is it pd?'"

His collection of public domain films included both 16mm and 35mm prints of American and foreign silent films, American films of the thirties and forties, foreign sound classics, and art house films. They came from different sources, including the dumpsters of the distribution centers in the area. "I once went with him to Fort Lee to the storage warehouses," Aronow remembered, "where he would literally dive into the dumpsters behind the warehouses for the old footage that they were always throwing out and that in some cases made their way into his movie, *Hollywood Out-Takes and Rare Footage*." At the end of his life, she wrote in an e-mail, her brother donated the bulk of his film collection to the UCLA Film & TV Archive. At the time, this legacy constituted the largest private film collection ever received by that archive. A much smaller collection of his early nitrate films stayed at MoMA, where they had been on deposit for some years.[11]

When he was working for Schwarz, Goldstein catalogued his collection, which numbered 500 to 1,000 prints at the time. "A lot was crap," Goldstein recalled, "but they were good prints, they were all good quality. He had a couple of really good films that were in public domain then, but aren't any more." Goldstein explained that a loophole in the copyright laws in those days allowed people to exploit films without paying for them: if the films didn't have a copyright notice on the main title, they were considered public domain. "So a lot of people jumped on this as a way to release films like *Grand Illusion* [1937]. A U.S. law changed that; foreign producers, Europeans mostly, are now able to recover their copyrights. For this reason, we're now able to show films in better prints. In those days we were showing them in these crappy prints."

Obsessed with getting the best quality print he could, Schwarz would stay up all night in the projection room, cannibalizing prints, combining the best parts of defective prints into one good print. "Sometimes it resulted in an unsatisfying hybrid," Goldstein said. "You'd be watching a beautiful print; all of a sudden it would become dupy for five minutes with bad sound, and then back to the good print. Sometimes I wondered if it was worth doing that way." But he had little choice; it was impossible in those days for most repertory houses to get new prints from the distributors. Repertory audiences, consequently, were used to prints with scratches throughout, splices, missing dialogue, and, sometimes, even missing scenes. "You were used to seeing scratches at the beginnings and ends of reels in just about every film," Goldstein remembered.

In addition to screening 35mm and 16mm films, Schwarz sometimes showed 3-D films. "He was obsessed with 3-D," said Goldstein. "He would get these old 3-D prints and fix them so they'd synchronize." Goldstein remembered the mending Schwarz did on the last remaining 3-D print of *The French Line* (1953) with Jane Russell. "He would put a slug in where there were missing frames. He wouldn't remove a frame, that was anathema to him; he'd put one back. So if he had a frame here and it's not on the right eye, he'd put a slug in. That's not the best way to do 3-D. The best way is to remove the frames." One patron who frequented the Thalia recalled seeing the 3-D *French Line* at the theater. "In the eighties," he wrote on the *Cinema Treasures* website, "Schwarz hunted down rare dual projector prints of *The French Line* (in Technicolor with the cut bubble bath sequence) and even borrowed a print of *Carnival of Souls* from [its director] Herk Harvey."[12]

The Thalia's sometimes less-than-satisfactory prints, however, were offset by its unusual programming. While Schwarz programmed the typical fare of a serious cinematheque—retrospective screenings, for example, of such art house favorites as Bergman, Truffaut, Kurosawa, and Fellini (one patron remembered that the audience of film buffs could always be engaged in stimulating conversations)—he mixed these with the quirky, rare films that he unearthed, such as the first movie treatment of a Frank Baum work, the 1914 *Patchwork Girl of Oz*, which he acquired from the Baum estate and played for the first time in sixty-four years in a triple feature with two other Oz pictures: *The Wizard of Oz* (1939) and a Wizard of Oz cartoon. Thalia patrons also saw the first revival of the Alan Freed Rock 'n' Roll movies; the first major retrospective of movies from the Poverty Row studios—Monogram, PRC, and Republic Pictures—that Godard and Truffaut lauded; and the first retrospective of silent screen legend Louise Brooks, including a rare showing of her bizarre B-Western swan song, *Overland Stage Raiders* (1938), opposite John Wayne.[13]

Especially appealing to the young was the lowbrow, "junk movie madness," the *New York Daily News* reported, "by such déclassé directors as Russ Meyer, Roger Corman, and the incomparable Ed Wood, Jr." The New York theatrical debuts of works of Wood, considered the worst director of all time—*Plan 9 from Outer Space* (1959), *Glen or Glenda?* (1953), *Jail Bait* (1954), and *Violent Years* (1956)—guaranteed enthusiastic audiences. "From the applause that greets his name in the opening titles," Delaney reminisced in his history of the Thalia, "to the last frame of madness, an Ed Wood audience is the most fun to be had at the movies." Other low-budget treats included the teenage exploitation picture, Renee Daalder's *Massacre at Central High* (1976), "an original, fascinating work" wrote the *Times*'s Canby, that was "not a movie for elegant East Side first-run houses but looks right at the Thalia," and *The Incredibly Strange Creatures Who Stopped Living and Became Mixed-UP Zombies* (1964), a legendary low-budget horror film about hideous goings-on at a carny sideshow, which shared billing with *Queen of Outer Space* (1958) in Cinemascope with Zsa Zsa Gabor. "The old Thalia used to run everything and anything," a patron reminisced. "I remember a triple bill of Zsa Zsa Gabor in *Queen of Outer Space*, *Plan 9 from Outer Space* and the one with Beverly Garland where the creature looked like a giant Asparagus, damn I can't remember the name. Those were fun times."[14]

One of Delaney's fond memories was what was "probably the theater's most famous offering"—the thirty-seven-hour, nonstop marathon of twenty-six horror movies starting at 2:00 in the afternoon on December 5, 1986, and ending at 1:49 in the morning two days later. "This marked the first and only time in movie history," he wrote, "that *Night of the Living Dead* was shown in a movie theatre at 7:30 in the morning."[15]

Schwarz's programming included uncommon thematic double features. A pairing of Paul Robeson's two films *Proud Valley* (1940) and *Song of Freedom* (1936) was one of the many revivals at the Thalia of African-American shorts and features from the 1930s. A double feature about the Hollywood blacklist—*Hollywood on Trial* (New York premiere of a 1977 documentary about the trial of the Hollywood Ten) and *The Front* (Martin Ritt's 1976 film about the blacklist and Hollywood)—explored this persecutory period of Hollywood history. Other double features tackled outré subjects of sexual orientation and gender identity, such as a double feature on homosexuality, *Boys in the Band* (1970) and *A Different Story* (1978), and another on transsexuality—*The Christine Jorgensen Story* (1970), the biopic of the first person notorious for undergoing a sex-change operation, and John Dexter's *I Want What I Want* (1972), about the sexual crisis in the life of a man who wants a sex-change operation. "The programs leaned a little kinky, sometimes,"

Premieres, cartoons, African-American features, Thalia Summer Film Festival, 1981.

Ford remembered. "It was nice to see films with sexual content occasionally. He wasn't afraid of that. He welcomed camp sensibilities. You wouldn't see that with a lot of repertory houses."[16]

On Fridays and Saturdays, New York premieres were slotted into the schedule. They ranged from foreign to American, from old to recent films. Goldstein claimed that most of the premieres were "really bad," but he explained that, because of the *New York Times*'s policy to review films that played two or more days, Canby of the *Times* regularly reviewed them. One instance of a "really bad" premiere film panned by Canby was a late film by Vittorio de Sica, *The Voyage*, 1973, based on a Pirandello novel. But a newspaper reporter and critic for *The Washington Post* and *L.A. Times* pointed out to Aronow that Canby must have wanted to see these films. As the chief critic for the *Times*, he would have sent an underling if he hadn't been interested in them. In newspaper interviews Schwarz said he hoped that these premieres would transfer to mainstream theaters for longer runs.[17]

One premiere that did transfer was Guy Enders's *Stevie* (1978) with Glenda Jackson, which received a rave review from Canby and then went to the 68th Street Playhouse, where it broke attendance records. Another transfer to a mainstream theater after a sell-out, two-day run at the Thalia was an obscure Robert Altman film, *Secret Honor* (1984), a one-character play with Philip Baker Hall portraying Richard Nixon. Ford had persuaded Schwarz to screen it in a single-film weekend booking (unusual for the Thalia) after Karen Cooper at Film Forum had turned it down. "Altman was so hot at the time, it broke the theater," recalled Ford. "They filled as many seats as they possibly could for two days; I'd never seen the Thalia have more people in it than those two days."

Other exceptions to the questionable films that Goldstein said constituted the majority of the premieres were some significant firsts. One of Schwarz's personal favorites was the original English language version of Josef von Sternberg's *Blue Angel* (1930) with Marlene Dietrich, which he screened in January 1980. He was very excited, Harvey remembered, with this premiere. "He couldn't find a record of anyone ever showing it. He loved that." Other successful screenings included Orson Welles's complete *Macbeth* (1948) and the 1963 *Uncle Vanya* starring Laurence Olivier.

In December 1980, as part of the theater's 50th anniversary celebration, the "New York Premiere" series held the world premiere of John Huston's documentary *Let There Be Light* (1946). Long-thought lost, the 1945 film depicted the problems of shell-shocked soldiers of World War II in treatment at Mason General Hospital on Long Island. Movie critics throughout the country praised the Thalia for its courage in finally screening the film, which had been suppressed by the government in the late forties for fear that it would scare off potential recruits. This screening, in Delaney's opinion, was one of the theater's finest hours. Canby's review described it as "a good, slickly made documentary … an amazingly elegant movie far different from the kind of documentaries we're now used to" and discussed the backstory of the film. According to Aronow, a number of the Vietnam veterans who were engaged in the heated national debate at the time about the psychological impact of the Vietnam War on soldiers were part of the audience.[18]

Contributing to the Thalia's reputation for adventurous, one-of-a-kind programming were its vertical series, which Tom Allen, film critic for the *Village Voice*, once declared "redefined thematic programming." The festivals often subverted conventional critical opinion. "Women Larger than Life," for example, called attention to the critically underrated films of major actresses like Bette Davis and Barbara Stanwyck, as well as of notable, minor actresses like Rhonda Fleming and Joan Leslie. A panned film like Davis's *Beyond the Forest* (1949), directed by King Vidor, was defended in the calendar as one of her best rather than worst films. Two little-known, B films from the fifties directed by Allan Dwan—the film noir *Slightly Scarlet* (1956) with Rhonda Fleming and Arlene Dahl, and the western *Woman They Almost Lynched* (1953) with Audrey Totter, Joan Leslie, and

12. A Temple to B Films

Thalia SUMMER FILM FESTIVAL

250 WEST 95th STREET
(at BROADWAY)
New York, N.Y. 10025
Phone 222-3370
• Doors Open Daily at 2 PM Daily •

FOUR-HANDKERCHIEF CLASSICS: 35 YEARS OF TEARJERKERS
EVERY MONDAY MAY 28 thru AUGUST 20

SUNDAY

SUNDAY, MAY 27
SEXUAL CURIOSITY
I AM CURIOUS YELLOW 1969
Directed by Vilgot Sjoman / With Vilgot Sjoman, Lena Nyman
The exploration of the role of women in modern society. "A genuine artistic and moral contribution."— John Simon
at: 2:00, 6:00, 10:00

I AM CURIOUS BLUE 1970
Directed by Vilgot Sjoman / With Vilgot Sjoman, Lena Nyman
The sequel, in which Lena continues her first-hand examination of the political, social, and sexual attitudes of contemporary Sweden.
at: 4:00 and 8:05

SUNDAY, JUNE 3
ORIGINAL TERROR
SWEENEY TODD,
THE DEMON BARBER OF FLEET STREET
1934
Directed by George King
With Todd Slaughter / This film, the first dramatic treatment of the legendary cut-throat barber, is the basis for the current Broadway musical hit. Meat pie, anyone?
at: 3:30, 6:45 and 10:00

NOSFERATU 1922
Directed by F.W. Murnau / Based on the novel Dracula by Bram Stoker, Photographed by Fritz Arno Wagner
With Max Schreck, Alexander Granach
The first silent film version of Dracula, albeit pirated without Stoker's permission. at: 2:15, 5:30 and 8:45

SUNDAY, JUNE 10
SAM PECKINPAH
STRAW DOGS 1971
Directed by Sam Peckinpah / With Dustin Hoffman, Susan George
A meek mathematician must defend his home against assault. A brilliantly edited film, contains a harrowingly violent sequence that has become notorious.
at: 2:20, 6:10, 10:10

JUNIOR BONNER 1972
Directed by Sam Peckinpah / With Steve McQueen, Robert Preston, Ida Lupino, Ben Johnson
A fading rodeo star returns to his hometown. Peckinpah's least violent film is an elegy for the lost frontier. Superb performance from Steve McQueen.
at: 4:20 and 8:10

MONDAY

MONDAY, MAY 28
SELF-SACRIFICE
MADAME X 1966
Directed by David Lowell Rich / Produced by Ross Hunter / With Lana Turner, Constance Bennett, Burgess Meredith, Ricardo Montalban, Keir Dullea
The celebrated saga of a neglected wife turned prostitute. Years later, charged with murder, she is defended by her lawyer son. at: 2:50, 6:35, 10:15

MAGNIFICENT OBSESSION 1954
Directed by Douglas Sirk / Produced by Ross Hunter / With Jane Wyman, Rock Hudson, Agnes Moorehead
Based on the Novel by Lloyd C. Douglas
A millionaire rake strives to become a surgeon so that he can try to restore the sight of a woman he has accidentally blinded. at: 4:40 and 8:25

MONDAY, JUNE 4
DOOMED ROMANCES
BACK STREET 1941
Directed by Robert Stevenson / With Margaret Sullivan, Charles Boyer, Richard Carlson / Photography by William Daniels / Based on the novel by Fannie Hurst
About the long-suffering secret mistress of a "respectable" family man. at: 4:20, 7:20 and 10:20

INTERMEZZO 1939
Directed by Gregory Ratoff / Produced by Leslie Howard and David O. Selznick / Photography by Gregg Toland
With Leslie Howard, Ingrid Bergman
Bergman's first American film, as a young pianist in love with a famous musician, who is a married man.
at: 3:00, 6:00 and 9:00

MONDAY, JUNE 11
SPOILED ROTTEN
DARK VICTORY 1939
Directed by Edmund Goulding / With Bette Davis, Humphrey Bogart, Ronald Reagan.
"A double order of prognosis negative" . . . Davis as a fast-living playgirl dying of a brain tumor.
at: 2:00, 6:05 and 10:10

HUMORESQUE 1946
Directed by Jean Negulesco / Screenplay by Clifford Odets / With Joan Crawford, John Garfield, Oscar Levant
A dissolute socialite falls in love with an aspiring violinist. Acerbic Levant steals the film.
at: 4:00 and 8:00

TUESDAY

TUESDAY, MAY 29
THE BATTLE OF CHILE
PART 1 & 2
Directed by Patricio Guzman

A high-powered, analytical documentary of the forces of military power confronted with those of a popular resistance in the vivid depiction of the demise of Allende and his progressive government.
at: 2:00, 5:20, 8:45

TUESDAY, JUNE 5
SHERLOCK HOLMES
HOUND of the BASKERVILLES 1939
Directed by Sidney Lanfield / With Rathbone, Bruce, John Carradine. The first appearance of Rathbone and Bruce in the roles with which they were forever-after identified. at: 2:00, 6:10 and 10:30

Adventures of SHERLOCK HOLMES
1939
Directed by Roy William Neill / With Rathbone and Bruce
A top secret bombsight and its inventor have disappeared. Is Professor Moriarty in league with the Nazis?
at: 3:20 and 7:40

THE SECRET WEAPON 1942
Directed by Alfred L. Werker / With Rathbone, Bruce and Ida Lupino. Mood chiller in which Holmes and Moriarty fight a battle of wits. at: 4:40 and 9:00

TUESDAY, JUNE 12
TRAGEDY
IPHIGENIA 1977
Based on the Euripides play / Screenplay and Directed by Michael Cacoyannis / Music by Mikis Theodorakis
With Irene Papas, Tatiana Papamoskou
The ancient drama Iphigenia in Aulis is the basis for this contemporary story of a man who choses between power and the life of his daughter, a young girl caught in the grip of war and political intrigue.
at: 5:15 and 9:45

STATE OF SEIGE 1973
Directed by Costa-Gavras / Music by Mikis Theodorakis
With Yves Montand, Renato Salvatori
An American "advisor" is kidnapped by revolutionaries. In the course of events the C.I.A. role in Latin America is disclosed. at: 3:00 and 7:35

A vertical series, "Four-Handkerchief Classics," Thalia Summer Film Festival, 1979.

154 Part Two: The Second Wave

Detour's (1945) Ann Savage—were touted as female genre films that were equal to their male counterparts. In his program notes on two of the films in the series—*Beyond the Forest* and Gerd Oswald's undeservedly obscure *Crime of Passion* (1957) with Barbara Stanwyck—Roger McNiven, who had run the Thousand Eyes Film Society with Mandelbaum in the late sixties and early seventies, provided a critical defense of the films.[19]

The most provocative series, though, and one closely identified with the Thalia was

Annual film noir festival, Thalia Spring Festival, 1983.

the annual film noir festival. Schwarz conceived the series and Harvey executed it. Schwarz loved the films of the fifties, which he considered the most critically neglected of the decades. "You pay high rental fees," he said in an interview with a *New York Times* reporter a few months after the opening of the Thalia, "to get the popular American films of the 30s and 40s, but if you look at the rental fees for the films of the late 40s and 50s, you would think they weren't worth two cents." The marginal films of the fifties, rather than such safer, critically favored ones as George Stevens's *Place in the Sun* (1951), comprised his first choices. "Richard would book *Kiss Me Deadly* [1955] in a second," said Ford. "Once my girlfriend [Ronnie Scheib, a mainstay New York *Variety* film reviewer] and I were setting up an Ida Lupino retrospective, and he asked, 'Can't we work in *Women's Prison* [1955]?' *Women's Prison* was to him the fun one, with Ida Lupino in the prison matron role." From this neglected decade he singled out the belittled films noirs produced from the late 1940s through the 1950s for special attention. "These were more realistic films," he said, "under the influence of German Expressionism and Italian neo-realism, more bleak, with more realistic dialogue and more work done on location."[20]

The first film noir series, "Film Noir: 1944–1958—The Great Hollywood Thrillers," appeared in the Spring Film Festival of 1978 calendar, advertised as this "whole school of downbeat melodramas, 'psychological' thrillers and mysteries, steeped in pessimism and fatality." A press release from the theater claimed that "the series will comprise the most extensive theatrical showing of film noir in the U.S. to date" and would include rare films that had not been shown theatrically or on television since their original release. As an indication of the low repute in which these films were held then, most of the "rare" films that are listed are now accepted parts of the film noir canon: *Criss Cross* (1949), *The Big Combo* (1955), *The File on Thelma Jordon* (1950), *They Live by Night* (1948), *Gun Crazy* (1950), and *The Line-Up* (1958).[21]

The double features were selected, the press release explained, "to reflect comprehensively the different aspects of this film style." The first one, for example, *Double Indemnity* (1944) with *Lady from Shanghai* (1948), highlighted "The film noir 'heroine'— haunting, dazzling and dangerous"; and the last in the series, *Out of the Past* (1947) and *Nightmare Alley* (1947), focused on "The poetic style: Lyricism and grotesquerie. The look and sound of doom itself." Harvey's film notes for each double feature described the films in relation to each other and the broader movement. In the double feature of Nicholas Ray's *They Live by Night* and Joseph H. Lewis's *Gun Crazy*, Harvey discussed their differences from other heist films in the genre as well as from each other; he also reviewed Ray's importance as a director. In the film notes for the Barbara Stanwyck double feature, *The File on Thelma Jordon* and *Sorry, Wrong Number* (1948), he wrote about Stanwyck's role as the quintessential noir heroine and its classic incarnation in *File on Thelma Jordon*. *Sorry, Wrong Number*, on the other hand, he wrote, shrewdly cast her against type in a hysterical feminine role. Allen declared that with this "extensive film noir retrospective, the Thalia was not only honoring cinema, it was helping to define it." Schwarz hoped, he told Allen in another interview, "to see the day when I gross as much with *Gun Crazy* and *Woman in the Window* [1944] as with *Rashomon* [1950] and *The Seventh Seal* [1957]."[22]

A box office hit the first year and the Thalia's first great success, the series continued every year as a popular annual event. "Whenever we showed a film noir," said Goldstein, "these guys would show up in black and I used to say that they must be from SoHo." The staff felt proprietary towards the series. Later, when Bingham Ray booked a film noir series at Talbot's neighboring repertory house, the Metro, the staff took it poorly. "We were really pissed," Goldstein recollected, "because it was kind of our thing."

While Schwarz programmed the daily repertory features, the various vertical series were mostly the creations of Schwarz's programmers, "a number of talented people who cycled through the Thalia," his sister remembered, with final approval by Schwarz. Harvey was his first programmer; at the time, he was a full-time professor in the English Department at the State University of New York, Stony Brook. He met Schwarz shortly after the Thalia reopened, at a screening of Josef von Sternberg's rarely seen last film, *Anatahan* (1953). The theater was empty, Harvey remembered in his Anthology tribute to Schwarz, but it didn't seem to bother Schwarz. "He was quietly elated because he had the Thalia, after all." They talked in the lobby after the film, and, while driving him to his subway station, Schwarz asked him if he would like to program for the Thalia. "I did. It was like a boyhood dream. So for three or four years, I was the chief programmer." Harvey, who had studied playwriting at the University of Michigan, had come to New York after a stint in the army to continue writing for the theater while teaching at Stony Brook. Later, after a play of his decisively bombed, he accepted an invitation from Alfred A. Knopf publisher Robert Gottlieb, who was impressed by his article in *Dance Life* magazine on Astaire and Rogers, to write a book on screwball comedy. He was writing this book when he met Schwarz. (The book, *Romantic Comedy in Hollywood: From Lubitsch to Sturges*, was published in 1987.)

Working with Schwarz was difficult at times for Harvey, "but he was a lot of fun, too," he remembered. "I was almost always happy to be going to the Thalia and to be there. He was its galvanizing presence, giving the place its odd contentious glamor. Richard was an idealist in a way. He never cared about getting his name in the papers or about being a public figure. He could be a jerk sometimes, but he had that kind of purity—and it was unyielding." Schwarz was always argumentative. "He loved to argue," Harvey remembered. "When he said 'no' to one of my suggestions, he was usually intransigent." One argument, though, on which Harvey remained adamant concerned the program notes, which were a standard part of all his series but which Schwarz regarded as a waste of time. "Richard was never in favor of the program notes," Harvey said, "but he never made any problems. He knew it would be a breaking point for me."

Programming for the Thalia gave Harvey opportunities to implement his ideas. "We did all kinds of series that I had wanted to do," he said. "We did many I was proud of." His particular favorites emanated from his work-in-progress on screwball, or romantic love, comedy, which placed the two filmmaking giants, Ernst Lubitsch and Preston Sturges, at the beginning and end respectively of the great era of the romantic comedy movie. The comprehensive Ernst Lubitsch retrospective, in the Winter Film Festival of 1979-80, ranged from the director's earliest films to his last one in 1948 and included such well-known ones as *The Shop Around the Corner* (1940), *Trouble in Paradise* (1932), and the Maurice Chevalier–Jeanette MacDonald operettas, as well as a rare Lubitsch film, *Angel* (1937), with Marlene Dietrich, "which was then a film nobody had seen," Harvey recalled, "including me, and which I wanted to see. My friend Samson Raphaelson had written it. It's an interesting film that I finally wrote about in *Romantic Comedy*." The screening of *Angel* involved one of those frequent, last-minute glitches that made repertory house programming challenging. "Richard said we can't show it because someone alive had gotten the rights somehow to one of the songs. He ran out and found the person in time for the screening. He just loved to confront and solve that kind of dilemma." Ironically, "there was [only] a small audience watching it and nobody knew what had happened behind the scenes."[23]

Harvey was especially proud of the Preston Sturges retrospective. Appearing in the 1979 Fall Film Festival and entitled "The Miracle of Preston Sturges: Writer-Director 1930–1949," it covered not only the well-known films for which Sturges was both writer and director (including the original version of *The Sin of Harold Diddlebock*, 1947, rather than the version re-edited by Howard Hughes and retitled *Mad Wednesday*, 1950), but also his screenplays for other directors: *Easy Living* (1937), *Never Say Die* (1939), *The Power and the Glory* (1933), *Port of Seven Seas* (1938), *Diamond Jim* (1935), and *The Good Fairy* (1935). "We were the first ones to do his screenplays," Harvey recalled. "Nobody thought of doing that before. We even did *Diamond Jim* with Jean Arthur, a wonderful film that was only available then on 16mm." The series was a great success, Harvey noted, with long lines around the block. It was the most comprehensive retrospective of the director's work ever held in New York and inspired the critic David Ansen's review of Sturges's career in the *Thousand Eyes* magazine.[24]

Another retrospective growing out of his research on the screwball genre was "La Cava Classics," a look at the films of Gregory La Cava, a director best known for his work in the thirties. La Cava's *My Man Godfrey*, 1936, with Carole Lombard as a dizzy rampaging heroine, was the inspiration for the term "screwball comedy," which was thought up by a publicist to describe the film. As with his other two series, Harvey included a number of the director's rarely seen films: *The Half-Naked Truth* (1932), a famed satire on show-business press agentry, with Lupe Velez and Lee Tracy; *The Primrose Path* (1940), a seldom-seen drama with Ginger Rogers, who called it her favorite vehicle; *Private Worlds* (1935), an early, acclaimed drama of a mental institution with Claudette Colbert and Charles Boyer; and *Affairs of Cellini* (1934), "a famous but long unavailable comedy" with Fredric March and Constance Bennett. Program notes for the series included Katharine Hepburn's elegant tribute to her *Stage Door* (1937) director, which Harvey solicited through his editor, Gottlieb, who was a personal friend of Hepburn's. Other contributions were written by film scholars William K. Everson and Elizabeth Kendall.[25]

While he was working on the romantic comedy book, Harvey had also become interested in the filmmakers of the fifties, especially Douglas Sirk and Nicholas Ray, both of whom were going through a "rediscovery" at that time, thanks to the auteurists and Sarris. The result was his series in the fall of 1978, "Fifties Melodrama: Post-War Auteurs and the Cinema of Hysteria," which focused on the films of the two directors and which later led to his second book, *Movie Love in the Fifties*, published in 2001. Harvey had arranged personal appearances by Sirk and Ray, both of whom he knew. He had met and interviewed Sirk in 1977 for three days at his home in Lugano, Switzerland, talking with him about his life and work—"almost two decades after he'd abandoned America and his Hollywood film career," Harvey noted in his book, " and four decades after he'd fled Hitler's Germany, with his Jewish wife, actress Hilde Jary."[26]

It was also in 1977 that he met Ray, who showed up unannounced one day at a screening of his film *In a Lonely Place* (1950), which Harvey was running for a film class at the New School's Fifth Avenue movie theater (formerly Martin Lewis's Fifth Avenue Cinema). Ray, who was living around New York and teaching a film class at SUNY Binghamton, had come on an impulse with his wife, who wanted to see the movie, and his usual entourage of four or five young people. The surprise visit was exciting for everyone present, and he answered questions afterwards. Two weeks later he returned for *Johnny Guitar* (1954). Both times he and Harvey talked afterwards in a diner surrounded by the entourage.[27]

Sirk's appearance at the Thalia was scheduled to coincide with his visit to New York for celebrations in his honor at MoMA and the City University of New York Graduate Center. When Harvey came to pick him up, however, just before his Thalia appearance, Sirk was unable to leave his hotel room. "Hilde [his wife had accompanied him on the trip] said that he couldn't go, he was sick," Harvey remembered. "He was sick a lot then, near the end of his life." Harvey was in a quandary since all this occurred right before show time. "They were all waiting at the theater. Sirk told me to say whatever I want. He claimed to know about the Thalia and to think highly of it. That may have been his politeness, but that's what I said—to a disappointed audience."

The scheduled appearance by Ray also turned into a fiasco, but this time because of Schwarz's tightfistedness and poor social and business skills. Carol Iannone, a former student of Harvey's and the theater's publicist at the time, was negotiating a fee for his speaking engagement, but Ray was asking for more than Schwarz was allowing. Without consulting her, Schwarz called Ray and offered him a very low fee. Later he realized his mistake and suggested to her that she call Ray back for future dates, offering a little more money. "I feel terrible," she wrote in a memo to Harvey, who was out of the country at the time. "I did try to do things step by step, and I didn't think Richard would suddenly back out like that. But of course I should have known better."[28]

Harvey continued programming until approximately 1981 when he began reducing his time at the Thalia as he was becoming more deeply involved with his book. "I never left entirely," he said, "because I was fond of Richard, I was fond of the whole thing."

Another of Schwarz's programmers, Greg Ford, was responsible for a further popular and profitable annual festival, "Cartoonal Knowledge," which was probably, Delaney wrote in his Thalia history, "the largest and most comprehensive review of animated films ... in a ... theatrical context of any theatre or film society in the world." Ford had done animation festivals for MoMA and the Zagreb Festival in what was then Yugoslavia, as well as a cartoon show, "Hollywood Cartoons," with Marty Rubin for the New York Cultural Center in 1973. Schwarz, who had seen "Hollywood Cartoons," asked Ford to do a similar program for the Thalia. "Hollywood Cartoons" had been a director-themed show. "This was in the era of Andrew Sarris and *The American Cinema* and the pantheon of directors," Ford explained, "and Lincoln Center had just had a big Walt Disney retrospective in '72 or '73." This gave Ford and Rubin the idea of doing a similar program on Chuck Jones, Fritz Freleng, and Tex Avery, major film animators whom Ford had known in Los Angeles. "I thought," Ford said, "that these guys are as great as Disney in a different way; and the studios aren't going to support them, but the public will." He was right; the program at the New York Cultural Center was very successful. "It got mentioned everywhere," he remembered.[29]

The Thalia's first "Cartoonal Knowledge" program, in summer 1980, replicated the auteurist focus on the non–Disney animators. Over two hundred short subjects and seven full-length features from such animators as Chuck Jones, Tex Avery, Robert Clampett, Max and Dave Fleischer, and Frank Tashlin, who later became a live action director, played in the thirteen-week program on Mondays. On one Monday, Ford coupled Tashlin's cartoons with his live action feature, *Son of Paleface* (1952) with Bob Hope and Jane Russell. "He had a lot of the same gags," said Ford. Each Monday's schedule was the equivalent of a double feature; for example, the first double feature was a Walter Lantz program of shorts coupled with a Chuck Jones program. Ford patterned each director's program in a particular way. "It opened big," he explained. "Then the middle cartoon, out of the 11 or 12 in each program, would be the most interesting aesthetically to me, but not necessarily to the audience. Finally, I'd build to a crescendo—cartoons ten, eleven, twelve usually killed, so they'd go out happy." The formula remained the same for all the subsequent years.

The first year was such a hit—"It was a shock to Richard and me," Ford recalled—that they scheduled a second show in the fall; but the fall show was thin because he ran out of material. They decided after that to do only one show a year, in the summer. Ford skipped the next year, 1980-81, since he was setting up a major show on Disney at the Whitney Museum. "It was gigantic," he said, "and almost killed me, so I was happy to go back to the Thalia." As a result of the Disney show at the Whitney, he was able to get Disney programs for the Thalia in following years. "I would do a double feature," he said, "of Mickey Mouse cartoons and Silly Symphonies." In summer 1981 the series returned under the heading "ThaliAnimation Fest!"[30]

Over the years he created a variety of cartoon programs. "We did theme shows," he said, "like one on the Depression. We did puppet animation shows, we did shows on thirties innocence and the screwball forties. Occasionally we'd do sociological shows. We occasionally did early Japanese anime stuff, like *Galaxy Express 999* (1979), which was the first time anyone saw those kinds of films. It was well before anime became this huge thing."

Notice was especially taken of the cartoons by once-important early animators who had been eclipsed by Disney. The first discovery was the films of Winsor McCay, a pioneer of movie cartoons. Already famous for his newspaper comic strips, *Little Nemo in Slumberland* and *Dreams of a Rarebit Fiend*, McCay produced his first animated film, *Little*

Noir patsy Porky Pig and "Dark City" dame Betty Boop in the "Cartoon Noir" series, 1984. Courtesy Greg Ford and Bruce Goldstein.

Nemo, in 1911 and a second one, *The Story of a Mosquito*, in 1912, both great successes. Two groundbreaking films followed: his most famous movie, *Gertie the Dinosaur* (1914), the first original character developed solely for the animated cartoon and not based on a preexisting comic strip; and *The Sinking of the Lusitania* (1918), featuring his most distinctive animation, one of the first films to use cels (short for *celluloid*, a transparent sheet on which objects are drawn or painted for traditional, hand-drawn *animation*). McCay made a total of ten animated shorts. *Little Nemo* screened at the Thalia as the second short on July 20, 1981, with a promise of "More McCay in the very exciting U.S. Premiere in our Animation Fest, 'Pioneers of American Animation' on August 3rd!"[31]

Ford followed up with *Felix the Cat* silent cartoons, a series by Otto Messmer for Pat Sullivan's Studios; these were the leading cartoons of their time until displaced by Mickey Mouse. Another major revival of Ford's was Lou Bunin's *Alice in Wonderland* (1949), a live action and animated puppet film that had appeared at the same time as Disney's film and had received better critical notices, but failed to gain wide distribution because of a lawsuit by Disney, who wanted no competition with his version. At the time of the opening of the film at the Thalia, Bunin told the *New York Times* reporter Janet Maslin, chain theaters, fearful of retaliation by Disney, refused to play the film; and because Technicolor would not process it, he was forced to use the Ansco process.[32]

Ford, who knew of Bunin and his film through his research, learned from an elderly animator, Joe Oriolo, that Bunin was living in New York. He visited him, saw his sculptures, and found out more about his print of *Alice*, which was the last surviving one. Finally, after a nearly thirty-year absence from the theaters, Bunin's *Alice in Wonderland* was screened on a weekend in April 1985. The response was so healthy that the theater repeated it a week later.

The film, a collaboration between stop-motion animation pioneer, Bunin and director Dallas Bower, begins with a live-action sequence, and then places the live actress Carol Marsh as Alice in a wonderland of stop-motion characters that, Gary Cahall wrote in his survey of the different film versions, "many now claim comes the closest to capturing the feel of the original text." Bunin explained in the *Times* interview that the denizens of Wonderland should not be cast with live actors, as the previous failed six features had done. For the inhabitants of Wonderland in his film, he used animated sculptures less than seven inches high, which were sized on film to suit the live-action Alice. While Disney also used animation, Bunin thought he did not understand Lewis Carroll and consequently ignored some of the best situations and the best lines.[33]

Ford's last year with the Thalia was 1986. Looking back on his years at the theater, he marveled at the difficulty of booking animation films for the theater's daily schedule. "Doing a different double feature every day was hard," he said, "but booking animation was especially hard, like doing twenty-four bookings for one day." In addition, he then had to splice the films of a program together, usually at home. "Literally, I'd be so covered in sweat," he said, "because at the last minute at home I'd be writing these program notes, then xeroxing them myself." Unlike with Harvey, Richard liked him to do program notes. The editing wasn't always finished at home. Sometimes, at the last minute, the show would be running too long and something had to be taken out. Then he would have to edit in the booth. "It was reel to reel in the booth," Ford recalled, "and Richard, who was very hands-on with the editing, would be helping me." The projection was good, he remembered. "Practically all my shows were 16mm, although occasionally I'd score a couple

Billboard ad for Lou Bunin's *Alice in Wonderland* premiere at Mayfair Theatre, 1949. Photofest.

of 35mm programs." Ford also brought in some animators for personal appearances: Bob Clampett, Chuck Jones, Faith Hubley, and Lou Bunin.

His annual series developed a dedicated following, including Jim Hoberman, film critic for the *Village Voice*. "Although Bruce had a lot to do with the good press that the series got, Jim Hoberman, who loved the cartoon shows, would often also give us a review. It was unusual because it was just repertory, but we often got reviews from him." Besides Hoberman, there were "a lot of repeat audience members, to an almost shocking extent over the years." The audience was like his classroom. "You got to see what people reacted to," Ford said, "what gags worked." He described an instance where Chuck Jones's "Feed the Kitty" started in the middle, and, as successive audiences expressed enthusiasm for it, he placed it gradually more toward the end until it finished as the top cartoon in the program. The series even developed a *Rocky Horror Picture Show* quality, where there would be audience participation for the more popular programs, like the Tex Avery ones—"Tex on Sex," "Tex Avery Fairytales," "Tex Avery Westerns," among others.

Despite the difficulties of programming at the Thalia—putting together the double features, putting up with Schwarz's outbursts—his experience there meant something special to him. "It's weird," he said. "I ended up writing, directing, producing television shows and millions of people would see them, and it didn't mean a fucking thing. But if we got 500 people into the Thalia, it was a wonderful achievement."

Both Ford and Harvey were programming at the Thalia when Goldstein became a full-time employee around 1980. Goldstein had first met Schwarz in Boston in the early seventies at Schwarz's equipment store. "There used to be a little street of Boston," Goldstein said, "where all the distributors were, including the branches of the big distributors, like MGM, as well as all the equipment places. Richard had a little equipment shop there; he had so much equipment that there was no place to sit inside, so he actually sat on the sidewalk." Schwarz bought prints from Goldstein for about $700, "which was a fortune to me at the time." Goldstein moved to London; but on his return to New York around 1980, Schwarz hired him. He worked at the Thalia for three or four years.

Goldstein's forte and unique contribution to the Thalia were marketing and publicity. "More than programming," Goldstein said, "what I contributed was the hype and the publicity. I tried to bring more showmanship to the exhibition." To compensate for the rundown look of the theater, he supervised the writing and design of the calendars to give them an elegant look. Most importantly, Goldstein brought an inventive level of publicity to the programs. In a tribute to Goldstein on his receiving the Mel Novikoff award at the San Francisco International Film Festival in 2009, Hoberman singled out the Fay Wray scream-alike contest, which "[o]ld hands at the Thalia still remember ... complete with man in monkey suit that he organized for the 50th anniversary of the original *King Kong*." The most successful promotion Goldstein ever did, perhaps in his entire career he opined, was the one for Alberto Cavalcanti's *Nicholas Nickleby* (1947). "Richard had a 16mm print of the 1948 Ealing film," recalled Goldstein. "At the same time on Broadway was the Royal Shakespeare Company's production of *Nicholas Nickleby*, which was the highest priced ticket in Broadway history at that time. I think it was $100. So I sent out a press release that said, '96 dollars cheaper than the Broadway show.' Every newspaper and magazine picked up on this line and we had lines wrapped four times around the block." For a series of black-and-white Porky Pig cartoons, a random bunch of cartoons that usually didn't sell as well as director-defined or theme series, Ford remembered that Goldstein turned it into a birthday party—"'Porky Pig, so many years old." The angle generated local news coverage and brought out a large crowd. "It was a very successful program in terms of attendance. He was very knowledgeable about film, unlike most publicists." But Schwarz was unenthusiastic about Goldstein's publicity efforts. "Bruce had to win Richard over," said Mandelbaum, "so there were endless discussions, arguments."[34]

Reflecting on his experience at the Thalia, Goldstein was critical of Schwarz's programming approach, which hampered his publicity efforts. Rather than curating his programs, Schwarz's approach, in Goldstein's estimation, resembled the booking approach.

"Programming is a high-falutin' idea for what was done at the Thalia," he said. "It would be like 'Hey, should we play this?' 'Nah, it stinks.'" Schwarz's scattershot programming—a different double feature each day in the week—did not afford Goldstein an opportunity to generate major publicity—like my series at Film Forum," he explained in an e-mail, "where my retrospectives often generate significant press attention. We treat the series as a museum would treat a major art exhibition." (This echoed the same argument he had made in a 1987 newspaper interview: the horizontal series approach spawned major newspaper articles that created public interest while daily changes generated only a listing in a newspaper's calendar of events.)[35]

Furthermore, Goldstein complained, Schwarz's approach led to the loss of potential business. Some premieres were instances of missed opportunities. "If Richard had sat down and watched *Stevie*," Goldstein clarified, "and said, 'Hey, this is a film of quality, maybe this could run a week at least,' it would have been good business for us. But because he just threw it in for those two days, we lost it after the opening run, we lost all this business." But Schwarz had a different mindset from Goldstein's marketing perspective. "If you want to do what he [Schwarz] wanted to do," said Ford, "a zillion films per month, 52 films a month on a 31-day month, films like *Secret Honor* and *Stevie* were too big for the Thalia. They weren't the right kind of films." Moreover, the Thalia was not atypical in scheduling vertical series with random double features each week. The Regency, in fact, was the only repertory theater to program only horizontal series—and generate the kind of publicity that Goldstein wanted for the Thalia.

Working with Schwarz wasn't easy for Goldstein, either. Their relationship was stormy, according to Mandelbaum, "because Richard admired Bruce's knowledge and enterprise, but at the same time was competitive." Nevertheless, Goldstein worked closely with him on a number of areas in addition to publicity. One major joint effort involved a filmmaking venture. Schwarz's love of digging up rarely seen films from the public domain led to his own moviemaking, putting together Hollywood outtakes from films in the public domain. Some of these outtakes came from the Fort Lee dumpsters; others were acquired in trades with other collectors or bought from them. "He edited three programs of outtakes from his own collection into a single, feature-length version," Aronow recalled. "He cropped together all this footage. They were very funny, fresh, almost all American, Hollywood stuff, a lot of it." Goldstein helped Schwarz professionalize the product. "We duped it and made a negative," Goldstein said. "We might even have blown it up to 35mm." In the end, according to Aronow, her brother hired a professional editor to put together the final, feature-length product. The editor, Doug Rossini, and Goldstein worked together on the final product, which was collectively called "Hollywood Out-Takes and Rare Footage," and contained, a *New York Times* reporter wrote, "snippets and boo-boos by such as Humphrey Bogart, Bette Davis, Errol Flynn that never made it to the finished product." Goldstein had director's credit on the released film.[36]

The response to *Hollywood Out-Takes and Rare Footage* was extraordinary, Goldstein related in an e-mail. It played at the Waverly (now IFC Center) in the Village as well as around the country. "We got calls from Hugh Hefner, Mrs. Walter Mirisch [wife of Walter Mirisch, the then president of The Mirisch Corporation, an independent filmmaking organization], and The White House [President and Mrs. Reagan], who all wanted to screen it. We turned them down."[37]

The programs became another of the Thalia's popular annual events, one that Schwarz and Goldstein marketed around the country. "We started a little distribution company called Manhattan Movietime," Goldstein said. "I think I was president; it didn't mean anything." Goldstein implied they had money disputes over their collaboration. "We made lots of money on this film, but I don't think I was paid anything beyond what I was getting paid at the Thalia."

Goldstein eventually left over several disputes with Schwarz. *Hollywood Out-Takes* was one, but the major one involved a company, Gopher Films, which Ford and Goldstein had formed to distribute Bunin's *Alice in Wonderland*. "This was the major reason Richard and I had a falling out," he explained in his e-mail. Finally, Goldstein was also starting his own publicity business, Falco & Goldstein.[38]

By 1985 the West Side building boom that was transforming much of the neighborhood was threatening the existence of the Thalia and the other small businesses in the area. New stores had opened in the last several years, and a sixteen-story luxury apartment building was going up across the street from the Thalia. "In 20 years," Pete Gonzalez, manager of F and G Discounts, told a reporter for the *West Side Spirit*, "this has gone from a poor, slum area to a gentrified, yuppie neighborhood. And it is old places like the Thalia that are the first to go." The two-story Symphony Space building that housed the Thalia became embroiled in litigation over its redevelopment. The current owner, Symphony Space, wanted to modernize the property and continue it as a performing arts center; but another group, whose principal partners, Pergola Properties and Bradford Swett, held a lease on the stores and offices in the building, was interested in straight redevelopment, demolishing the entire block front. An option to purchase the deed in January 1987 was held by Pergola Properties and Swett, but Symphony Space was contesting its validity.[39]

Schwarz was facing the same kind of adversary that Gould and Zlatkin at the Elgin had encountered—a hostile landlord—but one, according to Aronow, who was especially threatening. "Brad Swett," she remembered, "used to be in the *Village Voice* as one of the ten worst landlords in New York." Her brother told her he closed the Thalia not only because of his inability to renew his lease but also because of specific frightening events he said the landlord orchestrated to force his departure. One incident involved a private garbage truck that backed right into the Thalia's marquee and heavily damaged it. Right before the occurrence an employee at the theater saw someone paying off the driver. Schwarz viewed that as warfare. In the other episode, he said someone was paid to run around with a gun and chase him out of the theater. "That event scared the daylights out of him," Aronow said. "Our mother screamed at my brother to get out of there." Mandelbaum remembered that he had to hire a bodyguard.

Schwarz hung on to the Thalia for the full duration of his lease. Meanwhile, as backup in the event of losing the Thalia, he opened a second theater, the Thalia Soho, in November 1985, which he changed from a legitimate theater (the former Vandam) into a small movie theater. His life partner Jim Poling worked in the theater with him. In 1986, taking a big risk, he purchased another theater in Greenwich Village, the Cinema Village, and instituted repertory programming there. Nevertheless, the two newer theaters could not take the place of the Thalia. According to Aronow, he frequently made unfavorable comparisons of the audience at the Cinema Village to the Thalia's audience. "He loved the Thalia's, but barely tolerated the other."

Harvey described the Thalia SoHo as a mess and the Cinema Village as poorly managed. Mandelbaum reprimanded him once over his management of the Cinema Village, which led to the breakup of their friendship. "I visited him at the Cinema Village, and when I saw the condition of the theater, I said to him, 'Why don't you get a mop, it's filthy. You took a decent theater and changed it into the Thalia.' I guess I went too far. He thought it was charming, you were getting atmosphere."

What neither Harvey nor Mandelbaum knew at the time was that he had AIDS and was suffering a long and lingering end, physically and emotionally. "He never confided to me about his AIDS," said Harvey. "After years of close friendship, he was drawing away from me, and I didn't understand." Mandelbaum experienced the same rebuff. "I would like to have seen Richard," Mandelbaum remembered, "but he didn't want to see me, even though we had had happy times and were close romantically for a while." Yet, even though his life was ending and he was distancing himself from former friends, he operated his theaters as long as he could; they were his lifeline. After he closed Cinema Village, even though he knew he had almost no time left, his sister related, he began building new projection booths for Anthology Film Archives on a voluntary basis and with equipment he donated.

When his ten-year lease ended in January 1987, Swett put Schwarz, along with the other store owners in the building, on a month-to-month lease. "The fact that somebody is willing to demolish a building with the Symphony Space, the Thalia, and a bookstore is outrageous," Suzanne Zavrian, the owner of the pocket-sized Pomander Bookshop next door to the Thalia, complained on being informed of the closing. Four months later, in May 1987, Zavrian was told that her lease would run out at the end of the month, and she and the other tenants in the building would have to move. "They want everybody out" she said. "I can't believe it. There should have been a huge commotion. They're erasing all this wonderful cultural space to put up another stupid apartment building."[40]

On May 10, 1987, the Thalia closed after the 2:00 a.m. screening of its last double feature, Paolo and Vittorio Taviani's *Night of the Shooting Stars* (1982) and Roberto Rossellini's *Paisan* (1946). Three years later, in August 1990, the same month that the Bleecker Street Cinema closed, both the Thalia Soho and the Cinema Village shut their doors. Then, in October 1990, two months after the demise of his last two theaters, Richard Schwarz died at the age of thirty-nine of AIDS, complicated by a heart attack.

The Thalia's closing brought expressions of sadness and loss from many people: those from the film world, other repertory programmers, and former patrons of the Thalia. What the community of film lovers mourned the most was the loss of the theater's bold programming under Schwarz. "The Thalia booked films from independent sources," Harlan Jacobson, editor of *Film Comment*, told the *West Side Spirit* reporter, "and took all kinds of risks over a very long period of time. That's going to be very difficult to replace." A similar theme was expressed in the same article by Peter Biskind, editor of *American Film*: "It has an important place in cinema history. It singlehandedly allowed obscure films to flourish at a time when there was no place else to see them."[41]

The passing of the Thalia meant for many a loss for film history. Acknowledging that "[w]e certainly will pick up some business," Frank Rowley at the Regency nonetheless regretted its passing. "[W]e lose something, too," he said. "Every time a great revival theater closes, fewer people will get to see the classics, and a little more of film history is washed away." Echoing the sentiment in what is perhaps a fitting epitaph for the Thalia and repertory theaters in general, William Simon, a professor at the New York University film school, told a reporter, "A revival theater, in a way, is a living archive of a whole art form. The success of moviemaking, like painting, depends on a historical knowledge of it. This is very difficult without theaters like the Thalia."[42]

Chapter 13

Carnegie Hall Cinema and Bleecker Street Cinema: Classic Revivals, American Independents, Godard and Company—A Smorgasbord of Riches

In the second wave, the Bleecker Street Cinema in Greenwich Village and Carnegie Hall Cinema in midtown were taken over by Sid Geffen, who, together with his French-born, second wife, Jackie Raynal, herself a filmmaker and film editor, made the two theaters into centers for European and American independent films.

Geffen was a paradox. He loved running a repertory movie theater and championing the art of film, but he had no background in film, knew little about films, and had no interest in formally educating himself in the subject. He was always on the alert to drive a bargain, but heedless in his attitude towards money. He saw himself as an astute businessman, but was prone to making capricious decisions. He had ambitions for his theaters, even though he lacked the resources. Yet, somehow, he was able to expand the scope of his operations well beyond that of most other repertory owners. Geffen's ambitions mirrored the expansionary drive of the pioneering repertory owner, Martin J. Lewis. He created a chain of three theaters (a third, small auditorium, the James Agee Room, was later established in the Bleecker Street Cinema), published a literary-style magazine that, for a time, covered repertory movie theaters citywide, established a cinema bookstore in the Bleecker Street Cinema, and set up a Parisian-style café in the Carnegie Hall Cinema. "Sid was really an artist at heart," was how Barbara Nitke, a close friend and one of his first managers, described him, "maybe he didn't have a medium. I think he was an artist who was trying to be a businessman."[1]

Geffen came from Utica, New York, where he had worked in his father's car dealership. Married with four children, he had a troubled relationship with his wife. Nitke recalled Geffen's story that his father had handed over his paychecks to his wife because of her complaints that he was irresponsible with money. "He probably was," Nitke acknowledged, "but she had created a situation where he worked for his father and his paycheck went directly to her. That was the relationship they had. I could see both sides." Later, he would tell his staff that something had been missing in his life and that he came down to New York City wanting to do something different. Faced with a deteriorating marriage and discontented with his life, he left for New York City around 1972. He was about 47 years old.[2]

While in Utica, he had gotten his real estate license. In New York he became friends with Herb Nitke, Barbara's husband and the owner of a chain of adult movie theaters in upstate New York. According to Raynal, Nitke was operating the Carnegie Hall Cinema as one. (A former patron recalled, on the *Cinema Treasures* website, visiting the theater during its porn period. "I will never forget going to the bathroom," he wrote, "and it was really scary.... I felt very uneasy there and left.") Later rumors swirled among some Carnegie staff that Geffen was involved with Nitke in the porn business, but Barbara refuted this. "They were going in different directions," she remembered, "because Herb was interested in making money, but Sid was more interested in showing fine art movies. He didn't have Herb's entrepreneurial moxie; they were going in different directions."[3]

As Raynal remembered, Geffen told her that Herb Nitke was one of the partners in General Cinema, which, in addition to owning the lease to the Carnegie, owned a chain of drive-in theaters that it wanted to sell. Acting as broker, Geffen was able to sell the chain in a year to developers who turned them into shopping malls; in an agreement with Nitke, he gave up his fee of around $18,000 in exchange for the Carnegie Hall Cinema lease. The idea of running a repertory movie theater must have been gestating in his mind for some time; in the early seventies, in what seems to have been a test run, he had rented the Regency on the Upper West Side for a month to screen the Janus Film Festival.[4]

The arrangement was satisfactory with Carnegie Hall Corporation, the nonprofit organization chartered to manage Carnegie Hall for the owner, the City of New York. The corporation was pleased to rid itself of Nitke and hand it over to Geffen, who promised to operate an art cinema. Its executive director, Julius Bloom, "a very nice gentleman, an old-fashioned, nineteenth century type, with a cane and a hat," Raynal remembered, "was excited that Geffen was doing 'cultural stuff' and promised him the renewal lease when the current one expired." According to Raynal, Geffen persuaded Bloom to give him a 25-year lease at around $32,000 to $34,000 a year in rent, including electricity and a minimal two percent increase a year. He purchased the lease through a corporation he set up, Comico, Inc.[5]

Some details in the newspapers of the purchase differ from the above account as well as from each other. *Variety*'s account confirmed that he bought the Carnegie Cinema lease from the Carnegie Hall Corporation with fees he had earned selling theater screens. According to a *Villager* article, however, he bought the lease from the bankrupt Cinecom, which had purchased the theater in 1969 from F and A Theatres in the hope of launching a first-run policy at the Carnegie Hall Cinema; it failed.[6]

In any event, Geffen opened the 285-seat Carnegie Hall Cinema on October 12, 1973, with "The Ursula Lewis Film Festival," honoring the recently closed Thalia and its beloved former owner. Mrs. Lewis curated the inaugural program, *Children of Paradise* (1945), which was followed by double features every two days through December 13. *Cue* noted that "The Carnegie Hall Cinema has taken up where the Thalia left off ... a nonstop reprise of Ms. Lewis' movie-classics festival...." The Thalia was his model. "Sidney was interested in copying the Thalia Theater," Nitke recalled. "He liked playing art movies. That was really his love."[7]

Geffen was reinventing his life. He now had his own theater and soon met his future second wife. Their first meeting took place after a private screening of her award-winning film, *Deux Fois* (1968) at the Museum of Modern Art. He called to ask her to do a program of French New Wave films for the Carnegie Hall Cinema. Sometime before or after the reconciliation with his wife failed, they became romantically involved and married in 1976. "Jackie was such a different kind of woman [than his first wife]," Nitke remembered, "that he went head over heels in love with her. She was really the right kind of person for him. She was a filmmaker, an avant-garde person, somewhat flaky; they were perfect." They were an odd couple; Raynal was an attractive, young French hippie while Geffen was a middle-age, mustachioed Jewish businessman from upstate New York, who looked like a round-face Groucho Marx.

Raynal had begun her career in film as an assistant editor to Jean Renoir in the early sixties, then in 1964 met Eric Rohmer and edited his first three "Moral Tales," followed by an editing role for other New Wave filmmakers, like Jean Rouch, Jean-Luc Godard, and Claude Chabrol. By 1964, she was the youngest film editor in France. A director as well as a film editor, she had belonged to the Zanzibar Group, a radical filmmaking collective in France of about twelve young, leftwing members, who had made fifteen films, among them Raynal's *Deux Fois*. It was critically recognized as a pioneering work of the nascent feminist cinema. In 1969 she moved to the United States; and following a three-year sojourn living a hippie lifestyle, she obtained a job editing a gay film, *Saturday Night at the Baths* (1975), at Magno Sound, one of the East Coast's largest and most comprehensive post-production facilities. The film was released in 1975.[8]

Raynal introduced Geffen to filmmakers and other artistic types. They would host Sunday afternoon salons in their apartment on Central Park South for visiting filmmakers from Europe who were friends of Raynal's, as well as actors and other media personalities. "When we were premiering a film at one of the theaters," Bill Thompson, one of his programmers, recalled, "we'd sometimes have the film's director there, or the actor or actress. Isabella Rossellini came once." Jonathan Rosenbaum, another freelance programmer for Geffen, remembered the Sunday brunches as an important social event for visiting filmmakers. "It was a salon, social circle," he said. "There would be special lunches for people just coming through town, like Wim Wenders, Chantal Akerman." Raynal recalled that every Sunday she cooked a big brunch. "A lot of directors came from France, Switzerland, Italy. Everyone came. We often had to go on the roof, because we had 200, 300 people."[9]

Geffen had ambitions beyond just one theater. "He dreamed of having five screens," Raynal remembered, "even though he had no money." At one point in his career, he hoped to develop a network of repertory theaters with Carnegie Hall as the center, to screen the films he was importing. The idea, Thompson explained, was that with this network, it would be easier to distribute and screen them. A year after opening the Carnegie, Geffen acquired a second theater, the smaller, 180-seat Bleecker Street Cinema in Greenwich Village from Lionel Rogosin.[10]

According to Raynal, she gave him the idea of acquiring the Bleecker. One night in 1974, at dinner in a Village restaurant, Geffen was discussing his need for more screens. On the cab ride back to her apartment on the Upper East Side, they passed the Bleecker, and she pointed out the theater to him. It was lying fallow most of the time, except for use as a screening room for New York University film classes. Geffen wrote the address in his notebook and later called to tell her he had bought the lease to the theater from Rogosin for $12,000. Embarrassingly, the check for the lease bounced. "Lionel, who was a classy man," Raynal recalled, "kindly waited a week or perhaps two before redepositing the check." To earn enough to cover it, Geffen, "with always an eye on the box office," played a surefire hit, *Last Tango in Paris* (1972), for several days at the Carnegie and thus covered the check. Later, around 1978, when the block of buildings on which the Bleecker Street Cinema was located was put up for sale by New York University, Geffen bought the building with a business partner for $115,000. He later bought out the partner.

Jackie Raynal, in the period when her film, *New York Story*, was selected by Richard Roud for the New York Film Festival, ca. 1980. Photofest.

The Bleecker Street Cinema reopened on Wednesday, October 16, 1974, with a tribute to Jean Renoir and his 80th birthday. Beginning with a double feature of Renoir's *The Little Theatre of Jean Renoir* (1970) and *The Testament of Dr. Cordelier* (1959), the tribute continued for the next four days with a double bill of the former film and a different Renoir film each day. After the Renoir retrospective, the schedule, like that at the Carnegie, consisted of daily changes of double features, mostly of films of foreign directors like Jan Troell and Federico Fellini. "Business was okay," Raynal recalled. "We had the NYU students, but it wasn't established like the Carnegie."[11]

Six years later, in November 1980, Geffen opened his third, and last, theater, a small (82-seat), second auditorium in the Bleecker, the James Agee Room; it replaced the theater's Thousand Eyes Bookshop, which at its peak was one of the largest film bookstores in the city. But it had been losing money, much of it from stealing. On Raynal's recommendation, Geffen closed it in 1978 and converted the space to the Agee Room. "James Agee lived on Bleecker Street," Raynal recalled, "that's why we named it the James Agee Room. When we opened it, his three ex-wives came to the opening." The inaugural program appropriately was the local theatrical premiere of Ross Spears' award-winning *Agee* (1980), based on the life of the novelist, film critic, and screenwriter.

The idea behind the Agee, explained Thompson, "was to create an alternative screening space for films which would not get screened in New York under ordinary circumstances." Raynal made it her pet project; she took over its complete operation, including acting as its principal projectionist. It would run, she told *Variety*, on a split-week basis: on Tuesdays through Thursdays, the theater would be open only to members of the Center for Public Cinema (the nonprofit, subscription-based organization Geffen set up for his theaters), free of charge, to show obscure classics from nontheatrical distributors, including Audio-Brandon; and on weekends, Fridays through Sundays, regular admissions would be available both to members and the public, to see premieres of foreign and independent films.[12]

Of the three theaters, the Carnegie Hall Cinema was the class act, as befitted its location in the prestigious, high-culture Carnegie Hall building. The murals and gilded boxes on the side of the theater's auditorium gave it a touch of elegance. Its Parisian-style

Exterior of Carnegie Hall building. The canopy of the Carnegie Hall Cinema can be seen around the corner at the far right edge, on 57th Street. Photofest.

café lounge, which had been Geffen's idea, offered patrons sophisticated relaxation before and after screenings. Named Café Mille Yeux (Café Thousand Eyes), it served, the Fall 1979 calendar announced, "cappuccino, espresso, pastries, ice cream, natural fruit juices, bagels, yogurt, and more." Geffen hired a student from the School of Visual Arts, who, Raynal recalled, "painted it like a French old-fashioned café, and Sid put in the first espresso machine. There were coffee machines in movie houses a long time before, and Sid put that back." Carnegie Hall reminded a former patron of Edward Hopper's painting *New York Movie*, "because of the stairway that you used to use to descend to the basement-level auditorium."[13]

Geffen enhanced the prestige of the theater with periodic lectures in its lobby, even though, as Jim Harvey, a frequent patron, observed, "[t]hey certainly didn't add to the box office take." Harvey, in fact, presented a talk at the Carnegie on Robert Bresson's *Au Hasard, Balthazar* (1966).

Like a poor relation, the Bleecker "was a classy dump," Harvey remembered, "shabby, and smaller than the Carnegie." But it had the prestige of the Thousand Eyes Bookshop within its walls. "The bookstore was my idea," Raynal explained. "It was huge; we had about 1,200 titles. We used to sell foreign magazines and a lot of books." The theater continued to attract independent filmmakers, as it had done in Rogosin's time. One of the rooms on the second floor of the theater was rented for several years to First Run Features, a small, independent distribution company, whose ten-person staff, which included the future director Spike Lee, was squeezed into office space normally inhabited by one person.

The exterior of the Bleecker Street Cinema and 1000 Eyes Film Bookshop. Collection of the Cinémathèque de Toulouse.

David Denby, film critic for *New York* magazine, once characterized Geffen's enterprise as "an organization of utopian aims and minimal budget." His expansive ideas—two theaters, a bookstore—required money; and around the middle to late 1974 he devised a solution to his financial inconveniences. Buying the name of the Thousand Eyes Film Society from its owners, Howard Mandelbaum and Roger McNiven, (the name, according to Raynal, came from Fritz Lang's *The Thousand Eyes of Dr. Mabuse*, 1960), he created the nonprofit Thousand Eyes Film Club, under which he placed his two theaters and operated them as part of a nonprofit organization. "So instead of running the Bleecker Street as the Bleecker Street or the Carnegie Hall as the Carnegie Hall," Raynal explained, "they were under the umbrella of the Thousand Eyes." The Thousand Eyes Film Club sold membership subscriptions and offered membership benefits, including discount tickets, but it also sold individual tickets to nonmembers. It was an amalgam of a nonprofit and a for-profit theater. This setup enabled him to wring additional income from the box office at the expense of the distributors: the organization shared only a percentage of the discounted and regular admission tickets with the distributors while keeping the annual membership fees as clear profit.[14]

Distributors objected to this setup. In the summer of 1978, Columbia, Paramount, Warner Bros., United Artists, Universal, and 20th Century-Fox filed a lawsuit against the Thousand Eyes, alleging "systematic underreporting of box office grosses," in particular not reporting membership income as part of the box office gross and reducing admissions through the sale of member discount tickets. This was a violation, the lawsuit claimed, of the distributor's film licensing agreements; punitive damages were sought for over $79,000 in back rentals as well as damages and costs. (Raynal said that the companies eventually lost the suit.) That summer, Geffen then established another not-for-profit corporation, The Center for Public Cinema, as an end run around the lawsuit.[15]

The Center operated essentially the same as the Thousand Eyes, with one critical difference. Geffen gave both theaters a members-only policy (only members of The Center could buy tickets to the theaters, replicating the structure of the earlier Cinema 16), but then created a temporary membership, with which a nonmember could buy a temporary membership for $2.00 and an admission ticket for the member discount of $2.00. Geffen would then pay a percentage of the $2.00 admission ticket to the distributors. "If he were paying 35 percent for a double feature," Michael Silberman, who worked for Geffen in the early eighties, explained, "he'd be paying 70 cents to them. The $2.00 membership went to a separate fund for the Public Cinema." Some companies, he added, would not serve Geffen because of that loophole.[16]

Although also under the rubric of the Center, the Agee Room operated more legitimately since it showed only 16mm films that were obtained directly from the producers or from nontheatrical distributors. Fifty percent of the proceeds, reported *Soho Weekly*, would go to the producer of the film that was showing. "This policy," the article explained, "keeps the Agee's programming strictly noncommercial, since there will be no profits to share with commercial film distributors." In the reporter's view, this finally justified the Center for Public Cinema's nonprofit status.[17]

The income from the Thousand Eyes Film Club and, later, the Center for Public Cinema, went for good causes, Raynal insisted. In addition to supporting the two (and eventually three) theaters, it helped pay for his various projects. Creating a network of theaters was only one of his dreams. He set up a Cinema Information Service, according to Thompson, which was intended to provide free programming information to repertory theaters nationwide (it ended up, however, primarily serving the Bleecker and the Carnegie). Another was an attempt to organize all the repertory theater owners into an association. In the fall of 1979, the Center for Public Cinema and the Harold Clurman Theater, an Off Broadway theater that instituted a film program, began a relationship, which, according to John Pierson, the film programmer at the time for the Clurman, was "the first step in the Center for Public Cinema's broader-range project ... of trying to foster more collaboration among all of the repertory people in New York, including both commercial and nonprofit exhibitors and museums." Pierson recalled that Geffen tried "to bring all the repertory folks who were competitive and not necessarily that trusting of each other into a coalition. I remember going to those meetings and finding it fascinating." The project fizzled, though, other than creating a joint presentation by the Clurman and the Center of "A Tribute to Arthur Miller" for two days in November 1979 at the Carnegie.[18]

Cover of the November 1976 issue of *Thousand Eyes* magazine. Collection of the Cinémathèque de Toulouse.

His most innovative and successful ancillary creation was the *Thousand Eyes* magazine, which began around the first quarter of 1974. Much of the income from the Thousand Eyes Film Club, Raynal claimed, went to support the magazine. An especially ambitious venture to cover all of repertory programming in New York City, it started modestly as a stapled, letter-size, eleven-page pamphlet with a few articles and revival schedules of the various repertory theaters, then underwent different shapes and sizes, peaking in 1979 at its most expensive and ambitious incarnation—a pocket-size journal with a detailed calendar for twenty-one repertory and nonprofit theaters, plus short articles highlighting the main events of the month, and an index of every film by title, director, and language. This expansion into "a more comprehensive, regular publication that will include the schedule of every repertory cinema in New York" was probably part of Geffen's strategy to organize New York exhibitors.[19]

But this expanded version failed to motivate other theaters to organize and became too expensive for the Center alone, so in October 1980, it took on a tabloid format; a new name, *Focus on Public Cinema*; and a shrunken territory—it now focused its spotlight only on Geffen's three theaters. The more modest *Focus* carried the monthly schedules of all three theaters in the middle of each issue, and then devoted its remaining space to larger articles on the special film programs that Geffen's theaters were running. The February 1981 issue gives an idea of the breadth of information of even the reduced version: a full-page, in-depth article by Thompson discussing the two films of the Polish director Andrzej Wajda that were premiering at the Bleecker; a review of the work and joint careers of Lerner and Loewe in relation to the tribute to these songwriters in the Melody Makers series at the Carnegie; a discussion of the films then currently playing in the James Agee Room; and two more full-page articles, one on Roman Polanski by Tom Campbell, in anticipation of the forthcoming retrospective of his work, and the second, by Raynal, relating to the series in the James Agee Room, "Radical Images: World Politics in the Seventies."[20]

"Whatever money he made," Raynal explained, somewhat hyperbolically, "he spent it on the magazine. He had about ten people working on it. You had to have a staff to do a 28-, 30-page magazine. There was no internet or computers then." Bulk mailings were made to the approximately twelve thousand members of the Thousand Eyes Film Club, and free copies were laid out in both theaters, as well as at other repertory houses like Anthology Film Archives and Film Forum. But the income from his theaters and film clubs also supported his reckless spending. "The money would go quickly when it was there," Thompson remembered. "Several times we had particularly successful summers, but he would go ahead and spend it rather than save it for the colder months, January and February, when it got much harder to get people to come out." Geffen's chronic irresponsibility with money—Raynal characterized it as "he didn't care about money"—contributed to the chasm between his "utopian aims and minimal budget."

Despite this unpromising context, Geffen managed to build a complex, rickety structure that somehow stayed upright and became a preserve of film culture in New York.

Unlike other repertory house owners like Dan Talbot at the New Yorker, Frank Rowley at the Regency, and Howard Otway at Theatre 80 St. Marks, Geffen relied for the programming at his theaters on mostly young cineastes, a number of them New York University (NYU) students, whom he employed on a full-time, part-time, or freelance basis for minimal salaries (like all rep house owners).

Many of his staff found him to be an erratic micromanager, throwing them off balance with his last-minute decision reversals. "Sidney would get very involved, for instance, in what color the movie marquee letters should be," Barbara Nitke remembered, "and always changing his mind. He'd say, 'I don't know if we should put up the red letters today. Can you come up with black ones instead?' You'd just tear your hair out, because you're trying to get the letters up in time for the next day. I was the manager maybe six months." Thompson recalled that "[i]f something was working smoothly, he'd like to change it." There was the anguish he would cause Thompson and Raynal in putting out the *Thousand Eyes* magazine. "He always loved to change the format," recalled Raynal. "Well, the format was perfect. 'Why do you change it, it's more money,' I'd ask him. 'No, no, no,' he'd say. It was a strain all the time." The monthly calendars came out late a few times because Geffen decided he didn't like the layout. "He would say," Thompson remembered, "'I don't care about money, that's not the important thing, the important thing is to get it right.' But then he would become upset when the box office was doing poorly because people did not know what was playing."

Because of his immoderate spending, which often left him without even money for cab fare, Geffen resorted to tactics that gave him a controversial reputation in the film community. Delaying bill payments was one ploy. Mandelbaum, who worked at the Carnegie for a while after selling the name of his film society to Geffen, recalled that he ignored bills. "I used to answer the phone," he said, "and people at Easter time were calling from department stores for the money that he spent at Christmas for presents. Sid would say to me, 'Howard, don't you know, nobody pays bills anymore.'"

"Everybody in the city," Thompson remembered, "used to have a Sid Geffen story about how Sid had screwed them or something like that." A number of these stories centered on his propensity for firing staff to save money, particularly the seasoned managers, who were better paid than the other staff. (According to Raynal, Geffen followed the advice of Ben Barenholtz, who had advised him to pay his managers double the rest of the staff, so they would "keep an eye on the box office" in order to prevent stealing by the cashiers.) One such axed employee was Bingham Ray, Geffen's longtime manager of the Bleecker and Carnegie. Raynal remembered that he claimed to fire him for his own benefit—"he said he was better off doing other things. He could go to Hollywood, make a career." Ironically, in this instance Geffen was right. After spending some time working at Talbot's Metro Theater, Bingham moved to Los Angeles and had a prestigious career as a leading force in independent films for more than two decades.[21]

Other staff suffered the same fate as Ray. "I was hearing all these stories from people when I was being hired about this character Sid Geffen," Larry Chadbourne, an ex-graduate student from Brown University who managed the Bleecker and Carnegie in the eighties, recalled. "He was going through management and staff very quickly." Raynal thought the reputation was unwarranted; she insisted that he only fired people for good cause, like stealing. But some of his former staff remembered differently. Marty Rubin, who managed and programmed the Bleecker Street Cinema in the late 1970s, would hear him say that he had a flush system for flushing employees in and out. His strategy was to deliberately provoke an employee into quitting. In New York at that time there was a multitude of young film students and cineastes wanting to work in the repertory houses. "He knew that he had this constant pool of people," Rubin said, "who had the knowledge and the desire to do it."[22]

One young NYU student who escaped the usual fate was Penny Yates, his first programmer, whom he had selected from a list of recommendations provided by the university at his request. For approximately eight years until around 1978, Yates served as his longest-lasting and most valued employee. "He trusted Penny," Raynal recalled. "She could do whatever she wanted, carte blanche. She was extremely modest and extremely professional. She was a gift for Sid Geffen." Yates was one of the few staff who could get along with the difficult Geffen. "She had a serene, diplomatic personality," Rubin remembered, "and a certain amount of class."

The indispensable Yates was the author of the early success of the Carnegie and Bleecker. She took charge of most aspects of programming, from selecting films to negotiating with distributors, and even acting in a public relations capacity when necessary. In a letter to the *New York Times* editor in 1974, for instance, she responded to a complaint from a patron about the poor print of *A Night at the Opera* (1935) that played at the Carnegie with a defense of the theater, arguing that the blame lay with the indifferent distributors, who often sent butchered prints to revival houses close to the screening date (as they did in this case), thus leaving her little choice but either to show it in its poor condition or to play nothing at all. At the end of the letter, expressing the frustration

Penny Yates was editor of the *Thousand Eyes* magazine, 1978. Collection of the Cinémathèque de Toulouse.

common to most rep house programmers, she asked: "Why do distributors confirm 'bookings' of films when they have nothing to offer but butchered prints? Why do distributors fail to maintain or replace their prints when necessary?"[23]

In preparing programs, Yates perused *Variety* to keep current with film releases and maintained extensive files with notes on all the films. She was up-to-date on the availability of films, developed a sense of what kinds of films would work with the audience, and what types of combinations to put them in. Her standard format for each season at both theaters consisted of vertical series on specific days of the week and random double features for the rest of the week. "Yates's programming," wrote a *Villager* reporter in a look back at the two theaters, "soon established the mix of styles, periods, and nations which was to prove popular at both theaters."[24]

Typical of Yates's rich mix was the Summer 1975 schedule for the Carnegie, in which she scheduled a Jean-Luc Godard retrospective on Mondays from June 16 through August 25; a festival of Charlie Chaplin and Harry Langdon films, "Comedy Kings: Chaplin and Harry Langdon," on Wednesdays in July; and a Yasujiro Ozu special, "Yasujiro Ozu: Selected Features," on Wednesdays in August. The random double features in that season included a World War I–themed double feature, Lewis Milestone's *All Quiet on the Western Front* (1930) and Stanley Kubrick's *Paths of Glory* (1957); a pairing of two silent films, F.W. Murnau's *The Last Laugh* (1924) and E.A. Dupont's *Variety* (1925), both starring the great German actor Emil Jannings; and a director-themed double feature, Volker Schlondorff's *A Free Woman* (1972) paired with his *The Sudden Wealth of the Poor People of Kombach* (1970).

The festivals at the two theaters were frequently director retrospectives or mini-series (Jean-Luc Godard, Akira Kurosawa, and Ingmar Bergman were favorites, but older and contemporary American directors—John Ford, Howard Hawks, and Robert Altman, for example—also received notice). A miscellany of interesting festivals appeared sporadically, such as a series of gay festivals, which the Bleecker screened over several years, and festivals from the catalogue of individual distributors, Janus Films and Almi Cinema 5, which were screened in 1979 and 1982 respectively.

Often the retrospectives of directors and stars highlighted their earlier works or less familiar ones. The "Luis Buñuel Festival" at the Carnegie in the fall 1976 season, for example, included, in addition to familiar films like *Viridiana* (1961), such lesser known works as *The Adventures of Robinson Crusoe* (1954), *Illusion Travels by Streetcar* (1954), and *The Milky Way* (1969), an "irreverent satire by Buñuel that starts where *L'Âge d'or* left off." Periodically, a series would be shared between the two theaters. In the Winter 1976–1977 season, a Cary Grant retrospective began at the Bleecker and continued at the Carnegie.[25]

Jackie Raynal and Sid Geffen standing beneath the Bleecker Street Cinema marquee, ca. 1979–80. Photograph by V. Moszynski. Collection of the Cinémathèque de Toulouse.

The random double features ranged from classic American and foreign films (the films of Jean Cocteau and Orson Welles were frequently screened as was Marcel Carne's *Children of Paradise*), the films of auteur directors from the 1950s through the 1970s ("We used to play a lot of Buñuel films at both theaters," Raynal explained, "plus Resnais films, Godard, and John Ford, Fritz Lang, and of course Fellini"), the American New Wave films of the 1970s (Robert Altman's *Three Women*, 1977, for example, was on the schedules periodically), foreign and American independent films, and more recent Hollywood products, like Robert Mulligan's *To Kill a Mockingbird* (1962).

Although the Carnegie and Bleecker often screened the same or related films, there were differences between their programs. Both Raynal and Thompson attributed much of the distinctions to geography. The Bleecker, catering to the students from three surrounding colleges, could experiment with the more unconventional films that the students preferred, while the Carnegie, in the midst of a conservative, cultural bastion, concentrated on classic American and foreign films, such as musicals and older British comedies. The subway station next to the Carnegie brought in a large crowd of Russian-Americans from Astoria on Sundays for the Russian ballet films. Films that the staff thought would attract a large number of people were programmed at the larger Carnegie.

Representative of the Carnegie's more conservative approach were the "Melody Makers," festivals of the musicals of American composers such as Cole Porter and Rodgers and Hart. The highbrow Carnegie audience also enjoyed film adaptations of plays, such as *Noel Coward on Screen* and *Eugene O'Neill on Film*. The Carnegie especially favored festivals of stars—a Marlon Brando retrospective in the winter 1975-76 season surveyed his films from 1956 to 1972, and a Jean Seberg festival in October 1981 featured a number of her "Seberg and France" films, starting with Otto Preminger's *Bonjour Tristesse* (1958) and including Jean-Luc Godard's *Breathless* (1960) and Romain Gary's x-rated *Birds in Peru* (1968). Personal appearances by stars became a specialty of the Carnegie. In January 1982 Myrna Loy, Sylvia Sidney, and Tony Randall introduced their respective films in a series on forgotten films of the thirties through fifties, based on John Springer's book *Forgotten Films to Remember*; Joan Bennett made an appearance at a four-film tribute to her in December 1980; and for the Sophia Loren Festival in September 1980, Ms. Loren introduced her film *The Black Orchid* (1958). Finally, a special feature in the theater was the 2/9 Wurlitzer Theatrical Pipe Organ, which premiered at the Carnegie in March 1977, with organist Lee Erwin accompanying two silent film versions of *Camille*, the 1912 one starring Sarah Bernhardt and the 1927 version with Norma Talmadge. "Lee Erwin at the Organ" became a regular accompaniment to Carnegie's ongoing series of silent films.[26]

The Bleecker could be more experimental with the offbeat, avant-garde films favored by the students at the neighboring colleges: New York University, the New School for Social Research, and the School of Visual Arts. Picking up on the popularity of weekend midnight movies with the young crowd, for example, it began its own midnight specials; in winter 1977 it screened a "Surrealistic Animation Celebration" along with *High School Confidential* (1958), starring Mamie Van Doren, one of the first Marilyn Monroe imitators.

Early on, Geffen brought programs into the Bleecker that he thought would appeal to the younger crowd. Shortly after the Bleecker opened, he reached out to the Association of Independent Video and Film Makers (AIVF), the first postwar trade association for independent filmmakers, to enlist their help in programming independent films. Marc Weiss, who was then a young, leftwing activist and filmmaker and the vice president of the association, volunteered. It was a mutually satisfactory arrangement. Nurturing the independent movement was the organization's priority, exhibition was the key to this effort, and Geffen was presenting them with one of their first real opportunities. For Geffen, it would hopefully shore up the nascent theater's box office with little financial risk since a minimal investment of money was involved. "He was basically paying me some paltry amount per week," Weiss said, "and I think we weren't paying the filmmakers rent, we were splitting the box office or something like that with them." In addition, Weiss pointed out, he was tapping into the theater's identity as a venue for independent films. "It was consistent," Weiss said, "with the spirit of the Bleecker Street Cinema when Lionel Rogosin was there."[27]

Weiss's program consisted mostly of the issue-oriented, political documentaries of young filmmakers, who were politicized by the movements of the late sixties and seventies—the antiwar movement, the civil rights movement, the Women's Movement, the Black Power movement, and the beginnings of the environmental movement. Included among his selections was one on Indian rights (*Broken Treaty at Battle Mountain*, 1974); another on the countercultural lifestyle (*A Man, a Woman, and a Killer*, 1975); and a French film about a strike in a French factory (*Coup pour coup*, 1972). One of the first films to receive a *Times* review, *Men's Lives* (1974), embodied a feminist perspective on growing up male in America. The documentary was made by two young men, Will Roberts and Josh Hanig, while they were students at Antioch College. It explored "the masculine mystique in a competitive society," wrote the *New York Times* reviewer. Weiss, who had viewed the film while on a speaking engagement at Antioch, told Geffen on his return that he wanted to show it and would try to get publicity for it. Geffen liked that. Thanks to the positive review, "[t]hat film," Weiss said, "then became part of New Day Films [a feminist filmmakers' distribution cooperative]. It was a consciousness-raising film for men, the first of its kind, a really, really influential film."[28]

On the double bill with *Men's Lives* was *Janie's Jane* (1971), about a welfare mother in New Jersey, which was obtained through his personal connections with its filmmaker, Geri Asher, a member of Newsreel, a radical documentary film production and distribution collective. *Janie's Jane* was one of the first feminist films in the early seventies, a period, Sklar discussed in *Movie-Made America*, when women filmmakers who wanted to explore questions of feminism found a home in the alternative cinema. These early feminist documentaries, like *Janie's Jane*, focused on filming women talking about their lives.[29]

From December 1974 to March 1975, Weiss organized three separate programs of independent films that ran in different time slots. The Free Film-Makers' Showcase, similar to the setup that the Charles Theater had offered novice filmmakers in 1961, announced an open invitation to new, independent filmmakers who needed a free screening, *Newsday* reported, for "an incomplete or unsold film they must show to backers, distributors, family, cast, or crew." These unscheduled screenings ran from 2:00 p.m. to 4:00 p.m. on Tuesdays and Wednesdays. The second program, Film-Makers' Showcase, featured the world or U.S. premieres of new, independent films on weekdays at 4:00 p.m. and weekends at noon. The third program, Independent Cinema Spotlight, screened new films and independent classics with filmmakers present and ran every Monday night at 9:30. "I finally prevailed on Sid to give me one evening slot," Weiss recalled, "and Monday being the worst night of the week, that's what he gave me."[30]

Among the four premieres in the Film-Makers' Showcase was *The Bearding of the President* (1969), an 18½ minute film directed by and starring Rip Torn, which was repeated in the Monday night Independent Cinema Spotlight. "I programmed it with other shorts in the Film-Makers' Showcase," Weiss said, "and in the Independent Cinema Spotlight, I paired it with one of Rip Torn's feature films, *Pay Day* [1973], and brought in Rip for a special appearance. It was a strategy to use this already well known film and Rip's presence to get *Bearding* launched." Weiss was quickly learning programming strategies.[31]

Along with *The Bearding of the President,* Weiss screened four classic independent films in the Independent Cinema Spotlight: Al Maysles' *Salesman* (1968), an acclaimed cinéma-vérité account of a Bible salesman's life; Emile de Antonio and Dan Talbot's film

Point of Order!; and two films associated with Rogosin's Bleecker—Mekas's *The Brig* and Rogosin's *On the Bowery*.

The three programs ran through the end of March 1975, and then Weiss left. "I tried to organize a strike," he said. "Geffen would pay us almost nothing, but he would take us out to these big dinners at Rocco's and I would say, 'Don't buy me dinner, I need that money as salary. Please raise our salaries.' 'No, no,' he said. From my perspective, we were being exploited." Weiss organized five or six of the employees into a two-day strike, which ended when Geffen gave them an ultimatum. "A couple of them wanted to keep working there," Weiss remembered, "so they went back to work. And that's when I left."

With this hands-on experience in programming, promotion, and publicity, Weiss moved from filmmaking to programming, where he felt he could make a greater contribution to the independent movement. Shortly after, he opened *Union Maids* (1976) at the Elgin, one of the first independent documentaries to get national visibility, and in 1986 created the program *POV* on PBS, "probably the single most visible showcase," Weiss said, "for documentary films in the U.S. today." Although the Bleecker program was not a major box office success, one could say that Geffen and the Bleecker Street Cinema had a positive influence on the independent film movement.

Yates, as well as Geffen, was open to program ideas for the Bleecker that would appeal to the students in the area. In 1977, Bill Thompson, a recent arrival from the University of Michigan's Ann Arbor campus where he had been business manager and treasurer for the campus's film society, approached Yates with an idea for a Japanese series; his interest in doing it was partly for his own education. Yates was receptive, and together they decided to test it out on Tuesdays, generally the weakest day after Monday. "If nobody came to the theater," he said, "we weren't losing that much." The series did so well that it became one of the Bleecker's most popular festivals, running uninterruptedly for five years on Tuesdays until early 1983. "Throughout," Thompson said with pride, "it supported itself."

The first program took place in December 1977, and by January 1978, the series assumed its permanent title, "Spectrum of Japanese Cinema." The films came from art house distributors like Kino, Audio-Brandon, and Janus Films, as well as from the Japanese production companies with offices in the U.S. "Toho had an office on 1600 Broadway," Thompson recalled, "and Shochiku had one on the West Coast. We didn't have much money for shipping so we got a lot of films from Toho's New York office. But we did get some from Shochiku." Later, the head of Shochiku's Los Angeles office helped Thompson get Daiei [another production company] films, including good samurai films that had never been shown in New York. As Thompson explained, Daiei films were normally distributed by Shochiku only in a limited number of cities in the West and Midwest.

Over its five years Spectrum provided the education in Japanese film that Thompson wanted for himself and the public. The inaugural Winter 1977–1978 season included films from the 1930s and 1940s, such as a silent Ozu, *Passing Fancy* (1933), about a young boy and his disillusioned relationship with his father, as well as more recent genre films: samurai, ghost, detective, bizarre sexual practices, traditional family features, comedy, yakuza. Two special highlights were a Nagisa Oshima mini-series, including the New York premiere of *Violence at Noon* (1966), the portrayal of a violent rapist, and a Kinuya Tanaka tribute—Tanaka, who had died earlier in the year, was a quintessential Mizoguchi heroine—that included the East Coast premiere of one of her best films, *Aizen Katsura* (1938). In the Spring 1978 program, the series featured four works by Kurosawa (*Rashomon*, 1950;

Red Beard, 1965; *Dodes'Ka'den*, 1970; and *The Lower Depths*, 1957); Kenji Mizoguchi's *Ugetsu* (1953) and Keisuke Kinoshita's *The Ballad of the Narayama* (1958); and rarer but well-received works like Yasuki Chiba's *Downtown* (1957), an unsentimental account of the brief happiness found by a widow in postwar Japan. The spring season also presented the New York theatrical premiere of Ozu's *The Brothers and Sisters of the Toda Family* (1941). The goal, Thompson explained in the season's calendar, was "to demonstrate the breadth and depth of both classical and contemporary Japanese cinema."[32]

Thompson followed the usual repertory house programming strategy, pairing a familiar film with a little-known one. He was inventive in creating publicity for Spectrum. In mid–November 1982 he premiered *Mr. Radish and Mr. Carrot*, based on an original story by Ozu, as a companion to the Japan Society's Ozu retrospective. To help celebrate the fifth anniversary of the series, he arranged for Sawako Ariyoshi, Japan's leading female writer, to make a personal appearance at the Bleecker to discuss her novels, *The River Ki* and *Twilight Years*, whose filmed versions were both screened for the anniversary. Another special event in honor of the anniversary was a live demonstration of Japanese fencing on the Bleecker's stage by the Japan Swordsmanship Society.[33]

New York or East Coast premieres, such as Mizoguchi's *Story of the Last Chrysanthemums* (1939), were a specialty of Spectrum. "A lot of the films," Thompson said, "that we got from Audio Brandon had never been shown before theatrically in New York. When I wanted to go big in opening a film, I went for two days rather than one." He also introduced a number of interesting, little known, Japanese popular entertainment features. Many of the films in Japan's longest running series, the twenty-five Zatoichi movies that were made in Japan between 1962 and 1973, screened at the Bleecker Street. Zatoichi, explained a *New York Times* reviewer, was "a hero of Japanese action filmdom, a ronin, or masterless samurai who is tough, a superb swordsman, sometimes within the law and sometimes outside it." Another popular series that premiered at the Bleecker in December 1982 was the unfamiliar films of Raizo Ichikawa, a young actor who died early in his career in the late 1960s. Thompson introduced over twenty Raizo pictures, including the entire "Kyoshiro Nemuri" series featuring the actor as an alienated half-breed samurai, and the "Shinobi no Mono" ninja series, which were among Spectrum's most popular premieres.[34]

In an adroit programming strategy, Thompson booked mostly samurai and action films, a popular feature for the young during the summer months, while concentrating on films related to Japanese culture, family life, and literature during the rest of the year. Among the samurai double features in the summers were two of Hiroshi Inagaki's films starring Toshiro Mifune—*Rikisha Man* (1958) and *Duel at Genryu Island* (1956), the concluding film of Inagaki's *Samurai Trilogy*, about a peasant's rise to samurai fame. For the enthusiastic young, the summer series were the Japanese version of the Saturday cowboy features of an earlier day. Wendell Jamieson, who had been a devotee of the summer programs as a youngster, recalled in a 2011 *New York Times* article how his immersion in the samurai films featuring major samurai stars like Tatsuya Nakadai and Toshiro Mifune developed into a lifelong passion for the genre. "Spectrum of Japanese Cinema" lasted until Thompson left the Bleecker in 1983.[35]

One of Yates's most important projects for the two theaters involved organizing festivals of national cinemas under the auspices of the Thousand Eyes Film Club, in co-sponsorship with various foreign consulates and other cultural entities, like Goethe House in New York. Yates or Thompson would approach cultural centers offering them a theater

The March 1978 program at the Carnegie Hall Cinema was part of Geffen's focus on foreign imports. Collection of the Cinémathèque de Toulouse.

where their filmmakers and films could appear. "This was good business for both of us," Thompson explained. "If the people [mostly directors] were coming to New York and the cultural center could provide us with a print of their film, it wouldn't cost us much money. And they were happy to work with us. It was publicity for them as well as for us."

Yates, Thompson, and Raynal scheduled these programs for the theaters they best suited. A series of festivals at the Bleecker drew attention to the emergence of third world national cinemas, reflecting the passions of the Bleecker's left-leaning, young audience. In March 1976, the first Egyptian film program to tour the U.S. was arranged in cooperation with the American Film Institute and the Association of Arab-American University Graduates. Most of the films portrayed personal dramas within the social, political, and economic context of that country. Also in 1976, the "Cinema Novo: Brazil" festival highlighted the radical movement of young Brazilian filmmakers in the sixties. Yates followed up at the Bleecker with an "Iranian Cinema Festival" in spring 1977, and a "Middle Eastern

Film Festival" in spring 1978, representing, according to the blurb, the best work by Middle Eastern filmmakers "who broke from a film tradition of romantic melodrama to create provocative and expressive films exploring life in one of the most explosive and misunderstood regions of the world."[36]

In contrast to the Bleecker's spotlighting of third world cinema, the Carnegie inclined to the "style and intellectual content of European and American films." (This distinction was not hard and fast; the Bleecker also programmed contemporary independent films from Germany and Belgium.) Between midwinter 1977 and spring 1978, as Yates was probably reducing her work load, Thompson and Raynal negotiated with foreign consulates and cultural entities to stage special events at the Carnegie. "Berlin Now: Recent German Feature Films" was part of a major citywide cultural event sponsored by Goethe House in New York; "Soviet Cinema: Yesterday & Today" was presented in association with the American Film Institute with cooperation of Goskino in Moscow. The latter highlighted three crucial periods in the Soviet cinema since the Revolution: the late-silent, early sound years, 1927–34 (mounting such films as Sergei Eisenstein's 1927 *October*); the post–Stalin thaw of 1957–60 (with films like Sergei Bondarchuk's 1959 *Fate of a Man*); and the new directions of the past ten years (mostly premieres of films like Georgy Danelia's 1975 *Afonia*). In 1978 "Yugoslavian Cinema: Past, Present and Future," took place at the Carnegie in two parts: the initial program in the spring was a three-day series sponsored by Yugoslavian Film; the second program in the fall of that year, sponsored by the Federal Administration for International Scientific, Educational, Cultural and Technical Cooperation (JUZAMS), screened a retrospective of Yugoslavian films from the postwar period to date. With the second series the *Thousand Eyes* published a booklet on the history of Yugoslavian cinema.

In addition to these national cinema festivals, Yates and others also negotiated for the works of individual directors, mostly from Germany, Scandinavia, and Eastern Europe, who were famous in their native land but unknown in the U.S. In October 1977, "The Films of Reinhard Hauff," one of the more obscure New German Cinema directors, was presented in cooperation with Goethe House at Carnegie Hall; Hauff was on hand to discuss his films. Eugene Ionesco, better known as a playwright than filmmaker, discussed his film *La Vase* (1970), directed by Heinz von Cramer, on March 19, 1978, courtesy of the Académie du Cinéma. The Danish director Jorgen Leth, considered Denmark's leading avant-garde filmmaker, made a special appearance at the Carnegie in the fall of 1980 as part of a one-day presentation of premieres of three of his films. A year later Leth returned with three more films. By 1981 *Variety* was reporting that the Center for Public Cinema had an ambitious program of "exposing pics without distributors" and that its ongoing relationships with cultural entities such as the Danish and Yugoslav consulates "resulted in showing Jorgan Leth documentaries from Denmark and local bows of [leading Yugoslavian director] Aleksandar Petrovic's *The Master and Margarita* [1972] and his UA-produced (but unreleased in U.S.) *Group Portrait with Lady* [1977]."[37]

Raynal, meanwhile, was using her connections with the French film industry to stage annual festivals of French independent films at the Carnegie. For the midwinter 1977 season she worked with the Société des réalisateurs français, an organization of French film directors, to screen "Perspectives on French Cinema," which launched the premieres of eight new French independent films, as did "French Producer's [*sic*] Week" for six new French films in the spring of 1979. Another event, "Positif at 30," an elaborate eight days of screenings, directors' appearances, and critics' roundtable discussions, took place in October 1982 under the auspices of Unifrance, the French Film Office, and the Center for Public Cinema. It celebrated "thirty years of thought provoking [sic] film criticism published by the French film journal Positif," a leftwing magazine, which championed popular American cinema. The eight-day festival coupled American films, including Robert Altman's *Three Women* (1977), Jerry Schatzberg's *Scarecrow* (1973), and Martin Scorcese's *Mean Streets* (1973), with French ones, such as Bertrand Tavernier's *The Clockmaker* (1974), Claude Sautet's *Un Mauvais Fils* (1980), and Jacques Bral's *Exterieur Nuit* (1980). The idea behind the series, Michel Ciment, the editor of the magazine, explained in a *Focus* essay, was to combine contemporary films of French directors who had been neglected in favor of the New Wave ones with those of American directors.[38]

In the fall of 1977 Raynal brought in Serge Daney, a leading French film critic and editor-in-chief of *Cahiers du Cinéma*, to develop a series, this time at the Bleecker, entitled "Semaine des *Cahiers du Cinéma*" ("A Week of *Cahiers du Cinéma*"). Premieres of independent films by avant-garde European filmmakers with introductions by Daney were the feature presentations. Included were Godard's *Ici et ailleurs* (1976) and *Comment ça va* (1976), Chantal Akerman's *News from Home* (1977), Wim Wenders' *Kings of the Road* (1976), and Jean-Marie Straub and Daniele Huillet's *Fortini/Cani* (1976). Daney, whose writings had not yet been translated into English, was relatively unknown in the States, despite his prominent reputation in France. In an ambitious undertaking, Raynal and Geffen produced a special, glossy issue of the *Thousand Eyes* magazine, which included translations of *Cahiers* texts on the programmed films, plus the first English translation of Daney's seminal essay on Godard and an interview with Daney, which illuminated "how Daney and the *Cahiers* went from their 'passions for films like BABY FACE NELSON (Siegel) and RANCHO NOTORIOUS (Lang)' to 'films made in factories, ghettoes and armed camps all over the world.'" *Ici et ailleurs*, a film that contrasted a French family (*Ici*/Here) with a Palestinian family (*Ailleurs*/Elsewhere), was the cause of a minor crisis, when, Raynal said, an anonymous, "Zionist person" telephoned the Bleecker Street box office during

The premiere of *Cahiers du Cinéma* week at the Bleecker Street Cinema, fall 1977. Collection of the Cinémathèque de Toulouse.

Special *Thousand Eyes* magazine issue for *Cahiers du Cinéma* week. Collection of the Cinémathèque de Toulouse.

Cahiers du Cinéma week and threatened to put a bomb in the theater if it were shown. (Naming the threatening caller a "Zionist" is more a reflection of Raynal's political biases than of the reality. For one thing, his or her identity was never discovered.) Geffen hired a guard at night to patrol the theater. "We were afraid," wrote Raynal in an e-mail from Paris to the author, "that the same thing would happen to us that did happen in Paris at the Saint Michel Cinema [when *Ici et ailleurs* was shown there]: a group of Zionists bombed the auditorium and the fire destroyed the theater. Thank God no one was hurt as this act of violence happened at night." The Bleecker escaped any violence, and the series came off without incident.[39]

"The *Cahiers du Cinéma* Festival was a good idea," Raynal wrote in her e-mail, "[conceived] to give my great friend Serge Daney a sort of carte blanche. Who in New York would have ever wanted to program *Ici et ailleurs*, let alone buy it for distribution? Even if for no other reason, I wanted to give the Bleecker Street public what it was starving for." Sadly, the public did not seem to be starving for these avant-garde films, as Dan Talbot had also discovered; the series was not well-attended. "I recall distinctly Sid coming by the theatre in the evening," Chadbourne wrote in an e-mail. "He was disappointed by the poor attendance at that show and said, 'Today is "fuck your buddy" day.' I asked what he meant and he explained that the Bleecker and Carnegie had been friends to fans of interesting cinema, and instead the fans hadn't appreciated that."

Raynal, Rosenbaum remembered, was willing to entertain interesting ideas from different people; he credited her for supporting his ideas for two series and putting the time and energy into implementing them. Rosenbaum, whom Godard later judged "one of the best film critics in America," had first met Geffen and Raynal at the Edinburgh Film Festival, where she showed her film *Deux Fois*. By 1978, he had moved from California to New York, partly in the hope of working for the two. "John Hughes [not the director] helped to convince me to move to New York," Rosenbaum said. "The major thing he used as a bait was that I could do all this work for Jackie and Sid."[40]

His first series for Raynal, a retrospective on key sound films entitled "Sound Thinking," was programmed in collaboration with film critic and writer Carrie Rickey; unfortunately it turned out to be a disappointing failure. "It was a very ambitious series," he recalled, "but it got screwed up, because Carrie and I prepared program notes for every film and they didn't print them. The whole point of the series was to contextualize it with writing. So it was just a group of films without any rhyme or reason for most people unless they understood the sound aspect." The fault, Rosenbaum felt, lay with Geffen's "capriciousness in changing his mind. First he could afford it, then he couldn't. There had to be a lot of follow through and in the case of 'Sound Thinking,' there just wasn't that."

His second effort, "Rivette in Context," a retrospective of Jacques Rivette's films at the Bleecker in February 1979, was more successfully executed. This was the second incarnation of the retrospective, the first one having taken place at London's National Film Theatre in August 1977, to accompany the publication of a book Rosenbaum had edited for the British Film Institute, *Rivette: Texts and Interviews*. For the Bleecker retrospective, copies of the book, which included an introduction by Rosenbaum and translations, mostly by Tom Milne, of two lengthy interviews with Rivette, plus three key critical texts by Rivette and a detailed biofilmography, were sold at some of the screenings. The *New York Times* "Weekender Guide" explained that the retrospective was "in context" because it included films by directors such as Otto Preminger and Howard Hawks, whose works influenced Rivette. Rosenbaum, however, in an e-mail, amended this explanation: Rivette's films, he wrote, were contextualized with films that the director had written about and discussed in various interviews.[41]

The Rivette films included *Out 1: Spectre* (1974), a four-hour version of Rivette's over-twelve-hour film, *Out 1* (1971); *Paris nous appartient* (*Paris Belongs to Us,* 1960); and *Céline et Julie vont en bateau* (*Celine and Julie Go Boating,* 1974). Among the films in the series that influenced Rivette were three Val Lewton films (*The Seventh Victim*, 1943, *Cat People*, 1942, and *I Walked with a Zombie*, 1943), Robert Kramer's political-fictional narrative *The Edge* (1967), avant-garde Czech film director Vera Chytilova's *Something Different* (1963), French cinéma vérité director Jean Rouch's *The Lion Hunters* (1965), and Otto Preminger's *Angel Face* (1952). One important U.S. premiere was *Meditérranée* (1963), a major French experimental film by Jean-Daniel Pollet, which was also the first film Raynal had worked on as an editor. "I had included the film," Rosenbaum explained in an essay on the two versions of the retrospective, "specifically because of Rivette's reference to it ... in *Rivette: Texts and Interviews*."[42]

The retrospective received press reviews by Roger Greenspun, Andrew Sarris, David Sterritt, and Amy Taubin. "One thing I do remember," Rosenbaum said, "which was a kind of triumph for Jackie and me and Sid, was that the Rivette series got an entire page of the *Village Voice* from Andrew Sarris and a piece by Roger Greenspun in some kind of smaller version of the *Village Voice*." Sarris placed Rivette's career in the context of his times and summarized the essence of his dense, ambiguous, multi-hour films in a tone of respect for a serious artist, acknowledging that not every film scholar, including Rosenbaum, agreed with his lukewarm views of Rivette's work. Taubin's review in the *Soho Weekly News* seemed to especially upset Rosenbaum. She questioned why he chose Rivette instead of another director like Bresson for the context idea, which she thought had value, and dismissed Rivette's films ("Rivette is an interesting director," she wrote, "a director for whom I have more sympathy than any one of his films deserve") without further explanation. Rosenbaum believed she had an underlying bias. "Her attack," he said, "was almost like a turf war, 'How dare you come in and do something like this.' I wrote a response to her review, basically calling her an ignoramus. She was making absurd comments and baseless charges, I thought." Taubin responded with an equally angry rebuttal. Despite the tepid reviews, Geffen was pleased that it had received publicity.[43]

Around the summer 1981, Geffen was including New York premieres at the Carnegie. With Raynal's assistance, he obtained exclusive rights to Godard's *Numéro deux*, a 1975 experimental film about a young family in a social housing complex in France. The film premiered in June 1981 in a way different from the typical New York opening. Like Talbot's experiment with "One Dollar at All Times," it was Geffen's attempt to avoid the costs of a typical New York opening. "*Numéro Deux* was important to us," Thompson remembered, "because we wanted to have an alternative way to introduce new films to the repertory and to New York without the expense that would come with the normal opening. The idea was if you could just plug it into a schedule, then you could open it on very little money." Geffen generated publicity for the film through his magazine *Focus*, with a cover announcement of the film's American premiere at the Carnegie and significant space devoted to articles relating to the film and director—an essay by Rosenbaum on Godard's later works and another by Carlos Clarens on the film itself.[44]

The second film that Geffen obtained exclusive rights to with Raynal's assistance was Marguerite Duras's *India Song* (1975), which premiered in August 1981 at the Carnegie. *India Song*, based on an unproduced play by Duras about the promiscuous wife of the French vice-consul in India, received a strong, positive review in the *New York Times* and led to requests from mainstream art chains to move it to their screens full time. At its premiere, Richard Roud, the director of the New York Film Festival, introduced Duras. In his introductory remarks, Roud reminisced about her collaboration with Alain Resnais on *Hiroshima, mon amour* (1959). "I don't know if Roud had too much to drink," Rosenbaum conjectured, "but he said, 'This is a wonderful thing that I just learned, that tonight … is the actual anniversary of when the bomb fell on Hiroshima.'" Duras, he recalled, handled it very gracefully.[45]

Geffen was especially proud of the film's success and followed it up with *Cinéastes de notre temps* (*Filmmakers of Our Time*), a French television series composed of a collection of documentaries, each of which deals with one filmmaker and is filmed in the style of that filmmaker.[46]

The early 1980s also saw Raynal and Geffen giving a big boost at the Bleecker to the group of New Wave American independent filmmakers who were part of the downtown New York scene, a disorganized, but vibrant, collective of artists, filmmakers, and musicians who were exploring the juncture of avant-garde and pop. The scene included Warhol-influenced painters Keith Haring and Jean-Michel Basquiat, musical groups the Talking Heads and the B-52s, and filmmakers Eric Mitchell, Beth B and Scott B, and Charles Ahearn. Jim Jarmusch had made his NYU thesis film, *Permanent Vacation* (1981), and would soon start on the low-budget *Stranger than Paradise*, which would help define

The premiere of *India Song* at the Carnegie Hall Cinema, August 1981. Collection of the Cinémathèque de Toulouse.

nonstudio cinema for the next generation. NYU graduate Susan Seidelman was the first of the downtown crowd to break through with her film, *Smithereens* (1982), a clear portrait of the downtown art and music scene, which was a surprise hit at Cannes Film Festival; it was distributed by New Line.[47]

Raynal had met Jarmusch in the early eighties at one of the Open Monday Night screenings at the Agee Room, when, as she explained in an e-mail, "anyone walking down the street could bring his/her movie and we would project it." (It seems that Raynal was resurrecting a programming strategy for independent films originally used by the Charles Theater and later by Weiss). Jarmusch showed up with *Permanent Vacation* (1980). "I liked the film so much that I decided to give it a run," Raynal remembered. Using the posters that Jarmusch had already created for the film and funding from the Center for Public Cinema, she paid for an ad in the *Village Voice* and another in *The Soho Weekly News* promoting its commercial release in the Agee Room, in March 1981. "The film ran for two weeks," she wrote in her e-mail, "not generating a big audience, but the critics were more or less 'good.' Then later on when I was the representative for the Rotterdam Film Festival, I showed it there."

Another of the couple's friends among the New Wave American filmmakers was Amos Poe. Poe had co-directed with Ivan Kral one of the earliest punk films, *The Blank Generation* (1976), about New York's punk underground, and directed the two films—*The Foreigner* (1978) and *Subway Riders* (1981)—that signaled the birth of No Wave Cinema, a movement (1975–1985) that "grew out of the bustling East Village music and art scene." *Subway Riders*, starring Susan Tyrrell, Robbie Coltrane and Cookie Mueller, had its world premiere at the Carnegie in April 1981 and then moved to the Bleecker for an extended run.[48]

Raynal had met Poe at the CBGB music club on the Bowery in the East Village. "We met regularly at CBGB," she recalled. "I think we became very close initially through Eric Mitchell [an actor in two of Poe's films, which were shown at the Bleecker]. Amos was very popular in the Village and actually when the film *Subway Riders* did open at the Bleecker, he did very well, attracting a young audience." His films became a popular feature in the Bleecker's Independent Showcase on Thursday evenings at 10:30. (The Independent Showcase, in the Bleecker's main screening room, featured foreign imports, like Andrzej Wajda's *Birchwood*, 1970, as well as American independent films.) In addition to *Subway Riders*, his other features at the Bleecker were *The Blank Generation* (1976); *The Foreigner*; and *Unmade Beds* (1976), an updating of *Breathless*, about a young man living in New York in 1976 who believes that he is living in Paris in 1959. *Cahiers du Cinéma* regarded *Unmade Beds*, reported the *New York Times*, as the "first film of the American New Wave." Accompanying his films in the Independent Showcase was a full-page article on Poe and his work in the January 1981 issue of *Focus*. "I remember," Thompson wrote in one of his e-mails, "a poster we had for one of Amos Poe's films in which he was quoting some critic from the *New York Times*. The review said something like 'The cinematic equivalent of kindergarten scribble.'"[49]

Other young filmmakers whose works appeared at the Bleecker included Beth B and Scott B and their Super 8mm films and Errol Morris, a Californian who was not part of the downtown crowd but whose debut feature *Gates of Heaven* (1978), a documentary about a pet cemetery in Napa Valley, had its New York premiere at the Bleecker's Monday night Independent Filmmakers Series (a precursor to Thursday night's Independent Showcase) in October 1980. "I associate *Gates of Heaven*," Thompson wrote in an e-mail, "with Werner Herzog and Berkeley rather than New York." Peter Scarlet, who programmed the Bleecker for a few months, discovered Morris and his film while Raynal was shooting her film, *New York Story* (1981). "No one at the time wanted to open that film," Raynal recalled, "as the subject was so gloomy. The film got ok [sic] reviews, but did not do too well at the box office. But Sid and I loved the film and Errol."[50]

In January 1982 the *Village Voice*'s film critic, J. Hoberman, recognized Raynal for her contributions to film culture in 1981 with her "audacious, specialized" programming. In particular, he cited "three of the finest films to open theatrically this year"—Austrian filmmaker Valie Export's debut feature film *Invisible Adversaries* (1977), Marguerite Duras's *India Song*, and Godard's *Numéro deux*—along with her support of "assorted New York independents" and her organization of the "most provocative" film series of 1981, "Radical Images," a month-long juxtaposition of recent political documentaries and experimental films with political content.[51]

For some time Yates had been pulling back in her programming responsibilities, although she continued to curate individual festivals, like a Marilyn Monroe one at Carnegie Hall Cinema in summer 1979. Thompson thought she had left in 1977 or 1978 to return to school to study architecture, but she was still listed in the December 1979 issue of *Focus* as director of Information Services. She left most likely shortly after, since by the summer 1980 issue of *Focus*, she was no longer listed in the magazine's credits. (Sadly, she died some years later.) In late 1978, with Yates' gradual withdrawal and the resignation of Chadbourne as manager of both the Carnegie and the Bleecker, Geffen

Richard Roud and Marguerite Duras at the opening of *India Song*, August 1981. Collection of the Cinémathèque de Toulouse.

hired Marty Rubin to program and manage the Bleecker and Terrence (Terry) McAteer to program the Carnegie.[52]

Rubin had handled the film program at the New York Cultural Center from 1972 to 1975. In contrast to Rosenbaum and his intellectual approach, Rubin leaned more toward popular culture and campy topics, a natural fit for the Bleecker. His major mark as programmer began with the summer 1979 season and his first curated series, "I Lost It at the Bleecker—A Survey of Sexuality in the Cinema." The idea for the series stemmed from his observation that "people were saying at that time that alternative cinema had an erotic component, this is where you see something that is kind of risqué but at the same time it's kind of culturally uplifting. So I thought of doing a series that was both raunchy and culturally significant."

He and Greg Ford, who had worked with him at the New York Cultural Center and again partnered with him on the Bleecker series, considered a wide range of films, up to and including hardcore porn. "We couldn't get *Deep Throat* [1972]," Rubin said. "It was too tied up with what seemed like crime connections, but we were able to get *The Devil in Miss Jones* [1973] by the same director [Gerard Damiano]." *The Devil in Miss Jones* was paired with a film that Ford picked out, *Hot Circuit* (1971), a porno version of *La Ronde* (1950). The series also included soft core porn, including Just Jaeckin's *Emmanuelle* (1974) and Radley Metzer's *Lickerish Quartet* (1970). In a "Programmers Note" in the calendar, Rubin listed the films he would have liked to show but couldn't: Buñuel's *Belle de jour* (1967) and Roger Vadim's *And God Created Woman* (1956); Pasolini's *Decameron* (1971) and *Salo* (1975); the independent, animated *Fritz the Cat* (1972); and the graphic, experimental *Flaming Creatures*, among others.[53]

The primary focus was on the "culturally uplifting" art house films: vintage films like *Ecstasy* (1933), which screened with *The Fox* (1967); *The Scarlet Empress* (1934) and *Pandora's Box* (1929); and *Pretty Baby* (1978) and *Baby Doll* (1956). Unlike most series at the Carnegie and Bleecker, this one was scheduled by Rubin as a horizontal, rather than vertical, series, running each week of its ten-week run from Wednesdays through Saturdays. (The other series during this calendar period from July to September was the vertical one, "Japanese Spectrum," on Tuesdays.)

In a typical last-minute crisis, a stressful incident occurred while screening one of the porn films, *The First Nudie Musical* (1976). "We realized," Ford recalled, "when we started showing it that we didn't have the last reel. We had to get it and make it back within 80 minutes. We had this crazy taxi driver, who was going so fast we felt we were going to be run off the bridge two or three times. I remember being covered in sweat; I actually had a cartoon mental image of my gravestone: 'He tried to get the sixth reel of *The First Nudie Musical*.' But we just made it."[54]

Rubin's next series was "Horrors!—Part One," in the fall 1979 season. Ford again worked with him. "He was kind of my secret advisor," Rubin said, "somebody to bounce ideas off of." Assessing that horror films had popular appeal, Rubin experimented with an open-end, vertical series on Wednesdays. "There was an audience for the horror film at the Bleecker," Rubin remembered thinking, "not so much at the Carnegie, which was middle-brow; the Bleecker was more edgy. The horror series could go as long as the audience kept showing up."

The first double feature, *King Kong* (1933) and *I Walked with a Zombie* (1943), however, was a failure. "I thought it was brilliant," Rubin recalled, "and it totally flopped, and I was so depressed. I thought the exotic locations of the two films might work, but it didn't. I just picked the wrong films." After that, fortunately, the series blossomed with a wide-ranging assortment of classic and new wave horror films. *Phantom of the Opera* (1925) and *Phantom of the Paradise* (1974), *The Last Wave* (1977) and *The Cars That Eat People* (1974), *The Hills Have Eyes* (1977) and *Night of the Living Dead* (1968), and *Freaks* (1932) and *Dr. Jekyll and Mr. Hyde* (Rouben Mamoulian's 1932 version) were some of the features. One film that Rubin remembered with particular fondness was Larry Cohen's *God Told Me To* (1976). "It's a wonderful, low-budget, science fiction film," Rubin recalled, "crazy as shit, perfect film to do at the Bleecker—Jesus turns out to be a space alien. Larry could bring that kind of crazy concept off. He came in person. He was great; he was very articulate." Rubin said with some pride that he thought "Horrors!" was still going when he left. (The series lasted through June 1980; Rubin had left earlier that year.)

Rubin's tenure with the Bleecker covered four principal seasons—the spring, summer, fall, and winter seasons of 1979. The spring season from April through June carried less of his imprint, except for a scheduling pattern that he did not repeat in the subsequent seasons: two-day double features on the weekends—one on Fridays and Saturdays and the other on Sundays and Mondays. "I Lost It at the Bleecker" was the highlight of the summer season, while the fall season carried some special events in addition to the "Horrors!" series: a personal appearance by James Toback following the screening of his first film *Fingers* (1978); two trilogies—Satyajit Ray's *The Apu Trilogy* and Roberto Rossellini's *The Age of Medici* (1973); and a tribute to Nicholas Ray. A special event of the winter schedule was the series "Complete and Uncut!," which screened the uncut version of films that had been shortened in their original releases: the British version of Joseph Losey's *The Damned* (1963), which had previously been cut by eight minutes; Sam Peckinpah's *The Wild Bunch* (1969), also trimmed originally by eight minutes; and Roman Polanski's *The Fearless Vampire Killers* (1967), more drastically cut by twenty minutes in its first outing, with an altered soundtrack. "It was the time," recalled Rubin, "when the uncut version, the director's cut, became a selling point. I'm not saying it was the first time it was done, but it was the time when it became a big marketing tactic."

Rubin recalled in particular how certain films that the studios ignored proved to be hits. "I remember *1900* [directed by Bernardo Bertolucci, 1976] was really huge," he said. "That was a film that the studios didn't know how to exploit and they basically threw it away. It was long, it got mixed reviews, but there was totally an audience for it. Repertory theaters like us took it over and we cleaned up on it." This was the same point that Steve Gould from the Elgin had made and that Janet Maslin, in the *New York Times*, had noted in 1977: repertory houses, she had written, were beginning to revive recent unsuccessful movies like Hal Ashby's *Harold and Maude* (1971), Sidney Lumet's *Long Day's Journey into Night* (1962), and Robert Altman's *Three Women* (1977), films that had been prevented by Hollywood economics from reaching their proper audiences the first time around. These films were also marketed as the director's cut. The selling point, Rubin said, for films like *1900* and [Nicolas Roeg's] *The Man Who Fell to Earth* was "We're showing the version they wouldn't let you see."[55]

When Rubin left in early 1980 to return to school, Thompson took over the repertory programming of the Carnegie and Bleecker while Raynal was general director of programming and programmer for the Agee Room. In addition to developing the schedules, Thompson had to cope with Geffen and his sometimes negative interference. One time he had scheduled a double bill of Satyajit Ray films, *The Music Room* (1958) and *Devi* (1960), at the Carnegie; but Geffen, unfamiliar with this prominent Indian director and major art cinema attraction, called Thompson in a panic thirty minutes before the theater opened to complain that these "adventurous films" would not draw a sufficient crowd for the 300-seat Carnegie; it was better suited, he shouted, for the smaller Bleecker Street. The program, nevertheless, opened and drew the large crowd that Thompson had anticipated. Seeing this, Geffen automatically reversed course and excitedly told Thompson that "You gotta find more films like that." His idea of effective programming was to milk a profitable film dry. "Most of us," Thompson said, "had an idea of which were the big films that made money; but in order to continue making money, we couldn't be showing them that frequently. But Sid would want them to be shown much more often; and as a result they would be burnt out to a certain extent. The schedule was becoming somewhat stale."

The box offices at the three theaters were not doing well, and Geffen gradually instituted changes. Having begun the shift away from a strictly repertory approach at the Carnegie with *Numéro deux* in 1981, he formally announced a first-run policy at the Carnegie in late 1982 in *Focus*—"Beginning in December [1982]," the announcement read, "Carnegie Hall Cinema proudly inaugurates its new policy of presenting American premieres of first-run foreign films as well as features by independent directors." He also modified the Agee Room's alternative programs of "films not shown in other theaters" to include commercial features for weeklong runs. Finally, in early 1982, Geffen engaged John Pierson and his company, Road Movies, to program both the Bleecker and the Agee Room, in the expectation that their publicity skills would boost attendance at these theaters.[56]

Geffen had become acquainted with Pierson and his seven partners through Jack Garfein, the director of the Clurman Theater, where they were curating film programs in the summer. "Sid was impressed with the amount of press that we were always able to get," Pierson remembered, "when we did the Clurman, a little theater in the middle of nowhere [42nd Street between Ninth and Tenth Avenues]. One of the people in our company, Anne Thompson, who's still active in the industry, was great in getting us tons of coverage. That was probably one of the things that attracted him." Accepting Geffen's offer, the group programmed the Bleecker for the first half of 1982, after which Pierson took over as both the solo manager and programmer of the Bleecker and Agee Room. "Sid didn't like dealing with the group," Pierson remembered. He agreed to take over only if he had complete operational control. Geffen agreed to his terms. Pierson then pushed Raynal out of the Bleecker, ironically, soon after the tribute paid to her by Hoberman in the Village Voice. "He was very rude," Raynal said. "He told me to go away, that he was the one [who would run the Bleecker]; but he was right, because then I could do my *New York Story*. You can't do both."

Sensing that his time was up as well, Thompson resigned sometime in early 1983. "Things were changing," he said. "Pierson was coming in, programming was changing; there were longer runs, so there wasn't as much of a need for someone to do the daily changes of rep programming. It was no longer the rep house that I had worked with." Thompson went on to program his Japanese series at the Thalia for a year or two.

Pierson had an interesting, varied background in film distribution and exhibition. After finishing New York University film school in 1977, he was hired by a small distribution company, Bauer International, to help distribute films during the day and program films at night in the Jean Renoir Cinema on Seventh Avenue in the Village, where the company had its offices. "It was a teeny company with no money," he said. "They got their titles for distribution for a song. In contrast to us, Dan Talbot was one of the big buyers at that time; he could get any film he wanted for $10,000 and most of them for a lot less than that." The experience provided him with a crash course in distribution and exhibition—with little salary. "But those who knew New York then," he recalled, "knew how decently you could live next to nothing."

After working there for a year, he drove the German director, Wim Wenders, most of whose films Bauer International owned the rights to, on his first tour of America; Wenders was en route to California to work with Francis Ford Coppola on his American debut film, *Hammett* (1982). After that, Pierson worked as an assistant on an American independent film festival at the Intermedia Theater in the East Village, the first such film festival in New York. Later when Sam Kitt, who had run the festival, became chief of UA Classics, Pierson was employed at the company in distribution. "I did all the repertory stuff," he recalled. "UA released art movies, but they also had a deep catalogue and I was doing that. The UA catalogue contained all the MGM collection and all the pre-fifties Warner Bros. films. I was one of the repertory theatrical guys, who the revival houses would get in touch with if we had a film they wanted." Eventually he and his seven friends formed Road Movies, to program films at the Clurman.

Using the programming skills forged at Bauer International and the Clurman, Pierson set to work rescuing the Bleecker Street Cinema from its doldrums. From the second half of 1982 to around October 1983, he created a "mix of re-issues, distributor festivals, actor/director retrospectives, and premieres" that the neighborhood newspaper, *The Villager*, credited with gaining a renewed audience for the Bleecker. His most popular and

Sid Geffen and Jackie Raynal in a scene from Raynal's film, *New York Story*. Photofest.

profitable booking, the one that he remembered with special fondness, was the revival at the Agee of Godard's *Breathless*. "One of the things that was miraculously, disgustingly successful," he said, "was when the Jim McBride/Richard Gere *Breathless* [1983] opened; we got our hands on a print of the original Godard *Breathless* [it was in public domain by then] and opened it in the Agee Room, and it sold out every night for definitely three months." The *Villager* singled out the revival for special mention. "The Agee Room," it reported, "also found unprecedented success when nearly all of its 84 seats were filled for 20 weeks with Godard's *Breathless*. The run exceeded that of the Richard Gere remake." The film helped put the theater in the black for that year. "Sid would remind me when it was over," Pierson recalled, "that it was a good thing I had that *Breathless*. I think that was the big profit center for the year. The year would have been a little ahead, but *Breathless* put it way over the top. Film is a hit-driven business, but repertory is not supposed to be that. It [the film] warped things in a good way, so I'm not complaining."⁵⁷

Pierson did not take the same risks that he and his group had taken at the Clurman, where they had shown cutting-edge films and were sometimes sued over the rights to certain films. Instead, he paid attention to what he considered the bread and butter of repertory programming—the retrospectives on actors and directors. A retrospective of the films of the Swiss director Alain Tanner, for instance, ran for eight days in April 1983. Series on actors were also a big draw. "I remember," he said, "we did a big Altman and a big De Niro in late '82 [a Brando/De Niro series on Sundays and a Robert Altman series on Thursdays ran the entire month of December 1982]." Like those of most rep house programmers, his curatorial strategies were motivated by a mixture of artistic integrity and commercial considerations. "You want to be complete," he explained, "in putting together these series, but at the same time you try to pair things off so you put something that's super popular and will bring in people with something that's more of an obscure discovery. Sometimes it tricks you and it's the more obscure film that is what everybody wants to see. That's what's so beautiful about a double bill; strategically you can try to figure out how to hook people."

In addition to the retrospectives, there were other traditions that Pierson felt were well-worth keeping. The "New German Cinema" films of Werner Herzog and Rainer Werner Fassbinder, which were part of a big movement in the seventies, were a rich vein. Raynal remembered that the Fassbinder retrospective sold out. The Japanese films also always worked well. Pierson's series opened with the New York premiere of *Zatoichi Meets Yojimbo* (1970). It was Thompson's last month at the Bleecker; and as a farewell gesture, he played several Zatoichi films to complement *Zatoichi Meets Yojimbo*.

Pierson also programmed personal favorites, such as the films of Jean-Pierre Melville in January 1983. "*Bob le flambeur* [1956]," he said, "had been reissued, but nobody knew the other works. He was an amazing director, but he had been eclipsed. That was really fun. That went great." Through his personal relationship with Wim Wenders, he opened Wenders' latest film, *The State of Things* (1982), which the director had made in the midst of the fiasco with *Hammett* and which won the Golden Lion Award for Best Film at the Venice Film Festival of 1982. "It wasn't a big hit," he said, "but it was a notable thing to do." When Scorsese's *King of Comedy* came out in 1983, Pierson piggybacked with a two-week, fourteen-title Jerry Lewis retrospective in the Agee Room entitled "Jerry Lewis: The King of Comedy." "It was not quite like reopening the original *Breathless*," he recalled, "but I love those movies."58

Another of his personal favorites was rock and roll films. Although they had underperformed in their initial releases, they did well at the Bleecker. "That's the best thing in rep," Pierson commented, calling to mind Rubin's similar observation, "to be able to bring back a film that didn't click all the way. I remember Penelope Speeris's first punk music documentary, called *The Decline of Western Civilization* [1981]. I loved showing it and we got a huge audience for that. It had kind of played but not really."

Like Rubin before him, he no longer stayed exclusively with daily changes. Thompson had been prescient about the changes that were taking place. "I dabbled with some open-end runs at the Agee," Pierson recalled, "which was why we could let *Breathless* just play and play and play." He also scheduled some single films as well as series for a week or more on a horizontal basis, such as *Zatoichi Meets Yojimbo* (one week), *The State of Things* (two weeks), and the Melville festival (one week).

One of his most enjoyable experiences in his year at the Bleecker was the friendships he made with the New York independent filmmakers, some of whose films had already screened at the theater. Somewhat younger than he, many were still students at his alma mater, New York University. A number of them, like Jim Jarmusch, Spike Lee, and Amos Poe, would come to the theater fairly regularly; and if they had no money, he let them in for free. He met Spike Lee in the winter of 1983, when Lee was interning at First Run Features. "I played Spike's *Joe's Bed-Stuy Barbershop* [1983, his first featurette] in the Agee Room for a couple of weekends in April." In December 1982, Pierson programmed a month-long series of contemporary American independent films drawn from the catalogue of First Run Features. The series included *Soldier Girls* (1981), a documentary about life among women recruits, one of the highlights of the 1981 New York Film Festival. "It was fun to have it [the Bleecker] become a gathering spot," he reminisced, "for what would become this big wave of American indie, New York–based filmmakers. New York was ground zero for the rise of American independent films. In the eighties it was all just New York."[59]

Pierson's tenure at the Bleecker followed Geffen's normal pattern. His contract, the *Villager* reported, was not renewed in October 1983 because of differences with Geffen. What were these differences that led to the breakup? "I think he thought it was too good a deal for me," Pierson recalled, "and it was not a good enough deal for him. But," he added, "I think it was as much me as Sid. I was always thinking about what I wanted to do next, anyway." What he did next was work for Films, Inc., doing repertory-related distribution work while also programming the second screen at the nonprofit Film Forum until 1986, when Bruce Goldstein, who had been serving as the Film Forum's publicist, took it over.[60]

Unlike the bitter memories some people had of Geffen, Pierson looked back on his relationship with him with amused affection. "I kind of loved the guy," he said. "I found him both colorful and inspiring in certain ways. There was a used-car-salesman aspect to him, but there was something about the way he loved movies that was really charming. I didn't feel exploited by him because you could figure out what strategy he was using to take advantage of you, and you could stay one step ahead." One incident in particular summed up for him Geffen's personality. He was sitting with him and Raynal in the Greek diner next door to the theater, the Triumph, which had been ordered by the Health Department to properly vent the kitchen. The owner didn't want to run a venting pipe up to the roof of the seven-story building and asked Geffen if he could vent over the back of the two-story theater building. Geffen agreed on one condition. "I'll run up a monthly bill," Pierson remembered him saying, "and at the end of each month you'll cut it by fifty percent." They agreed. From then on all of his meetings took place at the diner. "One time," Pierson said, "we were yelling at each other. Jackie was there; she takes the check and pays it at the cashier. Right in the middle of shouting at me, he sees her paying the bill and jumps up and says, 'What are you doing?' He completely forgot what we were arguing about."

After Pierson left, Raynal again assumed the programming of the three theaters, with Geffen's blessing. By November 1983, in tandem with the theaters' accelerated move to first runs, Geffen closed the Center for Public Cinema. Open-end runs became a regular feature of the theaters. By May 1984 Carlos Saura's *Carmen* (1983) was in its 32nd week at the Bleecker; and in June 1984 *Beyond Good and Evil*, a 1977 film by Liliana Cavani starring Dominique Sanda and Erland Josephson, was in its seventh and last week at the Carnegie and scheduled to move to the Agee Room, which had become Bleecker 2 by 1985. Revivals still had a place in the programming. The Bleecker ran a series, "Sixty Years of French Films," in August 1984, at the same time that the Carnegie was screening a festival of Paramount films.[61]

Raynal and Geffen also continued, and, in fact, stepped up, the practice of cosponsoring events with the cultural entities of foreign countries. A string of successful Greek, Israeli, and Dutch film weeks played at the Carnegie in 1985. "We didn't make a lot of money," Raynal remembered, "but we made a nice living. And at the time the Berlin Film Festival and the Rotterdam Festival paid for our tickets to go pick out films. We did a festival with Goethe Haus after the Berlin Festival. I did the French Week. We started with Unifrance and at the same time Unifrance would bring in Jacques Rivette, pay for his ticket, so it was great for us."

Hoping to offer year-round national cinema events, Geffen traveled to Cannes in May 1985 to meet with representatives of foreign film boards, cultural ministries, and other organizations to establish the Carnegie as the U.S. beachhead for national film weeks. "Our role," he told a *Variety* reporter, "is to offer support services, providing contacts with professional New York publicists, as well as aiding in the advertising and promotion." In addition to interest expressed by the French, Greek, and Dutch consulates in returning to the theater the next year, the Scandinavians told Geffen they wanted to present their Nordic Film Series in spring 1986.[62]

Geffen's plans never materialized. He died eight months later, on January 9, 1986, from stomach cancer, at the age of 64.

Shortly after his death, Cineplex Odeon bought the lease to the Carnegie from Geffen's estate and closed it for renovations. The theater reopened a year later in June 1987 as a mainstream theater, with a second, 75-seat screening room, with Raynal as manager, for showing art films. Along with this screening room, Raynal and J. D. Pollack, who had begun at the Bleecker in 1985, also managed the Bleecker Street Cinema and Agee Room under their new company, I.C.N. (International Cinema Network) Bleecker, Inc. "When Sid passed away," Raynal explained, "the Carnegie was closed but we had an option to make a small screening room when we sold the Carnegie. So that's when we created I.C.N. Bleecker; but I didn't get along very well with J.D. Pollack. He was kind of a strange person."

By late 1987, with the demise of many of the rep houses and the conversions of others into first-run theaters, the heyday of revival was over, the *New York Times* declared. Elliott Stein reported for the *Village Voice* in June 1989 that the Bleecker "is no-frills, but it's a real theater, and with one nicely sized screen, it's a decent place to see a movie. *Wings of Desire* ran for nearly eight months, but many offbeat films fare less well." By 1990 the competition from the home videocassette (VCR) revolution was a matter of serious concern among revival house owners. In a *New York Times* article that year exploring the effect of the revolution on the future of revival houses, Raynal was among the more pessimistic interviewees. "I think the video situation has harmed the repertory houses very much," she was quoted. "People collect tapes like they used to collect books. Now they do not need to go to revival houses as much. They have the movies at home."[63]

The Bleecker Street Cinema closed in August 1990, with Aki Kaurismaki's *Ariel* (1988) in the 171-seat main theater, and Roger Stigliano's *Fun Down There* (1989) in the Agee Room. It was not the VCR revolution that did the theater in, as Raynal feared, but the real estate revolution. Much like the closing of the Elgin, the Bleecker's closing pitted a real estate developer who saw the property as a profitable investment against a theater owner who treasured it as a cultural resource. It was a doomed struggle. Raynal, who had remarried, had been engaged in a bitter struggle for control of the theater's building with her landlord and former partner, John Souto, a real estate mortgage broker, who informed her earlier in August that the rent would be raised to $275,000 a year from $160,000. "The increase came as a complete shock to me," she told a *Times* reporter. "The theater just isn't generating enough income to pay for the increase." Souto had become Raynal's partner after Geffen's death. Because Geffen had left no will, she explained to a *New York Post* reporter, she was forced to acquire a partner in order to buy out his children from his previous marriage. Souto had promised to provide $600,000 to renovate the building, including the theater, and convert it into commercial and residential condominiums. He had also pledged to sell her the first floor, which was occupied by the theater, at a reasonable price. But the money was never used for renovations, and the building—which was jointly owned by Raynal and Souto—was twice mortgaged to raise more money for improvements. Earlier in 1990 the building was placed in receivership by the banks holding the mortgage. Raynal and her second husband, Jean-Paul Sarre, as well as the film producer Jacques Dorfmann, had tried to buy the building, but Souto outbid them.[64]

After the Bleecker closed, Raynal kept the rent-stabilized apartment on Central Park South where she had lived with Geffen their entire marriage, and divided her time between Paris and New York until 2014, when she moved permanently back to Paris. Between 1992 and 1998, she briefly ran another small repertory movie theater, Le Cinématographe, in the former site of Thalia SoHo on Van Dam Street in Greenwich Village, and then programmed a number of international festivals (Colombian Film Festival, Israël Film Festival, Avignon Film Festival, among others) at the Angelika theater in the Village, which her third husband owned. She directed several documentaries, including *Notes sur Jonas Mekas* (2000), *Bandes à part* (2001), *Autour de Jacques Baratier* (2002), *Portrait de Simon Lazard* (2003), and a feature-length fiction film, *La Nuit de l'ours* (2005); participated in conferences at different American universities, where she showed her films; gave lectures on her films, as well as the New Wave films that she had edited and those of the Zanzibar group; and collaborated in a tribute to Jean-Daniel Pollet at the Anthology Film Archives in 2008. In 2010, for her work in the arts, she was awarded the Légion d'Honneur by Minister Frederic Mitterand and was named Chevalier of the Order of Arts and Lettres.[65]

Reminiscing about the Bleecker at its closing, a *Washington Post* reporter wrote that "It was never very comfortable. The sound system was bad and, usually so were the prints. People in line were always selling things: film magazines, old movie stills, and other, less legal commodities. [But] Bleecker was one of New York's cultural emblems." If a small-budget film succeeded with the Bleecker's savvy New York crowd, he explained, distributors would be encouraged to pick it up. Andy Warhol's experimental, twelve-hour shot of the Empire State Building showed without interruption at the Bleecker. Fittingly, the Bleecker was immortalized in celluloid four times: in Paul Mazursky's *Willie and Phil* (1980), Woody Allen's *Crimes and Misdemeanors* (1989), Susan Seidelman's *Desperately Seeking Susan* (1985), and Barbra Streisand's *Prince of Tides* (1991).[66]

The Carnegie likewise summoned up affectionate memories. "I remember seeing the *Miracle of Morgan's Creek* (1944) at the Carnegie," Jim Harvey recalled, "and I wasn't very familiar with the film then. It was a small theater, but the communal hilarity was something, people were just roaring with laughter. It was an extraordinary experience with an audience, one of the most extraordinary I remember. It was a very good place to see a movie." Another patron remembered on the *Cinema Treasures* website both the Carnegie Hall and Bleecker Street Cinemas with great fondness. "I used to go to these two theaters on a regular basis back in the late 70's. It was great. You could see films there you could see nowhere else in NY [sic]. 'Big Deal on Madonna Street.' 'The Bicycle Thief.' 'Blow-up.' ... At the Carnegie I remember there was once an organist present to accompany a silent film.... Great time in my life."[67]

The major contribution of the theaters, Thompson summed up, were the programs, "the opportunity to see so many titles, the film school aspect. This is where you could see all the films of a director. I think we were almost on the level of the Museum of Modern

Art, with our series, with presenting obscure titles, classics that would be barely in distribution, things like the Audio Brandon and Janus Films catalogues."

Credit for the rich cultural experience that the three theaters and the *Thousand Eyes* magazine gave New Yorkers belongs finally to Sid Geffen. Whatever his faults, none of this would have existed without him and his ambitions for his theaters. Raynal described him as an impresario who took gambles, even when he did not have the money. He was reckless, some would say irresponsible. But he and his theaters left a venerable legacy. "Sid Geffen," film scholar B. Ruby Rich wrote in her memoir, "was one of a series of men who made a huge difference in film history through their exhibition choices in New York City. Geffen…, along with Amos Vogel and Fabiano Canosa, significantly effected [*sic*] the course of film history." Summing up Geffen, Nitke said that "[h]e loved film. He and Jackie were very involved in running that theater. It was their life."[68]

Chapter 14

Repertory Programming: A Return to Its Roots

For a brief period from the sixties to the eighties, a once-in-a-lifetime confluence of social, economic, and aesthetic trends allowed repertory programming to flourish in the for-profit as well as nonprofit sectors. When this confluence evaporated, alternative programming could only survive in the nonprofit sector. With its opportunities for grants from government, foundations, and private individuals to supplement the operating budget and provide for capital needs, the nonprofit sector was the natural home for this type of programming, which was too specialized, too dependent on a limited audience to rely solely on the box office, especially in the new, less hospitable environment.

A *Village Voice* reporter looked at the new scene in 1995 with an unsentimental eye. In the changing times, with home video, video stores, and cable TV, and the radically different habits of consuming film, he asked whether the venues for watching the film canon did not also need to evolve from the "parabohemian New York experience of discovering *Shoot the Piano Player* or *Summer with Monika* ... in a smelly side-street theater with a cramped group of like-minded movieheads." The inescapable answer was that, of course, it had to.[1]

Only now, there would be no more Mama Cats sitting next to favored patrons or climbing the screen. No more marijuana smoking while watching a midnight screening. No more familiar faces staffing the ticket booth and candy stand. No more lively discussions in the lobbies before and after a screening with a Dan Talbot. No more personal greetings by a Howard Otway or Frank Rowley. And no more inexpensive tickets (although membership subscriptions would be offered); they would now be priced on a level equivalent to commercial tickets. The intimate, communal flavor was gone, but in its place were more professionally run operations. The theaters were now clean, the seats more comfortable, the prints pristine—and the films started on time.

While the nonprofit repertory theaters have become more professionally run, their programming has come to be mainstream. Many of the old studio films, which were once disposable, now constitute requisite parts of the film canon; documentaries, which once played mostly in nontheatrical venues like film societies, now sometimes screen in the multiplex theaters of the chains as well as in specialized theaters like Angelika in Greenwich Village. Even the avant-garde films are now considered by some as orthodox.

This mainstream repertory programming has recently migrated back to the for-profit sector in new, state-of-the-art settings, under the auspices of established, well-to-do businessmen, who, unlike the young, idealistic, inexperienced, impecunious entrepreneurs portrayed in this book, have the means to house their theaters in comfortable surroundings with amenities. New York's new commercial repertory movie house, Metrograph, favors 35mm projection of its repertory programming in its renovated warehouse on the Lower East Side of Manhattan, with the additional conveniences of a bar, restaurant, and bookstore. A similar enterprise, Syndicated, a restaurant-theater in Brooklyn, combines a fifty-seat theater screening Hollywood classics, independent films, and double features with a bar and restaurant, which serves in-theater food and drink while patrons watch the repertory program.[2]

The more risk-taking films have been pushed out of the repertory theaters in favor of the more palatable foreign and independent films. Taking programming risks has become more difficult, unlike in the heyday of Cinema 16 and the commercial repertory theaters, when Amos Vogel, Dan Talbot, and the other programmers could take chances with controversial or obscure films. Today's core audience for repertory programming, reported contributors to the *Cineaste* symposium on repertory programming, are older and more conservative, leaning towards the *Masterpiece Theatre*–type art film. Most of the programmers in the symposium, like Richard Pena, former program director of the Film Society of Lincoln Center, agreed they could not be too adventurous. "It's hard to imagine," he wrote, "films such as *L'Eclisse* or *Muriel* getting commercial releases nowadays."[3]

Where then are the alternatives to the alternatives being screened, the contemporary cutting-edge, nonmainstream films? In a 2007 article in *Cineaste*, Rebecca M. Alvin makes a case for the microcinemas, small venues, often arising in makeshift settings evocative of the second-floor lofts and church basements of the past, that screen small films that cannot be seen elsewhere for likeminded cinephiles. The term microcinema was first used in 1994 by filmmakers Rebecca Barten and David Sherman, who built a tiny, thirty-seat venue for showing old and new experimental films and video in the basement of their San Francisco apartment and named it TOTAL MOBILE HOME microCINEMA.[4]

Since the 1990s, microcinemas have sprung up throughout the country, in Winterset, Iowa, and Shreveport, Louisiana, as well as in San Francisco and New York. While arising in a variety of forms, they share common features: they began as do-it-yourself venues; they are unconnected to a larger institution like a museum or university; and they are run by one or two people, or a small collective. The microcinemas, Alvin wrote, have taken the place of the repertory theaters (which she refers to as art-house cinemas) in three ways: due to low overhead and a different business model, they are able to screen underground, risk-taking works that are not being seen on other screens; they provide the sense of community that the old repertory theaters did; and they operate in smaller suburban and rural communities as well as in major urban areas. Craig Baldwin, experimental filmmaker and programmer-manager of San Francisco's Other Cinema, sees the microcinema movement as "more electronic folk culture, more neighborhood, more underground, more contemporary, more a community kind of thing" than the older avant-garde movement, which he describes as having become "academicized."[5]

The microcinemas in New York, which are uniformly nonprofits, have followed this basic pattern. Most began in small, raw spaces outside the cultural centers of Manhattan, mostly in Brooklyn, but also in the Bronx, Long Island City, Queens, and Harlem. Some have not lasted, while others have graduated to long-term homes, usually in storefronts. Founded by one or two people with visions of what they wanted their infant organizations to be, these groups generally focus on screening independent films in an intimate, communal setting where the audience interacts with the film, the filmmaker (who is generally expected to be present at the screening of his or her film), and each other, providing a context for the film. The microcinemas are accessible to all, with admission fees ranging from nonexistent to suggested donations. Since they are oriented to their neighborhoods, which are often low-income, affordable admissions are critical.

Like the film societies and repertory houses of the past, each has its own identity. There is, for instance, the peripatetic Rooftop Films, which puts on an annual summer festival in outdoor locations in different boroughs. The underground version of such mainstream festivals as the Toronto and New York Film Festivals, its summer series draw on submissions from independent filmmakers of all levels, from experienced professionals to first-time filmmakers. Their common characteristic is that they are nonmainstream, "short and feature-length films underserved by conventional commercial distributors, industry-run festivals, art galleries, and repertory theater retrospectives."[6]

Covering the spectrum of fiction and nonfiction films, including videos, home movies, and found footage, Rooftop's programs have covered independent films slated for theatrical release, like Will Allen's *Holy Hell* (2016), a home-video document filmed inside the Buddhafield cult group over twenty years by the filmmaker, and more experimental features, such as cinematographer Kirsten Johnson's self-reflective feature film *Cameraperson*, a meditation on the relationship between storytelling and the camera frame.[7]

Two microcinemas in Brooklyn, Light Industry in Greenpoint, Brooklyn, and Union-Docs in Williamsburg, Brooklyn, favor multi-media presentations—film, video, photography, printed word, and performance—with a slant towards the documentary. While there is much overlap between the two, there are also differences in emphasis. Light Industry strives "to explore new models for presentation of cinema," while UnionDocs's goal is "understanding the complexities of contemporary life."[8]

Light Industry brings together related art forms "in a way that we haven't seen before," its co-founder Ed Halter told a *Brooklyn Rail* reporter. The first six months of its 2016 program, for instance, included a mix of events, from two programs of conversations—one with a media theorist, Wendy Hui Kyong Chun, and another with a multi-media artist, Lynn Hershman Leeson—to the avant-garde filmmaker Tony Conrad's multi-media presentation, *Paul Sharits: Prescription and Collapsed Temporality* + Paul Sharits's *Razor Blades*; this was a rare screening of avant-gardist Paul Sharits's 1966 double projection *Razor Blades*, followed by a re-creation of Conrad's lecture in October 1976 on Sharits, with the use of nine cassette players.[9]

One program echoed Jonathan Rosenbaum's "Rivette in Context," which had played in 1979 at the Bleecker Street Cinema. On March 22, 2016, Light Industry screened D.W. Griffith's *True Heart Susie* (1919) in tribute to Jacques Rivette, who had died two months before, in January 2016, because it was "a film he [Rivette] once cited as among cinema's greatest."[10]

UnionDocs's programs of documentaries frequently stress "the marginalized stories, underrepresented facts, and interdependent networks." Its 2016 schedule included Diego Echeverria's restored 1984 cinéma vérité documentary *Los Sures*, a portrait of the crime-ridden, impoverished Puerto Rican neighborhood of Los Sures in Southside Williamsburg in the 1980s; and *Every Fold Matters*, a hybrid of live performance and film, the co-creation of experimental filmmaker Lynne Sachs and playwright Lizzie Olesker, which tells the personal stories of underpaid, exploited, immigrant laundromat workers and customers.[11]

Other documentaries in the 2016 schedule explored new definitions and experiments with nonfiction film, such as the work of Portuguese filmmaker Salomé Lamas, which attempts to redefine nonfiction filmmaking. UnionDocs presented three of her early short films: "Teatrum Orbis Terrarum" (2013), a one-channel projection adapted from three-channel installation; "Encounters with Landscape" (3X, 2012); and "VHS—VIDEO HOME SYSTEM" (2010–2012), including video footage by Cristina Lamas, HD.[12]

Two microcinemas—Maysles Documentary Center (MDC) in Harlem (the only independent film house north of Lincoln Center in Manhattan), and Bronx Documentary Center (BDC) in the Melrose neighborhood of the Bronx—emphasize their connections to their respective low-income neighborhoods. Both groups concentrate on documentaries, which have the power, as the Bronx Center states on its website, "to help build community, expose injustices and create positive social change." The co-founder of the Bronx Center, Michael Kamber, a former *New York Times* photographer and writer, envisioned it as an educational space for South Bronx residents to be exposed to high quality journalism and documentaries, in order to expand their horizons beyond the restrictions of poverty.[13]

Two of the Bronx Center's principal events, screenings of documentaries and photography/slideshow exhibits, cover a panoply of local, national, and international social and political issues. In 2016, South Bronx residents and others (all events are open to all) learned about the "inspiring but messy world of job training" through a documentary, *City of Trees*, which tells the personal stories of unemployed people from Washington, D.C.'s Ward 8, who participated in a new, green job training program. Greg Constantine, an award-winning documentary photographer, presented his slideshow, *Nowhere People*, the result of his ten-year exploration into the lives of stateless people around the world.[14]

Photo exhibits and slideshows are sometimes connected to screenings. Bernardo Ruiz's *Kingdom of Shadows*, a documentary on the U.S.–Mexico "drug war," was held in conjunction with a photo exhibition on the contemporary migration in The Americas, *Via PanAm: The Pursuit of Happiness*, by Kadir van Lohuizen.[15]

The Center also nurtures local photographers and filmmakers. The first major exhibition of BDC's Bronx Photo League (a name evocative of the 1930s leftwing Film and Photo League in New York), composed of sixteen Bronx photographers "committed to documenting social issues and change in our borough," opened in October 2016—*The Jerome Avenue Workers Project*, a photo exhibition of the workers and trades people of Jerome Avenue, who are being threatened with gentrification. Another group, the Bronx Filmmakers, a collective of filmmakers who live and work in the Bronx, screened a series at BDC in 2016, "Made in the Bronx," six short films made by its members. The series included Estefania Chavez's *The Velvet Devil* (2013), about the quick journey of a girl at a party, who was at the wrong place at the wrong time; and Alvano Franco's *A Brief Portrait* (2014), about a queer woman of color who continues to school while trying to conceal the fact that she is homeless.[16]

The nationally renowned documentary filmmaker Albert Maysles founded the

Maysles Documentary Center in 2005, after his move with his family from the Upper West Side to Harlem, with the objective of showing documentaries that were tied to Harlem. (Maysles died on March 5, 2015.) In addition to its own programming, the Center hosts various events, such as *The People's Film Festival* 2006, and partners with local and cultural organizations and citizen activists who co-present or co-curate programs that provide "exposure for underrepresented social issues and overlooked artists and their works." Maysles Cinema's first film screening partner, longtime Harlem resident Hellura Lyle, curates *Doc Watchers*, which features independent documentaries on local, national, and international issues. In 2013, one of *Doc Watchers*'s presentations, *Real Stories from a Free South Africa* (2003), a project of South Africa's most popular channel, South African Broadcasting 1, examined the question, from the point-of-view of two South African women, of the effect of the ten years of freedom from apartheid on the lives of ordinary South Africans.[17]

The Maysles Cinema's programming has included films experimenting with film form. In its 2013 schedule, a documentary series, *Fiction-Non*, explored "hybrid" films that crossed the boundaries between fiction and nonfiction traditions. One of the hybrid films in the series, *The Arbor* (2010), directed by Clio Barnard, tells the true story of deceased British playwright Andrea Dunbar and her daughter Lorraine through recorded audio interviews over two years with Lorraine Dunbar, other members of the Dunbar family and residents from the Buttershaw Estate, where Dunbar and her daughter had lived. These interviews were edited to form an audio "screenplay," which forms the basis of the film as actors lip-synch to the voices of the interviewees. This footage was intercut with extensive archive clips as well as extracts from Andrea's first stage play, *The Arbor*, filmed as a live outdoor performance on the Buttershaw Estate, to an audience of its residents.[18]

In 2016, after undergoing renovations, the Maysles Cinema reopened with Jonas Mekas's *Reminiscences of a Journey to Lithuania* (1974), a landmark, avant-garde, diary film, which documents a trip that Mekas took to his ancestral village of Semeniskiai, Lithuania, after twenty-five years of exile in the United States. Following Mekas's film, the two-day *People's Film Festival* featured a pre-festival kickoff, *The Art of Storytelling*, a panel discussion of the new forms of storytelling in film. Within the context of the many forms that storytelling takes today—digital art, multimedia, gaming and virtual reality—the panelists looked at the broadened scope and storytelling platforms of film that have been developed for mobile phones, tablets, and other devices, and how the past and present elements are used to tell stories.[19]

Screening nonmainstream, cutting-edge films within a communal setting, where the audience feels part of a special place, the microcinemas are carrying on the tradition of the film societies of the past. In speaking to a *New York Times* reporter about Union-Docs, Scott MacDonald, the chronicler of Cinema 16, who had presented programs in UnionDocs's intimate, fifty-seat, storefront venue, may have been speaking for all the microcinemas in describing an energy in the post-screening, lively discussions with directors and filmmakers at UnionDocs that he seldom saw in established forums of experimental work. "A youthful home like UnionDocs," he said, "has a healthy sense that the older definitions of what constitutes 'experimental' cinema and what constitutes 'documentary' are up for grabs." This sense of a supportive, engaged community touches filmmakers as well. Lena Dunham, director of *Tiny Furniture* and creator and star of HBO's *Girls*, wrote as a testimonial to Rooftop Films that "Rooftop does more than program unusual films in remarkable locations (and vice versa)—it fosters a deep sense of community among

New York independent filmmakers, one that is sorely needed. As trite as it sounds, Rooftop has made a lot of indie dreams possible—including my own."[20]

Ed Halter told the *Brooklyn Rail* interviewers that he saw his microcinema, Light Industry, continuing the tradition that stretches from the cine-clubs of the twenties to Cinema 16 in the fifties, Mekas's Film-Makers' Cinematheque of the sixties, and the Collective for the Living Cinema from the late seventies to the early eighties. The commercial repertory houses were part of that tradition. The sense of adventure in seeking out obscure films, which Alvin describes as a key attraction of the microcinemas, reflects the similar appeal of the obscure that Lopate remembered drew him and his friends to the films of the repertory movie theaters.

Other similarities between the microcinemas and the old repertory houses abound. The neighborhood character of the Maysles and Bronx Centers, for instance, has its roots in the local orientation of the repertory houses—the opportunities for neighborhood organizations to use the Elgin Theater for their own programs; the Elgin's token admission fees for the neighborhood elderly; the New York punk underground films screened at Sid Geffen's Bleecker Street Cinema for its area's student population; the New Year's Eve celebrations at Theatre 80 St. Marks and the Regency. Rooftop Film Summer Series' openness to all levels of filmmakers evokes the monthly Film-Makers' Festival of the Charles Theater. The microcinemas' stress on open dialogues among audience members and with artists can be traced to the guest books of the New Yorker, the lively discussions that Dan Talbot conducted in the lobby of the New Yorker Theater with his audience, the guest appearances of Hollywood actors and directors at the Regency. Finally, the appeal of the microcinemas to the young and their passion for the fresh and new mirrors the attraction the repertory houses had once had for the young cinephiles of the past.[21]

In every field, Alvin summed up, a generational process takes place between its fringe and mainstream. The fringe, which had once challenged the complacent mainstream, eventually becomes more acceptable and part of the mainstream; in turn a new fringe to the fringe, an outer edge with new elements, emerges. Once the repertory movie theaters had been part of the fringe. They had rescued segments of film history from oblivion and did the same for the neglected films of their own era. With their series and retrospectives, they not only entertained but educated the general public in the art of film. And they did all this within an intimate setting where its audience felt part of a special community. Now, the outer limits of filmmaking and film exhibition are on the microcinema screens.[22]

Chronology of the Repertory Movie Theaters, New York City, 1960–1994

First Wave

Thalia: July 1939 (or April 1941)–September 1973
New Yorker Theater: March 1960–December 1973
Bleecker Street Cinema: April 1960–late summer 1974
Charles Theater: October 1961–December 1962
Windsor Theater: October 1962–November 1962
New York Cultural Center: August 1964–September 1975
Cinema Village: October 1965–August 1990
Garrick (renamed New Andy Warhol Garrick Theater): May 1965–unknown

Second Wave

Elgin: May 1968–March 1977
Theater 80 St. Marks: August 1971–April 1994
St. Marks Cinema: September 1971–February 1977, May 1977–September 1985
Quad Cinema: October 1972–September 2015
First Avenue Screening Room: January 1973–March 1975
Carnegie Hall Cinema: October 1973–winter 1986
Bleecker Street Cinema: October 1974–August 1990
Regency: fall 1976–September 1987
Cinema Village: December 1990–present
Thalia: January 1977–May 1987
8th Street Playhouse: May 1978–October 1992
Metro: October 1982–May 1985
Thalia SoHo: November 1985–August 1990
Biograph: February 1988–September 1991
Le Cinématographe: February 1992–unknown
Gramercy Theater: April 1993–November 1993

Chapter Notes

All material cited as being in the author's collection and the collection of Ed and Mary Maguire will, after publication of this book, be donated to the Museum of Modern Art Department of Film Special Collections, New York (MoMA Dept. of Film Archives, New York).

Preface

1. For some of these personal accounts, see John Pierson, *Spike, Mike, Slackers & Dykes* (New York: Hyperion, 1997), 8, 15–16, 45–46, and J. Hoberman and Jonathan Rosenbaum, *Midnight Movies* (New York: Harper & Row, 1983), 70, 72, 154; Toby Talbot, *The New Yorker Theater and Other Scenes from a Life at the Movies* (New York: Columbia University Press, 2009); Douglas Gomery, *Shared Pleasures: A History of Movie Presentation in the United States* (Madison: The University of Wisconsin Press, 1992), 194–95; Raymond J. Haberski, Jr., *Freedom to Offend: How New York Remade Movie Culture* (Lexington: The University Press of Kentucky, 2007), 110–116.

Chapter 1

1. The following description of the arts scene in New York in the first three months of 1960 comes from the following sources: Arthur Gelb, "Off-Broadway—Second Act Crisis," *New York Times*, March 13, 1960; Michael Smith, "Theatre: An A.R.T. 'Godot,'" *Village Voice*, March 2, 1960; Advertisements, *New York Times*, January 1, 1960 and February 29, 1960; Advertisements, *Village Voice*, January 1, 1960, March 2, 1960, March 10, 1960, March 16, 1960.
2. Jonas Mekas, "Movie Journal," *Village Voice*, April 6, 1960.
3. Jonas Mekas, "Movie Journal," *Village Voice*, March 9, 1960; Arthur Knight, "SR Goes to the Movies: A Managerial Revolution," *Saturday Review*, June 18, 1960.
4. Phillip Lopate, "When Foreign Movies Mattered," *New York Times*, August 13, 2000, sec. AR; David A. Cook, *A History of Narrative Film*, 3rd ed. (New York: W.W. Norton & Company, 1981), 919; Robert Sklar, *Movie-Made America: A Cultural History of American Movies*, revised and updated (New York: Vintage Books, 1994), 280.
5. Gomery, *Shared Pleasures*, 188; Phillip Lopate, "Anticipation of La Notte: The 'Heroic' Age of Moviegoing," in Phillip Lopate, *Totally Tenderly Tragically* (New York: Anchor Books/Doubleday, 1998), 37.
6. As early as 1926, Symon Gould, who established the first art cinema in the United States, referred to theaters that would present "worthwhile films," including box office failures such as European films that no distributor would buy, as repertory theaters. See Symon Gould, "The Little Theatre Movement in the Cinema," *National Board of Review Magazine*, September-October 1926, 4.
7. The definition of film societies comes from "Film Society," *Wikipedia*, last modified February 3, 2015, accessed February 24, 2015, http://en.wikipedia.org/wiki/Film_society.
8. Peter Haratonik, phone interview by author, New York, NY, October 7, 2011. All subsequent quotations from Haratonik will come from this interview, unless otherwise indicated.
9. David Schwartz, "Repertory Film Programming: A Critical Symposium," *Cineaste*, Spring 2010, 50–51; Jason Rapfogel, "Repertory Film Programming: A Critical Symposium," 38; Roger McNiven, "Women Larger than Life: Program Notes 2: King Vidor's *Beyond the Forest* (1949) / Gerd Oswald's *Crime of Passion* (1957)," *Bright Lights Film Journal*, July 31, 2009, accessed February 20, 2015, www.brightlightsfilm.com/65/65programnotes.php.
10. Phillip Lopate, interview by author, New York, NY, December 6, 2011. All subsequent quotes from

Lopate will come from this interview, unless otherwise indicated.

11. Haberski, *Freedom to Offend*, 100, described the obstacles that made it difficult to attend MoMA's film programs.

12. *Cinema Treasures* catalogues all past and present movie theaters in the U.S. and allows patrons to write anecdotes or information about a theater on the theater's listing. edblank on September 4, 2010 at 1:20 p.m., accessed November 6, 2014, http://cinematreasures.org/comments?page=2&theater_id=285; Howard Mandelbaum, "Letter from New York," *Bright Lights Film Journal*, Issue #9 (1980), accessed January 22, 2015, http://brightlightsfilm.com/66/66letterfromny.php.

13. The Little-Cinema-Theatre Movement, unpublished paper in the Thomas Brandon Collection (TBC), L233, 2, The Museum of Modern Art Department of Film Special Collections, New York; The Exceptional Photoplays Work of the National Board of Review, unpublished paper in TBC, R370a, 2, MoMA Dept. of Film Archives, NY.

14. Gomery, *Shared Pleasures*, 173; The Little-Cinema-Theatre Movement, 5.

15. Richard Abel, *French Cinema: The First Wave, 1915–1929* (Princeton: Princeton University Press, 1984), 241, 251–2; Ben Davis, "The Beginnings of the Film Society Movement in the U.S.," *Film & History: An Interdisciplinary Journal of Film and Television Studies* 24, nos. 3–4 (1994): 8.

16. *Ibid.*, 15.

17. *Ibid.*, 12, 14.

18. Frederic Delano, "Halls of Immortals," *Cue*, October 26, 1935, 3.

19. This description of the beginnings of MoMA's film department comes from Peter Catapano, "Creating 'Reel' Value: The Establishment of the Museum of Modern Art Film Library, 1935–1939," *Film & History: An Interdisciplinary Journal of Film and Television Studies* 24, nos. 3–4 (1994): 33–35, 36.

20. Eileen Bowser, "MOMA's Special Oscar," *Films in Review*, May 1979, 287.

21. Thomas M. Pryor, "Film Society Movement Catches On," *New York Times*, September 18, 1949; Bosley Crowther, "The Film Societies: Lively Interest Manifest in Cultural Groups," *New York Times*, September 19, 1954.

22. Scott MacDonald, "Amos Vogel and Cinema 16," *Wide Angle* 9, no. 3 (1987): 38; Alan Levy, "Gideon Bachmann: A Wandering Jew at Home," Posted: August 2, 1995, *The Prague Post*, accessed March 22, 2016, http://www.praguepost.cz/archivescontent/20419-gideon-bachmann-a-wandering-jew-at-home.html.

23. Scott MacDonald, "Cinema 16: An Interview with Amos Vogel," *Film Quarterly* 37, no. 3 (Spring 1984): 23–24.

24. Pryor, "Film Society Movement Catches On."

25. Camilo C. Antonio, "Amos Vogel, Saboteur," *The Vienna Review*, May 19, 2011, accessed January 31, 2015, http://www.viennareview.net/vienna-review-book-reviews/book-reviews/amos-vogel-saboteur; MacDonald, "Cinema 16: An Interview with Amos Vogel," 23, 26.

26. MacDonald, "Amos Vogel and Cinema 16," 38–51, Cinema 16 clippings file, Research Collection of the Billy Rose Theater Division of the New York Public Library for the Performing Arts (Research Collection, LPA); Jonas Mekas, "Movie Journal," *Village Voice*, September 14 1961; MacDonald, "Cinema 16: An Interview with Amos Vogel," 29.

27. "Film as a Subversive Art: Amos Vogel and Cinema 16," 4, accessed February 16, 2015, http://www.thestickingplace.com/wp-content/uploads/2014/08/FAASA-dialogue-transcript.pdf; William K. Everson, *The Theodore Huff Memorial Film Society: A Brief History*, accessed January 6, 2015, www.nyu.edu/projects/wke/notes/huff/huff briefhistory.

28. Harvey Deneroff, "Recovered Memories," accessed February 1, 2015, http://deneroff.com/blog/2008/03/19/recovered-memories/.

29. Ronald S. Magliozzi, "Witnessing the Development of Independent Film Culture in New York: An Interview with Charles L. Turner," *Film History* 12, no. 1 (2000): 87. For a more detailed description of the beginnings of the film society, see pages 85–87 of this interview.

30. William K. Everson, et.al., *History and Overview of the Theodore Huff Memorial Film Society*, in Theodore Huff Film Society clippings file, Research Collection, LPA; Program for October 18, 1955, in Huff Clippings File, Research Collection, LPA.

31. Ed Halter, "Taboo Revue: Tracking down Legendary Cineaste Amos Vogel," *Village Voice*, November 29, 2005, accessed February 16, 2015, http://www.villagevoice.com/2005-11-29/books/the-frames/; "Film as a Subversive Art," 10.

32. Haberski, *Freedom to Offend*, 104–105; Nat Hentoff, "Last Call for Cinema 16," *Village Voice*, February 21, 1963.

33. "Film as a Subversive Art: Amos Vogel and Cinema 16," 8; Haberski, *Freedom to Offend*, 98.

34. Programs in Huff Clippings File, Research Collection, LPA.

35. MacDonald, "Amos Vogel and Cinema 16," 51; Antonio, "Amos Vogel, Saboteur."

36. Newsletter for March 1957 in Huff Clippings File, Research Collection, LPA; William K. Everson, *A Brief History of the Theodore Huff Memorial Film Society*, in Huff Clippings File, Research Collection. LPA.

The Huff Society remained small for other reasons as well. It could not market itself for legal reasons, but had to rely on word-of-mouth to grow, since it operated in a legal gray area due to the lack of permission to show many of the films that appeared on his programs. "The companies for the most part know about us," he wrote in his brief history of the Huff Society, "and we have a good reputation, so they turn a blind eye; but any attempt to commercialise [sic] ourselves could ruin the good will we have, and cut off major sources of supply." *A Brief History of The Theodore Huff Memorial Film Society.*

37. MacDonald, "Amos Vogel and Cinema 16," 51; Antonio, "Amos Vogel, Saboteur"; Richard Roud interviewed by Richard Corliss, "70-Millimeter Nerves," *Film Comment* September—October 1987, 38; Greg Merritt, *Celluloid Mavericks: The History of American Independent Film* (New York: Thunder's Mouth Press, 2000), 156.

38. Independent films ranged from feature fiction films and documentaries to the avant-garde. Their common feature was their independence from financing and production by the major studios and usually without prior distribution arrangements. See Merritt, *Celluloid Mavericks*, xii; Jonas Mekas, *The Film-Maker's Cooperative: A Brief History,* accessed January 28, 2015, http://www.film-makerscoop.com/about/history; Merritt, *Celluloid Mavericks,* 183; Sheldon Renan, *Report on Short Film Distribution,* draft report, June 29, 1972, TBC, M255a, MoMA Dept. of Film Archives, NY.

39. "About Lionel Rogosin: Biography," *Lionel Rogosin, A Visionary American Maverick Filmmaker Humanitarian,* accessed February 18, 2015, http://www.lionelrogosin.org/AboutLR.html.

40. Gerald R. Barrett, "Jonas Mekas Interview," *Literature/Film Quarterly* 1, no. 2 (Spring 1973): 103;"Film-Maker's [sic] Showcase" flyers, Filmmaker's Cinematheque Programmes, 1–150, MoMA Dept. of Film Archives, NY; Jonas Mekas, "Movie Journal," *Village Voice,* November 19, 1964; Jonas Mekas, "A Note of [sic] Film-Makers' Cinematheque," New York Film-Makers' Newsletter, November 1967, 1, MoMA Dept. of Film Archives, NY; Jonas Mekas, "Movie Journal," Village Voice, March 31, 1966; "About Lionel Rogosin: Biography."

Chapter 2

1. Knight, "A Managerial Revolution."
2. Roger Ebert, "Bruce S. Trinz, Owner of Legendary Clark Theater, Dies," *Chicago Sun-Times,* July 13, 2011, updated July 14, 2011, accessed https://groups.google.com/forum/#!msg/alt.obituaries/AeDJ8qqCOaY/Zo5Jx1fah6gJ; In an e-mail from Ben Barenholtz to author, dated September 20, 2012, he wrote that the specialized exhibitors in the country, which had grown since its early days, had organized into an informal group with Bruce Trinz as its chairman at the first Telluride Festival in 1973. The group no longer exists.
3. Lopate, "The Passion of Pauline Kael," in *Totally, Tenderly, Tragically,* 232–5.
4. http://observer.com/2011/10/the-iron-lady-a-new-biography-of-pauline-kael/; Jim Lane, "Critical and Cultural Reception of the European Art Film in 1950s America: A Case Study of the Brattle Theatre (Cambridge, Massachusetts)," *Film & History: An Interdisciplinary Journal of Film and Television Studies* 24, nos. 3–4 (1994), 54.
5. Talbot, *New Yorker Theater,* 192.

6. Roger Greenspun, "The American Cinema," *New York Times,* February 16, 1969; Steve Neale, *Genre and Hollywood* (London and New York: Routledge, 2000), 10–11; Andrew Sarris, interview by author, New York, NY, October 18, 2003. All subsequent quotes from Sarris will come from this interview, unless otherwise noted.

7. Martin Scorsese, foreword in Talbot, *New Yorker Theater,* xi, xii.

8. Gerald R. Barrett, "Andrew Sarris Interview: October 16, 1972 (Part One)," *Literature/Film Quarterly* 1, no. 3 (Summer 1973): 196–197.

9. Gomery, *Shared Pleasures,* 247; Howard Mandelbaum, interview by author, New York, NY, May 13, 2011. Two other interviews were held with Mandelbaum on November 3, 2011 and November 8, 2012. All subsequent quotes from him will come from one of these three interviews, unless otherwise noted; Bosley Crowther, "Boom in Revivals," *New York Times,* January 21, 1962.

10. Walter Langsford, interview by author, New York, NY, February 13, 2012.

11. Ted Ostrow, interview by author, New York, NY, January 31, 2012; the rental figures for these films come from "Ledger from the New Yorker Theater," in Talbot, *New Yorker Theater.*

12. Bruce Goldstein, "Repertory Film Programming: A Critical Symposium," 42.

13. For information on the relation of the exchanges to the repertory houses, see Bruce Eder, "The Decline of Revival Cinema," *New York Newsday,* September 1, 1987.

14. Laurence Lerman, "Repertory Theaters Find New Life: Nonprofit Orgs Keep Classics Alive," *Variety,* October 14–20, 1996; Hoberman, *Midnight Movies,* 38; Elliott Stein, interview by author, New York, NY, November 17, 2011. All subsequent quotes from Stein will come from this interview, unless otherwise indicated; Elise DeCarlo, "Missing Manhattan," in *Metropolitan Diary,* Ron Alexander, ed., *New York Times,* November 30, 1988; Phillip Lopate, "The Thalia: A Fan's Notes," *New York Post,* November 2, 1998; Pete Delaney, "The Thalia Theatre," *Movie Collector's World,* June 4, 1993, in Thalia clippings file, Research Collection, LPA.

15. Michelle O'Donnell, "A Revivalist Revived: The Thalia Returns Kindling Memories in Black and White," *New York Times,* March 31, 2002; Laurence Kardish, "Repertory Film Programming: A Critical Symposium," 46–47; Lerman, "Repertory Theaters Find New Life."

16. Lopate, "The Thalia: A Fan's Notes"; Talbot, *New Yorker Theater,* 152–156; Paul Gardner, "Thalia's Classic Era Slips into Folklore," *New York Times,* August 31, 1973.

17. O'Donnell, "A Revivalist Revived."

Chapter 3

1. Knight, "A Managerial Revolution"; Dan Talbot, interview by author, New York, NY, December

13, 2000. Two more interviews were held with Talbot on January 31, 2001 and January 28, 2012. All subsequent quotes by Talbot will come from one of these three interviews, unless otherwise noted.

2. Haberski, *Freedom to Offend*, 110–112.

3. Knight, "A Managerial Revolution"; Talbot, *New Yorker Theater*, 5.

4. The description of the theater comes from the author's interview with Dan Talbot, December 30, 2000, and Talbot, *New Yorker Theater*, 10–13; Jonas Mekas, "Movie Journal," *Village Voice*, May 18, 1960.

5. The attendance figures in this paragraph come from Talbot, *New Yorker Theater*, 7, 14, while all the financial figures come from New Yorker Theater (NYT) box-office ledger on microfiche, MoMA Dept. of Film Archives, NY, unless otherwise noted; Jonas Mekas, "Movie Journal," *Village Voice*, April 13, 1960.

6. Both Toby Talbot (*New Yorker Theater*, 14) and Haberski (*Freedom to Offend*, 112) cite around $350,000 as the gross total for 1960. However, in an e-mail dated February 16, 2015, Dan Talbot wrote to author that the figure for the 1960 gross total from the ledgers was the correct one; Dan Talbot, interview by Ron Magliozzi on May 3, 1991, MoMA Dept. of Film Archive, NY. The interview serves as an introduction to the microfiche copy of the NYT box office ledger.

7. "The Thirties Exhumed," *Show*, June 1962, available in New Yorker Theater clippings file, Research Collection, LPA.

8. Eugene Archer, "Old Movies Fill January Dearth," *New York Times*, January 11, 1961.

9. Peter Bogdanovich, *Who the Devil Made It* (New York: Alfred A. Knopf, 1997), 20. This may have been true in New York, but full-time repertory theaters existed elsewhere in the nation since the forties; Andrew Sarris, "Bogdanovich, Archer, and Me: The Way We Really Were," *Village Voice*, May 15, 1978.

10. Talbot, *New Yorker Theater*, "Guest Book/Sample Pages." All subsequent quotes from the guest books will come from this source, unless otherwise indicated.

11. Eugene Archer, "Movie 'Failures' Will Be Revived," *New York Times*, May 31, 1961.

12. Magliozzi interview with Talbot. According to Magliozzi, this was probably the New York theatrical premiere of the film in its full-length version. The Museum of Modern Art had shown an edited version in 1943 and 1946.

13. *Ibid.*; Eugene Archer, "Nazi Film Listed for Fall Showing," *New York Times*, June 29, 1960.

14. Magliozzi interview with Talbot.

15. "Operation Abolition," *Village Voice*, January 18, 1962.

16. This list of programs came from New Yorker clipping files, Research Collection, LPA; Jonas Mekas, "Movie Journal," *Village Voice*, January 7, 1965; Jonas Mekas, "Movie Journal," *Village Voice*, January 3, 1974.

17. Talbot, *New Yorker Theater*, 37.

18. *Ibid.*, 10; Bruce Goldstein, interview by author, New York, NY, February 27, 2012; Ed and Mary Maguire, interview by author, New York, NY, May 31, 2011. All subsequent quotes from the Maguires will come from this interview, unless otherwise noted.

19. Magliozzi interview with Dan Talbot.

20. Talbot, *New Yorker Theater*, 33; James Monaco, "Dan Talbot, film distributor," *Take One*, Nov./Dec. 1973, 22.

21. Vincent Canby, "Is Busby Really Camp?" *New York Times*, April 12, 1970; Talbot, *New Yorker Theater*, 20.

22. This history of the New Yorker Bookstore came from Toby Talbot, *New Yorker Theater*, 143–147.

23. Magliozzi interview with Dan Talbot.

24. NYT ledger, MoMA Dept. of Film Archives, NY.

25. "Play It Again, Woody, Is Theme for a Festival," *New York Times*, November 9, 1979; Talbot, *New Yorker Theater*, 33.

26. Talbot, "Guest Book/Sample Pages"; Dan Yakir, "The New Yorker Redux," the *Thousand Eyes: The Magazine of Public Cinema*, Thru November 30, 1979, in the author's collection and also available in New Yorker Theater clippings file, Research Collection, LPA.

27. James Monaco, "An Interview with Dan Talbot," *Take One*, November/December 1972, 23.

28. Nora Ephron, "Closeup: Movie Man," *New York Post*, January 27, 1964; Daniel Talbot, "On Historic Hearings from TV to the Screen," *New York Times*, January 12, 1964.

29. Monaco, "Dan Talbot, Film Distributor," 23; A.H. Weiler, "Observations from a Local Vantage Point," *New York Times*, October 7, 1962; Vincent Canby, "Indies Yen Intro to Manhattan," *New York Times*, April 1963, available in New Yorker Theater clippings file, Research Collection, LPA.

30. Monaco, "Dan Talbot, Film Distributor," 23; Gomery, *Shared Pleasures*, 190–191.

31. Howard Thompson, "$1 Charge Is Set for Films in a Series at New Yorker," *New York Times*, January 11, 1969; Advertisement, *New York Times*, January 12, 1969; McCandlish Phillips, "8 Foreign Films to Open in a 'Test,'" *New York Times*, May 21, 1972.

32. Advertisement, *New York Times*, January 12, 1969.

33. The figure of $4,500 a week to operate the theater came from the interview with Phillips, "8 Foreign Films"; Yakir, "The New Yorker Redux."; NYT log book, MoMA Dept. of Film Archives, NY.

34. Talbot, *New Yorker Theater*, 127–128; Phillips, "8 Foreign Films to Open in a 'Test.'"

35. Calendar in the author's collection.

36. "Talbot Unloads Lease to Reade: Further Down-Trends 'Arter,'" *Variety*, December 26, 1973.

37. Monaco, "Dan Talbot, Film Distributor," 26.

38. Judith Crist, "A Heartwarming Housewarming," *New York* [after 18th] January 1973, 72.
39. Jonas Mekas, "Movie Journal," *Village Voice*, January 3, 1974.

Chapter 4

1. A.H. Weiler, "By Way of Report," *New York Times*, February 28, 1960; Jonas Mekas, "Movie Journal," *Village Voice*, March 23, 1960; Jonas Mekas, "Movie Journal," *Village Voice*, April 27, 1960. The article mistakenly states that the film would begin at the New Yorker on March 28.
2. "The Building of an Alternate Cinema: An Excerpt from Unpublished Biography of Lionel Rogosin," in "About Lionel Rogosin: Bleecker Street & Impact Films," *Lionel Rogosin, A Visionary American: Maverick Filmmaker Humanitarian*, accessed February 18, 2015, http://www.lionelrogosin.org/bleecker_street_LR.html.
3. This summary of Rogosin's early biography comes from two sources: "Rogosin," *Wikipedia*, last modified October 13, 2014, accessed February 18, 2014, http://en.wikipedia.org/wiki/Lionel_Rogosin; and John Wakeman, ed., "Lionel Rogosin," in *World Film Directors, Volume II 1945–1985* (New York: The H.W. Wilson Company, 1988), 913–915. In an e-mail dated December 19, 2012, Rogosin's son, Michael Rogosin, corrected one fact in the Wakeman entry on his father: his grandfather was a Jewish businessman based in New York and New Jersey, not Philadelphia.
4. Mary Kelly, phone interview by author, New York, NY, January 30, 2012. All subsequent quotes from Kelly will come from this interview, unless otherwise indicated; anecdote about Breathless came from Rudy Franchi's posting, Nostalgia Factory on November 28, 2004 (4:35 pm.), *Cinema Treasures*, accessed February 18, 2015, http://cinematreasures.org/theaters/6016. Franchi, in a phone interview with the author on May 13, 2010, attributed the holes to the prevention of billowing. But Ted Ostrow informed the author in an e-mail dated June 11, 2014, that the perforated screen was to allow unmuffled sound to emanate through the screen. "During the silent movie days," he wrote, "screens were unperforated and with the advent of 'talkies' the so-called 'sound screen' was developed."
5. Marco Acevedo on February 12, 2004 (8:29 pm), *Cinema Treasures*, accessed February 18, 2015, http://cinematreasures.org/comments?page=3&theater_id=6016.
6. Eugene Archer, "Documentary Set by Lionel Rogosin," *New York Times*, August 13, 1960.
7. Jonas Mekas, "Movie Journal," *Village Voice*, March 9, 1961; Eugene Archer, "Novels by Proust," *New York Times*, March 1, 1961.
8. Filmmaker's Cinematheque Programmes, 1–150, in Cinema Clubs/Cinema Societies, Misc. (CCCS), MoMA Dept. of Film Archives, NY.
9. Gary Morris, "Jack Smith in Retrospect," accessed January 18, 2015, http://www.ubu.com/film/smith_jack.html; Hoberman and Rosenbaum, *Midnight Movies*, 40; P. Adams Sitney, "Preface," *Visionary Film: The American Avant-Garde* (New York: Oxford University Press, 1974), ix; Sklar, *Movie-Made America*, 312.
10. Jonas Mekas, "Movie Journal," *Village Voice*, June 13, 1963; Mekas, "Movie Journal," January 3, 1974; Marshall Lewis to Mekas, "New American Cinema File," Anthology Film Archives. Quoted in Haberski, *Freedom to Offend*, 129; Jonas Mekas, "Movie Journal," *Village Voice*, June 13, 1963; Marianne Shaneen, "Jonas Mekas, interview by Marianne Shaneen," *SFAQ: International Arts and Culture*, 52, accessed November 12, 2014, http://www.sfaqonline.com/pdfs/SFAQ_issue_eleven.pdf. Mekas told Shaneen that after he, Ken Jacobs, Florence Jacobs, and Jerry Sims were arrested in March 1964 at the Bowery Theater, he was arrested again a week later for screening Jean Genet's *Un Chant d'amour* (1950). With the help of a top lawyer hired by Jerome Hill, they escaped with six months' suspended sentences and a few days in jail. Susan Sontag and Allen Ginsberg were defense witnesses; Leslie Trumbull, "Movie Journal," *Village Voice*, January 9, 1964. For a detailed description of Mekas's use of *Flaming Creatures* in his battle against the censors and licensing board, see Haberski, *Freedom to Offend*, 128–151.
11. Rudy Franchi, interview by author, New York, NY, May 13, 2010. All quotes from Franchi will come from this interview unless otherwise indicated.
12. Ben Barenholtz, interview by author, New York, NY, January 17, 2012; IMDb, *Bonnie and Clyde* (1967), Release Info, accessed March 28, 2016, www.imdb.com/title/tt0061418/releaseinfo.
13. Ted Ostrow, interview by author, New York, NY, January 31, 2012. All subsequent quotes from Ostrow will come from this interview, unless otherwise indicated.
14. "'Village' Shows Movie Classics," *New York Times*, January 1, 1964; R.M. Franchi, Press release, February 18, 1966, in Bleecker Street Cinema clippings file, Research Collection, LPA.
15. Eugene Archer, "Movie about Bigot Is Awarded Seal of Approval Once Denied," *New York Times*, March 7, 1962.
16. *Ibid.*; Paul Gardner, "TV Commercials Gain Art Status; with Documentaries, They Will Be Shown in Festival," *New York Times*, February 15, 1965.
17. Andrew Sarris, "Bogdanovich, Archer, and Me: The Way We Really Were," *Village Voice*, May 15, 1976; Nostalgia Factory on November 28, 2004 (4:35 p.m.), *Cinema Treasures*, accessed November 18, 2014, http://cinematreasures.org/comments?page=3&theater_id=6016; Lopate, "Anticipation of La Notte," 12.
18. Background of Lewis's relationship with Truffaut comes from author's interview with Franchi; Godard quote from "The Building of an Alternate Cinema: An Excerpt from Unpublished Biography of Lionel Rogosin."

19. Anecdote related in Nostalgia Factory on November 28, 2004 (4:35 pm); VistaVision was Paramount Studio's version of the widescreen method and was used only on films made and distributed by that studio. It was different technologically from CinemaScope and other widescreen methods. Franchi was mistaken in writing that it is now known as widescreen, seeming to imply that it was the only method.

20. "Rogosin," *Wikipedia*.

21. Archer Winsten, "Rages and Outrages," *New York Post*, March 14, 1966; Advertisement for *Good Times, Wonderful Times*, *Village Voice*, July 21, 1966; This summary of Janus Films was adapted from "A History of Janus Films," accessed February 18, 2014, www.brattlefilm.org/brattlefilm/series/2006/janus/history.html; "The Building of an Alternate Cinema: An Excerpt from Unpublished Biography of Lionel Rogosin."

22. Vincent Canby, "Offbeat Movies Get Selling Unit," *New York Times*, March 30, 1966. Rogosin in none of his writings explains why he formed his own distribution company so soon after participating in the creation of the Film-Makers' Distribution Center. He may have done so to concentrate on the "socially and politically conscious cinema" that the avant-gardists Mekas and Clarke were less interested in.

23. The Bleecker probably showed Downey's films several times, both together and in different combinations. According to Downey (Robert Downey, Sr., interview by author, New York, NY, June 2, 2011), *Chafed Elbows* ran for ten months. Hoberman and Rosenbaum (*Midnight Movies*, 73), put *Chafed Elbows* on a double bill with *Scorpio Rising* for an eleven-week run.

24. Michael Rogosin, phone interview by author, New York, NY, May 13, 2011. All subsequent quotes by Rogosin will come from this interview, unless otherwise indicated; David Ehrenstein on May 1, 2005 (3:00 p.m.), *Cinema Treasures*, accessed February 18, 2015, http://cinematreasures.org/comments?page=3&theater_id=6016.

25. "The Building of an Alternate Cinema: An Excerpt from Unpublished Biography of Lionel Rogosin"; Author interview with Barenholtz.

26. "The Building of an Alternate Cinema: An Excerpt from Unpublished Biography of Lionel Rogosin."

27. *Ibid*.; Marco Acevedo on February 2, 2004 (8:29 p.m.), *Cinema Treasures*, accessed January 14, 2012, http://cinematreasures.org/comments?page=3&theater_id=6016.

28. "The Building of an Alternate Cinema: An Excerpt from Unpublished Biography of Lionel Rogosin."

Chapter 5

1. Creighton Peet, "Amateur Night for Movie Makers," *New York Herald Tribune*, June 24, 1962; Walter Langsford, interview by author, New York, NY, February 13, 2012. Two further interviews were held with him on March 11, 2012 and April 24, 2012. In addition there were several e-mail exchanges between Langsford and the author. All subsequent quotes by Langsford will come from one of these interviews or e-mails, unless otherwise noted.

2. Jesse Zunser, "New Audiences for Old Films: Movies' Latest Phenomenon Is the Growing Vogue of 'Revival' Programs," *Cue*, April 14, 1962, 8.

3. Calendar, Charles Theater Collection (CTC), MoMA Dept. of Film Archives, NY. All subsequent listings of films at the Charles will come from this collection, unless otherwise indicated; Hoberman and Rosenbaum, *Midnight Movies*, 41.

4. Press release, CTC, MoMA Dept. of Film Archives, NY.

5. *Ibid*.

6. A.S., "Theatre: What Else Is There?," *Village Voice*, November 1, 1962.

7. Press release, CTC, MoMA Dept. of Film Archives, NY.

8. The term *underground movies* was coined by the experimental animator and social satirist Stan Vanderbeek to encompass all avant-garde or experimental films. Hoberman and Rosenbaum make a distinction between the older avant-garde filmmakers with roots in the 1940s and the newer group who first appeared in the 1960s in New York, such as Kenneth Anger and Jack Smith. Hoberman and Rosenbaum, *Midnight Movies*, 40; Ben Barenholtz, interview by author, New York, NY, January 17, 2012.

9. "Experimental Film," *Wikipedia*, last modified November 19, 2014, accessed February 19, 2015, http://en.wikipedia.org/wiki/Experimental_film; J. Hoberman, "The Short Happy Life of the Charles," *American Film*, March 1982, 22; Mekas, "Movie Journal," *Village Voice*, January 3, 1974; Hoberman, "The Short Happy Life of the Charles," 34.

10. *Ibid*.

11. The idea for one-person retrospectives came most likely from Mekas, who soon became its champion. In his *Village Voice* column of January 10, 1974, for example, he attacked Film Forum's emphasis on "potpourri" programming of a range of stylistic approaches in independent filmmaking instead of focusing on one-man, in-depth shows; press releases, CTC, MoMA Dept. of Film Archives, NY.

12. Eugene Archer, "Screen: 'Flower Thief,'" *New York Times*, July 14, 1962; Hoberman and Rosenbaum (*Midnight Movies*, 46) place Ron Rice at the top of the list of the 1960s avant-garde filmmakers, as one of the three most important protégés of Jonas Mekas.

13. Peet, "Amateur Night for Movie Makers."

14. *Ibid*.; Don Kirk, "Audience Adds Sound Effects at Film-Makers' Festival Here," *New York Post*, May 7, 1962; Eileen Zabotinsky, "Grab-bag of Talent in Film Festival," *Villager*, March 29, 1962.

15. Howard Thompson, "Theatre Showing Amateurs' Films," *New York Times*, March 24, 1962; Peet, "Amateur Night for Movie Makers"; Zabotinsky, "Grab-bag of Talent in Film Festival."

16. Thompson, "Theatre Showing Amateurs' Films."

17. Peet, "Amateur Night for Movie Makers."

18. Andrew Sarris, "Movie Journal: Hello and Goodbye to the New American Cinema," *Village Voice*, September 20, 1962; Jonas Mekas, "Movie Journal," *Village Voice*, September 27, 1962.

19. Eugene Archer, "Windsor Theatre to Revive Films," *New York Times*, September 5, 1962.

20. Letter to Edwin Stein, CTC, MoMA Dept. of Film Archives, NY.

21. "Lights Out for Charles?," *Village Voice*, November 22, 1962; Summary of debts, CTC, MoMA Dept. of Film Archives, NY; Letter from Jerome Hill, CTC, MoMA Dept. of Film Archives, NY; Jonas Mekas, "Movie Journal," *Village Voice*, November 22, 1962.

22. A.S., "Theatre: What Else Is There?"; Hoberman, "The Short Happy Life of the Charles," 34.

23. *Ibid.*; Hoberman and Rosenbaum (*Midnight Movies*, 50) wrote that "[a]ccording to one member of the cast, *Flaming Creatures* was shot 'in broiling sunlight' on the roof of the Windsor Theater. The performers were 'high as kites, Jack pouring ceiling plaster all over them ... and careening dangerously above on some swinging, homemade contraption.'" For a detailed description of the making of *Flaming Creatures*, see J. Hoberman, "Up on the Roof," posted January 5, 2012, Museum of the Moving Image, *Moving Image Source*, Co-presented with Reverse Shot, accessed February 19, 2015, http://www.movingimagesource.us/articles/up-on-the-roof-20120105.

24. Hoberman, "The Short Happy Life of the Charles," 22.

Chapter 6

1. Jay Levin, "Thalia Film Theater Needs a Revival," *New York Post*, August 23, 1973; mfarricker_1 on April 7, 2014 (9:10 p.m.), *Cinema Treasures*, accessed February 17, 2015, http://cinematreasures.org/theaters/285/comments; Delaney, "The Thalia Theatre"; Michelle O'Donnell, "A Revivalist Revived: The Thalia Returns, Kindling Memories in Black and White," *New York Times*, March 31, 2002.

2. Delaney, "The Thalia Theatre"; John Lewis, interview by author, New York, NY, February 22, 2016. All subsequent quotes from Mr. Lewis will come from this interview, unless otherwise indicated.

3. Winfield Scott Downs, Litt. D, editor, "Martin John Lewis," *Encyclopedia of American Biography*, New Series (New York: American Historical Company, 1957), 215.

4. Thomas Lewis, interview by author, New York, NY, February 25, 2016. All subsequent quotes from Mr. Lewis will come from this interview, unless otherwise indicated.

This précis of Martin Lewis's background is an amalgam of information from the interviews with Lewis's sons, Tom and John Lewis, from Ursula Lewis, "Memoir," I, 13; and from "Elias Bickerman and Hans (Yohanan) Lewy: The Story of a Friendship," accessed March 2, 2016, https://anabases.revues.org/1764, 1, 14.

Mrs. Lewis's unpublished memoir is divided into four parts. Part I contains the separate histories of Martin and Ursula Lewis before their meeting and marriage. Part II details their marriage and family life, as well as Lewis's work in the Thalia. Part III concerns the immediate years before his death, the details leading up to his death, her efforts to stabilize her situation after his death, and her management of the Thalia in collaboration with Max Zipperman. The fourth part (IV) describes her management of the theater after Zipperman's retirement when she was on her own. A copy of the entire memoir is in the collection of the author.

5. Ursula Lewis, "Memoir," I, 13–16; Downs, "Martin J. Lewis."

6. "Prologue to a Fifth Avenue Festival," *New York Times*, June 26, 1938; Jesse Zenser, "New Films: Revivals," *Cue*, June 18, 1938, 10; Thomas Schatz, *Boom and Bust: American Cinema in the 1940s*, History of the American Cinema, Charles Harpole, General Editor (Berkeley: University of California Press, 1997), 65; "Film Revivals of the Week," *Cue*, May 30, 1936, 16; *Cue*, May 28, 1938, 18.

In addition to the top three winners, the full list included, by order of preference, *It Happened One Night* (1934), *Louis Pasteur* (1936), *Captains Courageous* (1937), *The Good Earth* (1937), *Emile Zola* (1937), *Naughty Marietta* (1935), *The Informer* (1935), *Mutiny on the Bounty* (1935), *Lost Horizon* (1937), *Mr. Deeds Goes to Town* (1936), *San Francisco* (1936), and *David Copperfield* (1935).

Cue, which began listing weekly revivals at local theaters in 1936, refined the list in 1937 by rating the films according to their entertainment value. The ratings were A for definitely recommended; B for good; and C for moderately entertaining "If you like that sort of thing." Various types of drama, such as war dramas and historical dramas, topped the A list while melodrama and comedy, especially the screwball comedies, headed the B list.

7. Jesse Zunser, "New Films," *Cue*, July 2, 1938, 10; "Prologue to a Fifth Avenue Festival." The lease of the Fifth Avenue Playhouse included several other restrictive clauses: it was the only theater in the city without a marquee since it occupied the ground floor of an office building in a restricted residential area; it could only present pictures that would not "endanger the morale of youngsters in the neighborhood"; and its usherettes could not wear pants, only (unabbreviated) skirts. "Prologue to a Fifth Avenue Festival."

8. Zunser, "New Films"; "Prologue to a Fifth Avenue Festival."

9. *Ibid.*; Sike Randolph, "Cue Says Go!," *Cue*, June 24, 1939, 12.

10. Theodore Strauss, "Hunger Is the Mother of Invention," *New York Times*, February 1, 1942; "Television Is Planned for Little Carnegie," *New York Times*, June 12, 1941; A challenge could be made to the Thalia's claim as the first revival theater in New York. In a *New York Times* article, Stanley W. Lawton, who described himself as "the impresario of the revival business," claimed he had opened a commercial revival house at the Lyric, a 42nd Street grind house off Times Square, in 1932, first showing silent films as the "talkies came into being," then later branching into revivals of sound films. Alfred Clark, "Bring 'Em in Alive," *New York Times*, March 30, 1941.

11. Jesse Zunser, "New Films," *Cue*, February 18, 1939, 40; "Hollywood News and Screen Notes," *New York Herald Tribune*, July 5, 1939; Douglas W. Churchill, "A New Role Soon for Miss Shearer," *New York Times*, August 21, 1939; "Foreign Films," *Cue*, July 1, 1939, 29; "The People's Choice," *New York Times*, May 5, 1940. The 50 films in the program, mostly American, were grouped into categories: Comedy (*Bluebeard's Eighth Wife*, 1938, for example); Musical (*The Mikado*, 1939); Melodrama (*Elephant Boy*, 1937); and Drama (*The Citadel*, 1938); there were also two documentaries; Alan Bader, "Films in Fiesta: Revival Programs Form Local Success Story," *New York Times*, September 1, 1957, available in Thalia clippings file, Research Collection, LPA.

12. Strauss, "Hunger Is the Mother of Invention"; Archer Winsten, "Movie Revivals: A Quiet Boom," *New York Post*, December 20, 1977.

13. Strauss, "Hunger Is the Mother of Invention"; Delaney, "The Thalia Theatre"; "By Way of Explanation," Surrealist Film Festival calendar, in the collection of the author.

14. Ursula Lewis, "Memoir," II, 2.

15. 1947 Summer festival calendar, in the author's collection.

16. Delaney, "The Thalia Theatre"; Paul Gardner, "Thalia's Classic Era Slips into Folklore," *New York Times*, August 31, 1973.

17. William Wolf, interview by author, New York, NY, November 30, 2011. All subsequent quotes from Wolf will come from this interview, unless otherwise noted; O'Donnell, "A Revivalist Revived."

18. John Lewis interview; Ursula Lewis, "Memoir," III, 2, 5.

19. *Ibid.*, 11; Andre Sennwald, "American Debut of 'La Maternelle,' at the 55th Street Playhouse—'Little America,'" *New York Times*, October 15, 1935.

20. Thomas Lewis interview.

21. Ursula Lewis, "Memoir," III, 6–8.

22. *Ibid.*, II, 3, 4–5; Deborah Sutherland, interview by author, New York, NY, February 14, 2016. All subsequent quotes from Mrs. Sutherland will come from this interview, unless otherwise noted.

23. Ursula Lewis, "Memoir," III, 8–22.

24. *Ibid.*, II, 5–7; *Ibid.*, III, 10, 8–22.

25. "Janus Films," *Wikipedia*, last modified December 17, 2014, accessed February 17, 2015, http://en.wikipedia.org/wiki/Janus_Films.

26. Ursula Lewis, "Memoir," III, 32–34.

27. Ursula Lewis, "Memoir," III, 10–11, 26.

28. Gardner, "Thalia's Classic Era Slips into Folklore"; Calendar for Summer Film Festival, June 26–October 15, 1959, in Cinemas Repertory & Revival clippings file, Research Collection, LPA.

29. Ursula Lewis, "Memoir," III, 27, and I, track 2–3; Summer 1964 calendar, in the collection of Ed and Mary Maguire.

30. "Thalia Festival Starting Friday," *New York Times*, June 15, 1963; Mike Moore, "The Last Thalia Picture Show," *New York Times*, September 30, 1973; Ursula Lewis, "Memoir," III, 30.

31. LesW on December 3, 2010 (2:27 p.m.), *Cinema Treasures*, accessed February 17, 2015, http://cinematreasures.org/theaters/285/comments.

32. "The Thalia," *New Yorker*, September 10, 1973; Astyanax on September 4, 2010 (9:00 a.m.), *Cinema Treasures*, accessed November 6, 2014, http://cinematreasures.org/comments?page=2&theater_id=285; Joseph Michalak, "Thalia, West Side Muse of Reruns, is Revived," *New York Times*, August 12, 1977.

33. Ursula Lewis, "Memoir," III, 23.

34. *Ibid.*, 24.

35. *Ibid.*, 25.

36. *Ibid.*, IV, 1–2. Although she wrote that the weekly programs took place through the year (outside the summer festivals), she specifically assigned them to March through May and specified January and February as the months for "a review of the year." She made no mention of what November and December contained; Thalia clippings file, Research Collection, LPA.

37. Ursula Lewis, "Memoir," IV, 3–4.

38. *Ibid.*, 2–3.

39. 1969 and 1972 summer calendars, in the author's collection; Levin, "The Thalia Film Theater Needs a Revival."

40. Moore, "The Last Thalia Picture Show."

Chapter 7

1. Advertisement for the *New Republic*, *Village Voice*, January 13, 1966; Clyde Haberman, *New York Times: The Times of the Seventies: the Culture, Politics and Personalities that Shaped the Decade* (New York: Black Dog & Leventhal Publishers, 2013), vii; Vivian Gornick, "The Press of Freedom: An Ofay's Indirect Address to Leroi Jones," *Village Voice*, March 4, 1965.

2. Jeffrey A. Kroessler, *New York Year by Year: A Chronology of the Great Metropolis* (New York: New York University, 2002), 303.

3. Joshua B. Freeman, "The Fiscal Crisis," in *Working Class New York: Life and Labor Since World War II* (New York: The New Press, 2000), 256–257; Haberman, *The Times of the Seventies*, 88.

4. Marty Rubin, phone interview by author, New York, NY, December 6, 2012.

5. Freeman, "The Fiscal Crisis," 260; Adam Davidson, "Jane Jacobs Vs. Marc Jacobs," *New York Times Magazine*, June 10, 2012, 16, 18.

6. Lynda Cohen Cassanos, "Special Collections: Film Forum," *Sightlines*, Winter 1986/87, 5; Jonas Mekas, "Movie Journal," *Village Voice*, November 12, 1970; Kathy Davis, "The Return of Film Forum," *American Film*, September 1981, 62.

7. Robert Haller, "Introduction, Jerome Hill: Selected Correspondence," in *Perspectives on Jerome Hill & Anthology Film Archives*, ed. Robert A. Haller (New York: Anthology Film Archives, 2005), 11–14; "Stan Brakhage to Jerome Hill, Early September 1968," in Haller, "Selected Correspondence," 18; Genevieve Yue, "Jonas Mekas: Midwife of the New York Independent Cinema," *Senses of Cinema*, February 2005, accessed April 10, 2015, http://sensesofcinema.com/2005/great-directors/mekas/#senses; Barbara Rose, "Spotlight: Where to Learn How to Look at Movies: New York's New Anthology Film Archives," *Vogue*, November 1, 1971, 70; Mekas, "A Note of [sic] Film-Makers' Cinematheque," *New York Film-Makers' Newsletter*, November 1967; "Essential Cinema" blurb in all issues of the quarterly *Anthology Film Archives Film Program*; "Essential Cinema," *Anthology Film Archives Film Program*, April–June 2015; Sky Sitney, "Introduction, The Search for the Invisible Cinema," in Haller, *Perspectives on Jerome Hill*, 32; Marianne Shaneen, "Jonas Mekas, interview," *SFAQ: International Arts and Culture*, accessed October 7, 2014, http://www.sfaqonline.com/pdfs/SFAQ_issue_eleven.pdf, 56.

8. The history of the Millennium Film Workshop comes from its website, "History," accessed January 21, 2015, http://millenniumfilm.org/history.

9. RFH, "And Now, from the Commissioner of Acronyms: Tribeca," *Village Voice*, March 17–March 23, 1977; Amy Taubin, "The Collective for Living Cinema: Dark Night on White Street?," *Village Voice*, January 24, 1989; David Sterritt, "Adventurous Moviegoing," *Christian Science Monitor*, October 7, 1983; Susan Lepselter, "Emerging Artists at Collective for Living Cinema," *West Side Spirit*, February 21, 1988; Taubin, "The Collective for Living Cinema"; Amy Taubin, "Collective Problems," *Village Voice*, February 26, 1991.

10. Howard Thompson, "Going Out Guide," *New York Times*, July 25, 1978.

11. The descriptions of these small, apartment-based film societies, other than Don Coles's, come from Magliozzi, "An interview with Charles L. Turner," 87 (see Chapter 1, endnote 27).

12. Howard Thompson, "Going Out Guide," *New York Times*, July 25, 1978; Interview with Ed and Mary Maguire; Magliozzi, "An Interview with Charles L. Turner," 87; J.P. Coursodon, accessed April 14, 2015, http://www.movies.groups.yahoo.com/group/a_film_by/message/27369; posted by damiebona, Sun June 22, 2001 (11:45 pm.), accessed April 14, 2015, http://movies.groups.yahoo.com/group/a_film_by/message/154; For one person's impressions of the audience for these cineclubs, see Mandelbaum, "Letter from New York," *Bright Lights Film Journal*, Issue #9 (1980), accessed April 14, 2015, http://brightlightsfilm.com/66/66letterfromny.php.

13. Richard Schickel, "The Movies Are Now High Art," *New York Times*, January 5, 1969; Irving Howe, "Deeper into the Movies: Careful, Devastating, Enjoyable, Witty, Illuminating, Pauline Kael Should Write a Book," *New York Times*, February 18, 1973; Susan Sontag, "The Decay of Cinema," *New York Times Magazine*, February 25, 1996, SM60.

14. Lopate, *Totally, Tenderly Tragically*, 14; Sklar, *Movie-Made America*, 334; Gomery, *Shared Pleasures*, 193; Deac Russell, "Moving Pictures: Foreign Film in the U.S.: A Premature Obituary?," *Boston After Dark*, June 16, 1970 and June 23, 1970, in TBC, M255a., MoMA Dept. of Film Archives, NY.

15. Lopate, *Totally, Tenderly Tragically*, 14; Sklar, *Movie-Made America*, 334; Gary Crowdus, "The 7th New York Film Festival," *Film Society Review*, October 1969, 26.

16. Eric Breitbart, "Available Light: 20 Years of Social Issue Documentaries," *Sightlines*, Winter 1986–87, 10; Sklar, *Movie-Made America*, 333–334.

17. Cook, *History of American Film*, 920–922.

18. Sklar, *Movie-Made America*, 325; Cook, *History of American Film*, 931.

19. Peter Biskind, *Easy Riders, Raging Bulls* (New York: Simon & Schuster, 1998), 17; Sklar, *Movie-Made America*, 324.

20. John Pierson, *Spike, Mike, Slackers & Dykes* (New York: Hyperion, 1997), 8.

21. Manohla Dargis and A.O. Scott, "Mad about Her: Pauline Kael, Loved and Loathed," *New York Times*, October 16, 2011; Howe, "Deeper into the Movies."

22. William Wolf, "Wolf on Films: Can New York's Movie Institutions Avoid Obsolescence?," *Cue*, November 20, 1971 9; Charles E. Carley, "Manhatlan [sic] Film Buff," *Classic Film Collector*, Summer 1971, 28.

23. Advertisement for the first Whitney series, *Village Voice*, December 10, 1970; Mekas, "Movie Journal," *Village Voice*, February 1, 1973; David Bienstock, "Mekas in the '70s: Curator's Critique," *Village Voice*, February 22, 1973; Karen Cooper, Letter to the Editor, *Village Voice*, February 7, 1973; Mekas, "Movie Journal," *Village Voice*, February 15, 1973 and January 10, 1974.

24. William Wolf, "From Shakespeare to Cinema," *Cue*, Thru June 22, 1979; "Off-the-Beaten-Path Guide to Moviegoing," *New York Times*, November 30, 1979.

25. "A Talk with the Film Society of Lincoln Center," *Volvo Salutes the Film Society of Lincoln Center 25th Anniversary*, Film Society of Lincoln Center (FSLC) clippings file, Research Collection, LPA; An-

nette Insdorf, "New Director for New Directors," *New York Daily News*, March 25, 1984.

26. *Volvo Salutes the Film Society of Lincoln Center 25th Anniversary*.

27. Museum of the Moving Image, "Museum History," accessed March 29, 2015, http://www.movingimage.us/about/history; Richard Koszarski, Head of Collections & Exhibitions, "Creating a Collection," *Quarterly Guide to Exhibitions & Programs AMMI*, September/October/November/December 1993, American Museum of the Moving Image (AMMI) clippings file, Research Collection, LPA; Fact Sheet, AMMI, in AMMI clippings file, Research Collection, LPA; Paul Goldberger, "From Sound Stage to Strong, Silent Museum," *New York Times*, July 2, 1989; "American Museum of the Moving Image Unveils Permanent Installation, 'Behind the Screen,'" AMMI press release, AMMI clippings file, Research Collection, LPA; "Moving Images," *New Yorker*, October 24, 1988, 32; Koszarski, "Creating a Collection."

Chapter 8

1. McCandlish Phillips, "Repertory Movie Theaters Multiply in Manhattan," *New York Times*, December 15, 1971.

2. Dan Talbot, who opened another repertory house in this period, was still available, but the essentials of his philosophy and approach to repertory theater management had already been covered. Fabiano Canosa, who programmed the First Avenue Screening Room, was still living, but no longer available since he had moved back to his native country, Brazil; Phillips, "Repertory Movie Theaters Multiply"; Doug Block, "Reel Revival of 2nd Ave.," *East Side Express*, May 5, 1977, also available in St. Marks Cinema clippings file, Research Collection, LPA. The "reel" revival of Second Avenue, according to the *East Side Express* article, also included the opening of another repertory cinema in the area, the Jean Renoir Cinema, on Second Avenue and 10th Street, devoted to lesser known foreign imports and independent American films; Michael Musto, "Malling the St. Marks," *Village Voice*, September 3, 1985.

3. Phillips, "Repertory Movie Theaters Multiply"; Flyer, Olympia Theater clippings file, Research Collection, LPA.

4. Jonas Mekas, "Movie Journal," *Village Voice*, October 19, 1972 ; Allan Kozinn, "New Owner to Renovate and Upgrade Quad Cinema," *The New York Times*, August 21, 2014, accessed April 9, 2016, http://artsbeat.blogs.nytimes.com/2014/08/21/new-owner-to-renovate-and-upgrade-quad-cinema.

5. Judith Crist, "Condition Critical," *New York*, January 20, 1975, 51; "Buffs Not So Many (Or Loyal) for 'Screening Room' Profits," *Variety*, June 14, 1974, 7.

6. Bob Eimicke, "Balancing Art with Income in Downtown Film Houses," *Villager*, December 3, 1981; Matthew Flamm, "Eighth Street Theater Hits the Road," *New York Post*, October 22, 1992.

7. Stephen M. Silverman, "New York's Newest Theater Is All Ready to Roll," *New York Post*, October 1, 1982; Shawn Cunningham, "Metro Cinema Changes Policy," *Westsider*, June 6, 1985.

8. Wolf, "Wolf on Films." See Chapter 7, fn. 20; Michael Wolff, "So What Do You Do at Midnight? You See a Trashy Movie," *New York Times*, September 7, 1975; Pierson, *Spike, Mike, Slackers & Dykes*, 15–16.

9. Guy Flatley, "At the Movies: When Jean Arthur Was the Gem of Columbia's Ocean," *New York Times*, January 28, 1977; Tom Allen, "Art House Confidential: The Men Who Procure the Films," *Village Voice*, September 11, 1978; Janet Maslin, "Some Movies Born to be Revived," *New York Times*, August 26, 1977; Kathleen Carroll, "Requiem for the Film Lovers' Shrine," *New York Daily News*, January 27, 1974, Leisure section; Michalak, "Thalia, West Side Muse of Reruns, Is Revived."

10. Eleanor Blau, "Old-Movie Houses Dwindle," *New York Times*, August 13, 1987.

11. Bill Barol, et al., "The Last Picture Shows," *Newsweek*, June 8, 1987; Michael Klitsch, "New York's Revival Houses Face an Uncertain Future," *The New Manhattan Review,* May 6, 1987; Barol, "The Last Picture Shows"; Klitsch, "New York's Revival Houses Face an Uncertain Future."

Both sides, however, were arguing an absolutist position, either the horizontal series approach or the random double features one. But most repertory houses had been using the compromise trend, combining vertical series scheduled one day a week over a specific period with horizontal schedules of random double features.

12. Barol, "The Last Picture Shows"; Gomery, *Shared Pleasures*, 193.

13. Barol, "The Last Picture Shows."

14. Myra Forsberg, "Curling Up with a Good Double Bill," *New York Times*, March 14, 1986.

15. Anemona Hartocollis, "Fade to Black," *New York Times,* April 6, 2003, The City section.

16. Anne Thompson, "Rep-Cinema Yields to New Tastes and VCRs," *Chicago Tribune*, July 5, 1987, section 13; Talbot, *The New Yorker Theater*, 35; P. Adams Sitney, "Rear-Garde," *American Film*, July-August 1985, 13.

17. Lopate, "When Foreign Movies Mattered"; Pierson, *Spike, Mike, Slackers & Dykes*, 7; Louis Menand, *American Studies* (New York: Farrar, Straus and Giroux, 2002), 190.

Chapter 9

1. Vivian Gornick, "Chelsea Fights Back: The Elgin Wins ... for Now," *Village Voice*, April 4, 1977, 39.

2. Ben Barenholtz, interview by author, New York, NY, January 17, 2012. All subsequent quotes from Barenholtz will come from this interview, unless otherwise indicated.

3. Hoberman and Rosenbaum, *Midnight Movies*, 93.

4. Gornick, "Chelsea Fights Back."
5. Canby, "Is Busby Really Camp?," *New York Times*, April 12, 1970.
6. This brief history of Sam Clare comes from Pumpernick Eggburger, "Big Time Operator," *Elgin Marble*, Summer 1974, 1, available in the Elgin clippings file, Research Collection, LPA; Steve Gould, interview by author, New York, NY, September 22, 1996. All subsequent quotes from Gould will come from either this interview or additional ones with Gould on October 3, 1996, June 1, 2010 and November 2, 2011 or a joint interview with Chuck Zlatkin on November 17, 1996, unless otherwise noted.
7. Steve D'Inzillo, a member and organizer of the New York Projectionists Local 306 of the International Alliance of Theatrical Stage Employees since 1933, was its chief officer from 1992 until January 2000. He died in October 2000. See Eric Pace, "Steve D'Inzillo, 90, Is Dead; Led Film Projectionists' Local," *New York Times*, December 26, 2000, accessed February 20, 2015, http://www.nytimes.com/2000/12/26/nyregion/steve-d-inzillo-90-is-dead-led-film-projectionists-local.html.
8. Calendar listing Janus Film Festival in private collection of Ed and Mary Maguire; e-mail from Dan Talbot to the author on August 22, 2012; Vincent Canby, "Film View: New York Is Revival City," *New York Times*, July 27, 1975.
9. Alan Douglas was an American record producer who worked with Jimi Hendrix, Miles Davis, John McLaughlin, Lenny Bruce and the Last Poets. He ran his own record label, Douglas Records. See "Alan Douglas (record producer)," *Wikipedia*, last modified February 13, 2015, accessed February 20, 2015, http://en.wikipedia.org/wiki/Alan_Douglas_%28record_producer%29; According to Hoberman and Rosenbaum (*Midnight Movies*, 80), Barenholtz also took advantage of a festival of avant-garde films in December at the Elgin, to announce the midnight showing of *El Topo*.
10. Chuck Zlatkin, interview by author, New York, NY, October 14, 1996. All subsequent quotes from Chuck Zlatkin will come from this interview or the joint one with Steve Gould on November 17, 1996, unless otherwise noted; "80th Straight Weekend for Reggae Film," *New York Times*, April 30, 1976; Vincent Canby, "Is 'El Topo' a Con?," *New York Times*, May 23, 1971; Roger Greenspun, "'El Topo' Emerges," *New York Times*, November 5, 1971.
11. According to Hoberman and Rosenbaum (*Midnight Movies*, 95, 99), four more Manhattan theaters, in addition to the Elgin, soon began regular midnight screenings: St. Marks Cinema in the East Village, the Waverly in Greenwich Village, the midtown Bijou, and the uptown Olympia. The second film to enjoy a lengthy midnight run, which began shortly after *El Topo* started at the Elgin, was Tod Browning's 1932 *Freaks* at the Bijou.
12. "El Topo," *Wikipedia*, last modified November 22, 2014, accessed February 19, 2015, http://en.wikipedia.org/wiki/El_Topo.

13. Hoberman and Rosenbaum (*Midnight Movies*, 153) assert that *Pink Flamingos* had its world premiere at the University of Baltimore and its first commercial screening, after it was acquired by New Line Cinema, at a Boston gay-porn theater.
14. Ben Davis, "Children of the Sixties: An Interview," *Film Quarterly* 53, no. 4 (Summer 2000), 6–7.
15. Hoberman and Rosenbaum (*Midnight Movies*, 157) state that the film ran forty-eight weeks through January 1974. A *New York Daily News* article reported that it had lasted eleven months of Friday and Saturday late shows. Jerry Oster, "Midnight Madness," *New York Daily News*, October 21, 1975.
16. Marc Caro, "Hail and Farewelles [sic]," Part Two," *The Boston Phoenix*, Section Three, August 28, 1987.
17. "80th Straight Weekend for Reggae Film"; A sheet listing the March 1977 schedule ("March Movies," Elgin clippings file, Research Collection, LPA) lists Brother Theodore and Terri Hall in *Gums* as the Friday midnight show and Jimmy Cliff in *The Harder They Come* every Saturday night at midnight. The film was probably winding down by then; Oster, "Midnight Madness"; Wolff, "So What Do You Do at Midnight?" See Chapter 8, fn. 8
18. 1973 calendars, in the author's collection.
19. Pierson, *Spike, Mike, Slackers & Dykes*, 16.
20. Adrian Glick Kudler, "Behold Buster Keaton's Once-Lost Film Vault (and Gorge Estate)," *Curbed Los Angeles*, October 8, 2012, accessed February 20, 2015, la.curbed.com/archives/2012/10/behold_buster_keatons_oncelost_film_vault_and_lovely_estate.php; a fuller version of Rohauer's relation to Keaton and the Keaton collection can be found in the letters to and from John E. Hampton, the owner and operator of a well-known revival movie theater of silent films, "Dorothy and John Hampton's Shrine of the Old Time Silent Pictures," in Los Angeles. The letters are in the author's collection.
21. "Archivist Raymond Rohauer Kept Films by Keaton, Others," *LA Times*, November 20, 1987, accessed February 20, 2015, articles.latimes.com/1987-11-20/news/mn-15061_1_raymond-rohauer; *Ibid.*; Ibid.
22. Calendar in the private collection of Ed and Mary Maguire.
23. Ibid.
24. A sample of his distributors was listed in an advertisement in *Village Voice*, July 6, 1972, for the Elgin program "A Festival of the Worlds [sic] Greatest Films": Janus Films, which provided the majority of the films for the program; Altura for Akira Kurosawa's *Ikiru* (1952), Luis Buñuel's *Viridiana* (1961), and Carl Theodor Dreyer's *Passion of Joan of Arc* (1928); Pathé for Alain Resnais's *Hiroshima Mon Amour* (1959) and Godard's *Pierrot le fou* (1965); New Line for Robert Bresson's *Mouchette* (1967); Fox for F.W. Murnau's *Sunrise* (1927); Embassy for Federico Fellini's *8½* (1963); and United Artist for Ingmar Bergman's *Persona* (1966).
25. The film *Union Maids* was reviewed by *Times*

film critic Vincent Canby on February 4, 1977, with a mention that it was playing at the Elgin, making it at least a New York premiere. It was on a double bill with another social issue documentary *On the Line* (1976). Vincent Canby, "Film: 3 Women Who Didn't Wait for Lefty," *New York Times*, February 4, 1977; Zlatkin's brief biography came from Davis, "Children of the Sixties," 4.

26. Gould's brief biography also came from Davis, "Children of the Sixties," 4.

27. Chuck Zlatkin, "Elgin Thoughts (or: How I Lost My Summer Vacation), *Elgin Marble* [undated], Elgin clippings file, Research Collection, LPA.

28. Later in the decade this became a noticeable trend when once-inexpensive films became high-price commodities because of their boost from the repertory houses.

29. Richard F. Shepard, "Going Out Guide," *New York Times*, November 23, 1974.

30. Gornick, "Chelsea Fights Back."

31. Ibid.

32. Ibid.

33. Ibid.

34. Ibid.

35. "Ben Barenholtz," *Wikipedia*, last modified December 8, 2014, accessed February 20, 2015, en.wikipedia.org/wiki/Ben_Barenholtz.

36. Press release, MoMA Dept. of Film Archives, NY.

37. Guy Trebay, "Talking Heads: What's Playing at the Elgin?," *Village Voice*, August 26–September 1, 1981.

38. Gornick, "Chelsea Fights Back."

Chapter 10

1. Jerry Bartell, "Film: Theater 80 Owner Found Future in the Past," *The Villager*, August 30, 1984. Mrs. Otway related to this author the story behind Crawford's gift of the oil painting. In her last week of life, she offered Otway the painting, which he happily accepted; but because he was busy, he sent someone else to pick it up. She was furious. "She just gave him the devil, because she expected him to come himself," Mrs. Otway recalled. "But she gave him the painting. I have letters that she wrote to him that are charming."

2. Paul Power, phone interview by author, New York, NY, February 5, 2012. All quotes from Power will come from this interview, unless otherwise noted; William Reiss, letter to Florence Otway, April 21, 1994, in Theatre 80 Collection (T80SM), MoMA Dept. of Film Archives, NY.

3. Lorcan Otway and his mother, Florence Otway, interview by author, New York, NY, December 20, 2000. All quotes from Lorcan Otway and his mother, Florence, will come from this interview, unless otherwise indicated; Susan Brenna, "Theater 80 Fades to Black," *New York Newsday*, August 1, 1994; Jeff Kisseloff, "Star-Studded Sidewalks," *New York Post*, Oral History, April 16, 1989; Lisa Redd, "A Film House with Flavor," *New York Newsday*, October 14, 1985; "Howard Otway, 72; Ran Revival Theater," *New York Times*, April 21, 1994.

4. Albert Amateau, "Florence Otway, Shoe Designer, Theatre 80 Co-Founder," *The Villager*, July 24, 2014; "Howard Otway, 72; Ran Revival Theater."

5. Otway usually co-produced plays rather than acted as a single producer. For *One Night Stands of a Noisy Passenger*, his production partners were Lawrence Goossen and Susan Richardson. Lortel Archives: *One Night Stands of a Noisy Passenger*, accessed June 23, 2015, http://www.lortel.org/LLA_archive/index.cfm?search_by=show&id=5924.

6. Kisseloff, "Star-Studded Sidewalks."

7. Lorcan Otway, interview by author, April 17, 2013, New York, NY.

8. Dan Sullivan, "Theater: In a New House," *New York Times*, November 2, 1966; "'Charlie Brown' Due in Musical March 7," *New York Times*, January 24, 1967.

9. Louis Calta, "No Talks in 2d Day of Actors' Strike," *New York Times*, November 18, 1970. According to the article, the Actors Equity Association was seeking a minimum of $125 a week, increasing to $130 plus cost of living increases after three years and a wage scale that would increase on a sliding basis to as much as $405 a week for shows grossing $20,000 a week.

10. "The Editors Bless," *Show*, December 1971, available in Theatre 80 St. Marks clippings file, Research Collection, LPA.

11. "East Village Theater to Show Old Musical Films Exclusively," *New York Times*, August 21, 1971; Kisseloff, "Star-Studded Sidewalks"; Daniel B. Schneider, "Hollywood East," *New York Times*, May 4, 1997.

12. "Fashion Viewpoints" in Theatre 80 St. Marks clippings file, Research Collection, LPA.

13. Kisseloff, "Star-Studded Sidewalks"; Philip Roxbury, "A True Star—Joan Crawford," Movie Mailbag, *New York Times*, September 19, 1971.

14. Kisseloff, "Star-Studded Sidewalks"; Mitch Broder, "Dropping Names: New York Has Its Own Sidewalk Heroes," *Asbury Park Press*, October 21, 2000.

15. "The Editors Bless"; Calendars, T80SM, MoMA Dept. of Film Archives, NY.

16. Ibid.; T80SM, MoMA Dept. of Film Archives, NY.

17. The approximate year that Whitelaw left was deduced from the calendars in the Theatre 80 collection. From February to May 1972, the headings of the Theatre 80 calendars read *The Movie Musical Under the Personal Direction of Howard Otway and Arthur Whitelaw*. Then, from May 1972 to June 1973, there is no personal attribution. By June 27, 1973, the calendars read only "Under the Personal Direction of Howard Otway."; the financial figures come from T80SM, MoMA Dept. of Film Archives, NY.

18. Michael Konik, "Revival Theaters Survive," *West Side Spirit* Through 25 May 1987. Also available

in the Theatre 80 clippings file, Research Collection, LPA.

19. Bartell, "Film: Theater 80 Owner"; Konik, "Revival Theaters Survive."

20. T80SM, MoMA Dept. of Film Archives, NY.

21. Advertisement for the first showing of *Show Boat*, in T80SM, MoMA Dept. of Film Archives, NY; "The Movie Musical" Monthly Gross Receipts, T80SM, MoMA Dept. of Film Archives, NY.

22. Bartell, "Film: Theater 80 Owner"; Allen, "Art House Confidential."

23. March 8–28, 1972, calendar, T80SM, MoMA Dept. of Film Archives, NY.

24. Allen, "Art House Confidential."

25. Bartell, "Film: Theater 80 Owner."

26. Allen, "Art House Confidential."

27. Bartell, "Film: Theater 80 Owner."

28. Calendars in T80SM, MoMA Dept. of Film Archives, NY; Brenna, "Theater 80 Fades to Black."

29. Record book, T80SM, MoMA Dept. of Film Archives, NY; Bartell, "Film: Theater 80 Owner."

30. Mike Portantiere, "Theatre 80: Paradise for Movie Buffs," *Staten Island Register*, January 2, 1978

31. Jeff Sweet, "Trois for Two?," Movie Mailbag, *New York Times*, December 5, 1971.

32. Marcia Kaufman, "It's Not Always 'Fair Weather,'" Movie Mailbag, *New York Times*, February 27, 1972.

33. "Features Available from Theatre 80 St. Marks," a list of his films that were offered for rent to other theaters, in T80SM, MoMA Dept. of Film Archives, NY.

34. Elliott Stein, "The Screening of Lower Manhattan," *Village Voice*, June 20, 1989.

35. Former patron, letter to Mrs. Otway, in T80SM, MoMA Dept. of Film Archives, NY; skeeelz on December 23, 2004 (11:37 am), *Cinema Treasures*, accessed February 19, 2015, http://cinematreasures.org/comments?page=3&theater_id=4698

36. Marvine Howe, "After a Death, a Theater Lives," *New York Times*, May 15, 1994; "Gotham's Many Film Repertory Sites," *Variety*, November 19, 1980.

37. Irajoel on December 12, 2009 (10:10 a.m.), *Cinema Treasures*, accessed February 19, 2015, http://cinematreasures.org/comments?page=3&theater_id=4698; hardbop on February 16, 2006 (8:20 a.m.), *Cinema Treasures*, accessed February 19, 2015, http://cinematreasures.org/comments?page=2&theater_id=4698.

38. edblank on May 22, 2008 (9:46 p.m.), *Cinema Treasures*, accessed February 19, 2015, http://cinematreasures.org/comments?page=2&theater_id=4698.

39. Lawrence Otway, letter to patrons after the death of Howard Otway on behalf of the Otway family, in T80SM, MoMA Dept. of Film Archives, NY.

40. T80SM, MoMA Dept. of Film Archives, NY. The gross through July, the final month of the theater, was $136,233. Since the total gross of the last five months of the year was generally six percent less than that of the first seven months (based on calculations of grosses of four randomly selected years, 1974, 1976, 1988, 1992), the gross for the remainder of the final year would have been approximately $128,059, making the total gross for the year $264,292, just approximately $16,000 less than the gross of $280,860 for the highest year, 1987. Record in T80SM, MoMA Dept. of Film Archives, NY.

41. Evan Wiener, "Execrable," *Columbia Summer Spectator*, July 27, 1994; Brenna, "Theater 80 Fades to Black."

42. Kisseloff, "Star-Studded Sidewalks."

Chapter 11

1. Van Sommer, phone interview by author, New York, NY, October 10, 2011. All subsequent quotes from Sommer will come from this interview, unless otherwise indicated.

2. Frank Rowley, interview by author, New York, NY, October 6, 2011. All subsequent quotes from Rowley will come from this interview or a previous one held on January 15, 2004, unless otherwise noted.

3. The history of the Alden and Sommer's family was colorful. "It was my grandfather's theater," Sommer related to the author. "It used to be a neighborhood theater. He told me that he had done some live performances there. He said that the guy who played Guggenheim on the Jackie Gleason show performed there. I don't know if it's true or not, but it's possible they did have some live stuff. My family had done vaudeville shows in other locations. My father had taken a show called *Bagels and Yox* around the country after opening in New York. He was like a producer-manager. I know a good part of that time the people may have come in for the air conditioning. It was a time when people didn't have air conditioning in their own homes. You could go to the movies and sit there all afternoon."

4. Hoberman and Rosenbaum, *Midnight Movies*, 72; The "mistakes" in *Chelsea Girls* were intentional, according to the *Wikipedia* entry on the film. For details of their experiment, see "Chelsea Girls," *Wikipedia*, last modified December 6, 2014, accessed February 20, 2015, wikipedia.org/wiki/Chelsea_Girls.

5. Morton Tankus, interview by author, New York, NY, August 30, 2011. All subsequent quotes from Tankus will come from this interview, unless otherwise indicated.

6. "A Rash of Revivals," *New York Times*, November 27, 1977.

7. MarkieS on October 7, 2010 (10:31 pm), *Cinema Treasures*, accessed February 20, 2015, http://cinematreasures.org/theaters/1199/comments; Miller Lide, interview by author, New York, NY, May 4, 2013. All subsequent quotes from Lide will come from this interview.

8. Howard Thompson, "Going Out Guide," *New York Times*, March 11, 1980.

9. See Chapter 2, "The First Wave," 32.

10. Bruce Eder, "The Regency's Ripple Effect, *Village Voice*, September 29, 1987; *Variety*, November 19, 1980.

11. James Harvey, interview by author, New York, NY, May 25, 2011.

12. Tankus explained the mechanics of the carbon arc projector. "These were the old-fashioned carbon arc projectors where the projector did not have light bulbs. It had two carbon rods; a flame would spark between them and would reflect off a curved mirror at the back of the projector and the light would go on the screen. It was a warmer light, the difference between the light from a flame and the light from a bulb. Part of the expense with this projector was the carbon rods. Once in a blue moon we'd have to scramble to get a shipment or borrow from one of the few other theaters who still used this type of projector. A slight drawback was that there was a little motor that would keep the carbon rods in place. As they burned down, it would move to keep them closer together. If you started losing the flame and it got dimmer, there was a lever to move them closer together. If the projectionist didn't see or pay attention, then it might start getting dim and you'd have to call up to the projection booth and get the light back on. I loved that projector; on cold days I'd warm myself by the flame of the projector."

13. Rowley related that Bevilacqua "fixed his meals in the projection booth. He had a lady friend who would come to visit him on Friday, and she would bring food and they would cook the food. The people would complain because they could smell spaghetti or whatever it was."

14. Henry Fera, interview by author, New York, NY, May 13, 2011. All subsequent quotes from Fera will come from this interview, unless otherwise indicated.

15. Mervyn Rothstein, "Summer Salute to M-G-M on Its 60th Birthday at the Regency," *New York Times*, June 1, 1984; Guy Flatley, "At the Movies," *New York Times*, March 25, 1977.

16. Letter from Karen Alters to Frank Rowley dated September 1, 1987, in author's collection.

17. "Flickering Hopes for Small Theaters," *New York Newsday*, October 14, 1985, City Business section; Regency box office log covering the years October 1985 to September 1987, in author's collection; Bruce Eder, "The Decline of Revival Cinema," *New York Newsday*, September 1, 1987, Part II. Interestingly, at the time of the Regency's closing, the coalition fighting the closing compiled a list ("Interested in Economics?," *Variety*, September 2, 1987), which demonstrated that the Regency's revenues in its last two weeks of operation compared favorably with those of nine of the eleven Cineplex Odeon first-run theaters in the same period. For instance, it netted a profit of $18,611 as compared to a loss of $223.00 at the Carnegie (now part of the Cineplex Odeon chain), a higher net than the $10,250.00 at National 2, and a comparable net to the $20,192.00 at National 1. The list is also available in the MoMA. Dept. of Film Archives, NY.

18. Letter from Congressman Ted Weiss to Garth Drabinsky, dated September 8, 1987, letter from State Assemblyman Jerrold Nadler, dated September 17, 1987, and letter from the director of the Mayor's Office of Film, Theatre and Broadcasting, Patricia Reed Scott, dated August 24, 1987. Copies of the three letters are in the author's collection; Ellen Cohn, "ROAR of the Crowd: Fans Protest Regency Policy," *Village Voice*, September 29, 1987; Elizabeth Kolbert, "Goodbye Gable: Regency Is Mourned," *New York Times*, August 24, 1987.

19. Cohn, "ROAR of the Crowd"; Jere Hester, "Regency Draws a Protest," *Westsider*, September 10–16, 1987, available in Regency clippings file, Research Collection, LPA; the Tony Randall quote is an amalgam of two quotes by the actor on the same subject from the following sources: Hester, "Regency Draws a Protest" and Janet Sullivan, "Fans, Stars Come out to Save the Regency," *West Side Spirit*, Through September 14, 1987; Cohn, "ROAR of the Crowd."

20. *New York Post*, March 22, 1988, in Regency clippings file, Research Collection, LPA.

21. Eder, "The Decline of Revival Cinema."

22. Judith S. (Mrs. Seymour T.) Levine, letter dated August 24, 1987; Sandy Ferber, letter dated August 28, 1987; Ed Cannan, letter dated August 22, 1987. Copies of the three letters are in the author's collection.

23. Richard Schickel, "Letters," *New York Times*, September 14, 1987.

Chapter 12

1. Ricki Fulman, "Future of Thalia Is Uncertain: 95th St. Revival House May Fall Victim to Development," *New York Daily News*, January 15, 1987, Manhattan section.

2. David Miller, "Death of a West Side Cinephile," *West Side Spirit*, Through October 30, 1990; Gail Aronow, interview by author, New York, NY, August 1, 2011. All quotes from Aronow will come from the interview, unless otherwise noted.

3. Miller, "Death of a West Side Cinephile."

4. Tom Topor, "On the Town: A Home of Reel Classics," *New York Post*, June 16, 1979; e-mail from Aronow dated January 30, 2016.

5. James Harvey, interview by author, New York, NY, May 25, 2011. Two more interviews were held with Harvey on September 19, 2011 and June 7, 2013. All subsequent quotes from Harvey will come from one of these three interviews, unless otherwise indicated; e-mail from Aronow dated January 30, 2016.

6. Greg Ford, interview by author, New York, NY, October 21, 2012. One more interview was held with Ford on June 7, 2013. All subsequent quotes from Ford will come from one of these two interviews, unless otherwise indicated.

7. Bruce Goldstein, interview by author, New York, NY, February 27, 2012. All subsequent quotes from Goldstein will come from this interview, unless otherwise noted.

8. E-mail from Michael Silberman, April 3, 2013; notes from Harvey, dated December 17, 2015.

9. James Harvey, "Richard Schwarz/Film Noir/Jim Harvey," *Anthology Film Archives Film Program*, September-October 1996, Thalia clippings file, Research Collection, LPA.

10. Vincent Canby, "Film: Egos Beset Chekhov's 'Sisters,'" *New York Times*, June 30, 1977.

11. "Richard A. Schwarz Film Collection: Prints Available for Transfer to Anthology Film Archives," in the author's collection; e-mail from Aronow, January 30, 2016.

12. Richard Haines on March 13, 2005 (7:04 a.m.), *Cinema Treasures*, accessed February 20, 2015, http://cinematreasures.org/comments?page=4&theater_id=285.

13. Delaney, "The Thalia Theatre." See Chapter 2, endnote 14.

14. "Now Dis Is Class: The High and Low Brows Browse at the Thalia," *New York Daily News*, January 2, 1985; Delaney, "The Thalia Theatre"; Vincent Canby, "Film: 'Teen-Age Massacre,'" *New York Times*, December 5, 1980; *The Incredible Strange Creatures Who Stopped Living and Became Mixed-Up Zombies* had the dubious distinction of being named in Merritt, *Celluloid Mavericks*, 178, as an example of "independently made no-budget horror and fantasy dreck [that] would slither to the [drive-in] screen" in the early 1960s; Robert R on April 30, 2004 (12 p.m.), *Cinema Treasures*, accessed February 20, 2015, http://cinematreasures.org/comments?page=4&theater_id=285.

15. Delaney, "The Thalia Theatre."

16. Summer Film Festival, 1978; Spring Film Festival, 1978; and Summer Film Festival 1981, Thalia calendars in the collection of the author.

17. Vincent Canby, "Film: A Late de Sica: From Pirandello Novel," *The New York Times*, December 1, 1978; e-mail from Aronow, January 30, 2016.

18. Delaney, "The Thalia Theatre"; Vincent Canby, "'Let There Be Light, John Huston vs. the Army,'" *New York Times*, January 16, 1981; email from Aronow, January 30, 2016.

19. Allen, "Art House Confidential"; Winter Film Festival, 1979, calendar in the collection of the author; McNiven, "Women Larger than Life," www.brightlightsfilm.com/65/65programnotes.php.

20. Michalak, "Thalia, West Side Muse of Reruns, Is Revived." See Chapter 6, fn. 32.

21. Spring Film Festival, 1978, calendar and press release in collection of author.

22. *Ibid.*; film notes in the collection of the author; Tom Allen, "Sequels of Summer," *Village Voice*, July 3, 1978; Tom Allen, "Art House Confidential."

23. James Harvey, *Romantic Comedy in Hollywood: From Lubitsch to Sturges* (New York: Da Capo Press, 1998), xii; *Angel*, however, had been seen in a screening at the New Yorker Theater in February 1963. Advertisement in *Village Voice*, February 7, 1963.

24. David Ansen, "The Rise and Fall of Preston Sturges," *The Thousand Eyes: The Magazine of Public Cinema*, Thru October 26, 1979, in the collection of the author.

25. Harvey, *Romantic Comedy*, xi.

26. James Harvey, *Movie Love in the Fifties* (New York: Da Capo Press, 2002), 337–338.

27. *Ibid.*, 335–338.

28. Carol Iannone, letter to James Harvey, September 5, 1978, in the collection of the author.

29. Delaney, "The Thalia Theater."

30. Summer Film Festival calendar, 1981, in the collection of the author.

31. "A Brief Biography of Winsor McCay," Van Eaton Galleries, accessed April 25, 2016, http://vegalleries.com/winsorbio.html; Summer Film Festival, 1981, calendar in the collection of the author.

32. Janet Maslin, "At the Movies," *New York Times*, Late Edition (East Coast), April 19, 1985.

33. Gary Cahall, "Alice's Adventures in Filmland, 1903–1949," Movies Unlimited: Movie FanFare, accessed June 25, 2015, http://www.moviefanfare.com/alices-adventures-in-filmland; Maslin, "At the Movies."

34. J. Hoberman, "The Indispensable Man," San Francisco International Film Festival, Awards/Bruce Goldstein, Mel Novikoff Award, accessed February 20, 2015, http://fest09.sffs.org/awards/bruce_goldstein.php.

35. E-mail from Goldstein dated April 6, 2016; Klitsch, "New York's Revival Houses Face an Uncertain Future." See chapter 8, fn. 11.

36. Richard F. Shepard, "Going Out Guide," *New York Times*, September 21, 1981.

37. E-mail from Goldstein, dated April 6, 2016.

38. *Ibid.*

39. Barak Goodman, "Thalia Theater May Close Down," *West Side Spirit*, January 19, 1987; Christopher Gray, "A Closed Revival House that May Itself Be Revived," *New York Times*, July 5, 1987.

40. David W. Dunlap, "Literary Tenants," *New York Times*, February 9, 1987; Robert D. McFadden, "The Thalia, Offbeat Home of Classic Movies, Is Closed," *New York Times*, May 11, 1987.

41. Goodman, "Thalia Theater May Close Down."

42. *Ibid.*

Chapter 13

1. Barbara Nitke, phone interview with author, New York, NY, November 14, 2012. All quotes from Nitke will come from this interview, unless otherwise noted.

2. Bill Thompson, interview by author, New York, NY, March 9, 2011. A second interview was held with him on January 8, 2013. There were also several e-mails from him. All subsequent quotes from Thompson will come from one of these two interviews or the e-mails, unless otherwise indicated.

3. Jackie Raynal, interview by author, New York, NY, November 18, 2012. Three other interviews with Raynal were held on February 29, 2011, December 21, 2012, and January 21, 2013; there were also several e-mails from Raynal. All subsequent quotes from

Raynal will come from one of these interviews or e-mails, unless otherwise noted; Willburg145 on June 13, 2011 (2:51 pm), *Cinema Treasures*, accessed February 21, 2015, http://cinematreasures.org/theaters/6016/comments.

4. Geffen's rental of the Regency was mentioned to author by Van Sommer, the owner of the Regency, in our phone interview on October 10, 2011.

5. On May 16, 1960, New York City purchased Carnegie Hall through special state legislation. A new nonprofit organization, Carnegie Hall Corporation, was chartered to manage and rent the hall as well as present its own events. Julius Bloom was Carnegie Hall's executive director from 1960 to 1977. *Carnegie Hall: Then and Now*, accessed November 11, 2015, www.carnegiehall.org/history/Carnegie Hall Then and Now (PDF).

6. "Wider Art Pic Lure Backdrops Upgrade of Carnegie Cinema," *Variety*, January 12, 1983; Shawn Cunningham, "The Bleecker Outlook," *Villager*, March 15, 1984.

7. "About New York: Future Weeks," *Cue*, November 15, 1973, 88.

8. "Global Visions: Zanzibar Films and the Dandies of May 1968," *Harvard Film Archives*, accessed February 25, 2015, http://hcl.harvard.edu/hfa/films/2001mayjun/zanzibar.html; Advertisement, *Village Voice*, February 17, 1975.

9. Jonathan Rosenbaum, phone interview by author, New York, NY, November 27, 2012. All subsequent quotes from Rosenbaum will come from this interview, unless otherwise noted.

10. This idea of a network of cinemas nationwide to support independent filmmakers was first proposed in the 1930s by Harry Alan Potamkin, a left-wing film critic and theorist. Russell Campbell, *Cinema Strikes Back: Radical Filmmaking in the United States 1930-1942* (Ann Arbor, Michigan: UMI Research Press, 1982), 45.

11. Advertisement, *Village Voice*, October 17, 1974.

12. Raynal had joined the projectionist union earlier because of her displeasure with the union projectionists. As a film editor, she was particularly sensitive to the projection of the films. "I was horrified at the way they projected" she complained. "I remember at Carnegie Hall one time they put the film up the wrong way. Yet, you have to provide the projection booth with a telephone, a heater for food, and a special toilet. So I said to the union, 'I want to be a projectionist, I want to go in and at least rewind the film myself.'" In the opinion of Larry Chadbourne, one of the later managers of the Bleecker and Carnegie, she was too critical of the projectionists, who, he felt, did not always get the support they deserved and were under extra pressure with the constant changes and the unpredictable quality of the prints. "Jacques and especially Gary McVey at the Bleecker," he wrote in an e-mail to the author, "were professionals whom I learned much from about the technical aspects of film."; "Gotham's Many Film Repertory Sites: Supply Problems Shipping Costs," *Variety*, November 19, 1980.

13. Fall 1979 Program calendar for the Carnegie Hall Cinema. All calendars, articles and schedules in *Thousand Eyes* magazine and *Focus on Public Cinema* that are mentioned in this chapter are in the collection of the author, unless otherwise indicated; Benjamin on December 23, 2004 (4:38 p.m.), *Cinema Treasures*, accessed February 21, 2015, http://cinematreasures.org/comments?page=3&theater_id=6011.

14. David Denby, "Movies," *New York*, December 10, 1979, 138.

15. The details of the suit come from Cunningham, "The Bleecker Outlook"; the change was announced in the Summer 1978 calendar for the Carnegie Hall Cinema, available in the Carnegie Hall Cinema clippings file, Research Collection, LPA.

16. Michael Silberman, phone interview by author, New York, NY, February 10, 2012.

17. Seth Cagin, "Tracking," *Soho Weekly News*, November 12, 1980.

18. Email from Bill Thompson, January 17, 2013; Seth Cagin, "Tracking: Public Expansion," *Soho Weekly News*, September 6, 1979; John Pierson, phone interview by author, New York, NY, December 7, 2011. All subsequent quotes from Pierson will come from this interview, unless otherwise indicated; Fall Program 1979 calendar, in the author's collection.

19. *Thousand Eyes* magazine, as a guide to the alternative cinema in New York (similar to *Cue* for the mainstream New York cinema), was comparable to the *Elgin Marble*, published by the Elgin Theater in the seventies, and the *New York Film Bulletin*, published in the sixties, which, Jonas Mekas informed his Village Voice readers, was a monthly guide listing film society and museum screenings, unusual TV and theatrical revival screenings, "and full of other, most useful information." Jonas Mekas, "Movie Journal," *Village Voice*, June 27, 1963; Cagin, "Public Expansion."

20. *Focus on Public Cinema*, February 1981, in the author's collection.

21. Dennis McLellan, "Bingham Ray Dies at 57; Leading Force in Independent Films," *Los Angeles Times*, January 24, 2012, accessed December 18, 2014, http://articles.latimes.com/2012/jan/24/local/la-me-bingham-ray-20120124.

22. Larry Chadbourne, phone interview by author, New York, NY, January 2, 2013. All subsequent quotes from Chadbourne will come from this interview, unless otherwise noted; Marty Rubin, phone interview by author, New York, NY, December 6, 2012. All subsequent quotes from Rubin will come from this interview, unless otherwise noted.

23. "Mailbag," *New York Times*, August 18, 1974.

24. Cunningham, "The Bleecker Outlook."

25. Fall 1976 calendar, in the author's collection.

26. The originally announced premiere of the organ in the Fall 1976 calendar was delayed for unspecified reasons. According to the history of the organ in the Fall 1976 calendar in the author's col-

lection, it was originally a 2/5, but had four ranks added in recent years, making it the equivalent of a nine-piece orchestra. The original 2/5 Wurlitzer was the work horse of the silent picture houses; over seventy-five percent of movie houses in the 1920s had models similar to the Carnegie's. First built in the late 1920s, this particular organ was eventually bought by Ben Hall, "a significant figure in the American Theatre Organ Society." When plans for its use at the projected Harold Lloyd Museum fell through, Geffen "jumped at the opportunity to lease it from the American Theatre Organ Society."

27. Marc Weiss, interview by author, New York, NY, January 9, 2013. All subsequent quotes from Weiss will come from this interview, unless otherwise noted.

28. Richard F. Shepard, "The Screen: 'Men's Lives' Looks at Male Mystique," *New York Times*, January 22, 1975.

29. Sklar, *Movie-Made America*, 334.

30. The starting date for the first program, "Free Filmmakers Showcase," is inconsistent in the newspapers. The *New York Times* announced its opening in a December 1974 article (Howard Thompson, "Going Out Guide," *New York Times*, December 6, 1974) while *Newsday* announced its first official offering in January 1975 (Joseph Gelmis, "Movies: A Commendable Start for a Showcase," *Newsday*, January 24, 1975); the schedule came from a flyer in the possession of Marc Weiss.

31. Greg Merritt, in his history of American independent film (*Celluloid Mavericks*, 230), includes *Pay Day* (he spells it as one word) as one of the critically acclaimed, small independent films of the seventies that was overlooked by the general public.

32. Spring '78 calendar, in the author's collection.

33. *Focus on Cinema*, November/December 1982, in the author's collection.

34. Richard F. Shepard, "Going Out Guide," *New York Times*, February 2, 1983; *Focus on Cinema*, November/December 1982, in the author's collection.

35. July to September 1979 calendar, in the author's collection; Wendell Jamieson, "Slashing Samurai: A Culture Savored," *New York Times*, February 13, 2011.

36. The Bleecker Street New Year Program '76; Spring 1978 calendar. Both are in the author's collection.

37. Lawrence Cohn, "N.Y. Rep Sites Pull 'Lost' Pix Off Shelf, into Release," *Variety*, August 12, 1981.

38. Michel Ciment, Editor of POSITIF [*sic*], "A Positif Look at Today's Cinema," *Focus on Cinema*, September/October 1982, in the author's collection.

39. "A Week of *Cahiers du Cinéma* at the Bleecker Street Cinema," Fall 1977 calendar, in the author's collection; "Serge Daney," *Wikipedia*, last modified September 4, 2014, accessed February 21, 2015, http://en.wikipedia.org/wiki/Serge_Daney; "Daney on ICI ET AILLEURS: A Newly Unearthed Text and Some Known Ones," accessed February 21, 2015, kinoslang.blogspot.com/2009/01/preface-to-here-and-elsewhere-by-serge.html.

40. "Jonathan Rosenbaum," *Wikipedia*, last modified January 28, 2015, accessed February 21, 2015, http://en.wikipedia.org/wiki/Jonathan_Rosenbaum.

41. Jonathan Rosenbaum, "Reflections on 'Rivette in Context,'" Cinema Comparat/ive Cinema 1, no. 1 (2012), accessed February 21, 2015, http://www.ocec.eu/cinemacomparative/pdf/ccc01.pdf); Carol Lawson, "Weekender Guide," *New York Times*, February 2, 1979; e-mail from Rosenbaum to author, December 13, 2012.

42. Andrew Sarris, "Films in Focus," *Village Voice*, February 5, 1979; Amy Taubin, "The Other Cinema: Rivette in Context, Bleecker Street Cinema, 3 Weeks Beginning Feb. 4," *Soho Weekly News*, February 8–14, 1979; Cinema Comparat/ive Cinema 1, no. 1 (2012).

43. Sarris, "Films in Focus"; Taubin, "The Other Cinema."

44. The cover of *Focus*, June 1981 (in the author's collection), read "The American Premiere of Jean-Luc Godard *Numéro deux*."

45. In relating this anecdote to the author, Rosenbaum had mistakenly thought the screening was of *Hiroshima, mon amour* rather than of *India Song*, but Raynal corrected this in an email of October 7, 2015. Her memory of Roud's comment about the bomb was that it was less injudicious than Rosenbaum's account. She believed that he was noting the coincidence that "it was of course kind of strange that we did open her *India Song* on the day—I think it was in August—the day that the Hiroshima bomb came down in Japan!"

46. "Cinéastes de notre temps," *Wikipedia*, last modified February 21, 2016, accessed April 17, 2016, https://fr.wikipedia.org/wiki/Cineastes_de_notre_temps.

47. This description of the downtown New York independent film scene comes from Merritt, *Celluloid Mavericks*, 303, 307.

48. Amos Poe: "Film," accessed February 21, 2015, http://www.amospoe.com/cv.html.

49. C. Gerald Fraser, "Going Out," *New York Times*, January 29, 1981.

50. Thompson is referring to an anecdote in relation to Morris' debut feature, as described in "Errol Morris," *Wikipedia*, last modified February 3, 2015, accessed February 21, 2015, http://en.wikipedia.org/wiki/Amos_Poe. "In 1978 when the film premiered, Werner Herzog cooked and publicly ate his shoe, an event later incorporated into a short documentary by Les Blank. Herzog had promised to eat his shoe if Morris completed the project, to challenge and encourage Morris, whom Herzog perceived as incapable of following up on the projects he conceived."

51. J. Hoberman, "Confounding Commercial Expectations," *Village Voice*, December 30, 1981–January 5, 1982.

52. *Focus*, December 1979 and Summer 1980, in the author's collection.

53. *The Thousand Eyes*, Summer Supplement, July 1–September 22, 1979, in the author's collection.
54. Greg Ford interview. See chapter 12, endnote 6.
55. Janet Maslin, "Some Movies Born to be Revived," *New York Times*, August 26, 1977.
56. *Focus*, November/December 1982; "for members only…," *Focus*, September 1981. Both are in the author's collection.
57. Cunningham, "The Bleecker Outlook."
58. *Bob le flambeur* was Melville's fourth film, "often considered a film noir and precursor to the French New Wave because of its use of handheld camera and a single jump cut." "*Bob le flambeur*," *Wikipedia*, last modified January 10, 2015, accessed February 21, 2015, http://en.wikipedia.org/wiki/Bob_le_flambeur.
59. Winter 1983 calendar, in the author's collection.
60. Cunningham, "The Bleecker Outlook."
61. The exact dates of its closing are unclear. *Focus* stopped listing both the logo "The Center for Public Cinema presents" and a subscription application to the Center beginning with its January 1982 issue (in the author's collection); but on November 18, 1983, a *New York Times* advertisement listed Maxim Gorky's *Vassa* at the Carnegie as "an International Film Exchange, LTD., release in association with The Center for Public Cinema." This was the last ad listing the Center ("Display Ad 53," *New York Times*, November 18, 1983). By March 9, 1984 the Carnegie listing of Buñuel's *Wuthering Heights* makes no mention of the Center.
62. "Owner of Carnegie Hall Cinema to Seek More Series at Cannes," *Variety*, May 1, 1985.
63. Eleanor Blau, "Old-Movie Houses Dwindle," *New York Times*, August 13, 1987; Elliott Stein, "The Screening of Lower Manhattan," *Village Voice*, June 20, 1989; Richard Laermer, "Revival Houses in the Era of Videocassettes," *New York Times*, April 15, 1990.
64. Andrew L. Yarrow, "Another Prized Theater for Art Films Is Closing," *New York Times*, August 17, 1990; Frank Lovece, "The Last Picture Show," *New York Post*, September 8, 1990; This summary of the events leading to the closing is taken from Yarrow, "Another Prized Theater for Art Films Is Closing."
65. "Biographie," accessed February 21, 2015, http://www.jackieraynal.com/files/JR-BIO-FR.pdf; Barbara Matas, "Jackie Raynal: Biography," accessed February 25, 2015, http://www.jackieraynal.com/biography.
66. Michael Specter, "In House for Avant-Garde, the Ultimate 'The End,'" *Washington Post*, September 1, 1990.
67. boger on February 11, 2005 (3:38 pm), *Cinema Treasures*, accessed February 21, 2015, http://cinematreasures.org/comments?page=3&theater_id=6016.
68. B. Ruby Rich, *Chick Flicks: Theories and Memories of the Feminist Film Movement* (Durham: Duke University Press, 1998), 105.

Chapter 14

1. Michael Atkinson, "The Eternal Return," *Village Voice*, November 21, 1995, *Voice* Film Special.
2. Syndicated: Movie Theater, Bar, Restaurant, "About," accessed May 13, 2016, www.Syndicatedkb.com/about.
3. Richard Pena, "Repertory Film Programming: A Critical Symposium," 48. See chapter 1, endnote 9.
4. Rebecca M. Alvin, "A Night at the Movies: From Art House to 'Microcinema,'" *Cineaste*, Summer 2007, 5; Ed Halter, "The Small Screen," *Focus Features*, June 6, 2008, accessed May 15, 2016, http://www.focusfeatures.com/article/the_small_screen.
5. "Theaters and Screening Series: Underground Resources: Index," *Underground Film Journal*, http://www.undergroundfilmjournal.com/theaters-and-screening-series; Halter, "The Small Screen"; Alvin, "A Night at the Movies," 6.
6. "2016 Summer Series: For Filmmakers: Submit Your Film," *Rooftop Films: Underground Movies Outdoors*, accessed May 13, 2016, www.rooftopfilms.com/2016/info/submit/.
7. "Upcoming Shows," *Rooftop Films*, accessed May 30, 2016, http://rooftopfilms.com/2016/schedule/.
8. Light Industry, "About," accessed May 13, 2016, www/lightindustry.org/about; UnionDocs Center for Documentary Art, "About," accessed May 13, 2016, http://www.uniondocs.org/about/.
9. Rachael Rakes and Leo Goldsmith, "Cinema as an Event: An Interview with Light Industry's Ed Halter," *The Brooklyn Rail*, September 2011, accessed May 7, 2016, www.brooklynrail.org/2011/09/film/cinema-as-an-eventan-interview-with-light-industrys-ed-halter; accessed May 13, 2016, http://www.lightindustry.org/calendar/
10. *Ibid.*
11. UnionDocs, "About"; UnionDocs, "Screenings & Other Events Past," accessed May 30, 2016, http://www.uniondocs.org/about/.
12. *Ibid.*
13. Bronx Documentary Center, "About."
14. Bronx Documentary Center, "Past Events 2016," accessed May 30, 2016, http://bronxdoc.org/pastevents.
15. *Ibid.*
16. *Ibid.*
17. Maysles Documentary Center, "Maysles Cinema Programming," accessed May 13, 2016, www.maysles.org/mdc/; *Ibid.*, "Partners," accessed May 13, 2016, www.maysles.org/mdc/partners; *Ibid.*, "Mission Statement," accessed May 13, 2016, www.maysles.org/mdc/mission-statement; *Ibid.*, "Archives," accessed May 30, 2016, http://maysles.org/mdc/archive-january-2013.
18. *Ibid.*
19. *Ibid.*, Homepage, "Maysles Cinema Programming," accessed May 30, 2016, http://maysles.org/

mdc/; 5th Annual People's Festival, "Events," accessed May 30, 2016, http://thepeoplesfilmfestival.com/events/.

20. Dennis Lim, "Choosing Cinematheque over Cineplex," *New York Times*, September 2, 2011, accessed May 13, 2016, www.nytimes.com/2011/09/04/movies/microcinemas; http://rooftopfilms.com/2016/info/submit.

21. Rakes and Goldsmith, "Cinema as an Event."

22. Alvin, "A Night at the Movies," 7.

Bibliography

"About Lionel Rogosin: Biography." *Lionel Rogosin, A Visionary American Maverick Filmmaker Humanitarian.* Accessed February 18, 2015. http://www.lionelrogosin.org/AboutLR.html.

"About New York: Future Weeks." *Cue,* November 15, 1973.

Alvin, Rebecca M. "A Night at the Movies: From Art House to 'Microcinema.'" *Cineaste* 32, no. 3 (Summer 2007): 4–7.

Antonio, Camilo C. "Amos Vogel, Saboteur." *The Vienna Review,* May 19, 2011. Accessed January 31, 2015. http://www.viennareview.net/vienna-review-book-reviews/book-reviews/amos-vogel-saboteur.

Biskind, Peter. *Easy Riders, Raging Bulls: How the Sex, Drugs, and Rock 'n' Roll Generation Saved Hollywood.* New York: Simon & Schuster, 1998.

Bogdanovich, Peter. *Who the Devil Made It.* New York: Alfred A. Knopf, 1997.

Bordwell, David. *Making Meaning: Inference and Rhetoric in the Interpretation of Cinema.* Cambridge, MA: Harvard University, 1989.

Bowser, Eileen. "MOMA's Special Oscar." *Films in Review* 30, no. 5 (May 1979): 283–288, 315.

Breitbart, Eric. "Available Light: 20 Years of Social Issue Documentaries." *Sightlines* 20, no. 2 (Winter 1986-87): 10–13.

Cargni-Mitchell, Robert E. "Repertory Film Programming: A Web Exclusive Supplement to a Critical Symposium." Accessed February 20, 2015. http://www.cineaste.com/articles/repertory-film-programming-a-critical-symposium.

Cassanos, Lynda Cohen. "Special Collections: Film Forum." *Sightlines* 20, no. 2 (Winter 1986/87): 5–7.

Catapano, Peter. "Creating 'Reel' Value: The Establishment of the Museum of Modern Art Film Library, 1935–1939." *Film & History: An Interdisciplinary Journal of Film and Television Studies* 24, nos. 3–4 (1994): 29–44.

Cook, David A. *A History of Narrative Film.* 3rd ed. New York: W.W. Norton & Company, 1996.

Cook, Pam, ed. *The Cinema Book: A Complete Guide to Understanding the Movies.* New York: Pantheon Books, 1985.

Crowdus, Gary. "The 7th New York Film Festival." *Film Society Review* 5, no. 2 (October 1969): 25–35.

Davidson, Adam. "Jane Jacobs vs. Marc Jacobs." *New York Times Magazine,* June 10, 2012.

Davis, Ben. "The Beginnings of the Film Society Movement in the U.S." *Film & History: An Interdisciplinary Journal of Film and Television Studies* 24, nos. 3–4 (1994): 7–26.

———. "Children of the Sixties: An Interview." *Film Quarterly* 53, no. 4 (Summer 2000): 2–15.

Delaney, Pete. "The Thalia Theatre." *Movie Collector's World,* June 4, 1993.

Delano, Frederic. "Halls of Immortals." *Cue,* October 26, 1935.

"Film as a Subversive Art: Amos Vogel and Cinema 16." Accessed February 16, 2015. http://www.thestickingplace.com/wp-content/uploads/2014/08/FAASA-dialogue-transcript.pdf

"Foreign Films." *Cue.* July 1, 1939.

Freeman, Joshua B. "The Fiscal Crisis." In *Working-Class New York: Life and Labor Since World War II,* 256–287. New York: The New Press, 2000.

Gomery, Douglas. *Shared Pleasures: A History of Movie Presentation in the United States.* Wisconsin Studies in Film, edited by David Bordwell et al. Madison: University of Wisconsin Press, 1992.

Gornick, Vivian. "Chelsea Fights Back: The Elgin Wins … for Now." *Village Voice,* April 4, 1977.

Haberman, Clyde, ed. *The Times of the Seventies: The Culture, Politics and Personalities that Shaped the Decade.* New York: Black Dog & Leventhal Publishers, 2013.

Haberski, Raymond. *Freedom to Offend: How New York Remade Movie Culture.* Lexington: The University Press of Kentucky, 2007.

Haller, Robert, ed. *Perspectives on Jerome Hill & Anthology Film Archives*. New York: Anthology Film Archives, 2005.

Harvey, James. *Movie Love in the Fifties*. New York: Da Capo Press, 2002.

———. "Richard Schwarz/Film Noir/Jim Harvey." In *Anthology Film Archives* (September-October 1996).

———. *Romantic Comedy in Hollywood: From Lubitsch to Sturges*. New York: Da Capo Press, 1998.

Hoberman, J. "Explorations: The Short Happy Life of the Charles." *American Film* 7, no. 5 (March 1982): 22, 34.

Hoberman, J., and Jonathan Rosenbaum. *Midnight Movies*. New York: Harper & Row, 1983.

Knight, Arthur. "SR Goes to the Movies: A Managerial Revolution." *Saturday Review*. June 18, 1960.

Kroessler, Jeffrey A. *New York Year by Year: A Chronology of the Great Metropolis*. New York: New York University, 2002.

Lane, Jim. "Critical and Cultural Reception of the European Art Film in 1950s America: A Case Study of the Brattle Theatre (Cambridge, Massachusetts)." *Film & History: An Interdisciplinary Journal of Film and Television Studies* 24, nos. 3–4 (1994): 48–64.

"Lionel Rogosin." In *World Film Directors, Volume II 1945-1985*, edited by John Wakeman, 912–919. New York: The H.W. Wilson Company, 1988.

Lopate, Phillip. *Totally Tenderly Tragically: Essays and Criticism from a Lifelong Love Affair with the Movies*. New York: Anchor Books/Doubleday, 1998.

MacDonald, Scott. "Amos Vogel and Cinema 16." *Wide Angle* 9, no. 3 (1987): 38–51.

———. "Cinema 16: An Interview with Amos Vogel." *Film Quarterly* 37, no. 3 (Spring 1984): 19–29.

Magliozzi, Ronald S. "Witnessing the Development of Independent Film Culture in New York: An Interview with Charles L. Turner." *Film History* 12, no. 1 (2000): 72–96.

Mandelbaum, Howard. "Letter from New York." *Bright Lights Film Journal*, Issue #9 (1980). Accessed January 22, 2015. http://brightlightsfilm.com/66/66letterfromny.php.

"Martin John Lewis." In *Encyclopedia of American Biography* New Series, edited by Winfield Scott Downs, Litt. D, 215. New York: American Historical Company, 1957.

McNiven, Roger. "Women Larger than Life: Program Notes 2: King Vidor's *Beyond the Forest* (1949) / Gerd Oswald's *Crime of Passion* (1957)." *Bright Lights Film Journal*, July 31, 2009. Accessed February 20, 2015. www.brightlightsfilm.com/65/65programnotes.php

Mekas, Jonas. "The Film-Maker's Cooperative: A Brief History." Accessed January 28, 2015. http://www.film-makerscoop.com/about/history.

———. "Movie Journal." *Village Voice*, January 3, 1974.

Menand, Louis. *American Studies*. New York: Farrar, Straus and Giroux, 2002.

Merritt, Greg. *Celluloid Mavericks: The History of American Independent Film*. New York: Thunder's Mouth Press, 2000.

Monaco, James. "The Infrastructure of Film: An Interview with Dan Talbot." *Take One* 4, no. 2 (Nov./Dec. 1972): 22–26.

Neale, Steve. *Genre and Hollywood*. London: Routledge, 2000.

Pierson, John, with the Conversational Collaboration of Kevin Smith. *Spike, Mike, Slackers & Dykes: A Guided Tour across a Decade of American Independent Cinema*. New York: Hyperion Miramax Books, 1995.

Randolph, Sike. "Cue Says Go!" *Cue*, June 24, 1939.

Rapfogel, Jared, assoc. ed. "Repertory Film Programming: A Critical Symposium." *Cineaste* 35, no. 2 (Spring 2010): 38–53.

Rich, B. Ruby. *Chick Flicks: Theories and Memories of the Feminist Film Movement*. Durham: Duke University Press, 1998.

Rose, Barbara. "Spotlight: Where to Learn How to Look at Movies: New York's new Anthology Film Archives." *Vogue*, November 1, 1971.

Roud, Richard. "London and New York." *Sight and Sound* 50, no. 4 (Autumn 1981): 233–236.

Roud, Richard, interviewed by Richard Corliss. "70-Millimeter Nerves." *Film Comment* 23, no. 5 (September–October 1987): 36–54.

Schatz, Thomas. *Boom and Bust: American Cinema in the 1940s*. History of the American Cinema, Charles Harpole, General Editor. Berkeley: University of California Press, 1997.

Shaneen, Marianne. "Jonas Mekas, interview by Marianne Shaneen." *SFAQ: International Arts and Culture* 52. Accessed November 12, 2014. http://www.sfaqonline.com/pdfs/SFAQ_issue_eleven.pdf.

Sitney, P. Adams. "Rear-Garde." *American Film* 10, no. 9 (July-August 1985): 13, 61.

———. *Visionary Film: The American Avant-Garde*. New York: Oxford University Press, 1974.

Sklar, Robert. *Movie-Made America: A Cultural History of American Movies*. Rev. ed. New York: Vintage Books Edition, 1994.

Staiger, Janet. *Interpreting Films: Studies in the Historical Reception of American Cinema*. Princeton, NJ: Princeton University Press, 1992.

Strauss, Theodore. "Hunger Is the Mother of Invention." *New York Times*. February 1, 1942.

Talbot, Toby. *The New Yorker Theater and Other Stories from a Life at the Movies*. New York: Columbia University Press, 2009.

Vogel, Amos. *Film as a Subversive Art*. New York: Random House, 1974.

Index

Page numbers in ***bold italics*** indicate pages with illustrations

Abraham Lincoln Brigade 114
Abstract Expressionist painters 93
Académie du cinéma 183
Academy Award (Hollywood) 39, 104, 111
Academy of Motion Pictures Arts and Sciences 102
Actors Equity Association 117
Actors' Playhouse 114, 117
Adventures of Robin Hood 132
Afonia 183
L'Âge d'or 10
Agee 169
Agee, James 169
Agee Room *see* James Agee Room
Ahearn, Charles 187
Aherne, Brian 113
AIDS 165
Akerman, Chantal 168, 184
Alan Freed Rock 'n' Roll movies 150
Alden theater 64, 131; *see also* Regency
Alice Doesn't Live Here Anymore 83
Alice in Wonderland (director Lou Bunin) 160, ***161***, 164
Alice in Wonderland (Walt Disney version) 160
Alice's Restaurant 83
All About Eve 138
"All Night Show" 93
all-night shows 101, 109
Allen, Tom 89, 152, 155
Allen, Will 202
Allen, Woody 22, 31, 39, 107, 139
Alliance française 108
Allied Artists 148
Almendros, Nestor 58
alternative cinema *see* alternative exhibition
alternative exhibition 6, 10, 11; *see also* repertory film movement; repertory movie theaters

Altman, Robert 152
Alvin, Rebecca M. 201, 205
American Cinema 9, 19, 158; *see also* Sarris, Andrew
American Film Institute 183
American Museum of the Moving Image (AMMI) *see* Museum of the Moving Image
American New Wave 83, 187, 188, 189
American Underground Cinema 54
Americana: Four Centuries of America on Film Festival 134
Anatahan 156
Anderson, Lindsay 40
Angel 156
Angelika Film Center 88, 198, 200
Anger, Kenneth 12, 45, 80
animation *see* cartoons
Ansen, David 157
Anthology Film Archives 79–80, 84, 148, 165, 174
anti–Nazi boycott committees 65
Anticipation of the Night 15, 55; *see also* Brakhage, Stan
antiwar movement 104
Antonia: A Portrait of a Woman 82
Antonioni, Michelangelo 12
apartheid 39
The Arbor 204
Archer, Eugene 27, 56, 59
Aristocrats of the Cinema *see* Mindlin, Michael
Ariyoshi, Sawako 181
Armored Attack see North Star
Army-McCarthy Senate hearings 34
Aronofsky, Darren 111
Aronow, Gail 145, 146, 147, 148, 152, 156, 163, 164
Art (movie theater) 6
art cinemas 6, ***7***, 65, 68, 81, 86, 90

Art Museum (Worcester, Massachusetts) 11
Art of Storytelling 204
Arthur, George K. 67
Arthur, Jean 89, 123
Asher, Geri 179
Association of Arab-American University Graduates 182
Association of Independent Video and Film Makers (AIVF) 178
Astaire, Fred 122, 123, 139, 156
L'Atalante 43
Au hazard, Balthazar 169
Auden, W. H. 33
audiences 6, 36, 63, 81, 82, 86, 88, 91, 93, 94, 98, 99, 100, 102, 108, 127, 101, 147
Audio-Brandon 169, 180, 181, 199
auteurism 11, 19, 27, 28, 41, 43, 52, 82, 121
Autour de Jacques Baratier 198
avant-garde film 15, 16, 40, 45, 46, 54, 59, 62, 84, 91, 92, 201; mythopoeic strand 40, 45
Avedon, Richard 123
Avery, Tex 158, 162
Azteca Films 94

B, Beth, and Scott B 187
B-52s 187
B films 145, 148, 152
B.H. (Before Hitler) 65
Babenco, Hector 85
baby boomer generation 83
Bachmann, Gideon *see* Group for Film Study
Baird, Bil, and Cora 130
Baldwin, Craig 201
Baldwin, James 93
Bancroft, Anne 130
Band à part 198
Bankhead, Tallulah 113, ***115***

231

Index

Baraka, Amiri 77
Barenholtz, Ben 41, 46, 47, 54, 102–105, 108–109, 111, 175
Barkentin, Marjorie 65
Barnard, Clio 204
Barr, Alfred H., Jr. 10
Barretts of Wimpole Street 114
Barry, Iris 10
Barrymore, Ethel 134
Barrymore, John 134, 136
Barrymore, Lionel 134
Barrymore, Maurice 134
"Barrymores" series 133
Bart, Peter 83
Barten, Rebecca 201
Barton Fink 111
Basquiat, Jean-Michel 187
Battleship Potemkin 126
Bauer International 193
Beat the Devil 51
Beatles 98
Beaunit Mills 38
Beavers, Louise 124
Beck, Julian 56
Bed and Sofa 10
Before the Revolution 34
Behind the Screen: Producing, Promoting and Exhibiting Motion Pictures and Television 85
Belle de jour 131
The Bells of St. Mary's 139
Bennett, Joan 134
Benny, Jack 95
Bergman, Ingrid 127, 139
Berlin, Irving 123, 140
Berlin Film Festival 196
Bertolucci, Bernardo 34
"Best Film" award 58, 59
"Best of the Year" series 139
Betamax 109
Betty Boop cartoons 99, *159*
Beverly Hills Cop 92
Beverly Theater 24, 64, 68
Bevilacqua, Sal 137
Beyond the Forest 152, 154
Bicycle Thief 67
Bienstock, David 84
Bijou (Baltimore, Maryland) 1
Bijou (Cold Spring, New York) 146
Bijou (New York, New York) 86
Bijou *see* Charles Theater
Billy Jack 107
Bilowitz, Ira 58, 59
Biograph Theater 86, 127, 143
Birchwood 189
Birth of a Nation 65, 103
Biskind, Peter 83, 165
Bitter End 39
Bivers, Paul Charles 65
Black Orpheus 45
Black Power Movement 77
Black Roots 47
The Blank Generation 188, 189
Blasi, Rafe 43
Bleecker Street Cinema 1, 2, 6, *16*, 17, 19, 20, 30, 51, 53, 54, 62, 67, 86, 89, 90, 96, 104, 165, 168, 169, *171*, 181, *184*, 196, 197, 202, 205;

programs—under Lionel Rogosin 39, 40, 42–43, 45–46, under Sidney Geffen 177–180, 182–183, 184–*185*, 186–187, 190–192, 193–196
Bleecker 2 196
blockbusters 91
Blonde Cobra 41
Blondell, Joan 117, 119
Blood of the Poet 66, 124
Blood Simple 111
Bloom, Julius 167
Blue Angel (English language version) 152
Blue Dahlia 113
Blue Velvet 124
Bob le flambeur 195
Bobo, Suzuya 111
Bodine, William 74
Bogart, Humphrey 72, 124, 163
Bogart ("Bogey") festival *see* Brattle Theater
Bogdanovich, Peter 27, 83
Boles, John 122
bomb threats 101, 106
Bondarchuk, Sergei 183
Bonnie and Clyde 41, 82
Boston After Dark 81
Boston Resist 32
Bosworth, Patricia 134
Boule de suife 60
Bower, Dallas 160
Bowery Theater 41
Boys in the Band 108
Brakhage, Stan 12, 16, 40, 54, 55, 80
Brando, Marlon 134
Brandon, Thomas 10
Brandon Films 42, 45
Brattle Theater 18–19, 71
Breakfast at Tiffany's 124
Breathless (cat) 39
Breathless (1960) 34, 44, 189, 193
Breathless (1983) 194
Breer, Robert 54, 55
Brenner, Walter 69
Bresson, Robert 12, 187
Brico, Antonia 82
Bridge Theater 66
"A Brief Portrait" 203
Brig 45
Bright Lights Film Journal 8
British Artists' Protest 44
British Film Institute 186
British Free Cinema Movement 40
Brock, Harry 50
Bronx Documentary Center 203, 205
The Bronx Filmmakers 203
Bronx Photo League 203
Brooks, Louise 135, 150
Broughton, James 79
Brown, Rap 94
Brussell, Mae 106
Bulldog Drummond series 126
Bunin, Lou 160, *161*
The Burglar 52
Burkhardt, Rudy 55, 80

Buster Keaton Archives 102
Buster Keaton festival 101, 103; *see also* Keaton, Buster
Buster Keaton Productions, Inc. 102
Buttershaw Estate 204
Byron, Bruce 45

Cabinet of Dr. Caligari 94, 126
cable television 91
Café Cino 93
Café Figaro 39
Café Mille Yeux (Café Thousand Eyes) 171
Café Reggio 39
Cage, John 56
Cahall, Gary 160
Cahiers du cinéma 19, 43, 52, 154, 189
calendars 9
Cameraperson 202
Campbell, Tom 174
Canary Murder Case 123
Canby, Vincent 31, 32, 34, 94, 148, 152
Cannes Film Festival 111, 188
Canosa, Fabiano 84, 88, 199
Cantor, Eddie 95
Canyon Cinema Film-Makers' Cooperative 15
Capra, Frank 136
Captain Blood 132
Les Carabiniers 32, 46
carbon arc projector 137, 145
Carefree 122, 123
Carlisle, Kitty 119
Carmichael, Stokeley 94
Carnegie Hall 167, 168, **170**
Carnegie Hall Cinema 44, 47, 86, 88, 89, 90, 167, 168, 169, 171–176, **188**, 197; programs 176–178, *182*, 183–184, 192, 196
Carnegie Hall Corporation 167
Carnival of Souls 149
Carol (cat) 147
"Cartoon Noir" *159*
Cartoonal Knowledge 158
cartoonists 145
cartoons 147
Casablanca 90, 91
The Case Against Brooklyn 52
Casque d'or 49
Castro (movie theater) 136
Cat on a Hot Tin Roof 124
Cavalcade 65
CBGB 189
Cedar Bar 93
censorship 41
Center for Public Cinema 169, 172, 173, 183, 184, 188, 196
Central Theatre *see* Gould, Symon
Chabrol, Claude 168
Chadbourne, Larry 175, 185, 189
Chafed Elbows 45
Chaplin, Charles 84
Charles Theater 8, 16, 17, 21, 30, 40, 46, *52*, 80, 88, 110, 188; closing 61; programs of 51, 51–53, 55–59, 205
"Charlie Chan" series 126

Index

Chavez, Estefania 203
Chelsea (New York) 86, 94
Chelsea Girls 95, 131
Chevalier, Maurice 133
Chevalier of the Order of Arts and Lettres 198
Child Bride 99
Children of Paradise 6, 167
Chinatown 83
Chinese opera 94
Chun, Wendy Hui Kyong 202
Ciment, Michel 184
Cineaste 8, 201
Cinéastes de notre temps 187
cineclubs *see* cinematheques
Cinema 16 3, 11, 12, 14–15, 54, 109, 201, 204, 205
cinema art *see* film art
Cinema-Guild 18, 30
Cinema Information Services 172, 189
Cinema Studio 37
Cinema Village 17, 86, 88, 89, 90, 164, 165
Cinemages see Group for Film Study
Cinemascope 44, 110, 125
Cinémathèque française 44, 47, 135
cinematheques 80–81; *see also* film societies
Le Cinématographe 198
Cineplex Odeon 91, 130, 142, 197
Cinepolitical Age 82
Cineprobes (MoMA) 78
Cino, Joe 93
Circle in the Square Theatre 93
Citizen Kane 43
City College of New York 32
City Lights Bookstore 32
City of Trees 203
City University of New York Graduate Center 158
Civil Rights Movement 77
Clampett, Robert 158, 161
Clare, Sam 95
Clarens, Carlos 13, 127, 187
Clark, Ramsey 109
Clark Theater 18
Clarke, Shirley **55**
Cliff, Jimmy 100
Clift, Montgomery 134
Clockwork Orange 91, 108, 124
Club des amis du septième art 10
Cobra Woman 124
Coca, Imogene 117
Coen brothers 111
Cohen, Alexander 130
Cohen, Charles S. 87
Cohen, Larry 191
Cohen Media Group 87
Colbert, Claudette 124
Cole, Don 81
Coleman, Ornette 94
Collective for Living Cinema 80, 205
collectors, film 125
Coltrane, John 94

Coltrane, Robbie 189
Columbia Pictures 89, 107, 123, 126, 132, 135, 136, 137, 172
Columbia University 32, 77, 147
Combat Zone, Boston 146
Come Back, Africa (1959) 6, 38, 39, 40
Comico, Inc. 167
The Connection 55
Conrad, Tony 202
Constantine, Greg 203
The Conversation 83
Cooper, Janet 62
Cooper, Karen 78, 84, 152
Cooperative Film Society 81
Coppola, Francis Ford 193
copyright laws 149; *see also* public domain films
Corman, Roger 83, 100, 159
Cornell, Katharine 114
countercultural movie theaters *see* repertory movie theaters
counterculture 94, 101
Crawford, Joan 113, 117, 118, **122**, 133
Crime of Passion 154
Crist, Judith 37, 88
The Crowd 147
Crowdus, Gary 82
Crowley, Mart 108
Crowther, Bosley 20, 43
Cue poll 65
Cukor, George 124
cult films 91, 97, 98, 145
Cunningham, Merce 56
curatorial approaches 8, 14, 30, 42–43, 52, 66, 72, 75, 101, 194–195; *see also* dialectical editing; festival format; fragmented programming; open screening; random programming; repertory programming; series programming
The Cure 60
Curtis, Jamie Lee 88
Czech films 46

Da Costa, Morton 117
Dahl, Arlene 152
Daiei Film Company, Ltd. 180
Daily News headline 78
Dance Life magazine 156
Dancing Lady 118
Danelia, Georgy 183
Daney, Serge 184, 185
Dargis, Manohla 83
Davidson, Adam 78
D'Avino, Carmen 54
Davis, Bette 72, 113, 133, 138, 140, 152, 163
Day of Wrath 26
Dean, James 134
de Antonio, Emile 26, 34, 45
Dearie, Blossom 113
De Carlo, Yvonne 117
The Decline of Western Civilization 195
de Havilland, Olivia 132
de Kooning, Willem 93

Delaney, Pete 21, 63, 66, 67, 150, 152
Deluise, Dom 119
Demme, Jonathan 33, 47
Denby, David 172
Deneroff, Harvey 13
De Niro, Robert 114, *115*
de Palma, Brian 57, 58
Le Départ 46
depot *see* film exchanges
Deren, Maya 12
de Sica, Vittorio 6
Desperately Seeking Susan 90
Deux Fois 167
Devi 192
The Devils (film) 91
The Devils (play) 130
dialectical editing 14
Diamonds of the Night 46
Diary of a Lost Girl 145
Dickstein, Morris 31
Dietrich, Marlene 41, 72, 152
Digges, Dudley 65
Dinner at Eight 124
D'Inzillo, Steve 96
DiPillo, Gladys 22, 71, 72, 74, 76
Disney, Walt 158, 159
distribution, independent 6, 36, 44, 47, 67, 87, 104; *see also* Audio-Brandon; Film-Makers' Cooperative; Film-Makers' Distribution Center; Gopher Films; Impact Films; Janus Films; Libra Films; Manhattan Movietime; New World Pictures; New Yorker Films; Newsreel
distribution 38, 105
Divine 99
Doc Watchers 204
Dr. Jekyll and Mr. Hyde 64
Doctorow, E. L. 21
documentaries 82
Dog Star Man, Part I 40
Don Giovanni (film) 69, 71
Donen, Stanley 43
Dorfmann, Jacques 198
D'Orsay, Fifi 117, 118
double features 8
Douglas, Alan 98
Douglas Films 98
Downey, Robert, Sr. 45, 46, 52
Drabinsky, Garth 143
Dretzin, David 87
Dunbar, Andrea 204
Dunbar, Lorraine 204
Dunham, Lena 205
Dunne, Irene 121, 122
Duras, Marguerite 187, **190**
Durk, David 77
Dwan, Allan 52, 152

Eagle-Lion Films 148
East of Eden 136
East Side theaters 24, 87
East Village 50
Easy Rider 83
Easy Riders, Raging Bulls 83
Echeverria, Diego 203
L'Eclisse 201

Eddy, Nelson 124, 133, 139
Edgar G. Ulmer Festival 52
Edie 138
Edie the Egg Lady 99
8th Street Playhouse 86, 88
Eisenstein, Sergei 43, 183
Elgin Marble Film News and Comment 105, 106, 108
Elgin Theater 1, 2, 30, 45, 47, 86, 88, 89, **95**, 108, 110, 164, 192, 205; audience 111–112; countercultural reputation, origin of 97–98; legacy 111–112; programming 96, 97, 109; programs 96, 101, 103–104, 106, 109; publicity 107–108, 109; senior policy 108–109
Eliza's Horoscope 107
Emerson College 145
Empire Strikes Back 92
Emschwiller, Ed 14, 40
Eraserhead 111
Ernst Lubitsch retrospective 156
Essential Cinema 80
Estridge, Larry 106
The Eternal Jew 14, 29
European Artists' Protest against the Vietnam War 44
Euster, Roger 94, 96, 97, 109, 110, 111
The Evangelist 114
An Evening with the Royal Ballet 108, 111
Evergreen Bleecker Street Cinema 47
Everson, William K. 13, 14, 15, 30, 60, 157
Every Fold Matters 203
Exceptional Photoplays Committee 9
exchanges *see* film exchanges
experimental films *see* avant-garde films
Export, Valie 80, 189

F and A Theatres 167
F & G Discounts 164
Fairbanks, Douglas, Jr. 136
Falco & Goldstein 164
Family Games 111
Fanfan la Tulipe 51
Farber, Manny 31–32, 83
Farrow, Mia 139, 140
fascism 38
Fassbinder, Rainer Werner 79
The Fat and the Thin 12
Fate of a Man 183
FBI 53
Federal Administration for International Scientific, Educational, Cultural and Technical Cooperation (JUZAMS) 183
Feiffer, Ed 71, 72, 76
Feiffer, Jules 25
Feiffer, Teddy 22, 71, 72, 76
Feinstein, Peter 78
Fellini Satyricon 108
Fellini, Federico 169
feminist documentary 82; *see also* *Antonia: A Portrait of the Woman*
Fera, Henry 138
Ferlinghetti, Lawrence 32
festival format 105, 131; *see also* curatorial approaches
Fiction-Non 204
Fields, W. C. 72
Fieldston School 50
Fifth Avenue Cinema 6, 64, 65, 66, 67, 68
Fifth Avenue Playhouse Group *see* Mindlin, Michael
"Fifties Melodrama: Post-War Auteurs and the Cinema of Hysteria" 157
55th Street Playhouse 6, 10, 30, 64, 66, 67, **68**, 69, 70, 71
Le Figaro 48
Fight Game 57
Fillmore East *see* Village Theater
Film: An Anthology 25
Film and Photo League 203
film art 9, 10–11, 13, 85
Film at the Public 84
Film Circle *see* Theodore Huff Memorial Film Society
Film Comment 83
film criticism 83
film culture 6, 83, 92
Film Culture 16, 19
film depots *see* film exchanges
Film Directions 11
film exchanges 21, 34
Film Forum 1, 10, 11, 78–**79**, 84, 87, 88, 90, 126, 140, 152, 163, 174, 196
film history 13
film noir 145, 146, 155
"Film Noir" series 155
film notes *see* program notes
film societies 7, 11, 13
Film Society 10, 11
film society movement *see* film societies
Film Society of Lincoln Center 84–85, 201
Film Society Review 82
filmmakers, avant-garde 54
Film-Makers' Cinematheque 17, 29, 46, 54, 79, 80, 205
Film-Makers' Cooperative 15, 16, 45, 79, 95, 96, 97
Film-Makers' Distribution Center 45, 47
filmmakers, experimental *see* filmmakers, avant-garde
filmmakers, feminist 82
Film-Makers' Festival 56, 57, **58**, 59
filmmakers, independent 38, 46, 54, 82, 187, 188, 189; *see also* Association of Independent Video and Film Makers (AIVF)
Film-Makers' Showcase 16–17, 40, 179
filmmakers, underground *see* filmmaker, avant-garde
filmmaking trends 81–83
Films, Inc. 126, 196
films, nitrate 136
films of the fifties 155
films, rare 145, 148, 155
"The Filthiest Person Alive" 99
Finley, Randy 104
First Avenue Screening Room 84, 86, 87; programming 87–88
First International Film Festival 64, 65
The First Nudie Musical 191
First Run Features 171, 195
fiscal crisis (New York) 77–78
Fitzgerald, Ella 113
Fitzgerald, Geraldine 136, 139, **141**
Five Easy Pieces 83
Flaherty, Robert 38, 39
Flaming Creatures 40, 41, 62
flat rates *see* rental fees, film
Flatley, Guy 89, 140
Fleischer, Max, and Dave 158
Fleming, Rhonda 152
Flint, Peter 140
Florey, Robert 13
Flower Thief 56, 58
Fluxus 51
Flying Down to Rio 122, 123
Flynn, Errol 132, 163
Focus on Public Cinema 173, 174, 187, 189, 192; *see also Thousand Eyes* magazine
Follies 117
Follow the Fleet 122, 123
Fonda, Henry 113
Fonda, Jane 124
Foolish Wives 60
Ford, Greg 89, 147, 148, 151, 152, 155, 158, 159, 160, 162, 163, 190, 191
Ford Foundation 61
Forde, Walter 13
foreign films 6, 34, 35–36, 81, 87
The Foreigner 188, 189
"Forgotten Films" series 26–28
Forma, Harold 60
Forsaking All Others 113
Fort Lee 149
fragmented programming 30, **31**
Franchi, Rudy 30, 39, 42, 43, 44
Francis, Kay 127
Franco, Alvano 203
Frank, Robert *see Pull My Daisy*
Franklin, Joe 60
Free Speech Movement 77
Freedom to Offend: How New York Remade Movie Culture see Haberski, Raymond
Freleng, Fritz 158
The French Line 149
French New Wave 6, 28, 43, 52, 82, 168
From Caligari to Hitler see Kracauer, Siegfried
Fuchs, Jay 86
Fuller, Samuel 52

Gabor, Zsa Zsa 150
Gam, Rita 117

Index

Garbo, Greta 72
Gardner, Ava 121
Garfein, Jack 193
Garland, Beverly 150
Garland, Judy 95
Garrick (theater) **16**, 17, 86, 104, 105
Gates of Heaven 189
Geffen, Sidney 47, 86, 96, 131, 166–169, 171–175, **177**, 178, 180, 184, 185–187, 189, 192, 193, **194**, 196–199
The General 102
General Cinema 167
George Eastman House (Rochester, New York) 11
George M. Cohan Theatre *see* Gould, Symon
George's Greek Restaurant 50
Gerard, Lillian 66
Gerald McBoing-Boing 67
German Expressionism 155
German New Wave 79
Gettner, Victor 50
Gillespie, Dizzy 48
Girls 205
Les Girls 125
Gish, Dorothy 81
Gish, Lillian 81
Giuliani, Rudolph 127
God Told Me To 191
Godard, Jean-Luc 6, 44, 168, 184, 186
The Godfather 124
The Godfather Part II 83
Goethe House 181, 183, 196
"Gold Coast" East Side (New York) 87
Goldberg, Joseph 15
Golddiggers of 1935 117
golden age of American cinema 83
golden age of live television 82
golden age of the foreign film 6
Golden Lion Award 195
Golden Theater 116–7
Goldovsky, Boris 69
Goldstein, Bruce 21, 30, 90, 132, 140, 141, 147, 151, 152, 155, 161–164, 196
Der Golem (1936) 68
Gomery, Douglas 3
Gone with the Wind 135, 146, 147
Gonzalez, Pete 164
Good Times, Wonderful Times 41, 44
Goossen, Larry 123
Gopher Films 164
Gordon, Ruth 147
Gornick, Vivian 77, 93, 94, 108, 109, 110, 112
Goskino 183
Gottlieb, Robert 156, 157
Gould, Steve 2, 103–**105**, 106–109, 111–112, 164, 192
Gould, Symon 10
Gramercy Arts Theatre 17
Gramercy Theatre 86, 143
Grand Illusion 67, 149
Grauman's Chinese Theater 117

Great Imposter 49
Green, Joseph 66
Green, Paul 49
Greenspun, Roger 19, 60, 98, 186
Greenwich Village 8, 39, 93
Gregory, André 105
Griffith, Richard 14
Griggs, John 49, 59, 60, 81
grindhouses, 42nd Street 24
Group for Film Study 11
Group Portrait with Lady 183
Grove Press 47
Guare, John 93
guest books 28, 33, 51, 108
Guidice, Joe 81
Gulf Coast Film-Makers' Cooperative 15
Guttenplan, Howard 80

Haberski, Raymond 3, 14, 23
Haley, Jack, Jr. 122
Haliday, Bryan 18, 71
Hall, Philip Baker 152
Halter, Ed 202, 205
Hammett 193, 195
Hanig, Josh 179
Haratonik, Peter 7, 9, 20
The Hard Swing 59
The Harder They Come 100
Haring, Keith 187
Hark! Hark! the Clark see Clark Theater
Harlan County, U.S.A. 82
Harlow, Jean 123
Harold and Maude 90, 107, 108, 192
Harold Clurman Theater 172, 193
Harvest 26
Harvey, Cy, Jr. 18, 71
Harvey, Herk 149
Harvey, James 3, 136, 146, 147, 148, 152, 155, 156, 157, 158, 160, 162, 164, 165, 171
Hauff, Reinhard 183
Hawks, Howard 186
Head (film) 107
Heckart, Eileen 117, 118, 124
Hefner, Hugh 163
The Heights 64, 70
Hellman, Lillian 124
Hell's Angels 123
Henry V 20, 26, 28
Hentoff, Nat 14
Hepburn, Audrey 124
Hepburn, Katharine 113, 133, 139, 157
Herzog, Werner 79, 189
High Noon 127, 129
High Treason 10
Hildegarde 119
Hill, Jerome 61, 79, 80
Hippler, Fritz *see The Eternal Jew*
Hirsch, Steve 88
Hitchcock, Alfred **27**
Hitler, Adolf 29, 65
Hoberman, J. 21, 40, 51, 61, 131, 161, 162, 189, 193
Hoffman, Dustin 140

Hoffman, Frank 115
Holliday, Billie 127
"Hollywood Cartoons" 158
Hollywood films 113
Hollywood New Wave *see* American New Wave
Hollywood Out-Takes and Rare Footage 148, 149, 163, 164
Hollywood stars 113
Holm, Celeste 136
Holy Mountain 110
Hoodlum Priest 49
Hope, Bob 158
Hopper, Edward 171
horizontal series 132, 191
Horowitz, Vladimir 139
"Horrors!—Part One" series 191
House Un-American Activities Committee (HUAC) 29
Howard, Leslie 124
Howe, Irving 81, 83
Hubley, Faith 161
Huff, Theodore (Ted) 13
Hughes, Howard 123
Humphrey Bogart Festival 51
Hunter College 32
Huntington Hartford Gallery of Modern Art 102
Hurt William 140
Huston, John 51, 152

"I Lost It at the Bleecker" 190–191
Iannone, Carol 158
Ici et ailleurs 184, 185
I.C.N. Bleecker, Inc. 197
Ikiru 25
I'll Cry Tomorrow 117
Images Cinema 90
Imitation of Life (1934) 64
Impact Films 45, 47
In a Lonely Place 157
Independent Filmmakers Series 189
independent films 40, 44, 82, 84
Independent Showcase 189
India Song 187, **188**, 189, **190**
Information Services *see* Cinema Information Services
Intense Family Theater Company 106
Intermedia Theater 193
International Film Arts Guild *see* Gould, Symon
international movement of film 6; *see also* film culture
Intrator, Jerry 69, 71
Invisible Adversaries 189
Ionesco, Eugene 183
Irving Place Theatre 66
It Happened One Night 141
It's Always Fair Weather 125
Italian Critics Award 39
Italian neo-realism 6, 155; *see also* film culture
Ivan the Terrible, Part II 18
Ivens, Joris 45

Jackson, Glenda 152
Jacobs, Ken 80

Jacobs, Lewis 54
Jacobson, Harlan 165
Jacobson, Herman 70
Jamaica 100
James Agee Room 166, 169, 172, 174, 188, 192, 197
Jamieson, Wendell 181
Janus Film Festival 96, 105, 167
Janus Films 44, 45, 47, 96, 126, 180, 199
Japan Society 108
Japan Swordsmanship Society 180
Japanese series see Spectrum of Japanese Cinema
Jarmusch, Jim 187, 188, 195
Jary, Hilde 157, 158
Jason, Sandy 69
Jaws 91
"Jazz at the Charles Theatre" (program) **53**
Jazz on a Summer's Day 6; see also Stern, Bert
Jean Renoir Cinema 193
Jennings, Humphrey 55
Jerome Avenue Workers Project 203
Jewish Museum 78
Jezebel 138
Jodorowsky, Alejandro 98
Joe's Bed-Stuy Barbershop 195
Joe's Place 81
Joffe, Charles 107
Johnny Guitar 157
Johnson, Kirsten 202
Jones, Allan 119, 121, 136
Jones, Chuck 158, 161, 162
Jones, Leroi see Baraka, Amiri
Jones, Tommy Lee 107
Jordan, Larry 40, 55
Jost, Jon 80
Joyce Theater 86, **105**, 111
Jules and Jim 43, 44, 96

Kael, Pauline 18, 25, 30–31, 34, 43, 56, 83, 92, 140
Kaloostian, Vartoohi "Kay" 138
Kamber, Michael 203
Kameradschaft 66
Kanin, Garson 147
Kardish, Laurence 22
Katharine Hepburn Festival 132
Kauffmann, Stanley 31, 83
Kaufman Astoria Studios 85
Keaton, Buster 102, 103
Keeler, Ruby 117, **119**
Keeper of the Flame 139
Kelly, Gene 139
Kelly, Mary 39, 41, 42, 44, 46
Kelman, Kenneth 79
Ken Murray's Hollywood 130
Kendall, Elizabeth 157
Kennedy, Robert 82
Kennedy Center 137
La Kermessee héroïque 65
Kern, Jerome 121, 122
Kerouac, Jack see *Pull My Daisy*
Kerr, Walter 116
Kershner, Irv 52
King, Martin Luther, Jr. 82

King Kong 97
King of Comedy 193
King of Hearts 90, 104, 108
Kingdom of Shadows 203
Kino International 91, 135, 136, 143, 180
Kipps Bay theater 84
Kirkland, Sally 114
Kirschen, Florence see Otway, Florence
Kirstein, Lincoln 139
Kiss Me Deadly 155
Kitt, Sam 193
Klein, Allen 98
Kline, Franz 93
Knapp Commission 77, 106
Knight, Arthur 6, 14, 18, 23
Kopple, Barbara 82
Kracauer, Siegfried 14
Kral, Ivan 188
Krim, Donald 91, 131, 135, 136, 143
Kubelka, Peter 79
Kubrick, Stanley 13
Kurosawa, Akira 6

Laber, Austen 32
La Cava, Gregory 157
"La Cava Classics" series 157
Ladd, Diane 114
Lady for a Day 66
Lady with a Dog 43
Landberg, Ed 18
Langlois, Henri 135
Langsford, Walter **52**, 81, 110
LaPlante, Laura 14
Last Picture Show 83
Last Tango in Paris 169
Laurel and Hardy 14
Leary, Timothy 94
Lee, Spike 171, 195
Leeson, Lynn Hershman 202
Légion d'Honneur 198
Leigh, Vivien 81
Lennon, John 98
Lerner and Loew (Broadway composing team) 74
Leslie, Alfred see *Pull My Daisy*
Leslie, Joan 152
Let There Be Light 152
Let Us Be Gay 114
Leth, Jorgen 183
Levy, Julien 10
Lewis, Deborah see Sutherland, Deborah
Lewis, John 63, 64, 67, 69, 70
Lewis, Joseph H. 43
Lewis, Marshall 30, 39, 41, 42, 43, 44, 46, 67
Lewis, Martin J. 63–69, 166
Lewis, Thomas 70, 72
Lewis, Ursula 64, 67, 70, **71**–72, **75**, 76, 97, 146, 167
Lewy, Hans 64
Lewy, Yohanan see Lewy, Hans; see also Lewis, Martin
Libra Films 104, 111
Library of Congress 121

Lide, Miller 132, 133
Light Industry 202, 205
Lincoln Brigade 96
Lincoln Center for the Performing Arts see New York Public Library
Lincoln Plaza Cinemas 37, 143
Lindsay, John 77
Lindstrom, Pia 139
Little Big Man 82
Little Carnegie Playhouse 64, 65
Little Cinema Movement 10
Little Shop of Horrors 145
Little Theatre of Jean Renoir 169
Liveliest Art 9; see also Knight, Arthur
Living Theater 54, 56, 62
Loew, Marcus 60
Loew family 146
Loews, Inc. 102
Lombard, Carol 136
Long Day's Journey into Night 192
Look for the Silver Lining 117
Lopate, Phillip 6, 9, 26, 28, 31, 51, 81, 82, 92, 96, 121, 133, 139, 205
Los Angeles Film-Makers' Cooperative 15
Lower Depths (Kurosawa) 43
Lower East Side 50
Loy, Myrna 113, 118
Luddy, Tom 47
"Lullaby of Broadway" 117
Lulu in Hollywood 135
Luna 139
Lupino, Ida 155
Lyle, Hellura 204
Lynch, Richard 114
Lytess, Natasha 69

M 65
M*A*S*H 82
MacDonald, Dwight 31, 43, 61
MacDonald, Jeanette 124, 133, 139
MacDonald, Scott 204
Maciunas, George 51
Made in the Bronx 203
Madison theater 64
Maedchen in Uniform 65
Mafia 50
Magliozzi, Ron 2, 26, 125
Magnificent Ambersons 26, 30
Magno Sound 168
Maguire, Ed 9, 61, 81, 98, 102, 126
Maguire, Mary 30, 81, 111, 147
Mailer, Norman 93
Makavejev, Dusan 12
Makeba, Miriam 39
Malina, Judith 56
Malkames, Don 81
Malmfelt, Al 105
Malthete-Méliès, Madame 60
Maltin, Leonard 13
Mama Cat 95, 111, 200
Man of Iran 38
Man Who Fell to Earth 192
Man Who Knew Too Much (1934) 66, 126
Mandelbaum, Howard 9, 20, 21,

Index 237

30, 81, 89, 93, 94, 143, 146, 147, 148, 154, 163, 164, 165, 172, 175
Manhattan Movietime 164
Mann, Theodore 93
Mansour, George 90
Marijuana: The Weed with Roots in Hell 99
marketing 192; *see also* publicity
Markopoulos, Gregory 55
Markovich, Gregory 56
The Marrying Kind 147
Marsh, Carol 160
Martin, Peter 32
Martinez, Amador, Jr. 56
Martinson, Joseph 79
Marx Brothers 72
Mary Martin Does It 58
Marzano, Joseph 55
*M*A*S*H* 82
Maslin, Janet 89, 140, 192
Mason, James 102
Master and Margarita (film) 183
Masterpiece Theatre 201
La Maternelle 68
A Matter of Gravity 133
Mayer, Arthur 67
Mayfair Theatre **161**
Maysles, Albert 204
Maysles Documentary Center 203, 204, 205
Mazursky, Paul 9
MCA 135
McAteer, Terrence (Terry) 190
McCay, Winsor 159–160
McGavin, Darren 61
McKay, Ralph 145, 146
McNiven, Roger 20, 81, 89, 54, 172
McQueen, Butterfly 147
Mekas, Adolfas 15, 16, 40
Mekas, Jonas 3, 6, 12, 15–17, 25, 30, 37, 38, 40, 41, 46, 53, 54, 59, 61, 79, 84, 98, 204
Mel Novikoff award 162
Méliès, Georges 60
Melody Makers series 174
Melville, Jean-Pierre 195
Menand, Louis 92
Menken, Marie 55
Meshes of the Afternoon 54
Metro 36–37, 86, 88, 89, 90, 156, 175
Metzger, Radley 13
Meyer, Russ 150
MGM 102, 121, 122, 124, 126, 131, 135, 148
MGM Technicolor musicals 87
microcinemas 201, 202, 203, 204, 205
Midnight Film Society 50, 53, 55
"Midnight Movie" 93
midnight movies 3, 86, 88, 97, 99, 100
Midnight Movies (book) 21, 40, 51, 94, 131
Midtown *see* Metro
Mildred Pierce 94
Millennium Film Journal 80
Millennium Film Workshop 61, 78, 80, 84

Miller, Henry 109
Miller, Marilyn 117, 127
Miller, Sandy 78
Miller's Crossing 111
Million Dollar Movies 20
Milne, Tom 186
Mindlin, Michael 10
Miracle Woman 123
Mirisch, Mrs. Walter 163
Mirisch Corporation 163
mise-en-scène 91
Mr. Magoo 67
Mitchell, Eric 187, 189
Mitchell, Joan 116
Moby Dick (1930 film) 134
Monaco, James 32, 34
Monday evening series (New Yorker Theater) 29–30
"Monday Midnights" 40
Monk, Thelonius 39
The Monkees 107
Monogram Pictures 150
montage 91
Montez, Maria 41
Montreal Film Festival 41, 43, 46
Moore, Grace 139
Moose Jaw, Saskatchewan 114
"Moral Tales" 168
Morgan, Chesty 146
Morgan, Helen 121
Morris, Errol 189
Morris, George 132, 138
Morrissey, Paul 58
"Most Promising Filmmaker" award 58
Mostel, Zero 64
Movie (British film journal) 43
movie criticism *see* film criticism
"Movie Journal" 15, 16; *see also* Mekas, Jonas; *Village Voice*
Movie Love in the Fifties 157
Movie-Made America 6, 40, 179
Movie Watch 109
"Movies: The Desperate Art" 25
Mueller, Cookie 189
multiplex theaters 86, 87, 88, 91
Muriel 201
Murray, Bill 140
Museum of Art (Cleveland, Ohio) 11
Museum of Modern Art (MoMA), Department of Film 2, 10, 11, 60, 90, 98, 117, 125, 149, 158, 168, 198
Museum of the Moving Image 85
Music in the Air 122
Music Inn 146
Music Inn (film) 111
The Music Room 192
Musical Film Co. 117, **118**
My Man Godfrey 157

Nabwana, Isaac G. G. 111
Nagel, Conrad 94
Naruse, Mikio 12
National Board of Review (NBR) 9–10
National Board of Review Magazine 9

National Film Theatre (London) 186
The Navigator 102
Neale, Steve 19
Nelson, Gene 117
New American Cinema 16, 40, 59
"New American Filmmakers" series 84
New Carnegie *see* Biograph Theater
New Directors/New Films 85
New Filmmakers Showcase 80
New Forum 47th Street (movie theater) 83
New Hollywood 83
New Left 77
New Line Cinema 87, 99, 188
New School of Social Research 7, 15, 178
New World Pictures 100
New York Civil Liberties Union 50
New York Cultural Center 89, 158, 190
New York cultural institutions 84
New York Film Bulletin 43, 83
New York Film Critics 88
New York Film Festival 15, 34, 82, 84, 196, 202
New York in the 1970s 78
New York Movie 171
New York Premiere series 151–152
New York Public Library for the Performing Arts (LPA), Research Collection of the Billy Rose Theater Division 2
New York Public Library: Lincoln Center for the Performing Arts 138; Picture Collection Department 10
New York Story 189, 193, **194**
New York University 13, 14, 31, 41, 46, 47, 104, 158, 168, 169, 174, 178, 193
New Yorker Bookstore 32
New Yorker Film Society (add from New Yorker T) 53
New Yorker Films 34, 35, 37, 45, 101
New Yorker Theater 2, 6, 17, 18, 19, 20, 21, 38, 46, 49, 51, 54, 75, 77, 86, 87, 88, 89, 96, 205; beginnings of 25–26; programs of 26, 27–30, 34, 35–36
The New Yorker Theater and Other Scenes from a Life at the Movies see Talbot, Toby
Newman, Paul 124
newspaper strike (New York) 26
Newsreel 179
Nicholas Nickleby (film) 162
Nicholas Nickleby (play) 162
Nicholson, Jack 83
Night at the Opera 20, 175
Night Mail 12
Night of the Living Dead 150
Night of the Shooting Stars 165
Nimoy, Leonard 45
1985 Biennial Exhibition 92

92nd Street YMHA 6, 11
Nitke, Barbara 166, 167, 168, 174, 199
Nitke, Herb 167
Nixon, Richard 152
No Wave Cinema 188
noncommercial films 6
nonprofit cinemas 8; *see also* film societies; Museum of Modern Art (MoMA), Department of Film
Nordic Film Series 197
Normandie 24
North American Cinema Group 16, 40
North Star 124, 125
Northwest Film-Makers' Cooperative 15
Nosferatu 124, 128
Notes sur Jonas Mekas 198
Notorious 127
Nowhere People 203
La Nuit de l'ours 198
Nuit et bruillard 29
Numéro deux 187, 189, 192

October: Ten Days That Shook the World 126, 183
Odds Against Tomorrow 25
Off-Broadway movement 93, ii4
Off-Off Broadway 93
Olesker, Lizzie 203
Olivier, Laurence 136
Olympia Theater 86, 87
On the Beach 25
On the Bowery 39
"One Dollar at All Times" 87–88
One Night Stands of a Noisy Passenger 114, 117, 123
one-sheets *see* posters
Ono, Yoko 98
open screening 56–57, 62, 80, 188; *see also* Film-Makers' Festival
L'opéra de quat' sous 10
Operation Abolition 29
Operation Correction 29
operator *see* projectionists
Oriolo, Joe 160
Oroko Ambrosia 93
Orpheum 104, 105
Orson Welles Cinema 100
Oshima, Nagisa 12
Ostrow, Ted 20, 42, 44, 45, 46, 47
Oswald, Gerd 52
Other Cinema 201
Otway, Florence 2, 113, 115, 116, 117, 123, 126, 127, 128, 129
Otway, Howard 2, 90, 91, **115, 119**, **122**, 132, 174, 200
Otway, Lawrence *see* Otway, Lorcan
Otway, Lorcan 2, 114, 115, 116, 117, 121, 122, 125, 128
Otway, Thomas 114
Overland Stage Raiders 150

Palace *see* RKO Palace
Palmucci, Gary 22

Pandora's Box 135
Papp, Joseph 79
The Paradise Bird 114
Paramount (movie theater) 83
Paramount Pictures 135, 172
Paramount Studio East Coast production complex 85
Paris (movie theater) 24
Parlor, Bedroom and Bath 102
Partisan Review 25
Patchwork Girl of Oz 150
Pathé Cinema 68
Patton 146
Paulettes 83; *see also* Sarristes
PBS *see* Public Broadcasting System
Pearl Theater 128
Pena, Richard 201
Pence, Bill 96, 105
People on the Beach 58
The People's Film Festival 203, 204
percentages *see* rental fees, film
Perfect 88
Performance 108
Pergola Properties 164
Perils of Pauly 57
Perkins, Anthony 81
Permanent Vacation 187, 188
Perry, William 110
Persian Room 114
"Personal Cinema" series 80
Peter, Paul and Mary 39
Peters, Bernadette 140
Petrovic, Aleksandar 183
Pfeiffer, Wilhelmina **58**
Phantom India 101
Phillips, McCandlish 86
Picker, David 107
Pierson, John 83, 89, 102, 173, 192, 193–195, 196
Pink Flamingos 99, 100
Pinthus, Dr. Curt 65
"Piss Man" 111
Place in the Sun 155
Platinum Blonde 123
The Plaza 114
Poe, Amos 188, 189, 195
Point of Order 34
Polanski, Roman 12, 174
police raid 41
Poling, Jim 164
Pollack, J.D. 197
Pollack, Jackson 93
Pollet, Jean-Daniel 198
Pomander Bookshop 165
Pomander Walk 74
Porky Pig cartoons **159**, 162
pornography 167
Portrait de Simon Lazard 198
Portrait of Jason 46
post-baby boomer population 91
Positif 184
posters 137
Potemkin 44
POV (public television program) 180
Poverty Row studios 150; *see also*

Monogram Pictures; Producers Releasing Corporation
Powell, William 123, 127
Power, Paul 113, 125
Powers, Bill 57
PRC *see* Producers Releasing Corporation
Preminger, Otto 186
President's Analyst **16**
Preston, Richard 54, 55
Price, Leontyne 139
prints, film 20–21, 51, 73, 102, 123, 125, 135, 143, 149
Producers Releasing Corporation 150
program notes 8, 13, 14, 30, 155, 156, 157
Progressive magazine 25
projectionists 20, 25, 95, 96, 119
projectors 102, 125
Provincetown Playhouse 54
Public Broadcasting System (PBS) 126
public domain films 148, 149
Public Theater 79, 84, 88, 90, 127
Puente, Tito 48
Puerto Rican neighborhood *see* Chelsea
Pull My Daisy (1959) 6, 26, 30
punk underground, New York 188
The Pursuit of Happiness 203
Putnam, Michael 59
Putney Swope 45

Quad Cinema 86, 87, 88; programming 87
Quintero, Jose 93

racism 38
"Radical Images: World Politics in the Seventies" 174
Rafelson, Bob 83, 107
Raiders of the Lost Ark 149
Rainer, Yvonne 80
Rapfogel, Jason 8
Raphaelson, Samson 156
Rapper, Irving 136
Rashomon 155
Ray, Bingham 155, 175
Ray, Nicholas 80, 157, 158, 191
Ray, Satyajit 6, 192
Raynal, Jackie 166–**169**, 172–175, **177**, 182–186, 188–189, 192–193, **194**, 196–199
Reagan, Nancy 163
Reagan, President Ronald 163
real estate (New York) 91, 141, 197
Real Stories from a Free South Africa 204
rear projection 117, 125
Rebel without a Cause 136
Red Balloon 26
Reefer Madness 99
Reflections 57
Regency Theater 2, 86, 89, 90, 121, 128, 132, 148, 167, 205; audiences of 139–140; changes in format of 131–132; closing of, reasons for

Index

and public outcry at 141–143; distributors' relationship with 135–136; guest appearances at 136–*137*; programs of 132–135; publicity 102, 105, 135, 140–*141*, 162–163
reggae music 100
Reiss, William 113
Reisz, Karel 40
Reminiscences of a Journey to Lithuania 204
Renata Theater 39
Renoir, Jean 6, 168, 169
rental fees, film 148, 155
repertory movie theater movement (New York) 3, 6, 17, 18, 20, 89–90; causes of collapse 90–92
repertory movie theaters 6, 8, 9, 17, 18, 19–22, 86, 87, 88–89, 93; *see also* alternative exhibition; repertory programming
repertory programming 7, 8, 10, 22, 30, 42, 88, 90, 92, 200; series versus random programming 90, 120, 162–163; symposium on 8, 201
Republic Pictures 150
retrospectives *see* "programs" under individual theaters
revival movie theaters *see* repertory movie theaters
Revivals Only at the Regency *see* ROAR
Rhodes, Eric 136
Rice, Ron 56, 58
Richie, Donald 36
Richter, Hans 40
Rickey, Carrie 186
Rio Bravo 89
Rivette, Jacques 186, 187, 197
"Rivette in Context" retrospective 186, 202
Rivette: Texts and Interviews 186
RKO Goldwyn **133**
RKO Palace 95
RKO Pictures 135
Road Movies 192, 193
ROAR 142
Robards, Jason 130
Roberta 122
Roberts, Will 179
Robeson, Paul 121
Robinson, Bill "Bojangles" 95
Rochlin, Sheldon 46
Rocky Horror Picture Show 88, 90, 99
Rogers, Ginger 122, 156
Rogosin, Lionel 6, 17, 30, 33, 38, 45, 46, 48, 62, 75, 86, 96, 168, 178
Rogosin, Michael 46, 47
Rogosin Films *see* Impact Films
Rohauer, Raymond 101, 102, 105, 126
Rohmer, Eric 168
Rollins, Jack 107
Romantic Comedy in Hollywood: From Lubitsch to Sturges 156
Rome, Open City 67

Romero, George 111
Rooftop Films 202, 205
Rose theater 64
Rosenbaum, Jonathan 21, 40, 51, 131, 168, 185, 186, 187, 190, 202
Rosenberg, Henry 25, 26
Rosenwald, H.S. 64, 65, 66
Rosie Riveter 104
Ross, Lillian 67
Rossellini, Isabella 168
Rossini, Doug 163
Roth, Lillian 117, 118
Rotterdam Film Festival 188
Rouch, Jean 168
Roud, Richard 15, 187, **190**
Rowley, Frank 90, 91, 130, **137**, **141**, 143, 165, 174, 200
Roxy Theater 25
Royal Shakespeare Company 162
Rubin, Marty 78, 89, 175, 190, 191, 192, 195
Rudd, Mark 32, 77
Ruiz, Bernardo 203
Rules of the Game 44
Russell, Bertrand 44
Russell, Deac 81
Russell, Jane 117, 149, 158

Sachs, Lynne 203
St. Cyr, Lili 69
St. Marks Cinema 86, 87, 88, 90; programming 87
Saint Michel Cinema 185
Salute to Warners festival 131
Salvation Army 114
Samuel Goldwyn Company 143
San Francisco, California 201
San Francisco International Film Festival 162
San Francisco Museum of Art 11
San Sebastian International Film Festival 111
Sansho, the Bailiff 46
Sarre, Jean-Paul 198
Sarris, Andrew 9, 13, 19, 20, 27, 43, 56, 59, 83, 137, 138, 158, 186
Sarristes 83; *see also* Paulettes
Saturday Night at the Baths 168
Saturday Night at the Movies 20
Saturday Review see Knight, Arthur
Savage, Ann 154
Sayler, Oliver M. 65
Sayles, John 85
Scarface 124
Scarlet, Peter 189
Scheib, Ronnie 155
Scheib, Walter 114, 116
Schickel, Richard 81, 144
School of Visual Arts 171, 178
Schuyler (theater) 72
Schwartz, David 8
Schwartz, Russell 131, 132, 143
Schwarz, Richard 86, 145, 146, *147*, 155, 156, 158, 160, 162, 163, 164, 165
Scorpio Rising 44
Scorsese, Martin 9, 19, 41
Scott, A.O. 83

Scott, Helen 44
screwball comedy 156, 157
Second Avenue Courthouse 80
Second International Film Festival 65
Second World War 114
Secret Agent 126
Secret Honor 152
Seeger, Pete 39
Seidelman, Susan 188
series versus random programming *see* repertory programming
series *see* "programming" under individual theaters
Serpico (film) 77
Serpico, Frank 77
17th Parallel: Vietnam in War 46
Seventh Heaven 32
Seventh Seal 155
72nd Street Playhouse 64, 68, 70, 71, 84
Shame 124
Shane 128, 129
Shared Pleasures: A History of Movie Presentation in the United States see Gomery, Douglas
Sharits, Paul 202
Sharon Playhouse 49
Shaw, Wini 117, *118*
Shawn, William 67
Shaye, Robert 87, 99
Shepard, Sam 93
Sherlock Holmes series 126
Sherman, David 201
Shoah 34
Shochiku Company, Ltd. 180
Shoeshine 20
Shoot the Piano Player 96, 200
Shop around the Corner 156
Show Boat (1936) 121, **122**, 128, 136
Show Boat (1951) 121
Show Business magazine 58
Shreveport, Louisiana 201
sidewalk *see* Theatre 80 St. Marks Theater: sidewalk
Silberman, Michael 148, 172
Sills, Beverly 139
Simon, John 33, 83
Simon, William 165
Simone, Nina 94
Singer, Isaac Bashevis 29
Sirk, Douglas 157, 158
Sitney, P. Adams 79, 92
16mm film 12, 127, 128
16mm projectors 129
68th Street Playhouse 152
Sklar, Robert 6, 40, 179
Sky Lodge 115
Sleeping Wives see Laurel and Hardy
Slightly Scarlet 152
Smith, Alexis 117
Smith, Jack 40, 41, 54, 61, 62
Smith and Dale 95
Smithereens 188
Snow, Michael 80
Société des réalisateurs français 183
Soft Skin [*La Peau douce*] 44

Soldier Girls 195
Sommer, Van 130, 131, 132, 141, 143
Son of Paleface 158
Sonbert, Warren 46
Sontag, Susan 13, 31, 33, 81
"Sound Thinking" retrospective 186
South African Broadcasting 1 204
Souto, John 197, 198
"Soviet Cinema" 183
Spanish Civil War 114
"Spectrum of Japanese Cinema" 180
Speeris, Penelope 195
Spielberg, Steven 85
Stand In 124
Stanwyck, Barbara 123, 152, 154
Stapleton, Maureen 117, 118
Star! **137**
Star Wars 91
The State of Things 195
State University of New York, Binghamton 157
State University of New York, Stony Brook 156
Stein, Edwin **52**, 110
Stein, Elliott 21, 127, 197
Stephen Foster Story 49
Stern, Bert 6
Sterritt, David 80
Stevens, Craig 117
Stevie 152
Stranger Than Paradise 187
Strangers on a Train 20
Strawberry Statement 83
Striporama 69
student protest movements 77
Students for a Democratic Society (SDS) 32, 77
Sturges, Preston 157
Subway Riders 188, 189
Sudden Fear 128
Summer Film Festival *see* Thalia International Film Festival
Summer with Monica 200
Sunny 117
Sunset Boulevard 26, 28, 33, 49, 51, 126
SUNY Binghamton *see* State University of New York, Binghamton
Los Sures 203
Sutherland, Deborah **69**
Sutton Cinema Society 49, 59, 81
Sutton theater 24
Swan Lake 106
Swanson, Gloria 26, 113, 114, 117, **118**, 122, 126
Sweet, Blanche 134, 136
Swett, Bradford 164
Swingtime 123
Symphony Space 164
Symphony Theater 63, 86
Syracuse University 104

Talbot, Dan 2, 3, 9, 17, 20, 21, 23–25, **27**, 34, 42, 49, 75, 86–88, 96, 104, 105, 107, 143, 174, 185, 193, 200, 201–202; *see also* Chapter 3

Talbot, Toby 3, 19, 22, 30, 32, 135
Tale of Two Cities 20
The Talking Heads 187
Tanglewood Music Center 69
Tankus, Morton 132, 134, 135, 138, 140, 141, 143
Tanner, Alain 40
Tashlin, Frank 158
Taubin, Amy 80, 186, 187
taxpayer 50
Taylor, Elizabeth 124, 134
Tel-A-Gay Corporation 110
Ten Cents a Dance (film) 123
Tenth Muse, Inc. 50
10th Street Gallery 53
Testament of Dr. Cordelier 169
Testament of Orpheus 124
Thalia (Martin and Ursula Lewis) 2, 18, 19, 21, 22, 51, **73**, 86, 89, 107, 167; programs 63, 66–67, 75, 89, 90
Thalia (Richard Schwarz) 193: programs 150, **151**–152, **153–154**, 155–156, 156, 157, 159–162
Thalia International Film Festival 66–67, 72, **73**–74
Thalia Soho 86, 90, 164, 165, 198
ThaliAnimation Fest 159
That's Entertainment! 131, 135
theater chains 91; *see also* Cineplex Odeon
Theater of the Living Arts 105
Theatre 80 St. Marks 1, 2, 86, 88, 90, 92, **120**, 124, 132, 205; description of theater 113, 115, 116, 117, 119; "lost" films 121–124, 124–125; opening night 117–**118**; programming approach 120–121; programs 119, 121; sidewalk 117–**119**
Theodore Huff Memorial Film Society 11, 13, 14, 15, 121
Third International Experimental Film Competition 41; *see also Flaming Creatures*
Third World Movements 82
This Here Nice Place 116
Thompson, Anne 193
Thompson, Bill 89, 168, 169, 174, 175, 180, 181, 182, 187, 189, 192, 193, 195, 198
Thousand Eyes Film Bookshop 169, **171**
Thousand Eyes Film Club 172, 173, 174, 181
Thousand Eyes Film Society 81, 89, 154, 172
Thousand Eyes magazine 138, 157, **173**–174, **176**, 183, 184, **185**, 199
Thousand Eyes of Dr. Mabuse 172
3-D films 146, 149
"The Three Rebels" series 134, 136
Three Women 192
Threepenny Opera 124
THX 1138 107
Till the Clouds Roll By 121
Times Films 71
Tiny Furniture 204

Tire au flanc [*The Army Game*] 43
Title IV 109
TLA 104, 105
Toad Hall *see* Music Inn
Toback, James 191
Todd, Mike 134
Toho Company, Ltd. 180
Tokyo Story 35–36
El Topo (The Mole) 83, 98, 99, 100, 101, 110
Toronto Film Festival 202
TOTAL MOBILE HOME microCINEMA 201
Totter, Audrey 152
Touch of Evil 20, 21
Tourtelot, Madeline 57
Travels with My Aunt 108
Travolta, John 88
Treasury of Mountaineering Stories 25
Tresca, Carlo 32
A Tribute to Arthur Miller 173
Trinz, Bruce S. 18
Triumph diner 196
Triumph of the Will 28–29
Troell, Jan 169
Tropic of Cancer 109
Trouble in Paradise 156
Truffaut, François 6, 43, 44, 52
Tucker, Sophie 95
Turner, Charles 13, 81
Turner, Ted 135
Twentieth Century (movie) 64, 136
20th Century-Fox 36, 172
200 Motels 108
Two Men and a Wardrobe see Polanski, Roman
2001: A Space Odyssey 82
Tyler, Parker 14
Tyson, Cicely 124

U.S.O 114
UCLA Film & TV Archive 149
Ulysses 109
Under the Roofs of Paris 67
Undercroft Coffeehouse 80–81
Underground film *see* avant-garde film
Unifrance Film 44, 184, 197
Union Maids 104, 180
UnionDocs 202, 203, 204
United Artists Classics 131, 193
United Artists 104, 107, 131, 172
United Cerebral Palsy of New York City 106
Universal Studios 121, 135, 148, 172
University of California, Berkeley 77
University of Michigan 156
Unmade Beds 189
UPA cartoons 67
Upper East Side (New York) 68
Upper West Side (New York) 8, 25, 63–64, 164
Urania 12
Ursula Lewis Film Festival 167
Utica, NY 166, 167

Vali, the Witch of Positano 46
Vandam *see* Thalia Soho
Vanderbeek, Stan 16, 54, 55
Van Dyke, Willard 54, 55
van Lohuizen, Kadir 203
La Vase 183
Vaughan, Sarah 103
The Velvet Devil 203
Venice Film Festival 39, 45, 195
vertical series 107, 163, 191; *see also* curatorial approaches; horizontal series
Victoria's Secret 91
Victory **24**
videocassettes 91, 197
Vidor, King 152
Vietnam War 44, 77, 82, 94, 152
Village East Cinemas 88
Village Gate 39, 48
Village Theater 94, 97
Village Vanguard 77
Village Voice 6
VistaVision 44
Viva la Muerte 88
Vogel, Amos 12, 30, 54, 199, 201
"Voice of the Iowa Grain Exchange" 114
von Bernewitz, Fred 51
von Cramer, Heinz 183
von Sternberg, Josef 41
Votiv Kino 12
The Voyage 152

Wajda, Andrzej 174
Wakaliwood: The Documentary 111
Walter Reade Organization 36, 81
Walter Reade Theater *see* Film Society of Lincoln Center
Wang, Wayne 85

Warner Bros. 132, 136, 172
Wasn't That a Time 29
Watergate scandal 82
Waters, John 99
Waverly theater 88, 163
Webster, Nicholas 55
Weinberg, Herman G. 54, 58
Weiss, Marc 178–180, 188
Wenders, Wim 78, 85, 168, 193, 195
What Else Is There? 53
What's New, Pussycat? 107
Whatever Happened to Baby Jane? 113
White Horse Tavern 93
Whitelaw, Arthur 116, 117, **118**, **119**, **122**, 124
Whiteman, Paul 95
Whitman College 62
Whitney Museum of American Art 84, 92, 159
The Who 94
Who the Devil Made It? 27
Who's That Knocking at My Door? 107
Wild Bunch 82
Wild Strawberries 124
Wilson, Lanford 93
Windsor Theater 59, 62
Wings 83, 123
Wings of Desire 197
Winsten, Archer 26, 56
Winters, Shelley 114
Winterset, Iowa 201
Wise, Robert **137**
Wizard of Oz 150
Wolf, William 67, 83, 88
Wolf Entertainment Guide 67
Woman They Almost Lynched 152
A Woman Under the Influence 83

The Women 124
"Women Larger than Life" 152–154
Women's Prison 155
Wood, Ed, Jr. 150
Workers' Film and Photo League 10
World War II 104
Worldwide Theater 143
Wray, Fay 97
Wurlitzer Theatrical Pipe Organ 178

Yale University 50
Yale University Press 50
Yates, Penny 175, 176, 180, 181, 182, 183, 189
Yiddish vaudeville 94
York Theater 131
Yorktown Theater 25
You're a Good Man, Charlie Brown 114, 116
Youmans, Vincent 123
Young Man of Promise/Who the Hell Is Howard Otway? 113
youth culture films 83
"Yugoslavian Cinema" 183

Zagreb Festival 158
Zanzibar Group 168, 198
Zapruder film 106
Zarek, Walter 70
Zavrian, Suzanne 165
Zéro de conduite 43
Ziegfeld Theater 110
Zionist 184, 185
Zipperman, Max 72, 73, 74, 75
Zlatkin, Chuck 2, 102, 104, **105**–112, 164
Zunser, Jesse 51
Zurer, Oscar 62

www.ingramcontent.com/pod-product-compliance
Lightning Source LLC
Chambersburg PA
CBHW081550300426
44116CB00015B/2822